THE
COMMON LISP
COMPANION

THE
COMMON LISP
COMPANION

TIMOTHY D. KOSCHMANN
Southern Illinois University

WILEY
JOHN WILEY & SONS

New York   □   Chichester   □   Brisbane   □   Toronto   □   Singapore

Text and cover design: Laura Nicholls
Cover art: Art Resources

Library of Congress Cataloging in Publication Data:
Koschmann, Timothy D.
    The Common Lisp Companion   /   Timothy D. Koschmann
        p.   cm.
    Includes bibliographical references.
    ISBN 0-471-50308-8
    1. COMMON LISP (Computer program language)   I. Title
    QA76.73.L23K67   1990
    006.3--dc20   89-29216
                                                                            CIP

For my three sons.

Preface

Many Lisp texts seem to be designed for a reader who has had no prior programming experience. It has been my observation that few people take up Lisp as their first programming language. Usually, students have had a few years of programming experience in one of the more traditional languages before turning to Lisp. Most undergraduates get their first exposure to Lisp in an introductory course on Artificial Intelligence. Other authors seem to operate on the belief that the Lisp functional style is best learned by first forgetting everything you have ever known about programming. I believe that prior programing experience provides an educational foundation upon which one can rapidly construct a sound understanding of a new language.

This book was designed with several different audiences in mind. It can serve as an optional lab text for a graduate or undergraduate AI or Computational Linguistics course. Because it is sufficiently self-contained, students can use the book independently to learn Common Lisp in a few weeks in order to go on and do course-related projects. Because it is not wed to the AI curriculum, this book can also be used in a variety of other undergraduate computer science courses such as Data Structures, Algorithms, or a languages survey course. The book can also be used as a self-study text by the data-processing professional who wishes to learn Common Lisp. All of the exercises in the book can be done using one of the versions of Common Lisp that run on personal computers.

When an auto shop paints your car, they build up a finish using many coats of paint; they know that if they spray the paint on too thickly, it will run and sag. Similarly, in this book, the ideas of Lisp will be built up in several layers. Certain topics will be covered several times, each time adding a little more depth or detail. The real fundamentals of Lisp programming will be covered in Chapters 1 to 3: manipulating lists, defining functions, and recursion. Chapters 4 and 5 discuss the data structures available in Common Lisp. Object-oriented programming using the Common Lisp Object System (CLOS) is covered in Chapters 5 and 6. Chapter 7 provides a thorough grounding in Lisp I/O. Chapters 8 onward build on the topics covered earlier in the book and discuss more advanced features of the language. Chapter 10 provides an extended programming example written in Common Lisp. Chapter 11 assesses Common Lisp's contribution to the evolutionary history of Lisp.

The book is based on the Draft ANSI standard for Common Lisp described in ANSI, 1990. The fundamental features of the language have not been changed, however, and you should be able to follow the text even if you do not have access to an implementation of Common Lisp that conforms to the new standard. As of this writing, not all Common Lisp vendors are providing supported implementations of CLOS. However, there is a portable version of CLOS, called PCL, that will work with most commercial Common Lisp implementations. Consult your Common Lisp vendor for information about obtaining an copy of PCL. Not all aspects of the standard have been covered in this text. The "For Further Reading" sections found at the end of each chapter direct you to additional sources for more detailed information.

Throughout the text, there will be discussion of what constitutes good programming style. I believe that if you make a conscious effort to adopt these precepts, you will not only become a better Lisp programmer, but you will be able to learn more rapidly.

Let me say a brief word about the exercises. The exercises for each section appear at the end of the section (not at the end of the chapter, as in many text books). This is because it is important that you complete the exercises for one section before you move on to the next. It is my hope that you will do all of the exercises in the book. Many ideas, when first presented, may seem obvious and perhaps even trivial. You may be tempted to skip to the next section without trying the exercises. Resist please! There is a difference between knowing a concept and being able to use it. The exercises serve two purposes: to teach and to self-test. They reinforce the lesson and provide you with an opportunity to test your knowledge and explore the idiosyncrasies of the Common Lisp implementation in which you work.

Many of the exercises build on pieces constructed in earlier chapters; be sure to save all of your work in a file so you don't have to retype functions when they reappear in a later problem. Most problems should only take a few minutes to complete; if you find they are taking substantially longer, perhaps you should reread the current section or review the material from previous chapters. Programming projects, found in many of the chapters, are more involved and may take several hours or more to complete. The more challenging exercises are marked with an asterisk (*). Answers for all exercises are given in Appendix C. I've found Lisp to be a fun language to use, and I have tried to share that through the exercises. I hope you find them a pleasant diversion.

Many people have provided help and encouragement in the writing of this book. Joe Dougherty, my editor at Wiley, invested a lot of time and effort to get this project off the ground. I would also like to thank those who took the time to review chapters and give me useful feedback:

Ed Anderson, Georgia Institute of Technology
Danny Bobrow, Xerox PARC
Lowell Carmony, Lake Forest College
Mike Carter, Rockhurst College
Ken Danhoff, Southern Illinois University
Charles Dyer, University of Wisconsin–Madison
Lance Eliot, University of Southern California
Stewart Eldred, University of Portland
Morris Firebaugh, University of Wisconsin–Parkside
Bill Kornfeld, Lyon Park Systems
Sam Koschmann
Barry Kurtz, University of New Mexico–Las Cruces
John Lowther, Michigan Technical University
Dennis Martin, University of Scranton

Robert Meghee, Naval Post Graduate School
Keith Mountford, Sun Microsystems
Gordon Novak, University of Texas–Arlington
Kent Pitman, Symbolics, Inc.
Craig Sweat, Micrognosis, Inc.
James Turner
Steve Verhulst, University of Southern Illinois
The students of CS311L at Southern Illinois University

Their editorial input has improved the style of this text and
helped to eradicate many of the small errors that tend to creep into
a work like this. I alone, however, assume the responsibility for any
that may have slipped by undetected.

Timothy D. Koschmann

Foreword

No doubt about it: Common Lisp is a *big* language.

It's big for a very good reason. As programmers have become used to having more powerful and convenient facilities at their disposal, no matter what language they program in, these facilities become standard components of the programming environment.

The usual practice is to deny that such facilities are part of the language in which programs are expressed. Instead, they are segregated into "subroutine libraries" and thereby distanced from the core language and its documentation. This allows the designers of languages such as Pascal and C to claim that they are "small" and "easy to learn." But the programmer who has learned only the core language is in the same position as one who has learned all the pronouns, declensions, and tenses of French, say, or German, but has not yet mastered a substantial collection of verbs and nouns. Even with complete knowledge of grammar, it's hard to say anything interesting with a vocabulary of only fifty words. In the same way, it's hard to say much of anything in C without using the standard libraries. (Just try to say even "Hello, world" without using the studio library!) If one admits that these libraries provide indispensable additional vocabulary, then C suddenly must be considered a rather large language–which is exactly why it is so useful in its particular niche.

The designers of Common Lisp faced this phenomenon foursquare. Rather than defining a small, skeletal core language and a fragmented set of loosely affiliated libraries, they have found it convenient to design a large language with many carefully integrated features. Common Lisp includes about a thousand built-in functions and variables and a large set of data types. With a vocabulary like that, you can say quite a bit. Not every feature will be used in every program, just as not every word in the dictionary is used in every conversation, but those features or words must be there, ready for use when appropriate, if a language is to be flexible, convenient, and richly expressive.

It is possible to learn a new language by studying the grammar and then reading the dictionary. But a dictionary is organized for reference, not for learning; it has great breadth, but not much of a plot. How much better it is to have a guide that will lead you through the most useful parts first and provide an appropriate framework for organizing one's understanding and one's speech!

Let Tim Koschmann be your guide. He has been participating in the ongoing work by ANSI technical subcommittee X3J13 to produce an American National Standard for Common Lisp. He has seen the process of language growth and the evolution of Lisp programming practice. In this book he has sorted out the most useful elements of Common Lisp for presentation in a coherent order and illustrated their appropriate use in context. In short, he has provided a plot. Lisp programming can be a lot of fun. I hope you enjoy it , too.

Guy L. Steele Jr.
Cambridge, Massachusetts
December 1989

Contents

1

Introduction

1.1 WHEREFORE LISP?

Why have computer scientists been drawn to Lisp? What accounts for the language's remarkable longevity and widespread popularity? The fact that you are reading this book suggests that you may already have your own reasons for being interested in this elegant and powerful language. Nonetheless, let me digress a bit and share my own views on why I think Lisp has caught on as it has. I believe the answer lies in four features of the language—its flexibility, its extensibility, the rich set of data structures it offers, and the fact that it is a very high-level language.

Flexibility

Many people who program in Lisp are involved in what is known as *exploratory programming* (Sheil, 1983; Gabriel et al., 1989). Exploratory programming involves trying to solve complex software design problems by a process of writing progressively better ap-

1

proximations of the solution. You start by implementing a small prototype of the program that you wish ultimately to design. You then evaluate the prototype to see how close it comes to meeting the requirements of the problem and either refine the prototype or start over. As the programmer's understanding of the problem increases, each iteration of developing a prototype and then evaluating it should bring him or her closer to the final solution. Psychologists call this process *successive approximation*.

Languages like Ada and COBOL are strongly typed. This means that the type of every data object used in a program must be declared at compile time. Lisp is a weakly typed language. Variable typing is done dynamically at run time. Strongly typed and weakly typed languages take diametrically opposing views about the timing of design decisions in the development of a programming project. Ada and COBOL require that the specification of data types occur as the very first step of program development. In Lisp, decisions about how variables will be used can be deferred until the actual time of usage. The typing scheme used in Lisp is clearly preferable for doing exploratory programming. Although strong typing may present many advantages to the system programmer who is developing or maintaining a large, well-specified program, it would only prove to be a distraction when constructing prototypes.

Lisp has other sources of flexibility that make it attractive as an exploratory programming language. Memory management is handled automatically in Lisp, unlike languages such as Ada, which burden the programmer with the responsibility for releasing storage after it is no longer needed (Schwartz et al., 1980). It is possible in Lisp to generate code within a program and then execute it. This represents the ultimate in deferred decision making. The programmer can wait until run time to define the program itself.

Extensibility

Programming languages pass in and out of vogue as the technology advances and philosophies of software design change. Another reason for Lisp's popularity is that it tends to change with the times. This is possible because Lisp is a readily extensible language. Lisp has been extended in two ways.

First, the Lisp language itself has undergone a number of changes over the years. In fact, Lisp can be said to have been in a state of continuous evolution since the time of its introduction. It has acquired all the trappings of a modern computer language by simply picking up the best features of other languages: records from COBOL, structured control constructs from Algol, and objects

TABLE 1-1 *Types of Data Structures Available in Common Lisp*

Data Structures	Processing Strategy	Example
Indexed structures	Iterative	Fortran array
Strings	String operations, pattern matching	SNOBOL string
Records	Accessor functions	Pascal record
Linked lists	Recursive	Lisp list
Unordered sets	Set operations	SETL set
Associative data structures	Indexed retrieval, Hash keying	ICON table
Hierarchical data structures with procedural attachment	Inheritance, Message sending	Smalltalk objects

from Smalltalk. Lisp has been able to accommodate these new features and others without losing its coherence as a language.

The second way that Lisp has been extended is by inventing new languages on top of Lisp. This is easier to do in Lisp than it is with many other languages. In later chapters, we will see how easy it is to write an interpreter for another language in Lisp. Designing a special-purpose language is a very useful strategy for many types of problems. This approach has been used most successfully in artificial intelligence research, but it could be applied with equal validity in other areas as well.[1]

Data Structures

A third advantage of Lisp is that it has a rich collection of built-in data structures. The data structures available in a language dictate the processing strategies that the language will require. Fortran arrays and matrices require the iterative processing capabilities of Fortran DO loops, for instance. Table 1-1 shows some of the different types of data structures offered in Common Lisp. Well-known examples of each of the data structures from other lan-

---

[1] CLOS, the object-oriented programming language described in Chapters 5 and 6, is a good example of a special-purpose language developed on top of Lisp.

guages are also provided. Many programming languages offer only one or two of these types of data structures. Although Lisp is best known as a list processing language, Common Lisp supports all of the data structures listed in the table. Most of these data structures will be described in more detail in Chapters 4 and 5. The availability of this rich set of data structures makes the use of the language much more convenient.

High-Level Languages

One additional reason that programmers tend to favor Lisp is that it is a very high-level language. A language is considered high level if it allows you to perform complicated computations with a small number of instructions. The more that you can accomplish in a single instruction, the higher the level of the language. APL is an example of a high-level language. Low-level languages, on the other hand, require many instructions to accomplish certain tasks. When you program in a low-level language like an assembler, you have to do a lot of coding but you are given greater control over how the computation will actually be performed. Paradoxically, Lisp is considered to be both a high-level and a low-level language. Because Lisp has some very powerful built-in functionality and because things like memory management are handled automatically in Lisp, it is considered a high-level language. But it is also possible to do fairly low-level programming in Lisp. Many dialects of Lisp allow the programmer to code at a level similar to that of assembly-level programming. A lot of systems programming has been done in Lisp.

Hopefully, the reader, at this point, will have been persuaded that Lisp may have certain special advantages as an implementation language. To be fair, I should mention that there are probably situations in which Lisp would be a particularly unfortunate choice of language. In certain cases, a large amount of flexibility would be more of a hindrance than a help. It would be inadvisable, for example, to do a large team project like a payroll program or an accounts payable system in Lisp. Also, Lisp is usually not very good for real-time applications. But as a language for doing exploratory programming, Lisp has few peers.

1.2 LISP FAMILY TREE

Lisp has a long and distinguished history. Among the programming languages in current use, it is second in tenure only to Fortran. It was developed by John McCarthy at MIT in the late 1950s. Lisp was originally designed as a functional language based on Church's

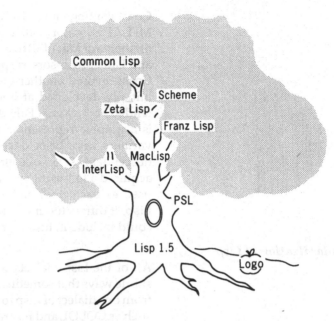

Figure 1-1 Lisp Family Tree

Lambda Calculus. The first implementation of Lisp that was distributed outside of MIT was Lisp 1.5. In its early incarnations, Lisp was a rather spartan language. The description of Lisp 1.5 (McCarthy, 1962) was only 42 pages long.[2]

Lisp and AI

The new Lisp language was especially popular with workers in the developing area of artificial intelligence (AI). The adoption of Lisp as the primary language for AI research in this country had a very positive effect on the development of Lisp. AI researchers were drawn to Lisp for a variety of reasons. These researchers tend to work on large and very hard problems and to foray in uncharted territory. They need the best programming tools available in order to make any progress at all. Lisp is a language with a simple syntax that is easily extensible. Over the years, more high-level tools have been developed for programming in Lisp than for any other language.

Lisp Dialects

Early on, a schism developed within the Lisp community. The East

[2]Compare this to the second edition of the Steele book (Steele, 1990), which has more than 700 pages!

Coast contingent tended to use a dialect of Lisp developed at the MIT AI laboratory called MacLISP. ZetaLISP and Franz Lisp were offshoots of MacLISP that were developed to run on Lisp machines and Unix processors, respectively. Their counterparts on the West Coast favored another Lisp dialect, known as Interlisp, that was initially developed at Bolt, Baranek and Newman and later extended at the Xerox Palo Alto Research Center (PARC). Figure 1-1 is a graphic representation of the Lisp family tree. Many other variants have been developed over the years. Scheme and its descendent, T, are two elegant versions of Lisp dialects that have acquired a following in academic circles. Logo was designed to be used to teach children how to program. Although it is related to Lisp, it differs too much from Lisp to be considered a dialect. We could include it, however, as a fruit of the tree.

Standardization of Lisp

All of the Lisp dialects were basically Lisp, but they differed in subtle ways that sometimes made the conversion of an application from one dialect of Lisp to another very difficult. Unlike languages such as COBOL and Fortran, Lisp has never had a standard. By the beginning of the 1980s, many developers were beginning to see the need for some kind of portable Lisp. The Department of Defense, which traditionally has provided the lion's share of funding for AI research, was particularly concerned about this problem.

PSL

An early effort to standardize Lisp had been made at the University of Utah (Marti et al., 1979). Their Lisp dialect, known as PSL (Portable Standard Lisp), consisted of the minimal set of primitive functions held in common by the other Lisp dialects in use at the time. Unfortunately, PSL failed to gain widespread acceptance within the Lisp community. This was probably due to the fact that most programmers were unwilling to live without (or to reimplement) the higher-level functionality that they had come to depend on in more elaborate but less portable versions of Lisp.

Development of Common Lisp

In 1981, at the urging of the Defense Advanced Research Projects Agency (DARPA), discussions took place concerning the development of a new, portable Lisp dialect, which came to be called Common Lisp. A description of the new dialect, edited by Guy Steele, was published in 1984. The designers of Common Lisp differed from the designers of PSL in that rather than trying to base the standard on a minimal subset, they chose to develop a whole new dialect (some would say a whole new language). As will be discussed later in the book, Common Lisp differs in significant ways from any of the earlier Lisp dialects. After the publication of the description of the language in 1984 (Steele, 1984b), Common Lisp was implemented on a wide variety of processors, including mainframes, workstations, specialized Lisp machines, and personal computers (see Appendix A for a list of vendors).

ANSI Standard

In 1986, the American National Standards Institute (ANSI) established a technical committee, known officially as X3J13, to develop a formal specification for CL (Mathis, 1988). A draft of this document will be circulated for public review in 1990 (ANSI, 1990). This book is based on the version of CL described in the Draft ANSI Specification.

1.3 CONVERSING WITH LISP

The means by which you start to use Lisp will vary, depending on the type of system you are working on. If you are working on a multiuser system like a VAX, you must ask the operating system (also known as the *monitor* or *executive*) to load and start the Lisp program. If you are running Common Lisp on a personal computer, you will probably have to insert a Lisp system disk into your machine in order to start up Lisp. If you have the good fortune to gain access to a Lisp machine, you won't have to worry about finding Lisp because everything is done in Lisp on a Lisp machine. In any case, there should be a reference manual (or perhaps a set of manuals) describing the implementation of Common Lisp on your system. Keep this material at hand as you work your way through this book.

Lisp Prompt

Most (but not all) Lisps use a special character or string of characters to inform the user that the system is working and awaiting input. The nature of this prompt was "purposely not rigorously specified" in the Steele standard. Consequently, different implementations of Common Lisp handle input from users in a variety of ways. In the examples presented in this book, I will use the string "CL>" as the Lisp system prompt. Furthermore, to make it absolutely clear who is typing what, text generated in the examples by the Lisp system will be presented in boldface. Do not be troubled if this differs slightly from the way that these examples would appear if you typed them into the Common Lisp implementation in which you have chosen to work.

Interpreted Lisp

Lisp is an interpreted language like BASIC and APL, which means

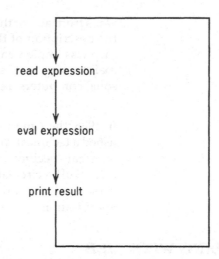

Figure 1-2 The Lisp Top Level

that each line is evaluated after it is typed instead of waiting until you have entered an entire program, as in Fortran or COBOL. Although Lisp and BASIC are both interpreted, there are some fundamental differences in the way that the languages work. In most BASIC implementations, if you enter a line of code, the code will be interpreted and checked for syntax errors, but ordinarily it will not be executed until a specific command is entered to tell the interpreter to commence execution. Lisp code is constructed of symbolic expressions, called *s-expressions* or simply *expressions*.[3] Unlike BASIC, Lisp code is evaluated as soon as the full expression has been typed. For example, if I type:

```
CL> (+ 2 2)
4
```

Lisp responds immediately with the expected result. The interactive facility in Lisp is referred to as the Lisp top level. It is also called the "read-eval-print" loop after the three system functions that are automatically invoked on each expression entered. Figure 1-2 shows the behavior of this loop.

Prefix Notation

If you look carefully at the preceding example, some other differences from BASIC become apparent. Expressions in Lisp are constructed in prefix notation (sometimes referred to as *Cambridge-*

---

[3]In Steele (Steele, 1990), the term *form* is used for a Lisp expression. In this book, the terms *form* and *expression* will be used interchangeably.

So What's a Lisp Machine?

Lisp machines are special-purpose, usually single-user workstations that were designed to execute Lisp code very efficiently. In a sense, Lisp is the assembly language on a Lisp machine, since there is no intermediate language between Lisp and the machine code for the processor.

Today's commercial Lisp machines are the products of two parallel and largely independent development efforts that occurred on the East and West coasts. In the early 1970s, a group of engineers at MIT were working on a custom-designed architecture to support Lisp (Steele and Sussman, 1979). Their first prototype, entitled the CONS machine, was completed in 1976. At roughly the same time, a group at the Xerox Palo Alto Research Center (PARC) developed microcode to support the Interlisp environment on an ALTO personal computer. In 1978 the PARC group ported Interlisp to a Xerox 1100 processor (perhaps better known as the Xerox Dolphin). The Dolphin was the first Lisp machine to be sold commercially and was used widely in universities and research centers. An ECL technology version of the Dolphin, known as the Xerox 1132 (or Dorado), was developed in 1979 (Pier, 1983). The MIT group produced a second-generation Lisp machine in 1978 known as the CADR. In 1981 two start-up companies, Symbolics and Lisp Machine, Inc. (LMI), introduced commercial versions of the CADR. Texas Instruments entered the Lisp machine market with the TI Explorer (derived from the LMI machine) in 1984. Texas Instruments and Symbolics have recently introduced VLSI implementations of their Lisp machines in which the entire central processing unit (CPU) resides on one chip (Dussud, 1988).

All Lisp machines share a number of architectural features (Graham, 1988b). Because real-world Lisp programs tend to be large, all Lisp machines are virtual memory machines. All Lisp machines use microcodable processors. Since large Lisp applications tend to be collaborative efforts and Lisp machines are usually single-user machines, a gracious means of communicating between machines is frequently required. All Lisp machines can exist as citizens of local area networks and can communicate using a variety of protocols. Many Lisp machines have special-purpose hardware to implement common run-time operations such as data typing and garbage collection.

Lisp machines have enabled programmers to achieve hitherto unprecedented levels of productivity. Some of the best programming tools extant were introduced on these machines. They are considered by most sophisticated Lisp programmers to be the premier vehicle for program development and debugging. Despite all of these accolades, however, the days of the Lisp machine may be numbered. The introduction of low-cost, general-purpose workstations has reduced the market for special-purpose architectures. Software vendors have rushed to develop Lisp programming tools to run on these new workstations. As the software tools on so-called stock hardware get better, the need for Lisp machines may ultimately disappear.

Polish notation) rather than in infix (e.g., 2 + 2), as we are used to seeing them in other programming languages. Note also that the expression is enclosed in parentheses. These parentheses must be balanced; that is, there must be an equivalent number of left and right parentheses. If you provide too many closing parentheses, the Lisp interpreter will complain; if you provide too few, it will obstinately refuse to read your input until it is complete.

Lisp Lists

The arithmetic example given previously is a Lisp list. So is this:

```
(able baker charlie)
```

Lists can be nested; that is, a list can consist of other lists. For example, all of the following are legal Lisp lists:

```
(x y z (1 2 3))
((a b) (c d) (e f))
((a) (b) (c))
(equal x y)
```

A list can be made up of symbols, strings, numeric constants, or any other Lisp form. Everything that is not a list is referred to as an *atom* in Common Lisp. Lisp expressions are constructed of atoms and lists of atoms.

Lisp Functions

Function calls are written as lists in Lisp. In other languages, such as Fortran or Pascal, the function name is separated from the list of arguments that are being passed to the function. In Lisp, the first element of the list is taken to be the function name; the remaining elements represent the arguments. We will see in Chapter 3 that function definitions are also constructed as lists in Lisp. Because Lisp functions are invoked by lists, can operate on lists, and are represented as lists, it is possible to write Lisp functions that create or modify other Lisp functions.

In the list

```
(+ 2 2)
```

the plus sign is the name of a Common Lisp system-defined function. Common Lisp has many other system-defined functions, which we will describe later in the text.[4] Everything is done with

---

[4]All of the Common Lisp system-defined functions are listed in Appendix B.

function calls in Lisp. In many languages, you are required to write a mainline program in order to invoke a function; not so in Lisp. As you can see from the preceding example, isolated functions can be invoked directly in Lisp. This makes it possible to test complicated programs one piece at a time.

If the arguments to a function are themselves lists, they are first evaluated as function calls and are replaced in the expression by their returned result. For instance, the formula

$$\frac{2+3}{7-2}$$

could be expressed in Common Lisp (using the addition, division, and subtraction functions) as

```
(/ (+ 2 3) (- 7 2))
```

In this example, `(+ 2 3)` is replaced by the value 5; then the form `(- 7 2)` is replaced by the value 5; and finally, the result of `(/ 5 5)` is computed and printed.

Lisp Variables

You now know enough to make Common Lisp perform like a simple four-function calculator, but in order to do anything really useful, you can't be limited to working only with numeric constants; you need to have some variables. Lisp variables are referred to as *symbols*. The `defvar` macro is used to define variables in Common Lisp. For example, you could type

```
CL> (defvar x 4)
X
```

to define the variable x and associate the value 4 with it. In the Lisp world, we say that the symbol x is now *bound* to the value 4. When we talk about a symbol's binding, we are referring to the current value that is associated with that symbol. We can easily find out what a symbol's binding is by simply typing the symbol name to the interpreter with no parentheses. For example, after the preceding call to `defvar`, you could type

```
CL> x
4
```

Since x is now a bound variable, you could use it in other expressions. You could, for instance, now type

```
CL> (defvar y x)
Y
```

defining a new symbol y and causing it also to be bound to the value 4. You could now type (using the Common Lisp multiplication function)

```
CL> (* x y)
16
```

Variable Assignment

Bindings remain in effect until the variable is reassigned. Variable assignment is performed using the Common Lisp primitive setf. If you typed

```
CL> (setf x "Some string")
"Some string"
```

the binding of x would be reassigned to the string "Some string". Notice that, on completion, setf always returns the value that was bound to its first argument (i.e., the value of the second argument).

Multiple Assignment

In Common Lisp, it is possible to effect several bindings within the same call to setf. For example, you could type

```
CL> (setf x 6 y 8)
8
```

When setf has multiple symbol-value pairs, it returns the value of the last pair evaluated. In Common Lisp, setf evaluates the symbol-value pairs in sequence from left to right.[5] The programmer can therefore use bindings that were previously established within the same call to setf. For example, you could type

```
CL> (setf var1 3 var2 var1)
3
```

and it would work well, whereas

---

[5]Forms that work this way are said to evaluate their arguments in a *sequential* fashion. There are other Common Lisp forms that evaluate their arguments in a *parallel* fashion.

```
CL> (setf var2 var3  var3 3)
```

would cause an *unbound variable* error to be signaled because `var3` has no binding when it is first evaluated.

Exercise 1.1

Explain the difference between the symbol X and the string "X".

Exercise 1.2

What do you predict the following Lisp expressions would return? Check your answers by typing the expressions to the Lisp interpreter.

a. `(* 5.(* 4 (* 3 (* 2 1))))`

b. `(/ (+ 5 (+ 6 (+ 4 7 ))) 4)`

Exercise 1.3

Convert the following formulas into Lisp functional form and then try them in Common Lisp.

a. $\dfrac{3}{2*3}$

b. $\dfrac{3}{2}*3$

c. $\dfrac{.5*10}{11+4}$

Exercise 1.4

In many languages, you can add parentheses to an expression with impunity. Do you think this is true of Lisp? Try adding an extra level of parentheses to a legal Lisp expression and see what happens.

Exercise 1.5 (*)

How does Common Lisp handle mixed-mode arithmetic? Consult the Steele standard or the programmer's reference manual for your implementation of Common Lisp for a description of the possible formats for representing numbers. Conduct some experiments in which you perform operations on combinations of integer and floating-point numbers.

SUMMARY

Lisp offers several advantages as a prototyping or exploratory programming language. Its weak typing, automatic memory management, and facilities for dynamic programming offer unusual flexibility. The language is readily extensible, as has been demonstrated over the last 25 years. Lisp supports an ample set of data structures suitable for many different applications. Paradoxically, Lisp can be considered both a high-level and a low-level programming language. Although it is not suited to all applications, Lisp has proven useful for a wide range of problems.

Lisp is one of the oldest programming languages still in active use today. It has evolved over time and has acquired many features from other languages. Over the years, factionalism has developed within the Lisp programming community, but Common Lisp promises to be a standard, device-independent version of Lisp. It is hoped that the availability of an industry standard will increase Lisp's popularity as an implementation language.

Lisp code is constructed of s-expressions or forms. A form can consist of either a single Lisp atom or a list of atoms. Lists are used in Lisp both as data structures and to represent programs. When a list is evaluated by the Lisp interpreter, the first argument is taken to be a function name, and the remaining elements of the list are evaluated and passed as arguments to the function. The arguments themselves may be lists, which are evaluated in exactly the same way. Lisp function calls are written in prefix notation.

New variables are defined in Common Lisp using the `defvar` primitive. It takes a variable name and an optional initialization value as arguments. Variables can be reassigned using the Common Lisp `setf` primitive. Multiple reassignments can be performed within a single call to `setf`.

NEW COMMON LISP DEFINED NAMES

```
*         +            /
-         defvar       setf
```

FOR FURTHER READING

The definitive reference for the Common Lisp is the draft ANSI Standard (ANSI, 1990). The updated edition of *Common Lisp: The Language* (Steele, 1990) (often abbreviated CLtL) is also very helpful. The book *Common Lisp: The Reference* (Franz, 1988) is also a convenient reference guide, even though it is not up-to-date with the proposed standard.

If you are interested in the history of Lisp, the McCarthy (McCarthy et al., 1978) and Stoyan (Stoyan, 1984) articles are good resources for the early years. *The Lisp 1.5 Programmer's Manual*

(McCarthy et al., 1962) is still in print and selling briskly. Although Lisp 1.5 is no longer used as a programming language, readers who are interested in Lisp as a language might like to see what it looked like in one of its earliest incarnations. Gabriel's benchmark book (Gabriel, 1985) provides some background on some of the pre-Common Lisp dialects of Lisp. Steele has written an article (Steele, 1984a) that covers some of the later history, especially as it relates to Common Lisp. There is also a brief history of Common Lisp in Chapter 1 of the draft ANSI Standard (ANSI, 1990).

For more in-depth coverage of the advantages of programming in Lisp, see the articles by Sheil (1983) and Allen (1985) and the technical report by Schwartz and Melliar-Smith (1980).

2

The Rule of Three

He looked again and found it was
A Double Rule of Three.
"And all its Mystery," he said,
"Is clear as day to me!"
Lewis Carroll, Sylvie and Bruno
Concluded

2.1 THE THREE RULES OF EVALUATION

So far, we have used Lisp to do some simple arithmetic. If this were all you were interested in doing, you would probably be better off using a language like Fortran or Pascal. Where Lisp really excels is in the area of symbol manipulation.

What happens when we try to bind a symbol to another variable? Well, let's try it. Type in the following

```
(defvar playwright shakespeare)
```

and see what happens. It doesn't work, does it? You will get an error message such as "unbound variable—SHAKESPEARE".[1] The in-

---

[1]The manner in which an error is signaled varies from implementation to implementation. Some versions of Lisp simply provide a message; others suspend execution and enter a debugging mode. You should become familiar with how it is done in your implementation now, because you are likely to see an error message or two before you finish this book.

17

terpreter is trying to replace the second argument with its binding. This is not what we intended. We wanted to bind the symbol shakespeare to the variable playwright. There are ways of overriding the standard evaluating behavior of the interpreter, but before we discuss them, I will make explicit what the standard evaluating behavior is.

Three Rules of Evaluation

The interpreter has three basic rules that it follows when evaluating expressions. The Three Rules of Evaluation are

1. Symbols are replaced by their current bindings.
2. Lists are evaluated as function calls.
3. Everything else evaluates to itself.

These arcane and seemingly arbitrary rules determine the interpretation of all Lisp code. In a sense, they *are* the interpretation of the code. Commit them to memory, because you need to know them in order to understand what Lisp code means. Learning the "Rules of Three" is the first step on the road to becoming a Lisp programmer.

Evaluating Symbols

According to the First Rule of Evaluation, when the Common Lisp interpreter encounters a symbol in an expression, it replaces the symbol with its current binding. This is why the example at the beginning of the chapter failed to work. When the interpreter attempted to replace the symbol shakespeare with its current binding, it discovered that shakespeare did not have a current binding, and so it grumbled. There are, however, many exceptions to the First Rule, some of which will become apparent when we examine the Second Rule of Evaluation.

Evaluating Lists

When the interpreter encounters a list in an expression, the list is treated as a function call. Functions in Lisp, like functions in Fortran and Pascal, return the value computed by applying the named function to the list of arguments. When the Lisp interpreter encounters a function call in an expression, it replaces the function call with the value returned by the function.

The first element of a list is treated as a function name. This is an exception to the First Rule of Evaluation. The first element of the list has to be a symbol, but it is not replaced by its current binding; instead, it is treated as the name of a function. If a function by that name has not been previously defined, the interpreter will signal an

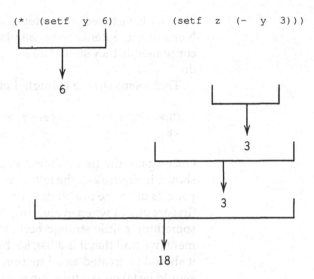

Figure 2-1 The Order of Evaluation of a Lisp Expression

error. The remaining elements of the list are evaluated in left-to-right order and passed to the function as arguments. Consider the following Lisp expression (assume that the value 4 is bound to x)

```
CL> (* x (+ x x))
32
```

The symbol * is taken to be the name of a defined function. The second element is evaluated using the First Rule and is replaced by the value 4. The third element of the list is another list. We apply the Second Rule of Evaluation to this list and replace it in the original expression with the value 8. The function * is then called with both of its arguments instantiated to return 32.

Third Rule of Evaluation

Everything that isn't a symbol or a list simply evaluates to itself. We call these *self-evaluating forms*. For example

```
CL> 10
10
CL> "This is just a sample string"
"This is just a sample string"
CL> #\k
#\k
```

Here we have typed in an integer, a string and a character constant.[2] None of these items are symbols, and they certainly aren't lists; consequently they should all self-evaluate, and as you can see, they do.

That seems simple enough. Let's look at another example:

```
CL> (* (setf y 6)(setf z (- y 3)))
18
```

Once again, the first element is taken to be a function name. As shown in Figure 2-1, the leftmost argument is evaluated first. This permits us to use the binding of y effected in the evaluation of the first argument when evaluating the second argument. But there is something a little strange here. When we evaluate the first argument, we find that it is a list; so, by the Second Rule of Evaluation, it should be treated as a function call. The first element of the list should be taken as a function name, and the remaining elements of the list should be evaluated and passed as arguments to the function. However, the variable y doesn't have a binding, so the interpreter should balk when it tries to evaluate the symbol. But in fact, the Lisp interpreter processes this expression without a peep. Why? This is another exception to the First Rule of Evaluation. This exception occurs because the Lisp primitive setf is not really a function.

Special Forms and Macros

All Lisp functions evaluate their arguments as described previously. There are two other groups of forms in Common Lisp that do not always evaluate their arguments in left-to-right order; in fact, they may not evaluate their arguments at all! These forms are referred to as *special forms* and *macros*, respectively. Special forms and macros are called just like functions—as a list. How do you tell the difference? You can't. You have to know which category the form belongs to in order to predict how it will evaluate its arguments. Fortunately, there are only a few dozen special forms defined in Common Lisp, and no more can be added. You can easily memorize their names. The list of Common Lisp macros is a little longer, but with time and practice, you will recognize them as well. All of the Common Lisp special forms and most of the macros are listed in Appendix B.

setf Macro

The setf form is an example of a Common Lisp macro. When the

---

[2]Note that character constants are preceded by a sharp sign and a backslash in Common Lisp.

Lisp interpreter encounters a call to setf, it evaluates the second argument but not the first.[3] This is reasonable if you think about it, because the motivation for calling setf in the first place is to assign a value to a variable. If the first argument must already have a binding before we can call setf, how are we to accomplish that without using setf? The designers of Common Lisp needed to have some routines that circumvented the standard evaluation procedures. That's fine for setf, but what do you do when you need to suppress the interpreter's tendency to evaluate all of the arguments to a function?

Preventing Evaluation

Now that you know the rules, let us return to the example given at the beginning of the chapter. You wanted to bind a symbol to a variable using the expression

```
(defvar playwright shakespeare)
```

but the interpreter would not cooperate. Because setf is a macro, the first argument is not evaluated but the second argument is.[4] Since the second argument is an unbound symbol, you ran into problems. How do you tell the interpreter that you don't want the current binding of shakespeare but the symbol shakespeare itself? Common Lisp has another form that handles its argument in an unusual way. It is called quote, and is an example of a special form. It takes a single argument and returns the argument unmodified and unevaluated. How does this help? Well, quote is used in places where you wish to override the normal evaluation behavior of the interpreter. By wrapping a call to quote around a symbol, you are, in effect, protecting it from evaluation. If you redo the example from the beginning of the chapter, you see

```
CL> (defvar playwright (quote shakespeare))
PLAYWRIGHT[5]
```

---

[3] Actually, since setf can perform multiple assigments, the rule is that even-numbered arguments are evaluated and odd-numbered arguments are not.

[4]If you do want the first argument evaluated, Common Lisp has a function called set for this purpose.

[5]The Common Lisp reader automatically converts our typed input into uppercase before it is evaluated by the interpreter. In this book, I follow the convention of typing examples in lowercase, but the examples would work exactly the same way if typed as uppercase characters.

Success! The call to quote is evaluated (because of the Second Rule), but since quote is a special form and does not evaluate its argument, the result returned is the unevaluated argument. This may seem like a roundabout method, but if you think about it, this is the only logical way to bypass evaluation. By quoting an expression, you don't prevent evaluation but you do nullify its effect.

Quoting Expressions

The special form quote can be used with whole expressions. For example, if you wished to bind a list to a variable name, you could type

```
CL> (defvar greeks (quote (homer socrates plato)))
GREEKS
```

This is a very useful thing to be able to do. In fact, the special form quote is used so frequently in Lisp that it has a shorthand form. The quote special form can be called by placing a single-quote character immediately before the expression you do not wish to have evaluated. So, the preceding example could be written equivalently:

```
CL> (defvar greeks '(homer socrates plato))
GREEKS
```

When quote is invoked using the shorthand form, it has no enclosing parentheses.

Indirect Variables

Suppose that you wish to create a variable y that would allow you to access the current binding of another variable x. We could say that y gives us an indirect reference to x. Do you now have enough tools to achieve this? Unfortunately, not. Let's try it once:

```
CL> (defvar x 99)
X
CL> (defvar y x)
Y
CL> y
99
```

So far, so good. But

```
CL> (setf x 100)
100
CL> y
99
```

Oh, oh! The symbol y doesn't pick up the new value of x. What would have happened if you had quoted x instead?

```
CL> (defvar y 'x)
Y
```

But this doesn't work either because

```
CL> y
X
```

the variable y is bound to the symbol x itself, not to its current binding. This brings out an important point about evaluation in Lisp. Evaluation applies only to what you see. If the result of evaluating an expression is another expression, it will not be automatically evaluated by the interpreter. In this case, the interpreter replaces the symbol y with its current binding, which happens to be another symbol. It does not then try to replace that symbol its current binding. Lisp evaluation only peels away the top layer. To penetrate an expression further, you must once again override the standard behavior of the interpreter.

Forcing Evaluation

The interpreter in Lisp is implemented as a function called eval. At times it is useful to be able to invoke the interpreter on a particular argument. This has the effect of calling for one more level of evaluation. We need eval in order to get our indirect variable example to work. Let's see how this is done:

```
CL> (defvar y 'x)
Y
CL> (defvar x 4)
X
CL> (eval y)
4
CL> (setf x 5)
5
CL> (eval y)
5
```

When we call eval with y as an argument, y is evaluated and is replaced by its binding, the symbol x. This is passed to eval as an argument, and eval causes it to be evaluated again to return the current binding of x. The ability to invoke the interpreter from within a program is a powerful feature of programming in Lisp.

Although the Three Rules of Evaluation seem simple enough, there are some subtleties that may take a while to appreciate. The Rules of Evaluation, however, hold the key to understanding Lisp. As you work your way through the book, you may wish to reread this section once or twice until you really understand the Rule of Three.

Exercise 2.1

Assuming that there are no previous bindings, predict whether or not the following Lisp expressions would succeed:

a. `(defvar var1 (+ var1 2))`

b. `(/ (setf var2 (* (setf var3 2)`
`                            4))`
`   (setf var4 (* var2 var3)))`

c. `(+ (defvar var5 4)`
`   (defvar var6 3))`

d. `(setf var6 (+ (setf var6 13)`
`                (setf var7 (- var6 13)))))`

e. `(setf var8 'var9`
`      var9 3`
`      var10 (+ var8 var9))`

f. `(setf 'bad-guy 'bluto)`

Exercise 2.2

Explain why `quote` couldn't be written as a function.

Exercise 2.3

Will the following examples work? Try 'em.

a. `(setf y '(+ 2 3))`
`   (+ (eval y) 4)`

b. `(setf z '(/ x z))`
`   (- (setf x 10)(eval z))`

c. `(setf x '*)`
`   ((eval x) 4 4)`

d. `(setf x 'x)`
`      (eval x)`

2.2 LISP STANDS FOR <u>LIS</u>P <u>P</u>ROCESSING

Lisp is renowned for its handling of lists. In fact, the name Lisp is a contraction for <u>Lis</u>t <u>P</u>rocessing. We've already encountered lists in some of the previous sections. In the last section, for example, we saw how to bind a list to a variable. If we wanted to have a list of composers, we could enter

```
CL> (defvar composers
           '(bach beethoven brahms))
COMPOSERS
```

The variable composers allows us to access the list whenever we need it without having to type out the list itself.

Constructing Lists

What if we wished to add another composer to the list? Common Lisp provides a function, cons, for constructing lists in this way. The first argument to cons is the item you wish to add to the list, and the second argument is the list to which the first argument is to be added. The function cons returns a new list with the item appearing as the head of the list. For instance, if you typed

```
CL> (cons 'mozart composers)
(MOZART BACH BEETHOVEN BRAHMS)
```

a new list would be created with mozart added at the beginning. Note that the atom mozart must be quoted to prevent the interpreter from trying to evaluate it. Note also that the list input to cons is not altered by the preceding call. If we evaluated the symbol composers, we would see that its binding was not changed by the call to cons. If we wished to change the list bound to composers, we would have to type

```
CL> (setf composers (cons 'mozart composers))
(MOZART BACH BEETHOVEN BRAHMS)
```

If the first argument to cons is a list itself, this list becomes the first element in the new list that is returned by cons. Consider the following interaction with Lisp:

```
CL> (defvar scary-things '(lions tigers bears))
SCARY-THINGS
CL> (defvar exclamation '( oh_my!))
EXCLAMATION
CL> (cons scary-things exclamation)
((LIONS TIGERS BEARS ) OH_MY!)
```

Building Lists from Scratch

Since cons only gives you the ability to add elements to the front of existing lists, how do you go about constructing a new list from disconnected atoms? Surely this is an operation that will be needed with some regularity. Fortunately, the designers of Lisp have recognized this need and have provided us with a function for making lists called, appropriately enough, list. This function will accept a variable number of arguments and return a new list consisting of the passed arguments. All of the arguments to list are evaluated. For example:

```
CL> (list 1 (+ 1 1)(+ 1 (+ 1 1)))
(1 2 3)
```

If one or more of the arguments to list happen to evaluate to lists themselves, the argument lists will be included intact in the list returned by list. For instance:

```
CL> (defvar list1 '( a b c ))
LIST1
CL> (defvar list2 '( d e f ))
LIST2
CL> (defvar list3 '( g h i ))
LIST3
CL> (list list1 list2 list3 )
((A B C)(D E F)(G H I))
```

Sometimes this is not what you really want to do. You may prefer to collapse all of the input lists into one simple list. This could be done using the function append. Using the same bindings as previously,

```
CL> (append list1 list2 list3)
(A B C D E F G H I)
```

Note that append expects all its arguments to be lists.

Accessing Elements of a List

In addition to building lists, we will frequently want to take lists apart. Common Lisp provides 10 functions that, when given a list, will return the element corresponding to a particular position in the list. These routines have names like `first`, `second`, `third`,... `tenth` that make it apparent which element they are intended to access. For example, suppose that there was a list that contained the first three finishers in the Kentucky Derby, such that

```
CL> place
(SWALE COAX-ME-CHAD AT-THE-THRESHOLD)
```

We could then retrieve various elements of the list `place` as follows:

```
CL> (first place)
SWALE
CL> (third place)
AT-THE-THRESHOLD
CL> (fourth place)
NIL
```

Since the first element of `place` was the atom `swale`, the result returned by the call to `first` was an atom. Note, however, that if the first element of the list was itself a list, then `first` would return a list. When we asked for the fourth element of a three-membered list, `fourth` returned the atom `nil`. This stands for the null or empty list in Lisp. In this context, when `fourth` returns `nil`, it means that there is no fourth element in `place`.

nth Function

Sometimes it would be convenient to pass the position of the element that we would like to extract as an argument to the function rather than specifying the position implicitly in the function name. The Common Lisp function `nth` accepts as its first argument the position of the argument that is to be accessed. Note that `nth` starts counting from zero, so that

```
CL> (defvar position 0)
POSITION
CL> (nth position place)
SWALE
CL> (nth (+ position 1) place)
COAX-ME-CHAD
```

Calling nth with its first argument equal to zero is equivalent to calling first, calling nth with its first argument equal to one is equivalent to calling second, and so forth.

Fetching Tails of Lists

There is another function in Common Lisp, called rest, that can also be used to extract a portion of a list. When a list is passed to rest, it returns a list consisting of everything in the input list except the first element. The rest function is the complement of the first function; it always returns a list. The following is an example of the use of rest:

```
CL> (rest place)
(COAX-ME-CHAD AT-THE-THRESHOLD)
```

If you wish to get the tail of a list starting after the nth element, there is a function in Common Lisp called nthcdr.[6] Like nth, nthcdr is zero-based. It always returns a list. For example:

```
CL> (nthcdr 2 place)
(AT-THE-THRESHOLD)
```

Note that none of the functions described for accessing parts of a list ever modify their arguments. They all extract the requested portion of the input list, but the input list itself is not affected; that is,

```
CL> breeds
(AIRDALE CORGI DACHSHUND SPANIEL TERRIER)
CL> (second breeds)
CORGI
CL> breeds
(AIRDALE CORGI DACHSHUND SPANIEL TERRIER)
```

There are some Common Lisp functions that do modify their arguments. We call these *destructive* list functions. They will be described in some detail in Chapter 4. An example is the rplaca function. It replaces the first element of a list with a new value. The list itself is changed. For example:

```
CL> (rplaca breeds 'doberman)
(DOBERMAN CORGI DACHSHUND SPANIEL TERRIER)
CL> breeds
(DOBERMAN CORGI DACHSHUND SPANIEL TERRIER)
```

---

[6]This function's name comes from combining nth with cdr. In earlier versions of Lisp, the rest function was called the cdr function. See Section 2.5 for an explanation of how cdr was named.

Exercise 2.4

Predict what will be returned by each of the following expressions:

a. (nth 1 `(a b c))

b. (first (second `((a b) (c d))))

c. (nth 1 (rest `(x y z)))

d. (first (rplaca

(rplaca

`(maclisp interlisp psl)
`zetalisp)
`common-lisp))

Exercise 2.5

Assume that the list (a b c d e) is bound to the variable test-list. Compose Common Lisp expressions that will return the following results:

a. B

b. (B C D E)

c. (C D E)

d. (E)

Exercise 2.6

Given the following dialogue with the Common Lisp interpreter, specify what is bound to the variable listx.

```
CL> (rest (second (first listx)))
(B)
```

2.3 COMMON LISP PREDICATES

In the last section, nil was discussed as a way of representing the empty list, but we will see that it has other meanings as well. Lisp has two logical constants, t and nil. Do they look more like symbols? See what happens when you evaluate them:

```
CL> nil
NIL
CL> t
T
```

However, since you know about the quote special form, you may still be suspicious that someone has just bound these symbols to

TABLE 2-1 *Truth Table for the Common Lisp Boolean Operators*

x	y	(not x)	(and x y)	(or x y)
t	t	nil	t	t
nil	t	t	nil	t
t	nil	nil	nil	t
nil	nil	t	nil	nil

themselves. Try this:

```
CL> (setf nil 99)
```

Convinced? It fails because you can't bind a value to a constant.[7] In Lisp, t and nil stand for the logical values true and false.

Boolean Operators

Common Lisp provides the three standard Boolean operators used in propositional logic: not, and, and or. The behavior of these operators is summarized in the truth table of Table 2-1.

Logical Negation

The function not takes a single, evaluated argument. If the value of the argument is nil, then the function returns t; otherwise, it returns nil. The not function basically inverts the truth value of its argument. Note that in Lisp there is only one way to represent the value false; false is always represented as the constant nil. True, on the other hand, can be represented by any non-nil expression. The logical constant t was provided merely to make code more readable.

Logical Conjunction

In logic, when two terms are joined by a logical and, the conjunction is true only when both terms are true (i.e., return non-nil values). The Common Lisp connective and provides this behavior (see Table 2-1). Like setf, and is an example of a macro. When the interpreter encounters a macro, it takes its (unevaluated) arguments and expands the macro definition to produce a form that is then evaluated. We will discuss macros in detail in Chapter 8. The

---

[7]MacLisp issued the error message *"Nihil est nihil"* in this situation.

important thing to realize about macros here is that the process of evaluation is a little different than it is for functions. Before calling a function, all of the arguments are evaluated and the values are passed to the function. Arguments to a macro are passed directly to the macro without evaluation. The macro determines when (if ever) an argument will be evaluated. The and macro, for example, uses a technique known as *lazy evaluation*. The first argument is always evaluated. If it returns a value of nil, the other argument(s) is (are) never evaluated. This is a reasonable thing to do, because if any argument to and evaluates to nil, the result returned by and will always be nil. If the value of the first argument is non-nil, the macro will continue evaluating arguments until it either finds one that does evaluate to nil or it runs out of arguments. If all arguments evaluate to non-nil values, the and macro returns the

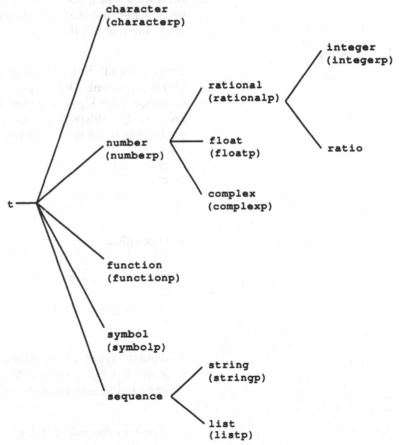

Figure 2-2   Common Lisp Type Hierarchy (Incomplete)

value of the last argument. The and macro can take any number of arguments.

Logical Disjunction

The third logical operator provided in Common Lisp is or. As seen in Table 2-1, the connective or returns a value of true whenever any of its arguments evaluate to a non-nil value. The Common Lisp or primitive, like and, is implemented as a macro. It also utilizes a lazy evaluation approach. The macro or evaluates its arguments from left to right. It returns the first non-nil value it encounters. If all of the arguments evaluate to nil, then the macro or returns nil.

Lisp Predicates

Lisp predicates are functions that return logical values. They are commonly used to test whether a pair of arguments are equivalent or represent a particular type. Several Lisp predicates can be combined using the Boolean operators presented earlier in this section. Because the use of predicates is ubiquitous in Lisp, we will cover them in depth.

Type Testing

There is a collection of built-in predicates for testing the type of a given argument. Data types are organized into a hierarchy in Common Lisp. Figure 2-2 shows part of the hierarchy of types that are available. Where applicable, the associated Common Lisp type-testing predicate is also shown. For example:

```
CL> (defvar var 10)
VAR
CL> (integerp var)
T
```

But note also:

```
CL> (rationalp var)
T
CL> (numberp var)
T
```

Because the types are organized in a hierarchy, an object can belong to more than one category. Most of the type predicate names are constructed by adding the letter p as a suffix to the type name.[8] One

---

[8]There is a convention in Lisp of naming all predicates with a p suffix. In fact, in Lisp programming circles, it is not uncommon around midday to hear the question, "Lunchp?"

exception to this rule is the type-testing predicate for atoms, which is simply called `atom`.

`typep` Function

If there is no built-in predicate for the type for which you wish to test, or if you want to supply the type as an argument, use the function `typep` instead. A call to `typep` has the following form:

```
(typep object type-specifier)
```

For example:

```
CL> (typep var 'ratio)
NIL
```

The *`type-specifier`* in `typep` can use logical connectives to combine types. For example, the following expression would return `t` if the current binding of `var` was a number or a symbol:

```
(typep var '(or number symbol))
```

While we're discussing type testing, here are two axioms of the Common Lisp type hierarchy. First, all data objects are considered to be examples of the type `t`. Second, the type, `nil` is considered to be a subtype of all types (Steele, 1990).[9]

List Predicates

As mentioned earlier, Lisp was designed to manipulate lists. It is perhaps not surprising that there are some special predicates for lists. There is, of course, the type-testing predicate, `listp`. There is a function, `member`, for testing to see whether its first argument is an element of a list. For example:

```
CL> (member 'b '(a b c))
(B C)
```

It returns the remainder of the list following (and including) the first *hit*. If there is at least one hit, the result will always be non-`nil`. Consequently, you can use `member` as though it were a predicate.

`null` Function

Because the need arises frequently, there is a special function `null`

---

[9]This may be a little confusing. The confusion arises from the fact that `nil` is used in at least three different ways in Lisp: as a named constant, as a list, and as a type. It is the last meaning that is being discussed here.

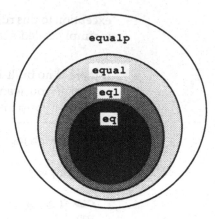

Figure 2-3   Venn Diagram Showing the Relationship Between Sets of Data Objects Possessing Different Degrees of Equivalence

for testing to see whether a list is empty. For example:

```
CL> (null ())¹⁰
T
```

The behavior of this function is identical to that of the not function. The two functions were provided to make it clear to readers of a piece of code whether the programmer wished to treat the argument as a list or a logical constant.

Testing Equivalence

Because there are so many data types and data structures in Lisp, there are a number of ways that two objects can be equivalent. In Common Lisp, you can determine not only that two objects are equal but also just how equal they are. There are four general equality predicates in Common Lisp. Figure 2-3 contains a Venn diagram portraying the relationship between the four predicates.

eq Function

The highest degree of equivalence occurs when two objects are in fact the same object. The Common Lisp predicate eq (pronounced either as the letters *e-q* or *eek*) will return a true result if its arguments are the same, identical object. The function eq can get you into trouble, however, if you are dealing with anything but symbols.

---

¹⁰The empty list can be written as nil or as a pair of empty parentheses.

Because you don't always know how individual Common Lisp implementations have chosen to represent constants, use of the function eq for testing numeric constants may give unexpected results. For example, in most implementations of Common Lisp:

```
CL> (eq 'x 'x)
T
CL> (eq 3.5 3.5)
NIL
```

eql Function

For this reason, eq is not a very good test of equivalence except when comparing symbols. Numeric and character constants can be compared using the eql (pronounced *e-q-l*) predicate. As seen in Figure 2-3, the set of objects that are equivalent by the eql test is a proper superset of the objects that are equivalent by the eq test. Two numeric constants that are the same are always guaranteed to be eql in any implementation of Common Lisp. For example:

```
CL> (eql 3.5 3.5)
T
```

in all Common Lisp implementations. But

```
CL> (eql (list 'a 'b 'c)
         (list 'a 'b 'c))
NIL
```

This unexpected result is due to the fact that every time you create a list with list, you get a brand new list. The two calls to list may look identical, but each one creates a different list. The created lists may look identical, but they are not the same list; as a result, eql indicates that they aren't equivalent.[11]

equal Function

As you can see, this could create some confusion if you were using this test in a program where you were sometimes dealing with lists and sometimes with nonlists. There is another test of equality, called equal, that considers two objects equivalent on the basis of their appearance (i.e., if they print out the same). This works well

---

[11]A similar problem occurs when you use eql to compare strings. For example:

```
CL> (eql "String" "String")
NIL
```

with lists and strings; for example:

```
CL> (equal '(a b c) '(a b c))
T
```

and

```
CL> (equal "String" "String")
T
```

But sometimes, an even more relaxed type of equality is required, such as

```
CL> (equal "XXXXX" "xxxxx")
NIL
CL> (equal 3 3.0)
NIL
```

The function `equal` treats two objects as equivalent if they are symbols and are `eq`, if they are numeric constants and are `eql`, or if they are two objects of the same type and print the same way. Clearly, the set of objects that are equivalent by the `equal` test is a superset of the set of objects that are equivalent by the `eql` test. The problem with using `equal` with strings is that, as mentioned earlier, the case is significant in strings. Consequently, when the strings "XXXXX" and "xxxxx" are evaluated, the results returned will look different and will not be `equal`. This may be exactly what you wanted, but if you wanted strings tested without regard to case, `equal` would be the wrong test. The problem with comparing 3 and 3.0 is that the two arguments are not of the same data type (one is an integer and the other is a float). If you just want to test the numeric value and don't care if the arguments are both of the same type, then again, `equal` is not the correct test to use.

equalp Function

The least stringent test of equality is used in the function `equalp`. It is true if its arguments are `equal`, or if the arguments are numbers and can be coerced to the same type and have the same value. When strings or characters are compared using `equalp`, discrepancies in case are ignored.

To summarize, `eq` and `eql` test to see if two objects are the same, `equal` tests to see if they look the same, and `equalp` tests to see if they have the same value (ignoring case and type differences). The test chosen will be determined by the types of data objects to which you anticipate the test will be applied. If you know that only symbols will be compared, `eq` is the fastest test to use. If comparison of numeric constants is possible, you may wish to use `eql` to ensure that your application will work the same way on all implementations of Common Lisp. If you must also consider lists or strings, `equal` is the best test. If you plan to encounter strings or characters and don't care about the case, or if you are working with numbers and are indifferent to the types of numeric arguments you might receive, `equalp` is the test for you. It would not be a good strategy to always use `equalp` because there are many situations in which you need a more stringent test. Also, `equalp` takes much longer to execute than `eql` or `eq`. In fact, a simple rule for remembering the relative computational efficiency of the equality predicates is "The longer the name, the longer it will take to execute."

If you are working with only one kind of data, like numbers or strings, it is often best to use more specialized tests. To those reading your code, this makes it clearer how you expected the program to be used. It also allows the system to do a little run-time type checking. Type-checking errors are often the first clue that your program is not working the way you had expected. A third consideration is that with numbers and strings you sometimes wish to do more than test for equality or the lack of it; sometimes you wish to test for inequality.

Arithmetic Comparisons

There are six predicates designed to compare two numeric arguments. They resemble the typical relational operators that you are familiar with from other languages. The six predicates are

```
=       ; equal to (actually equalp)
/=      ; not equal to
<       ; less than
>       ; greater than
<=      ; less than or equal to
>=      ; greater than or equal to
```

They are similar to `equalp` in that they compare two numeric arguments that are not of the same type. For example:

```
CL> (>= 3.2 3)
T
```

If the arguments are not numbers, however, these predicates will signal an error.

There are a few other numeric predicates that you may wish to know about. These come in handy in special situations. They all take a single argument that is always evaluated. The predicates evenp and oddp do the obvious. They accept only integer arguments. The predicates plusp, minusp, and zerop test to see if the argument is positive, negative, or equal to zero. They accept any type of number.

Special-Purpose Comparisons

There are analogous sets of comparison predicates for strings and characters. The names of the predicates are formed by concatenating the name string or char onto the appropriate test name. For example, the string comparisons have names like string=, string/=, and string>, the character comparisons have names like char>= and char=, and so forth. As with equal, the comparisons are based on the appearance of the arguments. We say that the arguments are compared *lexicographically*. For example:

```
CL> ( char< #\A #\B)¹²
T
CL> (char< #\A #\a)
T
CL> ( string> "some string" "SOME STRING")
0¹³
```

Case is significant for both character and string comparisons.

Character Predicates

There are also some special character predicates, like uppercase-p, lower-case-p, and alpha-char-p, that are useful when you are doing text manipulation. They operate only on character-type arguments. The first two do just what you would expect. The predicate alpha-char-p tests to see if its evaluated argument is an alphabetic character. For example:

```
CL> (lower-case-p #\T)
NIL
CL> (alpha-char-p #\?)
NIL
CL> (alpha-char-p #\g)
T
```

[12] A character is *not* the same as a string of length one.

[13] For string comparisons, if the comparison holds, Common Lisp returns a zero-based pointer to the place where the first difference occurred. Since the result is non-nil, it can still be used as a predicate.

Exercise 2.7

Write an expression to test to see if the current binding of x is

a. a symbol.

b. an integer or a ratio.

c. a character or a string.

d. a character between #\A and #\Z.

e. not a list

Exercise 2.8

What will the following predicates return?

a. `(listp nil)`

b. `(atom t)`

c. `(eql "S" #\S)`

d. `(typep 2/3 'ratio)`

e. `(eql "S" "S")`

f. `(eq '(a b c) '(a b c))`

g. `(equal '(A B C)(list 'a 'b 'c))`

h. `(eq (setf y 'x) 'x)`

i. `(member '(a  b c)(list 'a 'b 'c))`

j. `(typep  nil  t)`

Exercise 2.9

Are the following pairs of expressions equivalent? Create a truth table showing the four possible bindings of x and y. Use the interpreter to compute the values of the expressions.

a. `(and (not x)(not y))`

`(not (or x y))`

b. `(not (or x y))`

`(or (not x)(not y))`

2.4 CONTROL OF FLOW

With your new knowledge of Lisp predicates, you have the ability to test for a host of conditions, but you still lack the language tools to cause certain actions to occur based on the satisfaction of some set of conditions. In this section, you will be provided with those tools.

Common Lisp if Special Form

The simplest construct for conditional execution in Common Lisp is the if special form. It resembles the if statement found in virtually all modern languages. A call to the if special form has the following appearance:

```
(if condition-form then-form )
```

The *condition-form* is evaluated. If it returns nil, the if special form also returns nil; otherwise, if evaluates the *then-form* and returns its value. For example, you could type

```
CL> (setf  var 10)
10
CL> (if (numberp var)
       (*  var var))¹⁴
100
```

There is an optional third argument to the if special form that represents an *else-form*. Using this alternate form, a call to if has this appearance:

```
(if condition-form then-form else-form )
```

For example:

```
CL>   (defvar var 'x)
VAR
CL> (if (atom var)
        "this is an atom"
        "this is a list")
"this is an atom"
```

What if you had more than one form that you wanted to evaluate if the conditions were satisfied (i.e., a multiconsequent if)? You clearly couldn't put it inside the if form because it would be treated as an *else-form*. You could have multiple if statements, but this would be inefficient because the *condition-form* would have to be evaluated for each if form. Fortunately, Common Lisp provides two additional macros to solve this problem.

---

[14]Carriage returns are ignored by the Lisp interpreter within an expression. Often an expression can be made a little more readable by placing the arguments to a function or special form on separate lines. This has no effect on the execution of the form.

when and unless

Common Lisp provides a macro called when that will handle multiple consequents. It has the following form:

```
(when condition-form
      then-form-1
      then-form-2
           .
           .
           .
      then-form-n )
```

Like if, if the *condition-form* evaluates to nil, when goes no further and simply returns nil. If the *condition-form* evaluates to a non-nil value, however, all of the *then-forms* are evaluated in sequence and when returns the value of the last *then-form*. The unless macro is like a negative when. It is identical to writing

```
(when (not condition-form )
      then-form-1
      then-form-2
           .
           .
           .
      then-form-n)
```

For example:

```
(unless (atom p)
        (print (first p))
        (setf p (rest p)))
```

Constructs like unless are sometimes referred to as *syntactic sugaring* because, strictly speaking, their presence in the language does not provide the programmer with any new expressive capabilities. However, many programmers enjoy the convenience of having some of these extra constructs, and primitives like unless often make code easier to read.

Common Lisp **case** *Macro*

Common Lisp also offers a case macro, which behaves similarly to the case statement found in other languages, like Pascal. The form of a call to case is

```
(case key-form
    (clause-1)
    (clause-2)
        .
        .
        .
    (clause-n))
```

Each clause consists of a key or list of keys and one or more *then-form*. The keys are usually symbols or constants. A key can appear in one and only one clause. When the Lisp interpreter encounters a `case` macro, the *key-form* is evaluated and a match is sought among the keys in the clauses. The keys themselves are not evaluated. Matching is done using the `eql` function. If one of the keys in one of the clauses matches the result returned from evaluating *key-form*, all of the *then-form*s associated with that clause are evaluated and the value of the last *then-form* is returned for the `case` expression. If no match is found, `case` returns `nil`. If the key list for the last clause is replaced by either the symbol `otherwise` or `t`, then the last clause will be executed in the event that no other key matches the value of the *key-form*. For example, here is some code to compute the number of days in a given month:

```
CL> (setf month 'december)
DECEMBER
CL> (case  month
      (february  28)
      ((april june september november) 30)
      (otherwise  31))
31
```

The variable `month` is evaluated and returns the symbol `december`. The key for the first clause is the symbol `february`, which clearly is not `eql` with our key pattern (remember that all of the keys are converted to uppercase by the interpreter). The keys for the second clause are the symbols `april`, `june`, `september`, and `november`, which also fail to match. The third clause is selected by default. It has only one *then-form*, a numeric constant that self-evaluates. The `case` macro returns the value of the last *then-form*, which is just what we wanted.

The typecase Macro

Using a `case` form to test the type of an object is done so commonly that Common Lisp has a built-in macro, called `typecase`, for just this purpose. It resembles `case` in that it has a *key-form* and a set of clauses. It differs in that `typecase` uses the Common Lisp type of the evaluated *key-form* as the matching key rather than using the evaluated *key-form* itself. Also, the keys in the type-case clauses are Common Lisp type names. For example:

```
CL>  (defvar  my-object #\x)
MY-OBJECT
Cl>  (typecase my-object
        (integer t)
        (float t)
        (symbol t)
        ((or character string) t)
        (otherwise nil))

T
```

This typecase expression works like a kind of predicate that will return t when my-object is an integer, a floating point number, a symbol, a character, or a string and nil if it is anything else. The macro typecase, like the typep predicate, allows types to be combined using logical connectives. The fourth preceding clause, for example, says, "Select this clause if the type of the current binding of my-object is either a character or a string."

Exercise 2.10

Explain why the special form if cannot be implemented as a function in Common Lisp.

Exercise 2.11

What do the following expressions actually do?

a. (unless (atom x)
         (rest x))

b. (when (integerp x)
         (setf x (+ x 1))
       x)

c. (case rank
         (1 (quote ace))
         (11 (quote jack))
         (12 (quote queen))
         (13 (quote king))
         (t rank))

d. (typecase my-object
         (list (first my-object))
         (atom (list my-object))
         (otherwise nil))

Exercise 2.12

Write an expression that will test the current value of the variable `year` to see if it is a leap year. For our purposes, "a year is a leap year if and only if its number is divisible by 4, except that years divisible by 100 are not leap years, except that years divisible by 400 are leap years" (Steele, 1986, p. 445).

(Hint: The Common Lisp `mod` function takes two numeric arguments and returns the integer remainder after dividing the first argument by the second.)

Exercise 2.13

Write a `typecase` expression that will select an appropriate test of equivalency for two variables, `obj1` and `obj2`, depending on the current types of the variables. Use `eq` for a pair of symbols, `eql` for a pair of numbers, `equal` for lists, and `equalp` for everything else.

2.5 TRADITIONAL LISP

Some of the Lisp functions with which you are now familiar were known by different names in earlier versions of Lisp. The earlier names of these functions were nonmnemonic in the extreme. Nonetheless, Lisp programming initiates learned them while becoming full-fledged Lisp programmers. Because these names are used extensively in old Lisp code, Common Lisp recognizes both the old and the new names in order to provide backward compatibility. Since you are likely to encounter some of these more traditional expressions if you look at old code, you too must have some familiarity with these vestiges of Lisps past.

car and cdr

In Lisp 1.5, the name of the function that returned the head of a list was called `car`, not `first`. The function for finding the tail of a list was called `cdr` (pronounced *could-er*), not `rest`. These names were acronyms for assembly-level instructions on the IBM 704, the computer on which Lisp was first implemented (e.g., Contents of Address part of Register). Some Lisp programmers persist in using these function names, although the more mnemonic `first` and `rest` are probably preferable. One feature of the old names is that these functions can be composed together to define new functions for accessing parts of lists. The names of these functions have the form `cxr`, where *x* is replaced by a string of one to four characters chosen from the set `{#\a, #\d}`. A nested call to the `car` or `first` function is made for every `#\a`, and a nested call to the `cdr` or `rest` function is made for every `#\d`. For example, the function

```
(caddr some-list)
```

is equivalent to typing

```
(car (cdr (cdr some-list)))
```

or

```
(first (rest (rest some-list)))
```

This kind of naming convention can often be confusing, however, especially for the new programmer. Common Lisp has built-in functions that provide the same functionality but are much easier to read. For instance, the preceding `caddr` function is equivalent to the `third` function. (Prove that that is true.) For fetching tails of lists, the `nthcdr` function is easier to use than one of the functions composed of `car`s and `cdr`s. For example, to get everything in a list after (and including) the fourth element, you could type

```
CL> (nthcdr 3 '(a b c d e))
(D E)
```

Note that `nthcdr`, like `nth`, is zero based.

setq *Special Form*

Another commonly used special form that was used extensively in the past, but that has fallen into disuse in Common Lisp, is `setq`. This special form can be used in place of `setf` to assign values to Lisp variables. However, as you will learn in Chapter 4, `setf` can do a lot more than make assignments to variables. Since `setf` is a more general-purpose routine, the use of `setq` is no longer taught to new programmers. Chances are, though, that you will still encounter `setq` in the code of other programmers, so you should be familiar with its functionality.

cond *Macro*

One additional vestige of Lisp's colorful past is the `cond` macro. This macro served as the mechanism for conditional execution in early versions of Lisp. In Common Lisp, the use of `cond` has been largely supplanted by the more readable conditional execution routines: the `if` special form, the `when` and `unless` macros, and the `case` and `typecase` macros. The general form of a call to `cond` is

```
(cond cond-clause-1
      cond-clause-2
```

.
.
.
```
            cond-clause-n )
```

where a *cond-clause-n* would have the form

```
(condition-form-n   then-form-n-1
                    then-form-n-2
               . . . ))
```

For each *cond-clause* the *condition-form* is evaluated first. If it returns a non-nil value, the corresponding *then-form*s are evaluated in sequence. If the condition-form evaluates to nil, the *then-form*s are ignored and processing skips to the next *cond-clause*. Like a case form, only the first true clause is evaluated in a cond form. As an example of the use of cond, let us redo the case expression presented earlier in the chapter for computing the number of days in a given month. Using cond, the expression would appear as

```
(cond ((eq month 'february) 28)
      ((member month
          '(april june september november) 30)
      ( t 31 ))
```

Most programmers would agree that the case form is easier to read. Still, some programmers may prefer to use the cond macro instead of the newer forms for conditional execution. Unlike many of the language features in Common Lisp such as set f, which are more powerful than their predecessors, cond has greater expressive power than the newer if, when, unless, case, and typecase forms. Some programmers, therefore, may choose to always use cond because they only have to remember one form. Whichever approach you choose, you should be able to read both the new style and the old.

Exercise 2.14

Rewrite the following expressions, using compositions of cars and cdrs:

a. (second '(a b c))

b. (fourth '(a b c d e))

c. (nthcdr 3 '(a b c d e))

d. (rest (second '(a (b c d) e f g)))

Exercise 2.15

The macros when and unless are sometimes referred to as *syntactic sugar* because they don't allow you to do anything that you couldn't already do using the simple cond macro. To convince yourself of that fact, try rewriting the expressions in Exercise 2.11 using cond.

Exercise 2.16

There is a system variable in Common Lisp called *package* that points to the current package. (Packages are described in Chapter 8; You won't really need to know about them, however, to solve this problem.) If we call the Common Lisp function package-name on this variable, we will get back a string. For example:

```
CL> (package-name *package*)
"USER"
```

The string returned will vary, depending on the current assignment of *package*. Write an expression that will test the value of the returned string and do the following:

a.   Produce the string "Okay!", if the string returned by package-name is "CL-USER".

b.   Reassign *package* to the value returned by (find-package "CL-USER") and return the string "Package changed to CL-USER" if the string returned by package-name is "SYSTEM".

(Warning: Reassigning *package* can have surprising side effects; be careful to do it exactly as described earlier.)

c.   Otherwise, just return the string returned by package-name.

(Hint: Be sure that you are using the correct predicate for comparing strings.)

SUMMARY

The Lisp interpreter has three rules that it follows when evaluating Lisp forms. They are:

1.   Symbols are replaced by their current bindings.

2.   Lists are evaluated as function calls.

3.   Everything else evaluates to itself.

Exceptions to this general evaluation behavior occur in calls to Lisp macros and special forms. Some or all of the arguments to these Lisp forms are not evaluated.

You, as a programmer, can always prevent an argument from being evaluated by using the quote special form. In some situations, you may wish to force an extra round of evaluation. This is done using the eval function.

Lisp has a rich set of built-in routines for manipulating linked lists. Some of the most frequently used forms are the cons, list, and append functions for building lists; functions like first, second, and nth for fetching elements of a list; and functions such as rest and nthcdr for accessing tails of lists.

Lisp predicates are functions that return logical values. They are frequently used to test the type of an object or as relational operators to compare two or more objects. Lisp predicates can be combined using the Boolean operators not, and, and or. Common Lisp uses a lazy evaluation scheme when evaluating and and or expressions.

Testing equivalence in Lisp is complicated by the fact that two objects can be equal in different ways. Common Lisp provides four different equivalence predicates: eq, which tests for symbol identity; eql, which tests for identity of constants; equal, which checks for equivalent appearances (i.e., whether two things look the same when printed); and equalp, which tests for equivalent value, ignoring discrepancies in case or data type.

Common Lisp has several built-in forms for conditional execution. The simplest is the if special form. It can be used with or without an *else-form*. Multiconsequent if expressions can be implemented using the when and unless macros. Common Lisp also offers a case macro that behaves like the CASE statement found in other languages. The macro typecase is a special version of case for doing type testing.

For backward compatibility, Common Lisp supports a number of forms from earlier Lisp dialects. Many of these forms are still used by experienced programmers, and so you would be advised to become familiar with their usage.

NEW COMMON LISP DEFINED NAMES

=	eql	or
<	equal	plusp
<=	equalp	quote
>	eval	rationalp
>=	evenp	rest

alpha-char-p	first	rplaca
and	fourth	second
append	if	setq
atom	integerp	string=
cdr	list	string/=
car	listp	string>
case	lower-case-p	t
char=	minusp	third
char<	nil	typecase
char>=	null	typep
cond	nthcdr	unless
cons	numberp	when
eq	oddp	zerop

FOR FURTHER READING

For further information on topics covered in this chapter, read the following material in the Steel book (Steele, 1990): Section 5.1 (Rules of Evaluation), Chapter 15 (Lists), Chapter 6 (Predicates), and Section 7.6 (Control of Flow). Information on specific Common Lisp forms can be found in Chapters 6 and 7 of the Draft Standard (ANSI, 1990).

3

Forms and Functions

Form ever follows function.
Louis Henri Sullivan

3.1 DEFINING COMMON LISP FUNCTIONS

You now know quite a bit about how expressions are evaluated in Common Lisp. You have also examined the Common Lisp type hierarchy in some detail and have seen how to control conditionally the execution of parts of an expression. You know enough to produce some fairly complicated behavior from the Lisp interpreter, using the set of primitive forms and functions provided in Common Lisp. But how do you go about defining your own functions? That is the topic of this chapter.

Functions are defined in Common Lisp using the defun macro. As a simple example of how defun works, let's define a function for negating a numeric argument. The call to defun looks like this:

```
CL> (defun negate (number)
       (* number -1))
NEGATE
```

The first argument to defun is the name of the function to be defined. The second argument is a list of the function's parameters; in this case, we have only one, the parameter number. The rest of the arguments represent the body of the function. You can have as many Lisp expressions in the body as you wish. It is only necessary to multiply the number by a negative one, so we need only one form. The defun macro returns the name of the newly defined function.

The negate function is now part of our environment, as are all of the functions provided by Common Lisp itself. We could now type

```
CL> (negate 100)
-100
```

When the negate function is invoked, it returns the value of the last form evaluated in the function definition. In this case, the last (and only form) in the functional definition of negate is the call to the * function, so negate returns the value of number multiplied by minus one.

Value Returned versus
Side Effects

All Lisp forms (i.e., functions, macros, and special forms) return a value. In a functional language like Lisp, forms are usually called just to get the value that they return. Sometimes, however, what a function returns may be less important than what happens when the forms internal to the function are evaluated. Executing some forms may cause side effects. For example, the Common Lisp write function takes a single argument. The argument is evaluated and the value displayed on the terminal. The write function returns the value of its argument, but we are more interested in its side effect than its returned value. We say that write is called for *effect*, whereas negate is called for *value*.

Lambda Lists

Every Lisp function has a list of parameters, although the list can be empty. Parameter lists in Lisp are sometimes referred to as *lambda lists*. This term comes from the Lambda Calculus developed by Alonzo Church (Church, 1941). The elements of the lambda list become the names of variables, which can be used only within the function. When a function is called in Lisp, the arguments are evaluated from left to right and their values are passed to the function.[1] Inside the function itself, the passed values are bound to the parameter names. In the negate function, the parameter name, number, can be used to access the value of the argument given to the function.

Local and Global Variables

Variables in Lisp can be divided into two categories: *global* and *local*. Variables (like number in negate) that correspond to the elements of the lambda list are considered local. They are recognized only within the defining function, and their bindings are in force only while the function is being executed. For example, if you tried to evaluate the variable number after calling negate, you would get an undefined symbol error because number is defined only inside the function. This is different from the kinds of variables you encountered in the previous chapters. Variables created at the top level of Lisp are recognized across the system. We call them *global* variables. For example, let's create a variable at the top level like this:

```
CL> (defvar *last-value* 0)
*LAST-VALUE*
```

You can now use *last-value* in any function.[2] You can use this variable in a function that generates a new number every time it is called.[3]

```
CL> (defun generate-number ()
        (setf *last-value* (+ *last-value* 1 )))
GENERATE-NUMBER
CL> (generate-number)
1
CL> (generate-number)
2
CL> *last-value*
2
```

[1] Hence Common Lisp uses the argument passing convention of *call-by-value* instead of *call-by-name*. (This terminology is borrowed from Algol.) Actually, the situation is a little more complicated when lists are passed as arguments. This will be discussed in Chapter 4.

[2] Note the convention of enclosing the names of global variables in asterisks.

[3] This example illustrates how global variables work. A better way to write generators will be presented in Chapter 8.

Unlike the local variable `number`, the binding of `*last-value*` is preserved from one call to the next.

It may seem easier to work with global variables than with local variables. However, experienced Lisp programmers usually try to avoid using global variables for reasons that will be discussed later in the chapter. It is best to get into the habit of using local variables whenever possible.

Creating Local Variables with `let`

Sometimes you may need more local variables than are provided in the parameter list. The `let` special form can be used to provide all of the local variables you need. Its first argument is a list of the local variables. The remaining arguments are forms that are evaluated within the `let` expression. For example, you could type

```
CL> (let (local-var)
        (setf local-var 10)
            (+ 20 local-var))
30
```

Here we created a local variable, `local-var`. Local variables created in a `let` expression are recognized only inside the `let` form. The `let` form returns the value of the last expression evaluated within the form. You can initialize local variables by providing an expression to be evaluated. For example:

```
CL> (let ((x 100) (y 200))
      (+ x y))
300
```

The initialization of the variables in a `let` form is said to take place in *parallel*. This means that expressions like

```
(let ((x 100)(y  x))
   (+ x  y))
```

will not work. In situations where you want to use a local variable in subsequent initialization forms, you can use the special form `let*`. We say that `let*` evaluates its initialization forms *sequentially*. Using `let*`, the last example would work exactly as you wished.

The `let` and `let*` special forms are most commonly used to create local variables inside functions. For example, you could define a function that computes the average for a list of numbers as follows:

```
CL> (defun average (number-list)
       (let ((list-sum (sum-list number-list))
             (n (length number-list )))
         (/ list-sum n )))
AVERAGE
CL> (average '(10 20 30))
20
```

The let form here is used to create the local variables list-sum and n. They are used to store the intermediate values used in computing the mean of the numbers in the list. The sum-list function does just as its name suggests (you will write sum-list in Exercise 3.5). The length function is a built-in Common Lisp function that returns the number of elements in a list.

The Lisp World

Every time you define a new function or create a global variable, it becomes part of the environment in which you work. I will use the term *Lisp world* to refer to the totality of elements defined in the Lisp environment, including all of the Common Lisp forms and variables, as well as the functions and symbols contributed by you as a programmer. If a defined function does not work satisfactorily, you may redefine it using defun. You may, in fact, redefine functions and macros provided by Common Lisp if you wish, though I would not recommend it.[4]

Editing Function Definitions

So far, we have dealt with very small, simple function definitions. Very soon, however, we will be looking at longer, more complicated functions. If you are a bad typist (as I am), you probably may have to retype the function definition several times before the function will work. This becomes a bit wearing after a while. You would like a method of correcting mistakes without having to retype the whole definition. Most Common Lisp implementations provide editors within the Lisp world for just this purpose. The nature of the editors varies greatly from implementation to implementation. Some are very simple, line-based editors similar to the text editors used for other programming languages. Some are very sophisticated structure editors that have special knowledge of Lisp syntax. Consult the programmer's manual for your Common Lisp implementation for a detailed description of the features of your editor. Take time to familiarize yourself with the editor now,

---

[4] Most implementations will issue a warning whenever you attempt to redefine an existing form. You may redefine Common Lisp functions and macros but not special forms.

since you will probably use it more than any other program in your environment.

Storing Function Definitions

It would be exceedingly tedious if you had to retype the definitions of functions, like `negate`, every time you started Lisp. For this reason, every Common Lisp implementation provides a mechanism for storing function definitions in files for later use. Usually the Lisp editor provides a command for saving function definitions. Frequently, programmers will store several related functions in a single file. Common Lisp source files consist of expressions that, when evaluated, will redefine the forms. This situation is depicted in Figure 3-1.

Loading Functions from Files

The Common Lisp `load` function is used to load the definitions stored in a file. The `load` function is called with an argument that evaluates to a string specifying a file name. File-naming conventions are system dependent, so I will not provide an example of a call to `load`. When `load` is called, each form in the file is read and evaluated. The set of functions in your file then become defined (or redefined) in your current Lisp world.

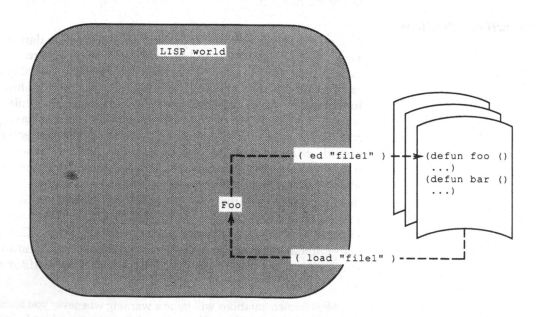

Figure 3-1 Saving Function Definitions to a File

Comments

As in all programming languages, it is usually desirable to insert some comments in your code, both as a courtesy to other programmers and for your own benefit when you have to revisit the code in the future. The semicolon is used in Common Lisp to set off comment lines. Anything that follows the semicolon is ignored by the Lisp interpreter. The Common Lisp standard basically allows for three levels of comments.[5] The highest level, designated by three semicolons, is usually used in files outside of functions to describe groups of functions. These comments start at column 1. The next level of comments is used to provide overall information for a function. They are designated with two semicolons and are indented to correspond to the indentation of the code in the function. The lowest-level comments are designated with a single semicolon. These correspond to inline comments. Typically, they document a single line of code. The single-semicolon comments appear to the right of the code, and all of them start in the same column. I have rewritten the average function to show how it would appear in a file with comments.

```
;;; Example of a commented function
(defun average (number-list)
  ;; This function computes the arithmetic mean
  ;; for a list of numbers.
  (let ((list-sum (sum-list number-list)) ;total value
        (n (length number-list)))          ; # of elements
    (/ list-sum n)))
```

Documentation Strings

Common Lisp allows a second type of documentation in functions other than comments. You may also include one string of documentation in the definition of a function. The previous example could be rewritten as

```
(defun average (number-list)
"This function computes the arithmetic mean
 for a list of numbers."
  (let ((list-sum (sum-list number-list))
        (n (length number-list)))
    (/ list-sum n)))
```

[5]The Common Lisp standard actually calls for four levels of comments. For our purposes, however, quadruple and triple-semicolon comments can be considered the same.

The documentation string is not executable; it serves only as documentation. The advantage of using a documentation string rather than a simple comment is that the documentation string can be retrieved at run time using the documentation function. For example:

```
CL>(documentation 'average 'function)
"This function computes the arithmetic mean
 for a list of numbers."
```

This information may be useful to later users of the function.

Exercise 3.1

Write a function called adiff that will return the absolute difference between two numbers. For example:

```
CL> (adiff 2 5)
3
CL> (adiff 5 2)
3
```

Exercise 3.2

Write a Common Lisp function, days-in-month, that will return the number of days in a specified month. For example:

```
CL>  (days-in-month 'september)
30
```

Exercise 3.3

Will the following functions work?

a.
```
(defun fun-with-local-vars ()
    (let (( x 100) (y 200))
        (let ((z x))
        (* z y))))
```

b.
```
(defun fun-with-local-vars-2 ()
    (let ((x 100) (y 200))
      (setf z (+ x y ))))
```

c.
```
(defun fun-with-local-vars-3 ()
    (let ((x 100)(y 200)))
    (let ((z x))
    (* z z)))
```

d.
```
(defun fun-with-local-vars-4 ()
```

```
(let* ((x 100)
       (y 200)
       (x (* x y)))
  (+ x y)))
```

Exercise 3.4

Write a Lisp predicate called `leap-year-p` to test to see if its argument is a leap year. Use the expression you wrote for Exercsie 2.12 to test the argument. For example:

```
CL> (leap-year-p 1989)
NIL
CL> (leap-year-p 1988)
T
CL> (leap-year-p 1800)
NIL
```

Exercise 3.5 (*)

Write the `sum-list` function used in `average`. Try it first using fixed-length lists; if you are feeling adventurous, try writing it for variable-length numbered lists.

3.2 FUNCTIONS THAT CALL THEMSELVES

If you tried to write the `sum-list` function for variable-length lists, you probably had a rough time extracting the numbers from the list. In this section, I will show you a general technique for taking lists apart (and putting them together). It is based on the simple but important idea of recursion.

Recursion

Recursion is nothing more than writing functions so that they can call themselves to solve a problem. Recursive functions solve problems in layers, like the process of peeling an onion. Many modern languages support recursion, so some of you may already be familiar with this concept. Recursion is one of the most powerful ideas in computer science.

Computing Factorials

The standard example of a recursive function is the `factorial` function. As you may recall, the factorial of a nonnegative integer is computed by taking the product of all the numbers from 1 up to the specified integer. It could be written as follows:

```
x! = factorial(x) = x * (x - 1) * (x - 2)...1
```

An elegant way of defining the factorial function is to define it recursively, that is, in terms of itself. We could rewrite the definition of recursion as

$$\texttt{factorial}(x) = \begin{cases} 1 & \text{when } x = 0 \\ x\big(\texttt{factorial}(x-1)\big) & \text{when } x > 0 \end{cases}$$

When stated in this way, we see that factorials are computed by two methods: the factorial of 0 is simply 1; the factorial of any other positive number is the number times the factorial of the number less 1. You can compute the factorial of any positive integer if you know the factorial of one less than the number. This second definition of the factorial function can be directly converted into a recursive Lisp function as follows:

```
(defun factorial (x)
  (if (zerop x
      1
    (* x
        (factorial (1- x)))))
```

In this function, the value of the parameter x is tested to see if it is equal to zero; If so, then factorial returns 1; otherwise, it returns the result of calling factorial on the value of x minus 1. The 1- function simply decrements its argument. It is equivalent to calling (- x 1).

Figure 3-2 shows how the factorial function could be used to compute the factorial of 6. The factorial of 6 is computed by multiplying 6 times the factorial of 5. The factorial of 5 is computed by multiplying 5 times the factorial of 4. This process is repeated until you reach the factorial of 1, which is computed by multiplying 1 times the factorial of 0. You can compute the factorial of 0 directly. This, in turn, permits you to compute the value of the factorial of 1. One by one, you can now complete the computation of each of the calls to factorial and produce the final result of 720.

Components of a Recursive Form

All recursive forms will have two parts: a termination test and a recursive part. If there were no termination test, most recursive forms would keep on recursing until the system stack overflowed.[6]

---

[6]Don't be concerned if you are not familiar with the term *system stack*. The stack data structure will be described in Chapter 4. System stacks will be discussed in Chapter 9 in the section entitled "Lexical versus Dynamic Scope."

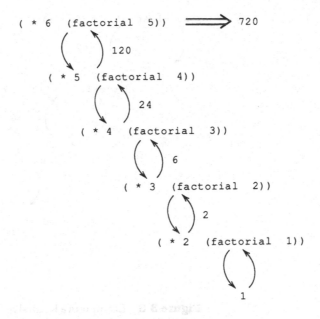

Figure 3-2   Computing the Factorial of 6

In the factorial function, termination occurs when the function is called with 1 as an argument. The recursive part of the form does all of the work. As in the factorial function, the arguments used for the recursive call are usually different from the parameter(s) accepted by the function. It is possible to have more than one recursive call within a recursive form. The recursive part may precede or follow the termination test. The order in which the components occur may have a dramatic effect on the behavior of the function.

Summing List Elements

Let's see how recursion could be used to solve the list-summing exercise in the last section. A version of sum-list that can handle variable-length lists could be defined as follows:

```
(defun sum-list ( number-list )
    (if number-list
        (+ (first number-list )
            (sum-list (rest number-list)))
        0))
```

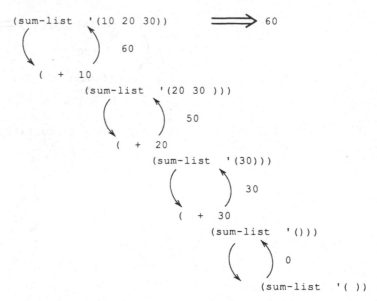

```
(sum-list  '(10 20 30))          ⟹    60

                      60
      (  +  10
           (sum-list  '(20 30 )))

                          50
           (  +  20
               (sum-list  '(30)))

                             30
               (  +  30
                   (sum-list  '()))

                                0
                   (sum-list  '( ))
```

Figure 3-3 Example of a Recursive Function for Summing the Elements of a List

We first test to see if number-list is empty.[7] If number-list is not empty, the first element of the list is added to the result returned when sum-list is called on the remainder of the list. If number-list evaluates to nil, then sum-list simply returns zero. Let's see how this works. If I called sum-list on the list (10 20 30), I would add 10 to the result returned when I call sum-list on the list (20 30). This would cause 20 to be added to the result of calling sum-list on a list with the single element 30. This would cause 30 to be added to the result of calling sum-list on the empty list. As we "unwind," back up the list of recursive calls, the last call to sum-list returns a zero, 30 is added to this and returned, 20 is added to this and returned, and finally, 10 is added to the last result to return the answer: 60. This whole sequence is portrayed graphically in Figure 3-3.

Building Lists

In sum-list the sum of the elements is created as we work our way back up the chain of function calls. This same technique can be used

---

[7]This is a Lisp colloquialism. The test is really

```
(not (null number-list))
```

but since the empty list and the truth value "false" share the same symbol (i.e., nil), it is frequently abbreviated to the symbol for the list.

to build lists. Consider, for example, a function to insert a number in a presorted list of numbers. We could write an `insert-sorted` function as follows:

```
(defun insert-sorted (item sorted-list)
   (if sorted-list            ; end of list?
      (let ((head (first sorted-list)))
         (if ( <= item head )       ;insert item at
                                    ;head of list?
            (cons item sorted-list)
            (cons head
                  (insert-sorted item
                        (rest sorted-list)))))
      (list item)))
```

In this function, we again test to see if the passed list is empty, indicating that we have reached the end of the list. If so, we return a new list consisting only of the new item. If we aren't at the end of the list, we create a local variable to store the first element of the current list. We then test to see if the item belongs at the head of the list. If so, we simply add the item to the beginning of the list and return the new list. If, however, the item does not belong at the beginning of the list, we need to move further down the list by

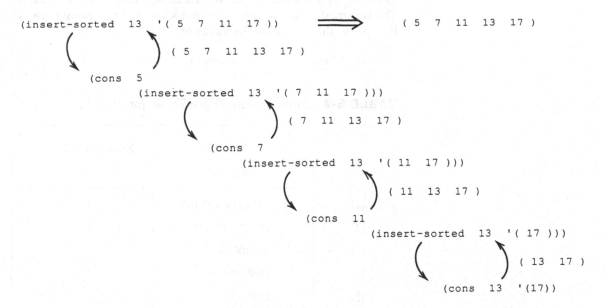

Figure 3-4 Recursively Inserting a Number in a Sorted List

TABLE 3-1 *Initial Trace Table for* `sum-list`

	Variables	Returned Value
	`number-list`	
[1]	(90 85 92 100 100)	?

recursively calling `insert-sorted` on the remainder of the list. Notice that `insert-sorted` is cleverly designed to reconstruct the list in sorted order as we work our way back up the chain of function calls. If this is not clear to you, work through the operation (as shown in Figure 3-4) to see exactly how this works.

Trace Tables

One way of studying a recursive function is to create a trace table to track the variable bindings and returned values for each recursive function call. For example, we could trace a call to the `sum-list` function, using

```
(90 85 92 100 100)
```

as the input list. Table 3-1 shows the initial state of the trace table. The returned value for this call is not known at this point because it requires that we know the value of

```
(sum-list '(85 92 100 100))
```

TABLE 3-2 *Intermediate Trace Table for* `sum-list`

	Variables	Returned Value
	`number-list`	
[1]	(90 85 92 100 100)	?
[2]	(85 92 100 100)	?
[3]	(92 100 100)	?
[4]	(100 100)	?
[5]	(100)	?
[6]	()	0

TABLE 3-3 *Final Trace Table for* `sum-list`

	Variables	Returned Value
	number-list	
[1]	(90 85 92 100 100)	467
[2]	(85 92 100 100)	377
[3]	(92 100 100)	292
[4]	(100 100)	200
[5]	(100)	100
[6]	()	0

This value is not known because, to compute it, we need to know the value of

```
(sum-list '(92 100 100)).
```

As we dig deeper, we eventually find the call

```
(sum-list '()).
```

This we can compute immediately, because we know that the sum of an empty list is zero. Table 3-2 shows the state of the table after five recursive calls to `sum-list`. The value of

```
(sum-list '(100))
```

TABLE 3-4 *Trace Table for* `insert-sorted`

	Variables			Returned Value
	Item	sorted-list	Head	
[1]	13	(5 7 11 17)	5	(5 7 11 13 17)
[2]	13	(7 11 17)	7	(7 11 13 17)
[3]	13	(11 17)	11	(11 13 17)
[4]	13	(17)	17	(13 17)

(line [5] in the trace table) can now be computed to be zero plus 100. This, in turn, allows us to compute the value returned in line [4], which is 100 plus the running sum of 100. Table 3-3 shows the final trace table after we have worked our way back to the original call and produce the final result: 467.

Table 3-4 contains the final trace table for the following call to `insert-sorted`:

```
(insert-sorted 13 '(5 7 11 17))
```

You may wish to work through this example yourself to see exactly how it functions. You will be asked to create some trace tables of your own in the exercises at the end of this section.

*CL **trace** Macro*

You will find that constructing trace tables is useful for studying the behavior of recursive forms. This must be done so frequently that Common Lisp comes with a built-in form for automatically computing a trace table for calls to specified functions. You could trace calls to `insert-sorted` by making the following call to the Common Lisp `trace` macro:

```
CL> (trace insert-sorted)
NIL
CL> (insert-sorted 13 '(5 7 11 17))
 Calling (INSERT-SORTED 13 (5 7 11 17))
  Calling (INSERT-SORTED 13 (7 11 17))
   Calling (INSERT-SORTED 13 (11 17))
    Calling (INSERT-SORTED 13 (17))
    INSERT-SORTED returned (13 17)
   INSERT-SORTED returned (11 13 17)
  INSERT-SORTED returned (7 11 13 17)
 INSERT-SORTED returned (5 7 11 13 17)
(5 7 11 13 17)
```

The format of the table produced will vary from implementation to implementation, but all of them should show at least the values of the arguments passed with each call to the function and the value returned. However, the availability of an automated facility for tracing functions does not mean that you will not need to know how to construct a trace table. The normal procedure for debugging a recursive function is to construct by hand a trace table for the function, using a set of test data. You could then compare the machine-generated trace for the function with your hand-generated version to see if the function is working properly. When you are satisfied that your function is working properly, you can turn off the trace facility, using the untrace macro as follows:

```
CL>(untrace insert-sorted)
NIL
```

CDRing Down a List

You may have begun to see a pattern emerging in the two recursive functions, sum-list and insert-sorted. The standard technique for taking apart a list is to process down the list recursively by calling the function on the remainder of the list after you remove the first element. Old Lisp hackers call this technique *CDRing down a list* after the cdr function described in Section 2.5. The standard technique for constructing a list is to cons elements onto a list as you back up the stack of recursive function calls. As with the function insert-sorted, the two techniques are often used together. Mastery of these two techniques will enhance your ability to manipulate lists.

Exercise 3.6

Make a trace table for the following call to insert-sorted:

```
(insert-sorted 12 '(6 8 9 10 12 14))
```

Exercise 3.7

Write a function called my-length that will compute the number of elements in a list.

Exercise 3.8

Write a predicate called member-p to search down a list of symbols looking for a match. If a matching symbol is not found, member-p returns nil; otherwise, it returns the list element. For example:

```
CL> (member-p 'x '(x y z)))
X
```

Do not use the Common Lisp member function.

Exercise 3.9

Write a function called insertion-sort that will sort a list using insert-sorted.

Exercise 3.10

Write a function called squash-list that, when passed a list of nested lists, will return a flat list. For example:

```
CL> (squash-list '((a) b ((c) d)))
(A B C D)
```

Exercise 3.11

Write a function that takes a list as an argument and returns a list with no redundant elements. For example:

```
CL> (remove-redundancies '(a a b a c b)))
(A C B)
```

Exercise 3.12

What do the following functions do? (Hint: A trace table may help.)

a. (defun mystery-fun-1 (x)
  (if (plusp x)
    (mystery-fun-1 (1- (print x)))
    'Lift-off!))

b. (defun mystery-fun-2 (x)
    (if x (append (mystery-fun-2 (rest x))
      (cons (first x) nil))))

c. (defun mystery-fun-3 (x)
    (if (< x 2) x
      (+ (mystery-fun-3 (1- x))
        (mystery-fun-3 (- x 2)))))

Exercise 3.13

The following function was developed by Ikuo Takeuchi (hence the name) as a Lisp benchmark:

```
(defun tak (x y z)
  (if (> x y)
    (tak (tak ( 1- x) y z)
         (tak (1- y) z x)
         (tak (1- z) x y))
    y))
```

Timings for the tak benchmark have been recorded for many Lisp implementations (see Gabriel, 1985). Using a trace table, predict the result for the following call:

```
(tak 3 2 1)
```

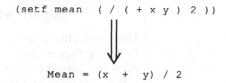

```
(setf mean ( / ( + x y ) 2 ))
```

$$\Downarrow$$

```
Mean = (x + y) / 2
```

Figure 3-5   Converting a Lisp Assignment Form into Fortran

3.3 RECURSION VERSUS ITERATION

Many of the examples we have considered up to now could have been implemented just as easily in any algorithmic language, like Pascal or C. Where Lisp really excels is in applications that require symbolic processing. When McCarthy wished to display some of the capabilities of the language he had just invented, he wrote an article describing the symbolic reduction of mathematical formulas using Lisp (McCarthy, 1960). Since then, Lisp has been used in a wide variety of symbolic processing applications, including work in expert systems, theorem proving, and computational linguistics.

Language Translation

As a simple example of a symbol-manipulating program, let's write a function to translate Lisp assignment forms into Fortran code.[8] Figure 3-5 shows a simple Lisp assignment form and the equivalent Fortran code. To perform the translation, we merely have to rearrange the expression a bit. Lisp expressions use prefix notation, whereas Fortran expressions are written in infix. The crux of the problem, then, is to rewrite the right-hand side of the expression in infix notation. We can start with the following simple function:

```
(defun lisp-to-fortran (expr)
  (let ((lhs (second expr))
        (rhs (third expr)))
    (write lhs)
    (write '=)
    (write (prefix-to-infix rhs))
    (terpri)))
```

The Lisp `write` function causes the value of its evaluated argument to be displayed to the user. The `terpri` function terminates a line of displayed output and starts a new line. In the function

---

[8]If you are averse to Fortran, this example would work just as well with Pascal, BASIC, C, or COBOL, with appropriate modifications.

High-Level Iteration Constructs

Historically, there has been an interest, within the Lisp community, in designing higher-level constructs for performing iteration. Lisp can express recursive algorithms in a fashion that is both simple and concise. Iterative algorithms, on the other hand, are a little more clumsy to express in a functional language like Lisp. Several approaches have been taken toward developing clearer, more readable iteration constructs for Common Lisp.

In the first edition of *Common Lisp: The Language* (Steele, 1984b), the iteration constructs were limited to do, do*, dotimes, dolist, and loop. The description of the loop macro was very simple. It was basically a form that repeatedly executed a body of expressions. In the Draft ANSI Standard (ANSI, 1990), the syntax of loop has been greatly extended. In the expanded version, loop will accept a variety of loop-keywords. These keywords can be used to create and initialize local variables, to specify termination conditions, and to define steps to be taken after the termination conditions are satisfied.

The extended loop macro can be used in place of the iteration constructs do, do*, dolist, and dotimes. For example, the expression:

```
(dolist (note '(do re me fa sol la te do))
   (print note))
```

could be written using loop as

```
(loop for note in '(do re me fa sol la te do)
   do (print note))
```

Similarly, the expression:

```
(dotimes (i 11)
   (print i))
```

could be rewritten as

```
(loop for i from 0 to 10
   do (print i))
```

The loop form may be a bit more verbose, but many people find it easier to read. It also provides you with greater control over where the loop index will start and finish and how the index will be updated. The following expression could not be implemented using dotimes (though it could be implemented using do):

```
(loop for j from 10 to 1 by -1
   do (print j))
```

The extended loop macro not only subsumes the powers of the simple iteration constructs, but it also performs most of the tasks normally done with mapping functions. For example, the expression:

```
(mapcar #'(lambda (x)
                  (* x x))
          '(12 11 8 7 9))
```

could be rewritten using `loop` as

```
(loop for x in '(12 11 8 7 9)
   collect (* x x))
```

In this case, each list element will be squared and results will be collected and returned as a new list.

The `loop` macro has many more capabilities than have been shown here. It is possible to produce very complex behavior using the new `loop` keywords. At the same time, it is also possible to use `loop` in very simple ways. In fact, if you do not supply any keywords, the `loop` macro will continue to work just as it did in the past.

In addition to the extensions to `loop` (which have been adopted into the ANSI CL Draft Specification), other more exotic approaches have been proposed for doing iteration in Common Lisp. One proposal uses a new type of data structure called a "series" and a set of functions that operate on such structures to implement iterative behavior (Steele, 1990). A series is conceptually similar to a stream, a data structure that we will be taking up in Chapter 7. A second proposal is based on a pair of data structures called "generators" and "gatherers" (Steele, 1990). Generators and gatherers, like series, are related to streams. They can be used to implement iteration in a particularly elegant way.

Obviously, there is more than one way to do iteration. Which is the best? The final test of a language construct is whether or not it is useful. Usefulness, in this context, depends on whether or not the construct permits you to write code in a way that makes it easier for you (and later readers) to understand what you are doing. A good construct not only allows you to express complicated ideas, but also gives you a medium in which you can conceptualize problems in new ways. A construct that "works" for one may seem obscure and confusing to another. As you become more proficient in Lisp, you will develop your own tastes in language features.

`lisp-to-fortran`, we create local variables to store what will be the left-hand and right-hand sides of the Fortran expression. We then simply display the assignment variable, the equal sign, and the rearranged formula.

Converting Prefix to Infix Notation

The real work here is being done in the `prefix-to-infix` function. This function can be defined as follows:

```
(defun prefix-to-infix (expr)
  (if (listp expr)
    (let ((operator (first expr))
          (operand-1 (second expr))
          (operand-2 (third expr)))
      (list (prefix-to-infix operand-1)
            operator
            (prefix-to-infix operand-2)))
    expr))
```

The function is recursive to handle nested expressions. It uses the combined techniques of CDRing down a list and constructing a new list as you unwind back up through the chain of recursive calls. It terminates when the argument passed to the function is an atom. The first element of every prefix form will be the operator; the second and third elements will be the operands. The `prefix-to-infix` function simply creates a new list in the proper infix order and returns it. Our recursive function ensures that elements of the Fortran expression will be put together in the proper order.

There are a few problems with our expression translation program as it stands. If we were to type:

```
CL> (lisp-to-fortran '(setf mean (/ ( + x y ) 2)))
MEAN=((x + y)/2)
```

we would get the appropriate answer. But if we typed

```
CL> (lisp-to-fortran '(setf mean (/ (+ x y z) 3)))
MEAN=((x + y)/3)
```

we would get an inappropriate answer. The `prefix-to-infix` function assumes that the expression will have three elements and can therefore handle only Lisp arithmetic forms with two arguments. In order to handle a variable number of arguments, we will have to add additional code to process down the list of operands. This could be accomplished by writing another recursive routine (see Exercise 3.12). Rather than do that, however, you can take advantage of the facilities that Common Lisp offers for iteratively processing lists.

The dolist Macro

The need to process down lists, performing one or more operations on each element of the list, arises so frequently that Common Lisp has a built-in macro for doing exactly this. The `dolist` macro can save us the trouble of writing a recursive routine every time we need to manipulate the elements of a list. The form of a call to `dolist` is as follows:

```
(dolist (var list-form result-form )
        body)
```

The *body* consists of one or more Lisp forms that will be evaluated once for each element of the list returned when *list-form* is evaluated. The dolist macro works like an implicit let form. It creates a local variable named *var*, which is bound, in turn, to the individual elements of the list as they are processed. After processing all the elements of the list, dolist returns the result of evaluating the *result-form* argument. For example:

```
CL> (dolist (element '(do re me fa sol la te do)
                      'Ciao!)
       (print element))
DO
RE
ME
FA
SOL
LA
TE
DO
CIAO!
```

The print function works like write, except that it always displays its result on a new line.

Using dolist, you could rewrite prefix-to-infix to accommodate variable-length operand lists. The new version would look something like this:

```
(defun prefix-to-infix-2 (expr)
;; this version handles optional operands
  (if (listp expr)
    (let ((operator (first expr))
          (new-expr (list (prefix-to-infix-3 (second expr)))))
      (dolist (element (nthcdr 2 expr) new-expr)
        (setq new-expr (append
                        new-expr
                        (list
                         operator
                         (prefix-to-infix-3 element))
                        ))))
    expr))
```

When lisp-to-fortran is changed to use prefix-to-infix-2, we get the following more satisfactory result:

```
CL> (lisp-to-fortran '(setf mean (/ (+ x y z) 3)))
MEAN=((x + y + z)/3)
```

Common Lisp Iterative Forms

Common Lisp has several built-in forms for defining iterative loops. In addition to the `dolist` macro that we just discussed, there is a `dotimes` macro and the more general-purpose `do` iteration macro.

The dotimes Macro

The `dotimes` macro is used to produce the behavior of a counted loop. It resembles a DO-LOOP in Fortran, although it is not quite as powerful. The form of a call to `dotimes` is

```
(dotimes (index-var
          upper-limit-form
          result-form)
    body)
```

Again, *body* is a collection of one or more Lisp expressions that will be evaluated once for each of the numbers from 0 to the value returned when *upper-limit-form* is evaluated. The variable *index-var* is locally bound to the current value of the loop index. After looping through the list of expressions the required number of times, the `dotimes` macro returns the value of the *result-form*. For example:

```
CL> (dotimes (my-index 4 'Ciao!)
       (print my-index))
0
1
2
3
CIAO!
```

If you want to advance multiple indices at once, or if you need to use a step size other than 1, you will need to use the more generic `do` iterative form.

The do Macro

The `do` macro is an extremely powerful instrument for affecting looping behavior. Its syntax is a little more complicated than that of `dolist` or `dotimes`. To use the `do` macro comfortably will require a bit of effort, but it will be worthwhile. The syntax of the `do` macro is

```
(do (index-specifier-1
     index-specifier-2   . . . )
```

```
                    (end-test result-form)
        body)
```

An *index-specifier* is a list of the form

```
    (index-var init-form stepping-form)
```

The *init-form* and *stepping-form* are both optional. In some ways, a do form resembles a let statement in that both have a list of local variables that are bound to their initialization forms. The major difference between a do form and a let form is that the expressions that comprise the *body* of the let form are executed only once, whereas the expressions in the *body* of a do form are executed over and over again until the *end-test* is satisfied.

The Computational Model for a do Form

How does the do macro work? These are the steps that are performed:

1. Each *index-var*s is locally bound to the result of evaluating its *init-form*. All of the bindings of the *index-var*s are done in parallel.[9]

2. The *end-test* is evaluated. If it returns a non-nil result, the do form returns the result of evaluating the *result-form*. Otherwise:

3. Evaluate each of the expressions in the *body*. All of the *index-var*s are available as local variables.

4. Update each of the *index-var*s, using the *stepping-form*s. Again, the new bindings are done in parallel.

5. Loop back to step 2.

In many cases, a do form may be invoked just for the *result-form* and the side effects of evaluating the *stepping-form*s. In cases such as these, there may be no *body* (see Exercise 3.16b and 3.16c for examples).

Defining dolist and dotimes

Anything implemented using dolist and dotimes can be redefined using the Common Lisp do macro. The converse is not necessarily true, since there are things that you can do with the do

---

[9]There is another macro called do* that performs the initialization step sequentially.

macro that cannot be expressed using dolist or dotimes. We could rewrite the previous dotimes example as

```
CL> (do ((my-index  0 (1+ my-index)))
            ((> my-index 3)  'Ciao!)
            (print my-index))
0
1
2
3
CIAO!
```

Note that calling

```
(1+ my-index)
```

has the same effect as calling

```
(+ my-index 1).
```

The example with dolist could also be rewritten using do as follows:

```
CL> (do ((to-do '(do re me fa sol la te do)
                (rest to-do)))
            ((null to-do) 'Ciao! )
            (print (first to-do)))
DO
RE
ME
FA
SOL
LA
TE
DO
CIAO!
```

The loop Macro

As general as the do facility is, there are still situations in which it will not suffice. One of the limitations of the do macro is that the *end-test* is always performed before evaluating the expressions in the body. There are many situations in which you would prefer to have the test occur after evaluating the forms that constitute the body of the loop. In these situations you would have to construct your own loop, using the Common Lisp loop and return macros. The loop macro causes a body of expressions to be repeatedly executed. In order to exit, you will need to invoke the return macro somewhere within the loop. The `return` macro has an optional argument with which you can provide a *result-form* for the loop. For example, the general form of a bottom-testing loop would be

```
(loop
     body
     (if end-test (return result-form )))
```

The `loop` macro is the most general iteration facility of all. By wrapping a `let` form around a `loop` expression to provide iteration variables, you can easily reproduce the behavior of any `do` form.

Efficiency of Recursion and Iteration

Any recursive function can be rewritten using one of the iterative forms, just as any iterative form could be reexpressed as a recursive function. For example, recall the `sum-list` function from the previous section:

```
(defun sum-list (number-list)
    (if number-list (+ (first number-list)
                          (sum-list (rest number-
list)))
                        0))
```

You now know how to rewrite this as

```
(defun sum-list-2 (number-list)
    (do ((to-do   number-list (rest to-do))
         (sum 0 ))
        ((null to-do) sum)
      (setf sum ( + sum (first to-do)))))
```

The question is, which is better? Many programmers prefer to use the recursive form rather than the iterative form for stylistic reasons. A recursive representation of a function is often shorter and easier to read than the iterative version.

Unfortunately, there may be a reduction in efficiency associated with always coding in a recursive fashion. Every time you call a function, a certain amount of overhead is incurred (e.g., to evaluate arguments and copy them to the stack). The amount of time needed for a single function call is negligible, but when the task involves many function calls (as in a deeply recursive function), the total cost can be substantial. When you loop within an iterative form, there is no overhead for function calling.

Does this suggest that the conscientious programmer should always use iterative forms? Probably not. Most smart Lisp compilers try to optimize recursive function calls. If they succeed, the optimized recursive code will run as fast as it would have run had it been written as an iterative form. When coding a function that needs to process over a list, I usually write it in the style that I find easiest to read and understand. In the simplest cases, this usually means using `dolist`. If the task is a little more complicated, I generally try to write it as a recursive function. If I produce a working version of the function, I then write the other parts of the program. Later, if I discover that the recursive function is causing the performance of the whole program to suffer, it is not difficult to go back and improve its performance.

Exercise 3.14

The arithmetic functions in Lisp can accept more than two arguments. We would like our `lisp-to-fortran` translator to be able to translate expressions like

```
(setf x (/ (+ 3 4 5 ) 3))
```

into the nice Fortran assignment statement

```
X = ((3 + 4 + 5 ) / 3)
```

The `prefix-to-infix` function could be rewritten as follows to handle variable-length operand lists:

```
(defun prefix-to-infix (expr)
  (if (listp expr)
      (let ((operator (first expr))
            (operand-1 (second expr)))
        (cons (prefix-to-infix operand-1)
              (build-infix-list operator
                                 (nthcdr 2 expr))))
      expr))
```

A recursive version of `build-infix-list` would look something like this:

```
(defun build-infix-list (operator operand-list)
  (if operand-list
      (append (list operator
                    (first operand-list))
              (build-infix-list operator
                                (rest operand-list)))))
```

Write an iterative version of `build-infix-list`.

Exercise 3.15

Rewrite `member-p` (from Exercise 3.8) as an iterative function.

Exercise 3.16

What do the following functions do?

a.
```
(defun mystery-fun-4 (x)
  (do ((i (1- x) (1- i))
       (result x))
      (( = 1 i ) result)
    (setf result (* result i))))
```

b.
```
(defun mystery-fun-5 (x)
  (do ((new-list x (rest new-list))
       (counter 0 (+ 1 counter)))
      (( null new-list) counter)))
```

c.
```
(defun mystery-fun-6 ( x )
  (do ((to-do x (rest to-do))
       (new-list nil (cons (first to-do)
                           new-list)))
      ((null to-do) new-list)))
```

Exercise 3.17

Write Lisp expressions, using the `loop` macro, that have the same behavior as the following:

a.
```
(dolist (element '( do re me fa sol la te do)
                'Ciao!)
  ( print element ))
```

b.
```
(dotimes (my-index 4 'Ciao!)
  (print my-index))
```

Exercise 3.18

Write a function called `combinations` that accepts three lists as input. It should return a list of all possible combinations, choosing one element from each of the input lists. For example:

```
CL> (combinations '(a b c) '(1 2) '(x y))
((C 2 Y) (C 2 X) (C 1 Y) (C 1 X) (B 2 Y)
 (B 2 X) (B 1 Y) (B 1 X) (A 2 Y) (A 2 X)
 (A 1 Y) (A 1 X))
```

Exercise 3.19

The right-hand side of the Fortran expression generated by `lisp-to-fortran` has an extra layer of parentheses around it. Although a Fortran compiler wouldn't mind, it's aesthetically unpleasing. Eliminate the problem.

Exercise 3.20

Our `lisp-to-fortran` translator works with binary operators. Make it work for unary operators like `negate`; for example:

```
CL> (lisp-to-fortran-4 '(setf z (negate y)))
Z = -Y
```

3.4 PASSING FUNCTIONS AS ARGUMENTS

Lisp allows you to pass functions as arguments. In certain situations, this is a very useful capability. For example, suppose that you want to write some functions to do arithmetic with vectors (i.e., a one-dimensional array). When you add a scalar, that is, a single number, to a vector, you simply add the number to each element of the vector. If we chose to represent a vector as a list, we can write a function for adding a scalar to a vector as follows:

```
(defun scalar-add (scalar vector)
  (if vector (cons (+ (first vector)
                      scalar)
              (scalar-add scalar
                          (rest vector))))) 10
```

We could then invoke this function by typing:

```
CL> (scalar-add 5 '(1 2 3 4 5))
(6 7 8 9 10)
```

---

[10]Note that there is no *else-form* for the `if` special form in this function. To be completely explicit, we could have written

```
(if vector
    (cons (+ (first vector)
             scalar)
          (scalar-add scalar (rest vector))
    nil)
```

But it turns out that the *else-form* is superfluous here. If the condition-form evaluates to `nil` (i.e., if we have worked our way down to the end of the list), then the `if` special form will return `nil`, which is just what we wanted.

Similarly, functions for doing subtraction, multiplication and division on vectors could be defined as follows:

```
(defun scalar-subtract (scalar vector)
   (if vector (cons (- (first vector)
                       scalar)
                 (scalar-subtract scalar
                           (rest vector)))))

(defun scalar-multiply (scalar vector)
   (if vector (cons (* (first vector)
                       scalar)
                 (scalar-multiply scalar
                             (rest vector)))))

(defun scalar-divide (scalar vector)
   (if vector (cons (/ (first vector)
                       scalar)
                 (scalar-divide scalar
                         (rest vector)))))
```

Careful scrutiny will reveal that with the exception of the arithmetic function called within the cons form, all of these functions are identical. Wouldn't it have been easier to define a single function with an additional parameter that specified which arithmetic function to use? One could envision a function such as this:

```
(defun scalar-arithmetic (scalar vector op)
;;;This doesn't really work!
  (if vector
      (cons (op (first vector) scalar)
            (scalar-arithmetic scalar
                           (rest vector)
                            op))))
```

This seems like a more reasonable approach, but there are a few problems. How do we pass a function as an argument? Merely quoting the function name, that is,

```
(scalar-arithmetic 3 '(5 10 15) '+)
```

won't give us what we want. First, when a symbol is evaluated, it is replaced by its current binding, not its functional definition. Second, the op symbol in the call

```
(op (first vector) scalar)                ;Doesn't work!
```

will not be evaluated anyway, because the first element of a list is assumed by eval to be a function name. (Remember the Second Rule of Evaluation?)

Fetching a Functional
Definition

We can solve the first problem using the Common Lisp function special form. Calling a function on a symbol returns the functional definition associated with that symbol. For example:

```
CL> (function +)
#<Compiled Function +>
```

The function special form is used so frequently that, like the quote special form, it has a shorthand way of being called. Preceding a symbol with a sharp sign (#) and a single quotation mark will invoke the function special form. Consequently, you could call the scalar-arithmetic function in the following way:

```
(scalar-arithmetic 3 '( 5 10 15 ) #'+)
```

This solves the first problem, but how do you get Lisp to execute the passed functional definition?

The funcall Function

Common Lisp has a function called funcall that will accept a functional definition as an argument and apply it to a specified set of arguments.[11] For example:

```
CL> (funcall #'+ 2 2)
4
```

In this case, funcall doesn't accomplish anything, but when the first argument to funcall is a symbol, you can select the function to use at runtime. This is exactly what you need to get the scalar-arithmetic function to work. You could rewrite it as

```
(defun scalar-arithmetic (scalar vector op)
  (if vector
      (cons (funcall op
                     (first vector)
                      scalar)
```

[11]There is a related Common Lisp function called apply that provides additional flexibility of allowing the number of arguments to be varied at runtime.

```
(scalar-arithmetic scalar
                   (rest vector)
                   op)))))
```

Now when you issue the call

```
CL> ( scalar-arithmetic 3 '( 5 10 15 ) #'+ )
( 8 13  18 )
```

you will get exactly what you want.

Mapping Functions

The need to apply a passed function to each of the members of a list occurs so frequently that Common Lisp provides a family of functions that do just this. These functions are known as *mapping functions.*

The **mapcar** *Function*

The simplest mapping function is mapcar. It takes as arguments a functional definition and a list. It iterates over the list and calls the passed function on each of its elements. Each result returned when the function is called on a list element is saved in a new list. The mapcar function returns the list of results. For example:

```
CL> (defun my-fun (x) (+ x 3))
MY-FUN
CL> (mapcar #'my-fun '(5 10 15))
(8 13 18)
```

That seems quite easy. Couldn't we simply rewrite the scalar-arithmetic function using mapcar? Once again, there is a slight hitch. In scalar-arithmetic we are passed both the functional definition and a numeric scalar argument. The my-fun function passed to mapcar can only accept one argument corresponding to the list element.[12] Consequently, to use mapcar in scalar-arithmetic, you would need to build a new function each time mapcar is called. How is this done?

Lambda Expressions

The standard technique is to use a lambda expression.[13] Lambda

---

[12]It is possible to use functions in mapcar that have more than one parameter. However, you are required to provide a list for each parameter.

[13]Lambda expressions, like lambda lists, derive their name from Church's Lambda Calculus (Church, 1941).

expressions resemble calls to the defun macro, but with one significant difference. They are lists of the following form:

```
(lambda parameter-list body)
```

where *parameter-list* (also known as *lambda-list*) is a list of parameters to the function and *body* is the set of Lisp expressions to be evaluated in the function. The major difference between functions defined with lambda and functions defined with defun is that lambda functions have no names. They are "disposable" functions that are used in only one place. Lambda expressions are perfect for constructing one-time functions for use in a call to mapcar. Using a lambda expression and mapcar, we could define the scalar-arithmetic function as follows:

```
(defun scalar-arithmetic (scalar vector op)
    (mapcar #'(lambda (element)
                  (funcall op element scalar))
          vector))
```

Other Mapping Functions

As mentioned earlier, mapcar is one of a family of mapping functions. There is a version of mapcar, called mapc, that works like mapcar but does not return the list of results. It is called strictly for its side effects. There is another mapping function, called maplist, that iterates over a list, like mapcar, but calls the passed function on the tail of the list (i.e., the list returned by rest) instead of the head. The difference can be illustrated with a simple example:

```
CL> (defvar colors '(red yellow blue))
COLORS
CL> (mapcar #'(lambda (x) x) colors)
(RED YELLOW BLUE)
```

If we call mapcar with a function that simply returns its argument, we will get back a copy of the input list. But if we call maplist with a similar function, we get back

```
CL> (maplist #'(lambda (x) x) colors)
((RED YELLOW BLUE) (YELLOW BLUE) (BLUE))
```

Filtering with mapcan

Another member of the family of mapping functions is mapcan. It is similar to mapcar in that it returns a list of the result of applying the passed function to each of the elements of the input list. It differs

TABLE 3-5 *Lisp Mapping Functions*

Returns	Operates on	
	(first input-list)	(rest input-list)
List of results	mapcar	maplist
Input-list (called for effect)	mapc	mapl
List of results (constructed w/nconc)	mapcan	mapcon

from mapcan in that it uses nconc to construct the result list. The nconc function, which will be discussed in the next chapter, is similar to the append function. Constructing the result list with nconc causes all of the nil results to be dropped from the list. This makes mapcan very useful when you need to filter a list. For example:

```
CL> (mapcan #'(lambda (x)
               (if (numberp x)(list x)))
          '("x" 2 #o100 3.141593 2/3 602e21))
(2 64 3.141593 2/3 6.02E23) 14
```

The differences among the Lisp mapping functions are summarized in Table 3-5. Each of the functions can be categorized based on whether it operates on the head or the tail of the list and on the value it returns.

Using mapcar to merge lists

Some even more interesting behavior can be achieved by passing more than one list to one of the mapping functions. The lists are then processed in a parallel fashion until the shortest input list is exhausted. In the case of mapcar, if we used more than one list, the passed function would be applied using one element from each list. For example, if we had an ordered list of states and another list with capitals, we could join the states to their capitals using mapcar in this way:

[14]The notation #o100 stands for 100 base 8 or octal. The default radix for output is base 10, so it prints as 64.

```
                              CL> (defvar states
            '(alaska wisconsin indiana michigan))
STATES
CL> (setf capitals
        '(juneau madison indianapolis lansing))
CAPITALS
CL> (mapcar #'list capitals states)
((JUNEAU ALASKA) (MADISON WISCONSIN) (INDIANAPOLIS INDIANA) (LANSING MICHIGAN))
```

Mapping as a Form of Iteration

Even the most complicated mapping forms can be expressed in terms of the do macro. For example, the scalar-arithmetic function could be rewritten one more time, using do instead of mapcar, as follows:

```
(defun scalar-arithmetic (scalar vector op)
  (let (result)
    (do ((to-do vector (rest to-do)))
        ((null to-do) result)
      (setf result
            (append result
                    (list (funcall op
                                   (first to-do)
                                   scalar))))))))
```

Some consider the mapping functions to be somewhat archaic, given the more powerful do iteration macro. They also argue that by using the do form, the programmer is able to spell out more explicitly how the computation should proceed. However, the syntax of do is somewhat more verbose and is a little harder to read for the uninitiated. Whether you choose to use the mapping forms or only do, you should be able to read code written either way, because both techniques are a part of standard practice.

Exercise 3.21

Do you think that the following would work?

```
CL> (defvar plus '+)
PLUS
CL> (scalar-arithmetic 3 '(5 10 15) plus)
```

Explain your answer.

Exercise 3.22

Write an expression using one of the mapping functions that, when passed the lists capitals and states, will produce the following output:

```
(JUNEAU ALASKA)
(MADISON WISCONSIN)
(INDIANAPOLIS INDIANA)
(LANSING MICHIGAN)
(ANCHORAGE MADISON INDIANAPOLIS LANSING)
```

Exercise 3.23

What will the following functions do?

a. (defun mystery-fun-7 (x y)

      (mapcan #'(lambda (z)

          (if (eq z x)

            nil

            (list z))) y))

b. (defun mystery-fun-8 (x y)

    (mapc #'(lambda (w z)

       (cons w z)) x y))

c. (defun mystery-fun-9 (x)

    (maplist #'second x))

Exercise 3.24

Write a function called `calculator` that will work like a simple four-function calculator. An interaction with the function should look something like this:

```
CL> (calculator)
100
+
100
+
50
-
75
+
67
=
242
```

Hint 1: You will need to use the Common Lisp `read` function to read in each line of input. The `read` function requires no arguments and returns the (unevaluated) Lisp expression typed in on the keyboard. For example, a function to input two numbers and add them could be written as follows:

```
CL> (defun adder ()
         ( + (read)(read)))
ADDER
CL> (adder)
100
150
250
```

Hint 2: Instead of using the `function` special form to retrieve the functional definition, use the `symbol-function` function, which evaluates its argument.

Exercise 3.25

Write a function called `my-maplist` that implements the mapping function `maplist` using the `do` macro. (Assume that `my-maplist` will accept only one input list.)

3.5 A SENSE OF STYLE

Now that you are beginning to write longer and more complicated functions, it's time to discuss good Lisp programming style. It is possible (in fact, quite easy) to write completely inscrutable Lisp code. This is obviously something that you as a programmer wish to avoid.

Master Coders

Some Lisp programmers are the masters of the craft. They are able to take a complicated problem and reduce it to a collection of easy-to-understand procedures. Because of their ability to decompose problems, they can code faster than their colleagues and produce a product that has fewer bugs and is easier to maintain. It is not surprising that employers place a high value on their services and go to great lengths to keep them happy.

These special programmers are made, not born. The skills needed to become such a programmer can be learned. They are part of what we call programming in a "good style." A good Lisp programming style is not developed overnight; it develops over time as your skills as a programmer mature. As a newcomer to Lisp, you are in a good position to learn to program well because you have not yet had time to develop any bad habits.

The Rule of Good Style

The secret to becoming a stylish coder can be summarized in one rule:

Make every function you write easily comprehensible.

In a way, this is just a corollary of the golden rule, "Do unto others as you would have them do unto you," because when you write bad code, you are doing a disservice to anyone who has to deal with that code in the future. Stated this way, the rule may seem simplistic, and you may wonder why so much bad code exists. Certainly no one sets out to write bad code, but it happens nonetheless. The reason is that we get careless. We usually work under pressure, and it is often tempting to cut corners. Doing careful design work and providing thorough documentation always takes a little more time, but often it saves time in the long run.

Some Suggestions for Achieving Good Style

Here are some suggestions for making your code more comprehensible:

- **Write moderate-length functions.** The larger the function, the more complicated it is to read. As a rule, functions should be no longer than a page (i.e., 18-20 lines of code). Note, however, that the suggestion to write smaller functions can be taken to absurd extremes. If you break up your code into too many function calls, it can actually make your code harder to read (not to mention run slower). Therefore, use common sense.

- **Choose informative names for functions and variables.** The names reveal a lot about how the programmer believes the functions and variables should be used. There is a convention, for example, to use a *p* suffix on function names for predicates.[15]

- **Provide sufficient documentation.** The term *documentation*, as used here, includes not only the comments in your source files, but also the organization of the source files, the formatting and indentation of the sources and any collateral documentation that may be available (e.g., users' manuals). Proper formatting of Lisp sources is essential to producing readable code. Most editors now have built-in *pretty-printing* capabilities that will automatically indent your code properly. If your editor does not have this facility, you will have to do it yourself. Remember that

[15]There are other function-naming conventions that are less universally adhered to. Many programmers prepend an n to the names of functions that destructively modify lists (e.g., nconc, nsubstitute). Some programmers add an f to the front of the names of "fast" versions of functions. A fast version of a function sacrifices safety in the interest of improving performance. Fast functions usually are written with few or no facilities for error testing.

too many comments in a function are as bad as no comments at all. Beginners often overdo it. Just provide the essential information.

- **Avoid the use of global variables.** Promiscuous use of global variables can lead to grief. There are situations in which the use of global variables is required. In these cases, follow the convention of adding an asterisk (*) at the beginning and end of the symbol name to declare your intent to use it as a global symbol.

- **Eschew programming tricks.** As you gain experience with Lisp, you will start to learn some of the quirks and nuances of your particular Common Lisp implementation. With time, you may learn how to exploit these idiosyncrasies to achieve modest improvements in performance or other gains. This is almost always a bad idea. Programming tricks are usually implementation dependent. The task of porting your code to other environments will be more difficult if the code is highly dependent on specific features of one implementation. Also, the use of tricks fosters obscurity and is antithetical to making functions comprehensible.

- **Work to achieve local transparency.** You should be able to understand the workings of a function by looking at the function itself, without referring to other pieces of code. Calling functions for their side effect and passing values between functions using global variables make it very difficult to understand the workings of a function in isolation. Therefore, these practices should be used with great discretion.

Some programmers use additional rules and practices they consider important to a good programming style. The foregoing list presents the most important points. If you keep these suggestions in mind as you write progressively more complicated programs, you will naturally develop a good programming style. Perhaps with time and practice, you too will become a master of the craft.

Exercise 3.26

The permute function takes a list as an argument and returns a list of permutations of the original list. For example:

```
CL> (permute '(a b c))
((A B C) (A C B) (B C A) (B A C) (C A B) (C B A))
```

Unfortunately, the following version of permute does not work properly, nor was it written in a very readable style. Correct this version so that it works; in the process, try to also improve the style of the code.

```
(defun permute (var)
  (if (> (length var) 1)
    (do ((n (length var) (1- n))
         (var2 var (append (rest var2)(list (car var2))))
         (result ()))
        ((<= n 0) result)
      (setq result
        (append result
          (mapcar  #'(lambda (x) (append (list (first
var2)) x))
            (permute (cdr var))))))
    (list var)))
```

SUMMARY

Functions are defined in Common Lisp using the defun macro. The form of a call to defun is

```
(defun function-name lambda-list
  [doc-string]
  body)
```

Where function-name is a Lisp symbol, lambda-list is a list of symbols representing the parameters for the function, doc-string is an optional documentation string, and body is one or more Lisp forms representing the body of the function. Argument passing in Lisp follows the convention of *pass-by-value*. All Lisp functions return a value; some functions may be called for value, others for effect.

Lisp variables can be divided into two categories: local and global. Global variables are bound at the top level and are accessible to all functions. Local variables are recognized only within a specific function. They can either be introduced in the lambda list or by using the special forms let and let*.

Functions that call themselves are called *recursive* functions. All recursive functions have two parts: a termination test and a recursive part. You can perform a hand simulation of a recursive function using a trace table. CDRing down a list is a general technique for recursively processing the elements of a list. A related technique can be used to build lists recursively.

Common Lisp provides three macros for iterative programming: dolist, dotimes, and do. Of the three, do is the most powerful. All of the iterative forms can be implemented using the do macro. There are trade-offs involved when implementing a function in an iterative or recursive style. Where performance is critical, an iterative implementation is often faster.

The mapping functions are a special family of iterative forms. They iterate over a list and apply a passed function to either the head or the tail of the list. If the passed function is used only in the call to the mapping function, it is convenient to define it as a lambda expression. In general, the `funcall` function can be used to invoke a passed function with a fixed number of arguments.

Good programming style involves making functions easily comprehensible. Comprehensibility can be enhanced by writing functions of moderate length, by choosing informative names for functions and variables, by avoiding programming tricks, and by seeking to make functions locally transparent.

NEW COMMON LISP DEFINED NAMES

apply	function	mapcar
defun	length	mapcon
documentation	let	map1
do	let*	maplist
dolist	loop	nconc
dotimes	mapc	1+
funcall	mapcan	1-

FOR FURTHER READING

For more detailed information on the topics covered in this chapter, see Section 5.3.1 for a description of the `defun` macro, Section 7.5 for the details of the `let` special form, and Section 7.8 for a description of iterative forms and mapping functions in the Steele book (Steele, 1990).

For a readable presentation of recursion and recursion theory, see the Touretzky (Touretzky, 1984) and Hofstadter (Hofstadter, 1979) books. The Lisp text by Brooks (Brooks, 1985) has a good chapter on programming style.

Project 3.1

There is a puzzle, known as the *Towers of Hanoi*, involving three spindles and three rings of different sizes. To solve the puzzle, you must find a way to move all three rings from one spindle to another. Only one ring may be moved at a time, and a larger ring may not be placed on a smaller one. Figure 3-6 shows the "start state" for the

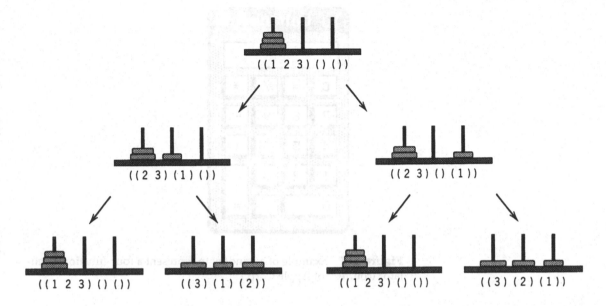

Figure 3-6   The Start State and Six Subsequent States for the Towers of Hanoi Problem

problem and all possible successive states that can be reached by moving a single ring. Write a function to solve the Towers of Hanoi problem.

(Hint: If the rings are assigned numbers corresponding to their sizes, each state of the problem can be represented as a list of three lists [see Figure 3-6].)

Project 3.2

If the Common Lisp implementation in which you have been working supports windows, you can make the `calculator` function from Exercise 3.25 easier to use. Design a program that will allow the user to interact with a window that resembles a four-function calculator. An example of how such a window might appear is shown in Figure 3-7. Since the proposed ANSI standard for Common Lisp does not cover windows, you will have to implement this project in an implementation-dependent fashion. Consult your reference manual to see how windows are handled in the implementation of Common Lisp that you are using.

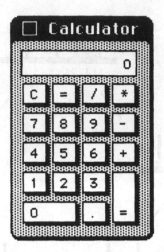

Figure 3-7 Example of a window to represent a four-function calculator (courtesy of Apple Corp.)

4

Inquisitor of Structures

Total grandeur of a total edifice,
Chosen by an inquisitor of structures
For himself. He stops upon this threshold
As if the design of all his world takes form
And frame from thinking is realized.
Wallace Stevens,
To an Old Philosopher in Rome

4.1 COMMON LISP SYMBOLS

One of the peculiarities of Lisp is that you can associate more than one thing with a Lisp symbol. In languages like Pascal or Fortran, variables are used strictly as repositories for storing values. In Lisp, the situation is a little more complicated. You may have noticed that symbols can be associated both with function names and with values. For example:

```
CL> (defvar foo 1000)
FOO
CL> (defun foo (x)
       (log x 10))
FOO
CL> (foo foo)
3.0
```

95

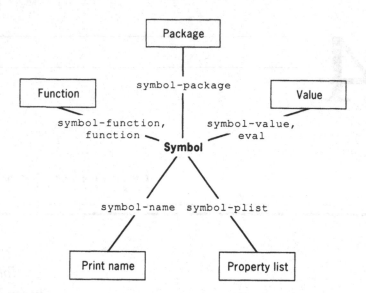

Figure 4-1 Accessing the Cells of a Common Lisp Symbol

In this case, the foo symbol is used both to hold a value and to name a function. The interpreter decides which association to use based on the context. If the symbol appears at the beginning of a list, by the Second Rule of Evaluation it is used as the name of a form (i.e., function, macro, or special form). If it appears elsewhere in a list or in isolation, it is replaced by its current binding (by the First Rule of Evaluation). The interpreter is able to keep the functional definition of foo and its current binding straight because it stores them in two distinct cells.[1]

Cells of a Symbol

In fact, every symbol in Common Lisp has *five* separate cells. As shown in Figure 4-1, there is a cell for storing a value, a cell for storing a functional definition, a cell for storing the print name, a cell for storing a pointer to the symbol's package, and a cell for storing a property list.

---

[1]If you wished, you could store a functional definition in the value cell of a symbol. You could, for instance, type

```
CL>  (defvar foo #'foo)
FOO
```

Note that you would only be able to invoke the function using funcall or apply.

Accessing the Cells of a Symbol

There are Common Lisp access functions corresponding to each of the cells of a symbol, as shown in Figure 4-1. You can, for instance, access the current value of a symbol by typing

```
CL> (symbol-value 'foo)
1000
```

Of course, you could get the same result by invoking eval on the symbol or simply by typing the symbol and taking advantage of the First Rule of Evaluation. By the same token, the symbol-function function offers nothing that we couldn't already do using the function special form, introduced in the last chapter. The series of functions—symbol-value, symbol-function, symbol-name, symbol-package, and symbol-plist—do, however, provide a consistent way of accessing the important information about a symbol. We need to look at the contents of the print name, package, and property list cells, since these are features that you have not encountered before.

Print Names

The print name for a symbol is simply a string representing the symbol's name. The contents of the print name cell will always show the exact representation of the name by which the system knows the symbol. In most circumstances, this will be the same as the name that you typed in, with all alphabetic characters converted to uppercase. It is possible in Common Lisp, however, to create nonconventional symbol names with embedded blanks or lowercase characters. Ordinarily, all lowercase characters are automatically converted to uppercase and spaces are treated as symbol terminators, but if you precede a character with a backslash (\), it will be inserted without modification into the symbol name. If there are several characters that you wish to have inserted in a literal fashion, it may be more convenient to enclose them in bars (i.e., | characters). For example:

```
CL> (symbol-name '\abracadabra)
"aBRACADABRA"
CL> (symbol-name '|a symbol name with embedded
blanks|)
"a symbol name with embedded blanks"
```

The backslash and bar characters are referred to as *escape characters* in Common Lisp.

Packages

In Common Lisp, symbols are organized into collections known as *packages*. Unless specified otherwise, whenever you create a new symbol, it automatically belongs to the current default package (i.e., the current binding of *package* the global variable). The details of working with packages will be covered in Chapter 9.

Property Lists

Property lists are the means by which a programmer can associate additional pieces of data with a symbol. They provide a facility for easily extending the set of things that are stored in the value, function, print name, and package cells of a symbol in order to accommodate new information. Each new piece of data is known as a *property* of the symbol. Each property has a name and a value. All of the properties of a symbol are stored on a property list. Many Common Lisp implementations use the property list of symbols to store implementation-specific information pertaining to each variable.

As an example of the use of the symbol property list, suppose that every time a symbol was updated, we wished to save the old value. You could do this by creating a property called old-value and writing the current value of the symbol to the property list before putting the new value in the value cell. You could retrieve the value of that cell by typing

```
(get 'foo 'old-value)
```

The get function evaluates its first argument expecting a Common Lisp symbol. It then evaluates the second argument expecting a property name and returns the current value of that property. If the property is not defined for the passed symbol, get returns nil.[2]

Setting Values of Properties

The value of a property is set using the setf macro. We could set the old-value property of foo to the current binding of foo by typing

```
CL> (setf (get 'foo 'old-value) foo)
1000
```

If foo did not have an old-value property, one would be created. If foo had a previous value associated with its old-value prop-

---

[2] It is sometimes difficult to discriminate between undefined properties and properties that have the value nil.

erty, it would be overwritten. The form of this `setf` expression is curious and deserves further explanation.

Generalized Variables

Up to now, we have used `setf` only to assign values to symbols. You will discover in this chapter, however, that `setf` has other interesting capabilities. In Common Lisp, the concept of variable assignment is generalized to embrace assignment of a value to any type of storage location. Possible storage locations include the value cell of a symbol, a position in a list array or string, or a property of a symbol. Assignment to these types of storage locations and others can all be effected using `setf`, which is, after all, a contraction of *set field*.

The execution of a `setf` expression proceeds in two steps. The form of a generalized call to `setf` is as follows:

```
(setf access-form  value-form)
```

Rather than evaluate the `access-form`, `setf` combines the `access-form` and the `value-form` to build an `update-form`. The `update-form` is then evaluated. For example, in the case of the simple variable assignment

```
(setf foo 1000)
```

an `update-form` similar to the following is generated

```
(setq foo 1000)
```

and then evaluated. The Common Lisp generalized variable facility requires `setf` to know what the appropriate `update-form` is for each type of `access-form`. Consequently, the set of possible `access-form`s is restricted; not all Lisp expressions can serve as legal `setf` `access-form`s.[3] So far, you have encountered `access-form`s consisting of symbol references and `get` forms. Others will be introduced in the following sections. As you will soon see, the `setf` macro plays an important role in the manipulation of data structures in Common Lisp.

incf and decf Macros

There are other Common Lisp macros that can also manipulate generic variables. The `incf` and `decf` macros take an *access-*

---

[3] The set of legal `setf` *access-forms* can be extended using the `define-setf-method` facility.

form and an optional numeric value as arguments. As a side effect, they increment or decrement the generalized variable indicated by the *access-form* by the specified amount. If the second argument is not provided, the default value is 1. For example, the form

```
(incf foo)
```

would have the same effect as calling

```
(setf foo (1+ foo))
```

Establishing Variables

Up to now, you have been using defvar to create new variables and give them an initial value. For example, you could create the *last-value* variable used in the generate-number function (from Section 3.1) as follows:

```
CL> (defvar *last-value* 0)
*last-value*
CL> *last-value*
0
```

Optionally, you can provide a third argument, which is a documentation string for the variable. For example:

```
(defvar *last-value* 0
        "Counter for generate-number")
```

You can retrieve the documentation string for a variable using the documentation function as follows:

```
CL> (documentation '*last-value* 'variable)
"Counter for generate-number"
```

Sometimes you want to associate a symbol with a value that won't change (i.e., create a constant). Common Lisp has another macro called defconstant that will perform this service:

```
(defconstant avogadro-number 6.023E23)
```

It is an error to try to reassign a symbol that has been defined with defconstant. Using defconstant to define new variables that will not change helps to make the programmer's intentions clear to later readers of the code.

Creating Symbols

Up to now, whenever you needed a symbol, the system accommodated you by creating one. When you first reference a symbol, if it has not already been defined, a new symbol with its five cells is created. There are situations in which you may wish to create a symbol within a function, usually because you need to compute the symbol name. In many cases, it doesn't matter what the symbol is named, as long as the name is unique. The Common Lisp `gensym` function will generate a new name every time it is called. For example:

```
CL> (gensym)
#:G10
CL> (gensym)
#:G11
```

If you want to specify the symbol name yourself, you can use the `make-symbol` function; for example,

```
CL> (make-symbol "BAZ")
#:BAZ
```

Symbols created by `gensym` or `make-symbol` are *orphans*, that is, they do not belong to any defined package. In Common Lisp they are referred to as *uninterned* symbols. Uninterned symbols are printed with a #: before their names to reflect their status. We will discuss how to make interned symbols in Chapter 9.

Exercise 4.1

Try reanswering Exercise 1.1, given the new information on Common Lisp symbols provided in this section.

Exercise 4.2

Define a property on a symbol called `time-of-creation`. Insert the current time as the value of `time-of-creation`. (Hint: The Common Lisp function `get-universal-time` will return the current time as the number of seconds since midnight, 1/1/1900. Store this integer as the value of the `time-of-creation` property.)

Exercise 4.3

Write a function to process down a list of symbols and record on the property list of each symbol its (zero-based) ordinal position in the list. For example:

```
CL> (enumerate-list '( a b c ))
2
CL> (get 'a 'list-position)
0
CL> (get 'c 'list-position)
2
```

Exercise 4.4

Write a function, my-set, that will work like the Common Lisp set function but will save the old value of the symbol on the property list. Because set is a function, it evaluates all of its arguments. Your version of set would work something like this:

```
CL> (my-set 'x 99)
99
CL> (my-set 'x 100)
100
CL> (get 'x 'old-value)
99
```

(Hint: You will probably need the Common Lisp boundp predicate to see whether or not the symbol has a previous binding.)

Exercise 4.5

Rewrite the generate-number function from Section 3.1 using the incf macro.

4.2 LISP LISTS

Lists in Lisp are implemented using a data structure known as *linked lists*. Each element of a list is represented by a cell, commonly known as a *cons cell* or simply a *cons*. Each cons cell has two pointers: one to its associated value and one to the next cons cell in the list.[4] In Lisp, the convention for terminating a list is to have the last cons cell point to the nil constant. Figure 4-2 is a diagram showing a cons-cell representation of the greeks list from Chapter 2. The first pointer (the CAR pointer) in the first cons cell points to the value HOMER; the second pointer (the CDR pointer) is directed to the next cons cell. The CAR pointers of the other two cons cells point to the

---

[4]The first pointer of the cons cell is sometimes referred to as the *CAR* pointer; the second pointer is sometimes referred to as the *CDR* pointer. These names were acronyms for assembly-level instructions on the old IBM 704.

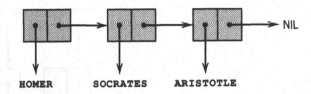

Figure 4-2 Cons Cell Representation of the Lost (homer socrates aristotle)

values SOCRATES and ARISTOTLE, respectively. The CDR pointer of the third and final cons cell points to the nil constant.

More complex list structures can also be represented using cons cells diagrams. For example, the cons-cell representation of the list

```
((lions tigers bears) oh_my!)
```

is presented in Figure 4-3. The CAR pointer of the first element points to the head of a second list. Note that both lists are terminated in the usual fashion, that is, with a pointer to nil.

cons Function

Cons cells derive their name from the cons function, whose name is short for *construct*. When you call cons on an item and a list, it creates a new cons cell with a CAR pointer pointing to the item and the CDR pointer pointing to the head of the list. For example:

```
CL> (defvar old-list '(a b c))
OLD-LIST
```

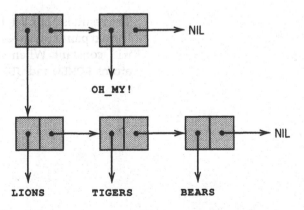

Figure 4-3 Cons-Cell Diagram for the List ((lions tigers bears) oh_my!)

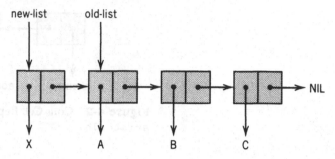

Figure 4-4   Adding a New Cons Cell to the Beginning of a List

```
CL> (defvar new-list (cons 'x old-list))
NEW-LIST
CL> old-list
(A B C)
```

This situation is depicted in Figure 4-4. The `old-list` symbol points to the cons cell at the head of the original list, and the `new-list` symbol points to the new cons cell added to the list. If the value cell of a symbol points to a cons cell, it is considered to be bound to the list corresponding to the chain of cons cells leading to a terminating cons cell.

Dotted Pairs

If the second argument to the `cons` function is not a list, a curious structure is created. For example:

```
CL> (defvar dotted-pair (cons 'romeo 'juliet))
DOTTED-PAIR
```

The result is not a list, but rather something known as a *dotted pair*. Dotted pairs are two-element lists that lack a terminal pointer to the `nil` constant. When we used the `cons` function to join the two atoms ROMEO and JULIET, it obligingly set up a cons cell with a

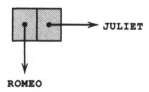

Figure 4-5   Cons-Cell Diagram of the Dotted Pair (ROMEO . JULIET)

CAR pointer to ROMEO and a CDR pointer to JULIET (Figure 4-5). But since JULIET is an atom, it has no terminal pointer to nil. The result is printed as a dotted pair to show that the two elements are joined but that they do not constitute a true list. Since the tail of a dotted pair is an atom and not a list, you might expect the behavior of the rest function to be different when called on a dotted pair. Indeed, that is the case; for example:

```
CL> (rest dotted-pair)
JULIET
```

When rest is called on a dotted pair, it returns an atom instead of a list.

Parenthetically, any list can be written as a nested set of dotted pairs. For example, the list

```
(homer socrates aristotle)
```

could also be written

```
(homer .(socrates  (aristotle  ())))
```

These are simply two different ways of writing the same thing. Although they are equally valid, Lisp programmers almost never write lists in the second form because dotted-pair notation is too much work to read and write.

List Surgery

There are Common Lisp functions that allow you to modify the structure of a list; we encountered one of them in Chapter 2. The rplaca function (short for *replace the CAR*) takes a list and an item as arguments and replaces the first element of the list with the item. The list argument is modified in the process. For example:

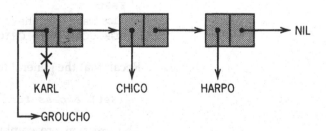

Figure 4-6 An Example of the Use of rplaca

```
CL> (defvar marx-brothers '(karl harpo chico))
MARX-BROTHERS
CL> (rplaca marx-brothers 'groucho)
(GROUCHO HARPO CHICO)
CL> marx-brothers
(GROUCHO HARPO CHICO)
```

A cons-cell diagram showing the effect of this call to rplaca is shown in Figure 4-6.

The list argument to rplaca can be any form that returns a list, so we could use a rest or nthcdr expression instead. This enables us to make changes in other positions within the list. For instance:

```
CL> (rplaca (rest marx-brothers) 'zeppo)
(ZEPPO CHICO)
CL> marx-brothers
(GROUCHO ZEPPO CHICO)
```

There is another Common Lisp function that offers the operation that is the complement of the rplaca function. The rplacd function (short for *replace the CDR*) takes two lists as arguments and replaces the tail of the first list with the second list. Like rplaca, rplacd modifies the first list. For example:

```
CL> marx-brothers
(GROUCHO ZEPPO CHICO)
CL> (rplacd marx-brothers '(harpo chico zeppo))
(GROUCHO HARPO CHICO ZEPPO)
CL> marx-brothers
(GROUCHO HARPO CHICO ZEPPO)
```

Treating List Positions as
Generic Variables

Another way of replacing elements of a list is to use setf and treat the list position as a generic variable. For example:

```
CL> (setf  (second marx-brothers) 'fred)
FRED
CL> marx-brothers
(GROUCHO FRED CHICO ZEPPO)
```

Recall that the general form of a call to setf is:

```
(setf access-form value-form)
```

The setf macro combines the *access-form* and the *value-*

form to produce an *update-form*. In the previous list example, the *update-form* would be

```
(rplaca (rest marx-brothers) 'fred)
```

Note that the *access-form* need not always access an atom. If the *access-form* is an expression that would ordinarily evaluate to a list, the whole list will be replaced instead of a single element. For example:

```
CL> (setf (rest marx-brothers) '(etc.))
(ETC.)
CL> marx-brothers
(GROUCHO ETC.)
```

In this case, the generated *update-form* would look like this:

```
(rplacd marx-brothers '(etc.))
```

Generally speaking, using setf is a more readable and convenient means of modifying pieces of lists than directly calling the lower-level functions rplaca and rplacd.[5]

Multiple **access-forms**

There are some macros that will accept more than one *access-form*. The rotatef macro, for example, will accept two or more *access-forms* as arguments. If called with two *access-form* arguments, the effect of calling rotatef is to exchange the values between the two generic variables. Observe the following:

```
CL> (defvar colors '(red blue green))
COLORS
CL> (rotatef (first colors) (second colors))
NIL
CL> colors
(BLUE RED GREEN)
```

If called with more than two *access-forms*, the effect is to "rotate" values between the locations. For example:

```
CL> (rotatef (first colors)
```

---

[5]There is a difference, however, in the values returned. The setf macro returns the value of its second argument, whereas rplaca and rplacd return the modified list.

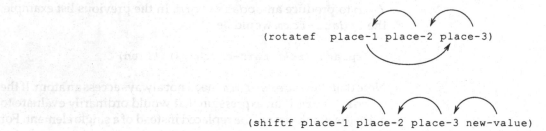

Figure 4-7 A Summary of the Behavior of `rotatef` and `shiftf`

```
                    (second colors)
                    (third colors))
NIL
CL> colors
(RED GREEN BLUE)
```

The related `shiftf` macro, takes one additional argument that provides a new value. Instead of rotating the values, `shiftf` shifts all of the values one place left and then inserts the new value in the location specified by the last *access-form*.

```
CL> (shiftf (first colors)
             (second colors)
             (third colors)
             'pink)
RED
CL> colors
(GREEN BLUE PINK)
```

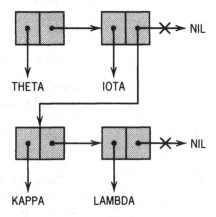

Figure 4-8 The Effect of Calling the `nconc` Function

What do you predict would be the value of `colors` if the preceding call to `shiftf` were repeated a second time? The behavior of `rotatef` and `shiftf` is summarized in Figure 4-7.

Destructive List Operations

Operations on lists that modify their arguments are referred to as *destructive* list operations. There are a number of destructive list forms in Common Lisp. In addition to `rplaca` and `rplacd` and using `setf` with a list position, you have encountered `nconc` (in the section on mapping functions). The `nconc` function is a destructive version of `append`. The `nconc` function actually changes the CDR pointer of the last cons in the first list. For example:

```
CL> (defvar greek-letters '(theta iota ))
GREEK-LETTERS
CL> (nconc greek-letters '(kappa lambda))
(THETA IOTA KAPPA LAMBDA)
CL> greek-letters
(THETA IOTA KAPPA LAMBDA)
```

The effect of calling `nconc` is shown in Figure 4-8.[6]

nconc versus append

Many programmers prefer to use `nconc` instead of `append` for reasons of efficiency. The `append` function copies the list passed as its first argument, whereas the `nconc` function does its work "in place." For example:

```
CL> (let (greek-letters)
       (dolist (element '(theta iota kappa lambda))
          (setf greek-letters (nconc greek-letters
                                  (list element)))))
       greek-letters)
(THETA IOTA KAPPA LAMBDA)
```

[6]You must be careful never to use quoted lists as the first argument to nconc within a function, or you may modify your code. This example was contributed by Gordon Novak:

```
CL> (defun taste (food)
        (write (nconc '(i like to eat) (list
food))))
TASTE
CL> (taste 'peanut-butter)
I LIKE TO EAT PEANUT-BUTTER
I LIKE TO EAT PEANUT-BUTTER
CL> (taste 'soup)
I LIKE TO EAT PEANUT-BUTTER SOUP
I LIKE TO EAT PEANUT-BUTTER SOUP
```

Note that even though `greek-letters` is modified as a side effect of calling `nconc`, `setf` is still used to reassign the variable. This is an idiomatic practice in Lisp that may seem wasteful to the uninitiated. It is done for two reasons, one stylistic and one practical. Many Lisp programmers think that it is a better functional style to not depend on side effects. Wrapping a call to `setf` around the call to `nconc` enables you to work instead with its returned value. A second reason is that `nconc` has some unusual boundary case behavior. If the previous example were redone without the call to `setf`, look at the result:

```
CL> (let (greek-letters)
      (dolist (element '(theta iota kappa lambda))
        (nconc greek-letters (list element)))
      greek-letters)
NIL
```

If the first argument to `nconc` is the empty list represented by the constant `nil`, `nconc` cannot modify it, so it produces no side effect.

Destructive Operations on Function Parameters

The programmer has to be very careful when applying a destructive operation to a parameter within a function, because changes made to the parameter will directly affect lists passed as arguments. You did not have this problem when dealing strictly with symbols. For example:

```
CL> (defun symbol-mod (arg)
        (setf arg nil))
SYMBOL-MOD
CL> (defvar x t)
X
CL> (symbol-mod x)
NIL
CL> x
T
```

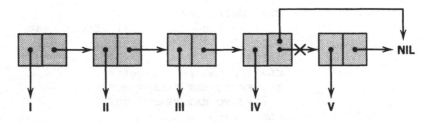

Figure 4-9   The Effect of Calling `nbutlast` on a List

When the function symbol-mod is called on the x symbol, x is evaluated and its value is passed to the function. Modifications to the arg parameter have no effect on the x symbol. Lisp follows the convention of call-by-value for symbols. This is not true of passed lists. When a list is passed as an argument, it follows the convention of pass-by-name. The function caller and the function itself both operate on the same list structure.

The nbutlast Function

As an example, consider the nbutlast function.[7] This is a destructive version of the butlast function that trims one or more conses off the end of a list. For example:

```
CL> (defvar roman-numerals '(I II III IV V))
ROMAN-NUMERALS
CL> (butlast roman-numerals 1)
(I II III IV)
CL> roman-numerals
(I II III IV V)
CL> (nbutlast roman-numerals 1)
(I II III IV)
CL> roman-numerals
(I II III IV)
```

Figure 4-9 shows how nbutlast actually changes the CDR pointer to shorten the list.

If you call nbutlast on a parameter of a function, it will cause the penultimate cons cell of the passed list to be modified. For example:

```
CL> (setf roman-numerals '(I II III IV V))
(I II III IV V)
CL> (defun ntrim-list (input-list)
        (nbutlast input-list 1))
NTRIM-LIST
CL> (ntrim-list roman-numerals)
(I II III IV)
CL> roman-numerals
(I II III IV)
```

This may not always be what we wished to do.

[7] Remember the convention of prefixing the names of destructive functions with an n. Unfortunately, this convention is not always followed rigorously. We see that nconc and nbutlast comply, but that rplaca and rplacd do not.

Many Lisp textbooks treat the use of destructive functions as an advanced programming technique and caution against their use. For this reason, many programmers are somewhat reluctant to use them. With care, however, the list-modifying functions are no more difficult to use than any other Lisp function. Nonetheless when you use list-modifying operations within a function, you must make sure that this is well documented so that future users of the function have no unpleasant surprises.

More Complex Data Structures

Lists can be used to represent a variety of other data structures. Sets, stacks, queues, and trees can all be implemented as lists. In many cases, Common Lisp provides built-in facilities for manipulating these other types of structures implemented as lists.

Lists as Sets

Lists can be viewed as ordered sets. There are a number of Common Lisp functions that allow you to do the standard set operations on lists. In Chapter 2, you encountered the member function. It can be used to test to see whether an atom is an element of a list. There are other functions for finding the intersection and the union of two lists. For example:

```
CL> (defvar greeks '(homer socrates plato ))
GREEKS
CL> (defvar philosophers '(plato socrates kant))
PHILOSOPHERS
CL> (setf greek-philosophers
          (intersection greeks philosophers))
(SOCRATES PLATO)
CL> (setf greeks-and/or-philosophers
          (union greeks philosophers))
(HOMER PLATO SOCRATES KANT)
```

There is also a set-difference function. (Note that this operation is not commutative.)

```
CL> (setf non-greek-philosophers
          (set-difference philosophers greeks))
(KANT)
CL> (setf non-philosophical-greeks
          (set-difference greeks philosophers))
(HOMER)
```

Finally, there is a Common Lisp predicate that allows you to test to see if one set (implemented as a list) is a subset of another.

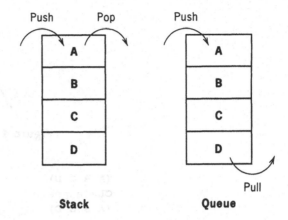

Figure 4-10 Comparison of the Workings of a Stack and a Queue

```
CL> (subsetp greek-philosophers greeks)
T
CL> (subsetp greek-philosophers philosophers)
T
```

Lists as Stacks and Queues

Stacks and queues are two structures that are used frequently as storage mechanisms. They differ in the way in which items are recovered. When items are placed on a stack, or *push-down*, the last item placed will be the first one recovered. The formal name for a stack is a *LIFO list*, where LIFO stands for "last in, first out." Stacks work exactly like the spring-loaded plate dispensers you sometimes find in cafeterias. When the plates come from the dishwasher, they are placed on top of the current stack. When you need a plate, you take the one on top; the plate below is then pushed up to the top of the stack. Queues, on the other hand, are *FIFO lists* (for "first in, first out"). In a queue, the next item recovered is the one that has been on the list the longest. Queues work just like the line at a box office window—first come, first served. Figure 4-10 graphically represents the difference between the two types of structures.

Manipulating Stacks in Common Lisp

Adding an element to a stack is referred to as *pushing* the element onto the stack. Common Lisp has a push macro that takes as arguments an atom and a list. For example:

```
CL> (defvar alphabet '( b c d))
ALPHABET
CL> (push 'a alphabet)
```

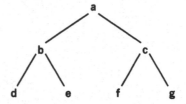

Figure 4-11   A Simple Example of a Tree

```
(A B C D)
CL> alphabet
(A B C D)
```

Similarly, things can be taken off a list using the pop macro.

```
CL> (pop alphabet)
A
CL> alphabet
(B C D)
```

Both push and pop modify their list argument. The list argument can be an expression that returns a list. This can have interesting side effects. For example:

```
CL> (pop (rest alphabet))
C
CL> alphabet
(B D)
```

Lists as Trees

Trees are another commonly used data structure. A tree is defined by a set of nodes, one of which is designated the *root* node. The root node can have one or more *child* nodes. Each of the child nodes can also have children. Figure 4-11 shows an example of a simple tree. Trees can easily be represented using lists. For example, the tree in

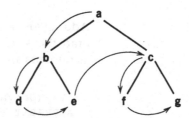

Figure 4-12   A Depth-First Transversal of a Tree

Figure 4-11 could be represented as the list

```
(a (b (d)(e))(c (f)(g)))
```

Using this format, each node is represented as follows:

```
(parent-node child-1 child-2 . . . child-n )
```

The child nodes are optional. If there are no children, the node is represented by a single-element list.

Traversing a Tree

Walking through a tree structure visiting all of the nodes is referred to as *traversing* a tree. There are two well-known techniques of traversing a tree: *depth-first traversal* and *breadth-first traversal*.[8] Both are guaranteed to visit every node. They differ in the order in which the nodes are visited. In a depth-first traversal, you start at the root node and then visit one of its children, followed by one of the children of the child node, followed by one of the children of the child of the child node, and so forth. It sounds rather recursive, doesn't it? Indeed, we could write a simple recursive function to do a depth-first traversal as follows:

```
(defun dft (tree)
  (when tree
    (visit-node (first tree))
    (dolist (subtree (rest tree))
        (dft subtree))))
```

This routine will cause us to visit each of the nodes in a depth-first fashion. What we actually do when we visit the node will be determined by the visit-node function. In the current case, we simply need to be notified when a node visit occurs, so the following definition of visit-node would suffice:

```
(defun visit-node (node)
  (print node))
```

As shown in Figure 4-12, the dft function would cause the nodes in the preceding tree to be visited in the following order: a-b-d-e-c-f-g. To see how this would actually work, we could trace the call to dft as follows:

[8]Breadth-first traversal is discussed in Exercise 4.15.

```
CL> (trace dft)
NIL
CL> (dft '(a (b (d) (e)) (c (f) (g))))
Calling (DFT (A (B (D)(E)) (C (F)(G))))
A
  Calling (DFT (B (D) (E)))
B
    Calling (DFT (D))
D
    DFT returned NIL
    Calling (DFT (E))
E
    DFT returned NIL
  DFT returned NIL
  Calling (DFT (C (F) (G)))
C
    Calling (DFT (F))
F
    DFT returned NIL
    Calling (DFT (G))
G
    DFT returned NIL
  DFT returned NIL
 DFT returned NIL
NIL
```

The dft function descends recursively into the tree structure until it reaches the node containing d. Since it can go down no further, it unwinds back to the second recursive call to finish processing the list. We then visit the other child of b and wind back again, but this time the list is finished, so we go all the way back to the first call to dft. Here we have another list to complete, which causes us to explore the other subtree, (c (f) (g). In this way, all of the nodes of the original tree are visited in the proper order.

Depth-first traversal is a general technique for manipulating trees in the same sense that CDRing down a list is a general and powerful technique for manipulating lists. Make it part of your programming repertoire because trees are commonly used data structures.

Exercise 4.6

Produce a cons cell diagram for each of the following lists:

a. (apples peaches pears plums)

b. ((tinker) (tailor) (soldier) (spy))

c. ((madison . wisconsin)

```
(indianapolis . indiana)
(springfield . illinois))
```

Exercise 4.7

If Lisp uses `nil` to mark the end of a list, how does it discriminate between the list

```
(nil nil nil)
```

(i.e., a list of three empty lists) and the empty list? Justify your answer with a cons cell diagram.

Exercise 4.8

Write a function called `swap-elements` that will exchange the position of two elements in a list and return the updated list. For example:

```
CL> (swap-elements 1 2 '( a b c d ))
(A C B D)
```

Exercise 4.9

Write your own versions of the `intersection` and `union` set functions. (Hint: You may use `member-p` from Exercises 3.8 and 3.14.)

Exercise 4.10

Draw a cons cell diagram to show the effect of the following call to the pop macro:

```
CL> (defvar alphabet '(a b c d))
ALPHABET
CL> (pop alphabet)
A
CL> alphabet
(B C D)
```

Exercise 4.11

Write a new version of the `calculator` function (from Exercise 3.23) that will work with prefix operators instead of infix operators. For example:

```
CL> (prefix-calculator)
/
+
+
3
*
```

```
2
2
5
4
```
13/4

Note that if you assume that all operations are binary, you will not need to use the "equals" sign to terminate input.

(Hint: If you do this as an iterative function, you will need to use a stack to store intermediate results.)

Exercise 4.12 (*)

Rewrite the `squash-list` function from Exercise 3.10 as an iterative function. (Hint: Use a stack to store your intermediate results.)

Exercise 4.13 (*)

When working with queues, there is an operation analogous to performing a pop on a stack. It is called a `pull`. Try writing a function that will take a list as an argument and return the last element of the list. The list itself should be modified as a side effect. What is the problem with your version of `pull`?

Exercise 4.14 (*)

One of the standard algorithms for sorting a list is known as a *bubble sort*. In this operation you make several passes through the input list, comparing each element with the one immediately succeeding it. If an element is larger than the following element (assuming that you are sorting in ascending order), you reverse their positions in the list. Eventually, all of the small-valued elements will "float" to the top of the list, hence the name *bubble* sort. Continue making passes through the list until you have made one complete pass without any exchanges. Write the function called `bubble-sort` to sort a list of numbers.

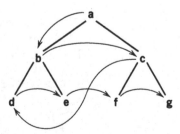

Figure 4-13   A Breadth-First Transversal of a Tree

Optional: Write a function called `character-bubble-sort` that will sort a list of characters; for example:

```
CL> (character-bubble-sort '( #\d #\a #\c #\b ))
( #\a #\b #\c #\d )
```

Exercise 4.15 (*)

There is another standard way of traversing a tree, called *breadth-first* traversal. As shown in Figure 4-13, a breadth-first traversal of the preceding tree would cause the nodes to be visited in the following order: a-b-c-d-e-f-g. Write a function to perform a breadth-first traversal of trees. (Hint: Use a queue to keep track of nodes that have not been visited.)

4.3 SEQUENCES

Common Lisp Vectors

All modern computer languages have facilities for representing vectors, and Common Lisp is no exception. There is a function called `vector` that works just like the `list` function, except that it creates a vector instead of a list. For example:

```
CL> (defvar my-vector (vector 'x 'y 'z))
MY-VECTOR
CL> my-vector
#(X Y Z)
```

The sharp sign before the left parenthesis in the returned result indicates that the result is a vector and not a list.[9] Common Lisp vectors are zero-based, which means that you start counting positions from zero. You can access elements of a vector using the `svref` function. For example:

```
CL> (svref my-vector 1)
Y
```

To change an element of a vector, you would use the `setf` macro. Positions in a vector, like positions in a list, can be treated as generic variables. Consequently, to change the second element of a vector,

---

[9]There is a shorthand way of creating a vector in which you type the vector directly. The preceding example could be written equivalently:

```
(defvar my-vector '#(x y z))
```

you would type

```
CL> (setf (svref my-vector 1) 'a)
A
CL> my-vector
#(X A Z)
```

Vectors versus Linked Lists

So far, vectors don't seem very different from the linked-list data structures that we have been working with in Lisp. You might wonder why we need another type of structure. Although it is true that both vectors and linked lists represent the same thing, that is, an ordered set, they differ in the way they are implemented. The implementation of linked lists was discussed in the previous section. Vectors are usually implemented by preallocating a block of contiguous memory slots. When we wish to reference the fifth element of a vector, we can immediately compute its address given the offset (i.e., 5) and the address of the beginning of the vector. With a linked list, on the other hand, to reference the fifth element, we must go to the beginning of the list and work our way down the chain of cons cells to the desired element. In a linked list the time required to access any particular element depends on the position of that element in the list; the farther down the list, the longer it will take to reach the item. In a vector, the amount of time required to access any element will be constant. For some applications, the use of vectors may offer clear performance advantages. Why not always use vectors? The problem with vectors is that you have to decide in advance how big the vector will be before using it. With lists you can always add another cons cell, but vectors have a fixed size.[10] The differences between vectors and linked lists are summarized in Table 4-1.

Processing Vectors and Lists

In addition to the issues of storage allocation and access times, there are differences in the processing strategies for vectors and lists. Vectors are usually processed in an iterative fashion. The dotimes macro is particularly convenient for manipulating elements of a vector because it computes an index for us. For example, a function to zero out all the elements of a vector could be written as follows:

---

[10]Actually, the situation in Common Lisp is a little more flexible than you have been led to believe. There is a facility for using *fill pointers* that makes the length of vectors somewhat more dynamic. There is also a function called adjust-array that allows you to redimension an array at runtime.

TABLE 4-1 *Comparison of Linked Lists and Vectors*

	Access Time	Storage Allocation	Processing Strategy
Linked lists	Variable	Adjustable	Recursive and Iterative
Vectors	Constant	Fixed	Iterative

```
(defun zero-out (vector)
  (dotimes (index (length vector) vector)
    (setf (svref vector index) 0)))
```

With lists, on the other hand, it is often more straightforward to use a recursive processing strategy. There are, of course, many exceptions to this rule. We have seen examples where lists can be processed most readily in an iterative fashion, and if you wished, you could always write a recursive function to process down a vector. But for the most part, vectors lend themselves to iterative processing, and linked lists tend to be most easily manipulated in a recursive fashion.

Common Lisp Strings

We encountered strings in earlier chapters, but we have not discussed how they are actually implemented. Strings in Common Lisp are implemented as vectors of characters. You can create a string (as we have done all along) by simply wrapping a pair of double quotation marks around a sequence of characters. For example:

```
CL> (defvar my-string "Matson, I need you!")
MY-STRING
CL> my-string
"Matson, I need you!"
```

Alternatively, there is a make-string function to create a string under the control of a program. Elements of a string are accessed using the char function. The function takes a string and an index as arguments and returns a character. For example:

```
CL> (char my-string 1)
#\a
```

Just as with vectors (and lists), the positions of a string can be treated as generic variables and their contents modified using setf. For example:

```
CL> (setf (char my-string 0) #\W)
#\W
CL> my-string
"Watson, I need you!"
```

Common Lisp Arrays

Common Lisp supports multidimensional arrays as well. Vectors are just a special case of a Common Lisp array that has only one dimension. Arrays are created using the make-array function. This function has one required argument: a list of integers specifying the dimensions of the array. For example, to create a 4 x 4 matrix, you would type

```
CL> (defvar my-array (make-array '(4 4)))
MY-ARRAY
```

The value returned by make-array will be a Common Lisp array. The way that an array is printed may vary from implementation to implementation.[11]

Optional Keywords

There are additional arguments that can be supplied to make-array. In Common Lisp, many functions allow the use of keywords with optional arguments. The keyword specifies how the optional argument will be used. Common Lisp keywords are special symbols that have a colon before their name.[12] There are a number of possible keyword arguments for make-array. The most commonly used are :element-type, :initial-element, and :initial-contents. You can declare that your array will be restricted to a certain type of data object using the :element-

---

[11]Arrays may be printed in two ways: using the #< form, as shown, or using #nA syntax. The former is for printing only; you cannot access the array by retyping the sequence of characters. Typing a printed representation of the second form, however, will actually create a new array with the specified contents. The current assignment of the global variable *print-array* determines which syntax will be used.

[12]Common Lisp keyword symbols are associated with the built-in package keyword.

type keyword. For example,

```
(make-array '(4 4 ) :element-type 'integer)
```

specifies that the array will only accept integer values. The keyword :initial-element specifies how the array will be initialized. If you wanted the array initially to contain all zeros, you would type

```
(make-array '(4 4 ) :initial-element 0)
```

If an initial element is not provided, the contents of the array will be undefined. Some implementations use the default value of nil, but this is not always true. If you want to specify an initial value for each position in the array, you should use the :initial-contents keyword and provide a list with values. The list of values should be nested to correspond to the dimension list for the array. An example of the use of :initial-contents is

```
CL> (defvar my-array
         (make-array '(4 4 )
             :element-type 'integer
             :initial-contents '((1 2 3 4)
                                  (5 6 7 8)
                                  (9 10 11 12)
                                  (13 14 15 16))))
MY-ARRAY
```

Accessing Elements of an Array

Common Lisp provides a function called aref for referencing the elements of an array. It takes as arguments a Common Lisp array and a numeric argument for each of the array indices. Note that, like list and vector positions, array indices are zero-based. To reference the array element in the fourth row of the fourth column of my-array, you would have to type

```
CL> (aref my-array 3 3)
16
```

Modifying the Elements of an Array

The elements of an array can be modified using aref in an access form as the first argument to the setf macro. This pattern should look very familiar by now, since it is similar to the mechanism used to update the positions of lists, vectors, and strings. For example, to change the value of the fourth element of the fourth row of my-array, you would type

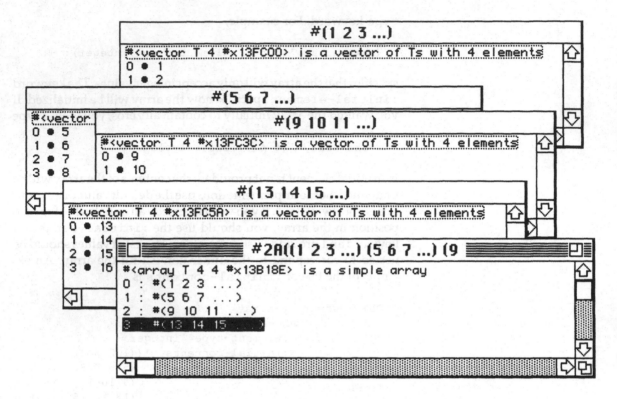

Figure 4-14   A Set of Inspector Windows (from Procyon™ Common Lisp)

```
CL> (setf (aref my-array 3 3 ) 99)
99
CL> (aref my-array 3 3)
99
```

inspect *Function*

There is a useful Common Lisp function called inspect for interactively examining the contents of data structures such as arrays, vectors, and lists. A call to this function would look like this:

```
CL> (inspect my-array)
```

The way in which a particular data structure is displayed may vary depending on the data type and the Common Lisp implementation.

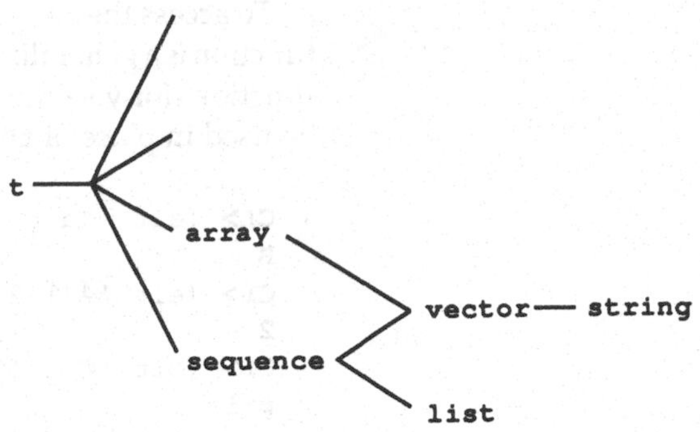

Figure 4-15   A Further Elaboration of the Common Lisp Type Hierarchy (from Figure 2-2)

A sample of the output from the inspect function for an array is given in Figure 4-14. The inspect function can be called recursively to inspect composite structures like nested lists or lists of vectors.

Common Lisp Sequences

Figure 4-15 shows a further elaboration of the Common Lisp type hierarchy introduced in Chapter 2. It shows strings as a subtype of vectors, which is reasonable, since strings in Common Lisp are character vectors. It also shows vectors as a subtype of arrays, which is equally reasonable, since vectors are nothing but one-dimensional arrays. One new element in Figure 4-15 is that lists and vectors are shown as subtypes of sequences. In Common Lisp, a sequence is a generalized structure that could be a list, vector, or string. The significance of having this more generic type of data structure would probably be strictly academic were it not for the fact that Common Lisp provides a selection of functions that operate on sequences. By using these functions instead of the more specialized list and vector functions, you can write code that will work with both.

Accessing Elements of a Sequence

You can create a sequence using the functions described for creating vectors, lists, and strings, since they are all subtypes of sequences. There is also a function called make-sequence that will create a sequence. You must specify the type and size.

To access the elements of a sequence, use the `elt` function. This function is a generalization of the `nth` function (for lists), the `svref` function (for vectors) and the `char` function (for strings), and can be used in place of any of them.[13] For example:

```
CL> (elt '(a b c) 1)
B
CL> (elt '#(1 2 3) 1)
2
CL> (elt "Ciao!" 1)
#\i
```

As you might expect, positions within a sequence can be treated as generalized variables and updated using `setf`.

Sequence-Manipulating Functions

Common Lisp provides a number of other useful sequence functions. Some of them are simple extensions to functions we are already familiar with as list functions. The `length` function, which we encountered in an earlier chapter, is actually a sequence function and will work with lists, vectors, and strings. The `concatenate` function joins together two or more sequences. It is a generalization of the `append` function. There is a general search function called `position` that works with sequences in much the same fashion that `member` works with lists. Finally, there is a function called `map` that does for sequences what `mapcar` does for lists. There are a number of sequence functions for which there is no analogous list function. These include the `reduce` function, the sequence predicates, and the sequence-modifying functions.

reduce Function

The `reduce` function performs a binary operation on all pairs of elements in a sequence. It performs the operation on the first two elements of the sequence and then performs the operation on the result and the third element. It continues in this fashion until all of

---

[13]Note that the order of arguments is not entirely consistent. The order of arguments for `svref`, `char`, and `elt` is

```
(svref vector index)
(char string index)
(elt sequence index)
```

but the order for `nth` is

```
(nth index list)
```

TABLE 4-2 *Sequence-Modifying Functions*

Function	Destructive Version	Behavior
—	`fill`	Sets all elements of a sequence or subsequence to a specified value
—	`merge`	Merges two sequences in sorted order
`remove`	`delete`	Removes an element from a sequence or subsequence
`remove-duplicates`	`delete-duplicates`	Removes redundancies from a sequence or subsequence
—	`replace`	Replaces a sequence (or part thereof) with another sequence or subsequence
`reverse`	`nreverse`	Reverses a sequence
—	`sort`	Sorts a sequence
`substitute`	`nsubstitute`	Substitutes one item for another in a sequence or subsequence

the elements have been processed. Using `reduce`, the `sum-list` function from Chapter 3 could be written as

```
(defun sum-list (number-list)
   (reduce #'+ number-list))
```

Sequence Predicates

The four predicates `some`, `every`, `notany`, and `notevery` can only be applied to sequences. The predicates with which you are already familiar will test a single argument, but the sequence predicates allow you to perform a test on all the elements of a sequence taken collectively.[14] The first argument to a sequence predicate is another predicate to be applied to each of the elements of the sequence. For example:

[14]Students of mathematical logic will recognize these as the existential and universal quantifiers and their negations.

```
CL> (defvar mixed-vector '#(a b c 3.12 100))
MIXED VECTOR
CL> (some #'numberp mixed-vector)
T
CL> (every #'numberp mixed-vector)
NIL
```

One of the elements of my-vector has to satisfy the numberp predicate in order for the some predicate to be true, but all elements of my-vector would have to be numbers in order to make the every predicate true.

Sequence-Modifying Functions

There are various functions that modify the contents of a sequence. There are also built-in sequence functions for sorting and merging and substituting pieces of sequences. These functions are summarized in Table 4-2. Some of them are provided in both a destructive and a nondestructive form. You should also note that some of the functions operate on subsequences as well as on sequences.

Working with Subsequences

When working with lists, we have found it convenient to work with heads and tails of lists. This is easy to do because of the way lists have been implemented in Lisp. Suppose we wanted to work with an arbitrary part of a list that wasn't the head or the tail? There is no easy way to do that using the list functions. There is a function called subseq that will allow you to reference a subsequence by specifying a starting position and an ending position. For example:

```
CL> (subseq '(a b c d e f g) 2 5)
(C D E)
```

The subseq function can be used with setf to modify a sequence destructively.

Many sequence functions, such as reduce and remove, allow the optional use of the :start and :end keywords, permitting you to limit the range of their effect. For example:

```
CL> (remove 'a '(a b c a b c a b c a b c )
                :start 3 )
(A B C B C B C B C)
```

Exercise 4.16

In matrix algebra, a pair of vectors of equal length can be multiplied to produce an *inner product* and an *outer product* (Searle, 1982). The inner product is computed by multiplying together the corresponding elements of the vectors and then taking the sums of the products. For example, the inner product of the vector

```
#(1 2 3)
```

and the vector

```
#(5 10 15)
```

would be

```
1(5) + 2(10) + 3(15) = 70
```

Write a function to compute the inner product of two vectors.

Exercise 4.17

There is an algorithm attributed to Floyd [Bentley, 1987] for taking random samples within a specified range of values. It is referred to as *sampling without replacement* because each value can occur only once in the sample set. A recursive version of this algorithm is

```
(defun sample (m n)
  (if (> m 0)
    (let((selections (sample (1- m)
                             (1- n)))
         (next (random  n)))
     (if (member next selections)
      (cons n selections)
      (cons next selections)))))
```

The m parameter is the number of items to sample; sample values can range over 0 to n (inclusive). The `sample` function uses the Common Lisp `random` function. Test to see if the random number generator in your implementation of Common Lisp really works by writing a function called `random-test` to call `sample` a large number of times (say, 10,000). Use a sample size of 5 and allow the values to range between 0 and 10. Create a vector to keep a tally of the number of times that each possible value is selected. If the random number generator is good, the distribution of values should be fairly uniform after 10,000 trials.

Exercise 4.18

A palindrome is defined as a sequence of letters that read the same both forward and backward. "Able was I ere I saw Elba" is the standard example of a palindrome. Write a predicate called palindrome-p, which, when passed a string, will test whether or not it is a palindrome.

Exercise 4.19

For many of us, our first exposure to another language was when we learned pig Latin in elementary school. Actually, pig Latin is more like an encryption scheme than a language. There is a simple two-step procedure for converting a word into pig Latin:

a. Take all the characters preceding the first vowel and move them to the end of the word.

b. Concatenate the string *ay* to the end of the new word.

Write a function that, when passed a symbol, will return a string representing its pig Latin translation. For example:

```
CL> (translate-to-pig-latin 'scram)
"AMSCRAY"
```

Exercise 4.20

Write a function to convert an Arabic number into a Roman numeral. The returned result should be a string. For example:

```
CL> (roman-numeral 1989)
"MCMLXXXIX"
```

(Hint: You may wish to use the Common Lisp floor and mod functions for this exercise. When called with two arguments, floor returns the integer part of the quotient of dividing the first argument by the second. The mod function returns the integer remainder of the division.)

Exercise 4.21

The outer product of two vectors of length n is an $n \times n$ matrix. For example, the outer product of the vector

```
#(1 2 3)
```

and the vector

```
#(5 10 15)
```

is

$$\begin{bmatrix} 1*5 & 1*10 & 1*15 \\ 2*5 & 2*10 & 2*15 \\ 3*5 & 3*10 & 3*15 \end{bmatrix}$$

Write a function to compute the outer product of two vectors.

Exercise 4.22

In general, we can compute the matrix product of two arrays, A and B, if the dimensions of A are $r_a \times c_a$ and the dimensions of B are $r_b \times c_b$ and $c_a = r_b$ (Searle, 1982). The matrix product, P, would be an $r_a \times c_b$ matrix. Each element of P, $p_{i,j}$, would be computed by taking the sum of the products of the corresponding elements of the ith row of A and the jth column of B. For example, the result of the following call

```
CL> (matrix-multiply (make-array '(3 2)
                        :initial-contents
                         '((1 2)
                           (3 4)
                           (5 6)))
                      (make-array '(2 2)
                         :initial-contents
                         '((10 20)
                           (40 50)))))
#2A((90 120) (190 260) (290 400))
```

would be equivalent to the matrix

$$\begin{bmatrix} 1(10)+2(40) & 1(20)+2(50) \\ 3(10)+4(40) & 3(20)+4(50) \\ 5(10)+6(40) & 5(20)+6(50) \end{bmatrix}$$

Write a function that, when passed two arrays, will test to see if they conform for multiplication and, if so, compute their matrix product. (Hint: There is a function called `array-dimension` that will return a specified dimension for an array.)

Exercise 4.23

There is a chessboard problem known as the *8-Queens* problem. In chess, a queen can attack any opposing piece that is situated on the same rank (i.e., column), file (i.e., row), or diagonal. The 8-Queens problem is to position eight queens on an 8 x 8 chessboard in such a way that no queen is attacking any other queen (Figure 4-16). If we represent the chessboard as an 8 x 8 array, can you write a function that, when passed an array representing a board, will return a list of all legal positions in which a queen could be placed? (A position is represented as a dotted pair consisting of a rank and a file.) For example:

Figure 4-16   A Possible Solution for the 8-Queens Problem

```
CL> (safe-squares (make-array '(8 8)
             :initial-contents
             '((QN nil nil nil nil nil nil nil)
               (nil nil QN nil nil nil nil nil)
               (nil nil nil nil QN nil nil nil)
               (nil nil nil nil nil nil QN nil)
               (nil nil nil QN nil nil nil nil)
               (nil nil nil nil nil nil nil nil)
               (nil nil nil nil nil nil nil nil)
               (nil nil nil nil nil nil nil nil)))))
((7 . 5) (7 . 1))
```

Exercise 4.24

Rewrite the `bubble-sort` function (from Exercise 4.14) to work with sequences instead of lists. For example:

```
CL> (bubble-sort-2
      '#(100 55 77 4 13 12 13 69))
#(4 12 13 13 55 69 77 100)
CL> (bubble-sort-2
      '("able" "baker" "charlie"))
("able" "baker" "charlie")
CL> (bubble-sort-2
     "the quick brown fox jumped over the lazy dog")
"        abcddeeeefghhijklmnoooopqrrttuuvwxyz"
```

4.4 DATA TABLES

Before we leave the topic of data structures, we need to consider the problem of how to deal with collections of data items. Sequences will accommodate collections of data items, of course, but to retrieve an item from a sequence, we must first know its position. More often, we would like to be able to retrieve an item using a search key. When you want a number from the telephone book, you don't need to know the page and line number to retrieve the phone number; you only need to know the name of the party you wish to call. We say that the phone book is *keyed by name*. Data structures that allow you to retrieve items using a search key are referred to as *associative retrieval tables* or simply *data tables*. Common Lisp has some built-in facilities for manipulating data tables. For special applications, it is quite easy to build your own customized data storage facilities using the other data structures described in this chapter.

Property Lists

Earlier in the chapter, we encountered the notion of property lists in the plist cell of a symbol, but property lists can be used as database structures as well. Property lists have the format

```
( key-1 item-1 key-2 item-2 . . . )
```

in which the keys and the data items alternate. Common Lisp provides some functions for manipulating key-item pairs in lists of this format. The getf function is used to retrieve an item from a property list. For example, to create a database of telephone numbers for Common Lisp vendors, we could type

```
CL> (defvar vendors '(Gold-Hill "(617)492-2071"
                       Franz "(415)548-3600"
                       Lucid "(451)329-8400"
                       Symbolics "(800)527-3500"))
VENDORS
```

To retrieve a phone number for one of the vendors, we could then type

```
CL> (getf vendors 'Franz)
"(415)548-3600"
```

Note that the values used for keys must be symbols, since `getf` uses `eq` to match keys.

Updating Property Lists

The property list can be updated by using a `getf` expression as an *access-form* in a call to the `setf` macro. For example:

```
CL> (setf (getf vendors 'Lucid) "(415)329-8400")
"(415)329-8400"
CL> vendors
(GOLD-HILL "(617)492-2071"
 FRANZ "(415)548-3600"
 LUCID "(415)329-8400"
 SYMBOLICS "(800)527-3500")
```

This is a destructive operation. The vendors' property list is modified by `setf`; the old key-item pair is lost.

Association Lists

An alternative way to construct databases is to use association lists. Association lists, or a-lists for short, have a different form from property lists. A-lists are lists of dotted pairs of the following form:

```
((key-1 . item-1)(key-2 . item-2). . .)
```

Common Lisp also provides built-in functions for manipulating lists of this form. To fetch an item from an a-list, you use the `assoc` function. For example:

```
CL> (defvar vendors-2 '((DEC . "(800)344-4825")
                        (Franz . "(415)548-3600")
                        (Lucid . "(415)329-8400")
                        (Symbolics . "(800)527-3500")))
VENDORS-2
CL> (assoc 'dec vendors-2)
(DEC . "(800)344-4825")
```

Note that `assoc` returns a dotted pair consisting of a key and an item. To get the actual item, you need to call `rest` on the result returned by `assoc`. There is a `:test` keyword for `assoc` that allows you to select the test used to match the keys; it defaults to eql.

You can retrieve keys from an association list given an item using the `rassoc` function (for *reverse association*). For example, you could retrieve a vendor name given a telephone number by typing

```
CL> (rassoc "(800)527-3500" vendors-2 :test #'equal)
(SYMBOLICS . "(800)527-3500")
```

Updating an Association List

A-lists are updated in an unusual way. There is a function called `acons` that adds a key-item pair to an a-list. For example:

```
CL> (setf vendors-2
          (acons 'Envos "(800)228-5325" vendors-2))
((ENVOS . "(800)228-5325")
 (DEC . "(800)344-4825")
 (FRANZ . "(415)548-3600")
 (LUCID . "(415)329-8400")
 (SYMBOLICS . "(800)527-3500"))
```

In a property list, if the key from the new key-item pair coincides with a previous key, the old key-item pair is overwritten. In an a-list, the new key-item pair is added, but the old key-item pair is retained. The new pair will be returned if you call `assoc` on the a-list. The old key-item pair is said to be *shadowed* by the new pair.

Hash Tables

Common Lisp has a third kind of built-in database facility called *hash tables*. Hash tables are used for large databases where an efficient retrieval mechanism is required. Property lists and a-lists are searched by working down the chain of cons cells looking for a key match. The retrieval time for any given item will vary, depending on the position of the key-item pair in the list. This can be very inefficient if the list is long.

Hash Keys

When an item is stored in a hash table, a hashing function is run on the item to produce a numeric *hash key*. The hash key specifies where the item will be stored in the table. The hashing function is carefully selected to produce a different hash key for each data item. Like arrays, items can be retrieved from a hash table in a fixed amount of time. Retrieval time is independent of the length of the list or the position of the item in the list (Knuth, 1973).

If we anticipate that our vendor list will grow much larger, we may choose to implement it using a hash table as follows:

```
CL> (defvar vendors-3
        (make-hash-table :size 1000
                              :test #'eq))

VENDORS-3
```

You may optionally specify the size of the table (in key-item pairs) and the test that will be used when matching keys.

Retrieving Items from a Hash Table

Common Lisp provides a function called `gethash` for retrieving items from hash tables. Items are added and updated by calling `setf` with a `gethash` form as an *access-form*. Updates to hash tables are done destructively. To provide a quick demonstration of how this works, let's convert the `vendors-2` a-list into a hash table. This can be done by typing the following expression:

```
CL> (do ((to-do vendors-2 (rest to-do)))
             ((null to-do))
        (let ((dotted-pair (first to-do)))
           (setf (gethash (first dotted-pair)
                              vendors-3)
                 (rest dotted-pair))))

NIL
```

You could then fetch the phone number for one of the vendors by typing

```
CL> (gethash 'Envos vendors-3)
"(415) 966-6200"
```

Note that we get the old number for Envos because it was the last to be installed in the hash table.

Putting It All Together

In the data table examples given earlier, the items were simple atomic data structures, but this did not have to be the case. The item could just as easily have been a list, an object, an array, or even another data table. In fact, this composition of data structures could be applied to all the data structures presented in this chapter. You could envision lists of objects, objects with vectors or lists as slot items, arrays holding lists or objects, and so forth. Indeed, the selection of primitive data structures provided in Common Lisp is so rich, and the possibilities for combining them are so vast, that the programmer should have no problem designing data structures in Lisp for any conceivable project.

Exercise 4.25

List three important differences in the operating characteristics of property lists and association lists.

Exercise 4.26

Draw cons cell diagrams to portray the vendors property list and the vendors-2 association list.

Exercise 4.27

The following is a list of airport abbreviations and the cities in which they are located:

Code	Location
BOS	Boston, MA
DCA	Washington, D.C.
JFK	New York, NY
LAX	Los Angeles, CA
ORD	Chicago, IL
SEA	Seattle, WA
SFO	San Francisco, CA

Represent this information in

a. a property list.

b. an association list.

c. a hash table.

(Hint: You will probably want to store the locations as strings.)

SUMMARY

In this chapter, we have looked more carefully at some of the Common Lisp built-in data structures and explored some of the things you can achieve using these structures. Figure 4-17 shows an updated view of the Common Lisp type hierarchy reflecting some of the new data types encountered in this chapter.

We began the chapter by considering how symbols are implemented in Common Lisp. Every Common Lisp symbol has five cells for storing a value, a function definition, a print name, a

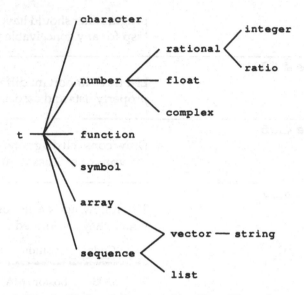

Figure 4-17 An Updated Common Lisp Type Hierarchy

package, and a property list. This explains how a symbol can serve both as a variable name and as a function name without causing a conflict.

We also discovered some of the secret powers of the setf macro. Using setf, we can treat a wide variety of storage locations as though they were simple variables and assign values to them. In addition to assigning values to symbols, setf can be used destructively to change elements of a list, to write new values into vectors and arrays, and to modify items in hash tables. Storage locations treated in this way are referred to as *generic variables*.

Common Lisp provides a number of macros that manipulate generic variables in addition to setf. The incf and decf macros can be used to increment and decrement generic variables. The rotatef and shiftf macros take multiple generic variables as arguments. They can be used to exchange values between storage locations.

Lisp lists are implemented as chains of cons cells. List structures can be represented using cons-cell diagrams. Some of the list functions destructively modify their arguments. This violates the call-by-value argument-passing convention described in Chapter 2. Data structures such as sets, stacks, queues, and trees can be implemented using lists.

Common Lisp sequences represent a generalized data type that includes lists, vectors, and strings. By writing functions that operate on sequences instead of one of their subtypes, you can create general-purpose functions that will handle all of the sequence subtypes.

There are built-in facilities for constructing data tables in Common Lisp. Data tables can be implemented using property lists, a-lists, or hash tables. Property lists and a-lists are specially formatted lists. Common Lisp provides built-in functions for retrieval and update of items stored on such lists. Hash tables are used for larger data tables. They use a hash key to compute a hash for each item to allow for efficient retrieval.

NEW COMMON LISP DEFINED NAMES

acons	gethash	rassoc
array-dimension	get-universal-time	reduce
aref	incf	remove
assoc	inspect	rotatef
boundp	make-array	rplacd
butlast	make-hash-table	shiftf
char	make-sequence	some
concatenate	make-symbol	subseq
decf	mod	svref
elt	nbutlast	symbol-function
every	notany	symbol-name
floor	notevery	symbol-package
gensym	pop	symbol-vlue
get	push	vector
getf	random	

FOR FURTHER READING

For more information about linked lists, stacks, and trees, consult the Horowitz text (Horowitz and Sahni, 1976) or any other data structures book. The Knuth volume on nonnumeric algorithms (Knuth, 1973) is also a good reference. A more detailed discussion of data abstraction can be found in the Abelson, et al. text (Abelson, et al., 1985).

For more detailed information in the Steele text (Steele, 1990) on the topics covered in this chapter see Chapter 10 or a description of Common Lisp symbols, Chapter 15 especially Sections 15.1 and 15.2) for more information about functions for manipulating lists, Chapter 14 for a discussion of sequences, Section 15.5 for a description of additional Common Lisp set functions, Chapter 16 for hash tables, Section 10.1 for property lists, Section 15.6 for a-lists, and Section 7.2 for generalized variables.

Project 4.1

The *magic square* is a 3 x 3 matrix with cells containing the digits 1 through 9, each digit appearing in only one cell. The sums of the cells in each column, row, and diagonal should equal one number. Write a program to find all arrangements of the matrix that qualify as magic squares.

Project 4.2

The Triangle Puzzle uses a triangular board with 15 holes, as shown in Figure 4-18. You begin the puzzle with pegs in all of the holes except the center hole (hole 5). You can eliminate a peg if another peg can jump over the peg to a free hole. A solution to the problem is a sequence of jumps that eliminate all pegs but one. Write a program that will solve the Triangle Puzzle.

Project 4.3

The Japanese abacus consists of (usually) 12 upright rods, each holding 6 beads or *counters* (Yoshino, 1963). The six counters on each rod are divided with a crosspiece so that one of the counters is separated from the other five. The upper partition of the abacus

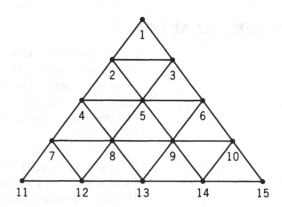

Figure 4-18   The Triangle Puzzle

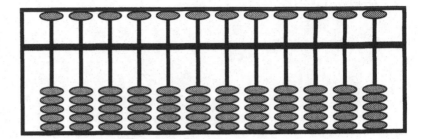

Figure 4-19   Japanese Abacus

is referred to as *Heaven*; the lower partition is referred to as *Earth*. Earth counters represent a value of 1, and Heaven counters represent a value of 5. The Earth counters are initially pushed to the bottom of their rod, and the Heaven counters are pushed to the top of their rod, as shown in Figure 4-19. Each rod represents a place in the decimal number system. When working with integers, we use the rightmost rod to represent the numbers 0 to 9, the next rod to represent the 10s place, and so forth. The numbers 1 through 4 are represented by pushing Earth counters up to the crosspiece. The number 5 is represented by returning all Earth counters to their initial positions and moving the Heaven counter to the crosspiece. The number 6 is represented by adding one Earth counter to the Heaven counter representing 5.

Design a data structure to represent an abacus as described. Write a function called abacus-value that will return the numeric value associated with an abacus structure. Write a second function, called abacus-add, that will take as arguments an abacus structure and an integer value and return an updated abacus. The passed abacus may be destructively modified as a side effect, if you wish.

5

Objects All Sublime

My object all sublime
I shall achieve in time.
W.S. Gilbert, The Mikado, II

5.1 COMMON LISP STRUCTURES

Often we have to invent special data structures to meet the particular requirements of an application. Those of you who have programmed in Pascal are familiar with the facility provided by that language for defining records. Pascal records allow you to define new data structures with predefined, named slots. Common Lisp provides a similar record definition facility. Common Lisp records are referred to as *structures*. These structures allow us to augment the set of built-in Common Lisp data structures with new data structures of our own design.

Chess Positions

As shown in Figure 5-1, any position on a chessboard can be specified using two numbers, known as the *rank* and the *file*. Chess players refer to this as *algebraic notation*. In the 8-Queens Problem (Exercise 4.23), you used dotted pairs to hold these numbers. This

143

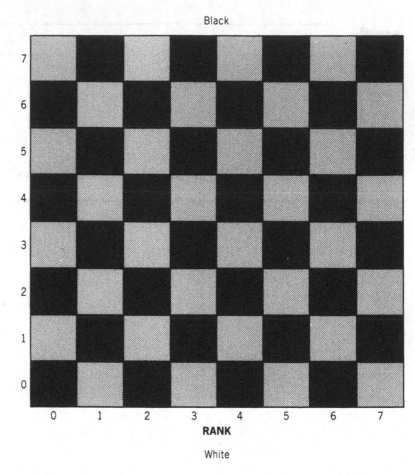

Figure 5-1   Defining Chessboard Positions Based on Rank and File

seemed to work adequately, but it can be confusing because there is no way to tell, simply by looking at a dotted pair, which element represents a rank and which represents a file. The Common Lisp structure facility allows us to create a new type of data object that has appropriately labeled slots. In this case, you can define a type of structure called a *position* with two slots labeled *rank* and *file*.

Defining a Structure

New structures are defined using the Common Lisp defstruct macro. You could define a structure similar to the one shown in Figure 5-2 for representing chess positions as follows:

```
(defstruct position
   rank
   file)
```

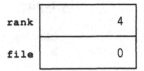

rank	4
file	0

Figure 5-2 A `Position` Stucture Used to Represent a Chess Position

The first argument to `defstruct` is the name of the new data structure being defined. It is not evaluated. The remaining arguments are slot descriptors.

Creating Instances of a Structure

The `make-position` function (which was automatically created by the `defstruct` macro) can be used to create instances of the new structure. For example, we could type

```
CL> (defvar king-position (make-position))
KING-POSITION
```

The `make-position` function returns a position structure that, in this case, is bound by `defvar` to the `king-position` symbol. The slots have an initial value of zero. If you wish to install values in these slots at the time that the instance is created, you could type instead

```
CL> (defvar king-position (make-position :rank 4
                                         :file 0))
KING-POSITION
```

The slot names can be used as optional keyword arguments for installing values in the slots of the newly created structure.

Accessing Slots of a Structure

You can inquire about the contents of the `rank` and `file` slots by using the `position-rank` and `position-file` functions (also generated by the call to `defstruct`). For example:

```
CL> (position-rank king-position)
4
```

Structure slots can be treated as generic variables and, as such, can be updated using `setf`. You could put a new value in the `rank` slot by typing

```
CL> (setf (position-rank king-position) 5)
5
```

Isn't that easy? Try changing the value stored in the `file` slot of `king-position`, just to convince yourself that you know how it works.

Doubly Linked Lists

Let's look at a slightly more complicated example using structures. Suppose that you were writing an application in which you not only needed to process down a list but to work your way up the list as well. Linked lists, as you will recall, are connected with forward pointers; each cons cell has a pointer to the next cons cell. In order to move up a list from back to front, you also need a pointer to the previous cons cell. Lists with pointers in both directions are called *doubly linked lists*. Figure 5-3 provides an example of such a list. We will term the cons cells with pointers in both directions *double-cons* cells (or *dcons* for short).

Common Lisp Structures

Lisp has no built-in facilities for handling doubly linked lists, but it does provide the capability to create new types of data structures when we need them. We can represent dcons cells using structures as follows:

```
CL> (defstruct dcons
        predecessor
        contents
        successor)
DCONS
```

As in the previous example, `defstruct` is called to define a new type of data structure. In this case, there are three slot descriptor

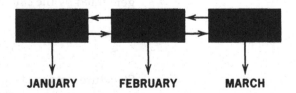

JANUARY   **FEBRUARY**   **MARCH**

Figure 5-3   A Doubly Linked List

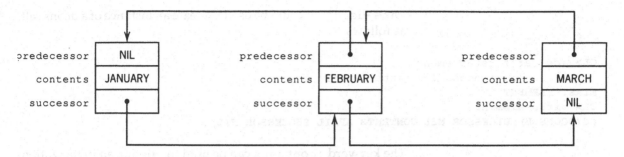

Figure 5-4   Representing a Doubly Linked List Using Dcons Objects

arguments. Slot descriptors can take the form of a list when an optional initialization form is to be provided. For this example, there is no initialization form, so a simple slot name will suffice. The predecessor slot in a dcons structure is intended to hold a pointer to the previous dcons cell. The successor slot holds a pointer to the succeeding dcons cell, just like a regular cons cell. The contents slot stores the value associated with the dcons cell. Figure 5-4 shows a doubly-linked list implemented using dcons structures.

Side Effects of a Call to
defstruct

Calls to the defstruct macro have a number of side effects. In addition to defining a structure to the system, a call to defstruct generates several useful functions. Specifically, the call to def-struct causes four things to occur:

- A new data type of the prescribed form is declared to the system. After calling defstruct, the symbol dcons becomes a recognized data type like a list, a symbol, or an integer.

- A constructor function called make-dcons is generated for creating instances of this new data type.

- Three additional functions known as *accessor functions* are generated for accessing the slots of doubly linked list structures. They are given the names dcons-predecessor, dcons-contents, and dcons-successor.

- A predicate called dcons-p is automatically defined for performing type testing.

Using Constructor Functions

As in the chess position example, a constructor function called make-dcons.[1] It could be used to create an instance of a dcons cell as follows:

```
CL> (defvar first-element
         (make-dcons :contents 'april ))
FIRST-ELEMENT
CL> first-element
#S(DCONS PREDECESSOR NIL CONTENTS APRIL SUCCESSOR NIL)
```

The keyword :contents can be used to provide an initialization value for the contents slot of the dcons being created. This is another little service that defstruct performed for us. It created keyword symbols corresponding to each of the slots of the newly defined structure. These keywords can be used to provide optional initialization values when the structure is created.

Constructor functions return an instance of the specified structure type with slots appropriately initialized.[2] Structures are printed as lists preceded by the symbol #S. The first element of the list is the name of the structure type, the remaining elements consist of slot names followed by their corresponding values.[3]

Using Accessor Functions

Just as you did in the position example, you can use the accessor functions created by defstruct to fetch values from the slots of a structure. For example:

```
CL> (dcons-contents first-element)
APRIL
```

[1]By convention, names of constructor functions are created by concatenating the "make-" string with the structure. There is an option to defstruct that will override this default behavior.

[2]Slot values provided as arguments to a constructor function have priority over any initialization form given at the time the structure was defined by defstruct. If a slot value is not provided in the call to the constructor function and no initialization form was provided when the structure was defined, the initial contents of the slot will be undefined. In many implementations it is set to nil, but woe to the programmer who depends on this always being the case!

[3]Typing in a list of this form will also create an instance of a Common Lisp structure. For example:

```
CL> (defvar first-element
      #s(dcons predecessor nil contents nil successor nil))
FIRST-ELEMENT
```

This provides an alternative to using constructor functions.

The argument to dcons-contents must be a dcons structure. Using the symbol first-element, we can access the dcons that we created earlier. The dcons-contents function returns the value stored in the contents slot. Calls to the accessor functions can be used as an *access-form* and passed as an argument to setf. For example:

```
CL> (setf (dcons-contents first-element)
                              'january )
JANUARY
CL>  (dcons-contents first-element)
JANUARY
```

Now that you know how to insert values into slots, you should be able to chain together a doubly linked list. You can create a couple of additional dcons cells like this:

```
CL> (defvar second-element
             (make-dcons :contents 'february ))
SECOND-ELEMENT
CL> (defvar third-element
             (make-dcons :contents 'march ))
THIRD-ELEMENT
```

You can now start to link the pieces together. The first element only needs a pointer to the second element. This can easily be accomplished by typing

```
CL> (setf (dcons-successor first-element)
          second-element)
#S(DCONS PREDECESSOR NIL CONTENTS
    FEBRUARY SUCCESSOR NIL)
```

The second element needs a pointer to both its predecessor and its successor. To install the pointer to the preceding dcons cell, type

```
CL> (setf (dcons-predecessor second-element)
          first-element)
#S(DCONS PREDECESSOR #S(DCONS PREDECESSOR
#S(DCONS PREDECESSOR NIL CONTENTS JANUARY
SUCCESSOR #S(DCONS PREDECESSOR #S(DCONS
PREDECESSOR NIL CONTENTS JANUARY SUCCESSOR
#S(DCONS PREDECESSOR #S(DCONS PREDECESSOR NIL
CONTENTS JANUARY SUCCESSOR #S(DCONS PREDECESSOR #S(DCONS PREDECESSOR NIL
CONTENTS JANUARY
SUCCESSOR #S(DCONS PREDECESSOR #S(DCONS
```

```
PREDECESSOR NIL CONTENTS JANUARY SUCCESSOR
#S(DCONS PREDECESSOR #S(DCONS PREDECESSOR NIL CONTENTS JANUARY SUCCESSOR
#S(DCONS  PREDECESSOR
(and on and on)
```

What happened here? When you type an expression in Lisp, it performs three steps: it reads in the expression, evaluates it, and prints the result. This is often referred to as the "read-eval-print" loop. The problem here occurs in the third step when the interpreter tries to print the result returned by setf. It tries to print the current value of first-element. The contents of the successor slot of first-element, however, contain a reference to second-element. When the interpreter tries to print second-element, the problem becomes apparent because the predecessor slot of second-element now points to first-element.

Circular Data Structures

Our doubly linked list is an example of a circular data structure. As you can see, these structures are very easy to create. The problem with circular data structures is that they may send the print function into an infinite loop. You can direct the printer to print circular data structures by setting the global variable *print-circle* to a non-nil value. This will enable the print function to handle circularities appropriately. The preceding example would look like this with *print-circle* reassigned:

```
CL> (setf (dcons-successor second-element)
          first-element)
#1=#S(DCONS PREDECESSOR NIL CONTENTS JANUARY SUCCESSOR #S(DCONS PREDECESSOR
NIL
CONTENTS FEBRUARY SUCCESSOR #1#))
```

Here the symbol #1# is substituted for the circular reference to second-element. By printing second-element this way, the print function can avoid going into an infinite loop.

Inspecting Structures

In the last chapter, we introduced the inspect function for inspecting the contents of arrays. The inspect function also comes in handy when debugging programs that create and manipulate structures. Figure 5-5 shows an example of an inspector window for the dcons structures created earlier. The inspect function is particularly powerful in window-based Common Lisp implementations. Experiment with this function in your implementation and see how it works.

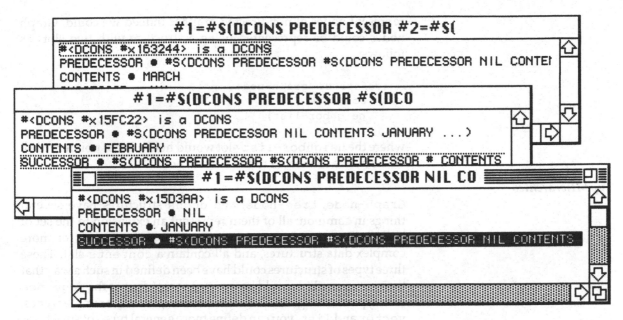

Figure 5-5   Inspecting a CL Structure (from Procyon™ Common Lisp)

Representing Tree Nodes

The strategy of building complex data structures from Common Lisp structures works with more than doubly linked lists. For example, a Common Lisp structure could be defined to represent a tree node:

```
(defstruct tree-node
   parent
   contents
   child-list )
```

In this case, we need a slot (contents) to store the data associated with the node, a slot to store a pointer to the parent node, and finally, a slot to store a list of child nodes.

This way of representing trees offers several advantages over the list-based representation described in Chapter 4. Many programmers find trees constructed of structures easier to read and manipulate than nested lists. Also, as with doubly linked lists, having a pointer to each node's parent makes it possible to move both up and down the tree.

Representing Graphs

In fact, why stop with lists and trees? Couldn't we use structures to represent nodes of nondirected graphs? Indeed we could. Graph nodes could be represented using a structure with two slots as follows:

```
(defstruct graph-node
    contents
    neighbor-list)
```

where the `neighbor-list` slot would hold a list of pointers to all of the nodes connected to the current node.

Type Hierarchies

`Graph-node`, `tree-node`, and `dcons` structures have several things in common: all of them represent an extension to the set of built-in Common Lisp data types, all are components of more complex data structures, and all contain a `contents` slot. These three types of structures could have been defined in such a way that their commonality would be more apparent. Just as the `sequence` data type is more general than and encompasses the simpler types, `vector` and `list`, you can define more general types of structures in Common Lisp that encompass more specific structures. You could, for example, define a more generic type of structure called a `data-node` that encompasses graph nodes, tree nodes, and dcons structures.

Inheritance

The `data-node` structure would be an abstract entity that captured the common features of the three more specialized types of structures. It would have only a `contents` slot and be defined as

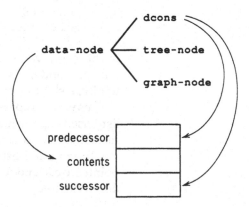

Figure 5-6 A `dcons` Structure Inherits Its Contents Slot from the `data-node` Structure Type

follows:

```
(defstruct data-node
    contents)
```

To show that graph-node, tree-node, and dcons are meant to be subtypes of data-node, you would have to redefine them using the :include keyword. For example, the dcons structure could be redefined as follows:

```
(defstruct (dcons :include data-node)
    predecessor
    successor)
```

As before, we have slots labeled "predecessor" and "successor." Since all dcons structures are data-node structures in the same sense that all squares are rectangles, it is not necessary to specify that dcons structures will have a contents slot. They will automatically have a contents slot because they are, by definition, data-node structures as well, and all data-node structures have a contents slot. We say that a dcons structure *inherits* its contents slot from the data-node structure. This relationship is illustrated in Figure 5-6. Tree nodes and graph nodes could be defined in a similar way:

```
(defstruct (tree-node :include data-node)
    parent
    child-list)
(defstruct (graph-node :include data-node)
    neighbor-list)
```

The notion of inheritance is central to the style of programming known as *object-oriented programming*. The subject of object-oriented programming will be described in the next section.

Data Abstraction

Defining a Common Lisp structure declares to the system your desire to have a new kind of data structure and specifies how the elements of that structure will be accessed. We could have implemented dcons cells in a number of ways without using def-struct. The advantage of working with structures, however, is that it makes the programmer's intent very clear. If we had instead implemented the dcons cells as a three-element list, it might be considerably less clear what the lists were intended to represent and how they should be used. How the Common Lisp environment ultimately implements the structure is usually not a matter for concern. The Common Lisp structure-defining facility provides us with an interface by which we can create instances of structures and manipulate their components. Because the other side of this interface is hidden from our view, it is sometimes referred to as an *abstraction barrier* (Abelson et al., 1985). Defining things like dcons structures to make their use apparent is referred to as *data abstraction*. Judicious use of data abstraction helps make your code easier to use and is considered good programming style.

Exercise 5.1

Redo your solution to the 8-Queens Problem (Exercise 4.23), using position structures instead of dotted pairs to represent positions on the chess board.

Exercise 5.2

Finish making the doubly linked list described in this section.

Exercise 5.3

Define a structure to represent a date. Create an instance of this structure corresponding to today's date.

Exercise 5.4

Define a structure to represent a playing card. Write a function called deal-hand that will return a list of five playing card structures. Use the sample function from Exercise 4.17 to draw cards randomly from a 52-card deck.

Exercise 5.5

Rewrite dft (from Chapter 4) to work with trees defined as connected structures instead of lists.

5.2 OBJECTS: CLASSES AND INSTANCES

ANSI Common Lisp offers a second type of record-like data structure called an *object*. Common Lisp objects resemble structures in that they have named slots and constructor and accessor functions. Objects are conceptually more complicated than structures, however. Their name is derived from a popular style of programming known as *object-oriented programming*. This type of programming involves organizing your code around sets of objects called *classes*. It differs from the more traditional style of programming, which we will call *procedure-based programming*, for want of a better name. The Common Lisp Object System (CLOS) is a general-purpose facility for doing object-oriented programming in Common Lisp.

Classes of Objects

CLOS (pronounced either *kloss* or *see-loss*) objects are organized into classes. Each class represents a set of objects that have the same set of slots. For example, a class of objects meant to represent automobiles may have slots for things like the auto's owner, the manufacturer, the model, and so on. Objects belonging to a class are referred to as *instances* of the class.

defclass Macro

In CLOS, instead of using `defstruct` to describe the structure of an object, you use the `defclass` macro. The general form of a call to `defclass` is

```
(defclass class-name supers-list slot-list )
```

The `class-name` is a Common Lisp symbol; it is not evaluated. Object classes can be organized in hierarchies, like the hierarchy of types in Common Lisp and the hierarchies of structures seen in the previous section. The `supers-list` is used to specify inheritance. Instead of using an `:include` keyword, as with structures, classes specify other classes from which they inherit slots by inserting them in the `supers-list`. A class from which another class inherits slots is called a *superclass*. The list of classes from which a class inherits slots is therefore called the *supers-list*. The `slot-list` consists of a list of `slot-specification`s. A `slot-specification` can be simply a slot name or a list containing a slot name and various slot specification options. Optionally, after the `slot-list`, you can add a `documentation-list` of the following form:

```
(:documentation documentation-string )
```

where `documentation-string` is a string of text describing the class.

Motor Vehicle Example

For example, let us assume that you needed to write an application involving various kinds of motor vehicles. You could define a class to represent motor vehicles as follows:

```
(defclass motor-vehicle ()
    ((year                :initform 1990
                 :initarg :year)
     (make     :initarg :make)
     (odometer :initform 0
                :type 'integer
```

```
                            :initarg :odometer)
          (fuel        :initform 'gasoline
                            :initarg :fuel)
          (fuel-capacity :initarg :fuel-capacity)
          (fuel-volume :initform 0
                            :initarg fuel-volume))
    (:documentation
      "General class for motor vehicles"))
```

Here the *class-name* is motor-vehicle and the *supers-list* is empty. The *slot-list* here specifies that all motor-vehicle objects will have six slots named year, make, odometer, fuel, tank-capacity, and current-fuel-volume. The slot option :initform allows the programmer to specify a form that will be evaluated when an instance of this class is created. This is how you specify default values for a slot. The :initarg option associates an initialization argument with the slot. Initialization arguments will be discussed further when the creation of instances is described. The third slot specification option shown is :type. As you might guess, its purpose is to specify the type of data that may be stored in a slot. There is another slot option, :documentation, which allows you to annotate a specific slot with a documentation string.

Subclasses

A class that inherits from another class is called a *subclass*. We could define a subclass of motor-vehicle to represent automobiles as follows:

```
(defclass auto (motor-vehicle)
   ((mileage-rating :initarg :mileage-rating)
    (model :initarg model))
   (:documentation
     "Class for automobiles"))
```

Because the motor-vehicle class is specified to be a superclass of the auto class, instances of the auto class will inherit all of the slots

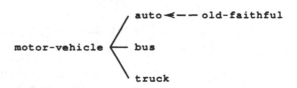

Figure 5-7   Class Hierarchy for the motor-vehicle Class

of the motor-vehicle class. Additional classes could be defined to represent buses and trucks as follows:

```
(defclass bus (motor-vehicle)
    ((number-of-passengers :initarg
                      :num-of-pass))
    (:documentation
     "Class for buses"))

(defclass truck (motor-vehicle)
    ((fuel         :initform 'diesel))
    (:documentation
     "Class for trucks"))
```

The relationship between the classes is shown in Figure 5-7. In this figure, solid lines join the subclasses with their superclass, and the dashed lines join instances to their class. Graphs of this sort are referred to as *class hierarchies* or *class inheritance lattices*. Note that the default initialization form in the definition of the truck class will override the default initialization form for motor-vehicle, as shown in Figure 5-8. We say that the specification at the class level *shadows* any specifications inherited from superclasses.

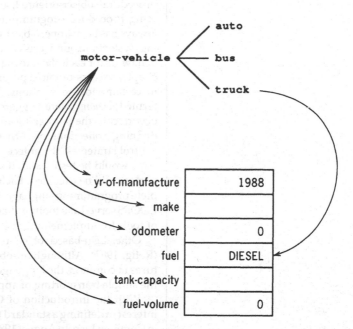

Figure 5-8 The Default Initialization for the Fuel Slot of a Truck Object Overrides the Default Initialization Provided by the Superclass motor-vehicle

The History of
Object-Oriented Programming in Lisp

Object-oriented programming was first developed as a convenient approach for implementing simulation problems and distributed operating systems. The notions of objects, classes, and inheritance were first introduced in the Simula language. Organizing code and data around the objects they represent proved to be a very general and natural means of conceptualizing computer applications. The Smalltalk project at the Xerox Palo Alto Research Center (PARC) was initiated as an attempt to couple a high-quality graphic interface with a general-purpose, object-oriented programming language (Goldberg and Robson, 1983).

The first efforts to incorporate object-oriented programming in Lisp were made by the MIT Lisp Machine Group in the late 1970s (Moon, 1986). H. I. Cannon developed a Lisp-based, object-oriented language called Flavors. The name was derived from the fact that attributes and behavior of classes (which they call *flavors*) can be blended together via inheritance mechanisms. Flavors has been used extensively to do systems programming on Lisp machines. It is still used today by many programmers.

In 1981, a second Lisp-based, object-oriented programming language, named LOOPS, was introduced at Xerox PARC (Stefik et al., 1983). LOOPS integrated several programming paradigms, including procedural, object-oriented, access-oriented, and rule-based programming. Procedural programming was simply programming in Lisp, as it always has been done. Object-oriented programming involved designing systems around classes of objects and defining a repertoire of behaviors for each class, using methods that will be covered in the next chapter. Access-oriented programming involved attaching procedures to certain storage locations. These attached procedures, sometimes termed *demons*, were triggered whenever a read or write operation occurred to the storage location. Rule-based programming involved defining collections of if-then rules called *rule sets*. Using various control strategies, the antecedent conditions of the rules (i.e., the "if" part) would be tested and, if satisfied, the consequent (i.e., the "then" part) would be executed. Each of these paradigms represented a complete programming language, but each was best suited for certain tasks. LOOPS served as a toolbox that provided the programmer with a choice of tools for implementing the various subtasks of a project.

Other Lisp-based, object-oriented languages were later developed (Retig, 1987). Although all object-oriented languages have some features in common, the languages were sufficiently different to preclude the simple transporting of applications from one language to another.

With the introduction of Common Lisp in 1984, there was great interest in defining a standard to support object-oriented programming in Common Lisp. In August 1985, there was a meeting at the International Joint Conference on Artificial Intelligence (IJCAI) in Los Angeles to discuss the nature of this impending standard. Three proposals, sponsored by LMI, Hewlett-Packard, and Xerox PARC, were presented.

Eventually a proposal was put together that synthesized ideas taken from a variety of sources. This proposal was known as the Common Lisp Object System (CLOS). Xerox PARC has distributed several versions of a portable implementation of a system called PCL, which is based on CLOS. In 1986, an ANSI subcommittee was established to draft a formal specification for Common Lisp. This subcommittee, known officially as X3J13, voted to make CLOS a required component of all conforming Common Lisp implementations. Thus, for the first time, it was possible for the Lisp programmer to implement portable applications in an object-oriented style.

Creating Instances

In CLOS, instances of a class are created using the `make-instance` function. This differs from Common Lisp structures that have different constructor functions for each type of structure. When using `make-instance`, you must specify what class of object you would like to create. For example, you could create an instance of the `auto class` by typing

```
(defvar old-faithful (make-instance 'auto))
```

The result returned by `make-instance` will be an auto object. By wrapping a call to `defvar` around the `make-instance` form, you provide a handle for accessing the newly created instance.

Initializing the Slots

The `defclass` macro allows you to specify the values that will be placed in the slots when instances of the class are later created. This can be done in two ways. Using the `:initform` keyword, you can provide a form that will be evaluated to produce a default value when the instance is created. The `year` slot, for example, will be initialized with the value 1990 because of the `:initform` keyword in the class definition for `motor-vehicle`. Evaluation of the initialization form takes place when `make-instance` is called. You can use any legal Lisp form as an initialization form. If not specified, the default value installed in a slot is undefined.

Initialization Arguments

Alternatively, you can define an *initialization argument* that will allow you to specify the initialization value for a slot in the call to `make-instance`. This is done using the `:initarg` keyword. You must provide an initialization argument for each slot for which you will allow initialization at instance creation time. For example, using the initialization arguments from the previous class definitions, the call to make-instance could be redone as follows:

```
(defvar old-faithful (make-instance 'auto
                          :year 1968
                          :make 'Volkswagon
                          :model 'Bug))
```

The slot value provided in the call to make-instance will take precedence over the default initialization form. In this case, for example, the value stored in the year slot will be 1968.

Accessing Object Slots

Unlike structures that have different accessor functions for each slot, objects use a single function, slot-value, to fetch the contents of an object's slot. To see what is stored in the year slot of old-faithful, you could type

```
CL> (slot-value old-faithful 'year)
1968
```

Calls to slot-value can be passed as an *access-form* argument to setf. This means that, like the slots of a structure, object slots can be treated as generalized variables. For example:

```
CL> (setf (slot-value old-faithful
                        'year)
         1969)
1969
```

Objects and Structures

So far, objects appear to have many of the same capabilities as structures. You may wonder why the designers of Common Lisp decided to add CLOS to the standard, since it may seem redundant. You should recognize, however, that we have told only one-half of the story. The other half of object-oriented programming, which you will encounter in the next chapter, has to do with methods and generic functions. These provide important capabilities not available with structures. Does this mean that CLOS makes structures obsolete? By no means; many experienced programmers continue to use structures in their code. Guidelines for when to use structures and when to use CLOS objects will be discussed in Section 6.3.

Object-Oriented Programming and Structured Programming

Object-oriented programming offers a number of advantages over the traditional procedural approach. It provides an alternative scheme for organizing the code within programs. Although opinions vary, many designers find it conceptually easier to decompose a problem into its component objects rather than into its component procedures. For some reason, it seems easier to work with the "nouns" of a complex problem than with the "verbs." Programming in an object-oriented style also encourages and, to some degree, enforces a form of structured programming. Indeed, some consider object-oriented programming the next evolutionary stage in software engineering. It has been said that object-oriented programming is to the 1980s and beyond, what structured programming was to the 1970s!

Exercise 5.6

Make an instance of an `auto` object and fill in its slots. Use the `inspect` function to view the object you have created.

Exercise 5.7

Redo Exercise 5.4 (the playing card problem), using objects instead of structures.

Exercise 5.8

Following is a list of airport codes with their associated names and locations:

Code	Name	Location
BOS	Logan	Boston, MA
DCA	Dulles	Washington, DC
JFK	Kennedy	New York, NY
ORD	O'Hare	Chicago, IL
STL	Lambert	St. Louis, MO

Define a structure to represent a location with slots for the city and state. Define an object to represent an airport with slots for a name and a location. Create objects for each of the airports listed here, and store them in a hash table using the airport code as a key.

Exercise 5.9

Write a function named `drive-vehicle` that takes as arguments an instance of the class `motor-vehicle` and an integer specifying the number of miles driven. The function should increment the vehicle's odometer reading by the number of miles driven.

Exercise 5.10

Design a class or set of classes to represent chess pieces.

5.3 REPRESENTING THE PROBLEM

In Exercise 5.10, you were asked to design a set of structures to represent chess pieces. Even a relatively simple task such as this involves some difficult design decisions. What information is required to represent a chess piece? To begin with, you need to know what kind of piece you are dealing with—a king, a pawn, or a rook. You also need to know what color the piece is (black or white) and where it currently sits on the board. If you were going to represent the piece as an object instead of a structure, you might define the chess-piece class as follows:

```
(defclass chess-piece ()
   (type
    color
    position))
```

However, this design may prove limiting, especially when you wish to start associating methods with classes. Alternatively, you could represent the type of a piece by using its class membership rather than by storing it in a slot. The classes could instead be defined in this way:

```
(defclass chess-piece ()
   (color
    position))
(defclass king (chess-piece) ())
(defclass queen (chess-piece) ())
(defclass rook (chess-piece) ())
(defclass bishop (chess-piece) ())
(defclass knight (chess-piece) ())
(defclass pawn (chess-piece) ())
```

This will produce a class hierarchy, as shown in Figure 5-9. All of the subclasses will inherit color and position slots from the chess-piece superclass. Using this scheme, the type of a chess piece can be determined by testing its type without having to consult one of its slots.[4] The same information is stored in either

---

[4]As you will discover in Section 6.3, you can test CLOS objects for class membership using typep, just as you do for Common Lisp data types.

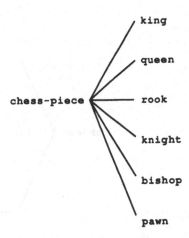

Figure 5-9   An Alternative Way of Representing Chess Pieces

case, but, as you will find in the next chapter, the latter approach provides the information in a more useful fashion.

Designing Class Descriptions

When you set out to define class descriptions, you are creating data structures that in some way model an external reality. You must first consider what information you will need to capture in order to represent accurately the real-world objects you are trying to model. You need only capture information that is relevant to the task you are trying to accomplish in your program. When representing automobiles in the last section, one could include hundreds of possible attributes, but not all of them are required. You need also think about how the information will be stored. In the automobile example, the odometer reading was stored as an integer. One might argue that it would be more appropriate to use a floating-point representation, but it would probably not be useful to store this information as a string. In making decisions about issues of this kind, the application designer must anticipate how the instances of the class will be used in order to produce an optimal design.

These considerations pertain to the structure of the class itself. You also need to determine how many classes are required and the nature of the relationship between them. One class can be related to another class in a number of ways. The relationship between a superclass and a subclass was discussed in the previous section. There are also other possible relationships to be considered.

Representing Vehicle Parts

As an example of another kind of relationship between two classes, consider how to extend the class hierarchy in Figure 5-7 in order to

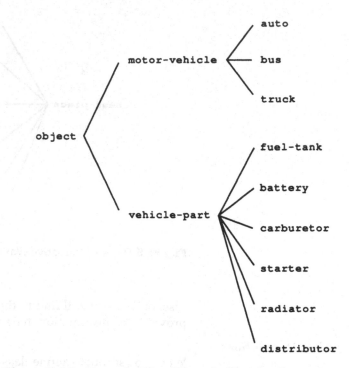

Figure 5-10   Expanded Class Hierarchy Showing the `motor-vehicle` and `vehicle-part` Classes

add classes for vehicle parts like water pumps, batteries, carburetors, starters, radiators, and distributors. One way of doing this is shown in Figure 5-10. Why do we need to add a new class (i.e., `vehicle-parts`) to handle parts? Wouldn't it be easier to designate the parts classes as subclasses of the `motor-vehicle` class?

Part-of and Is-a Relationships

When people begin to program using objects, a common mistake is to confuse the relationships between classes. The fundamental ideas of object-oriented programming come from set theory. The relationship between a class and a subclass is similar to the relationship between a set and a subset. We will call it an *is-a* relationship. The relationship between a class and one of its instances resembles set membership.

Is the relationship between the `motor-vehicle` class and the `fuel-tank` class an is-a relationship? No, of course not. An instance of the `fuel-tank` class could be considered part of a `motor-vehicle` object, not an instance of a `motor-vehicle`. Sometimes it is easy to confuse is-a relationships with part-of relationships. There is nothing wrong with having objects that are defined as parts of other objects. In complex systems, these part-of relationships are quite important, but they must be handled in a different way than is-a relationships. The important thing to remember is that inheritance works properly only when the relationships between all subclasses and their superclasses are true is-a relationships.

Representing Part-of
Relationships

One common way of representing a part-of relationship is to provide the class of the composite object (in this case, `auto`) with a slot in which to store a pointer to the component object. For example, if the `vehicle-part` and `fuel-tank` classes are defined as follows:

```
(defclass vehicle-part ()
  ((vehicle :initarg :vehicle)
   (purchase-date :initarg :purchase-date)
   (manufacturer :initarg :manufacturer))
  (:documentation
   "Class of motor vehicle parts"))

(defclass fuel-tank (vehicle-part)
  ((fuel-capacity :initform 20)
   (fuel-volume :initform 0))
  (:documentation
   "Class of motor vehicle fuel tanks"))
```

the class of `motor-vehicle` objects can be redefined as follows:

```
(defclass motor-vehicle ()
  ((make     :initarg :make)
   (odometer :initform 0
             :type 'integer
             :initarg :odometer)
   (fuel     :initform 'gasoline
             :initarg :fuel)
   (fuel-tank :initarg :fuel-tank
             :initform (make-instance 'fuel-tank))
   (year    :initarg :year))
  (:documentation
   "Class of motor vehicles"))
```

This automatically creates a new `fuel-tank` object every time a `motor-vehicle` object is created. The pointer in the `fuel-tank` slot of the vehicle can be used to access the slots of the object representing the part. For example, to see how much gas an `auto`

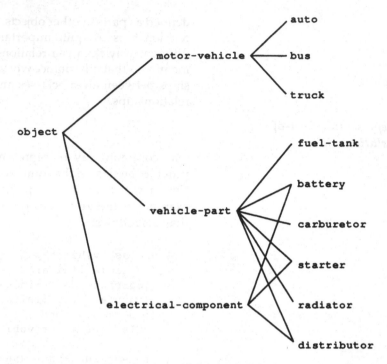

Figure 5-11   A Class Lattice with Multiple Inheritance

(a subclass of motor-vehicle) object has, you would have to do something like this:

```
CL> (slot-value (slot-value old-faithful
                           'fuel-tank)
            'fuel-volume)
0
```

The fuel-tank class inherits a slot for storing a pointer back to the motor-vehicle object, with which it is associated. Often it is convenient to have pointers in both directions. Just for practice, write a setf form to instantiate properly the vehicle slot of the fuel-tank object just defined.

Multiple Inheritance

Figure 5-11 shows another elaboration of the class hierarchy for motor vehicles. Another superclass, electrical-component, has been added. Note that some of the classes (i.e., battery, starter, and distributor) are subclasses of both electrical-component and auto-part. A CLOS class is allowed to have more than one superclass. The technical term for this situation is *multiple inheritance*. Why add another superclass? A subclass inherits structural characteristics in the form of slots and initial slot values from its superclasses. As you will learn in the next chapter, a subclass can also inherit functional characteristics from its superclasses. As shown in Figure 5-12, by adding electrical-component to the class hierarchy, you make it possible to add some new slots (e.g., voltage and amperage) that apply only to electrical auto parts. Extra superclasses like electrical-component are sometimes referred to as *mixins* because they allow the designer to mix in new data storage and functional capabilities with an existing class hierarchy.

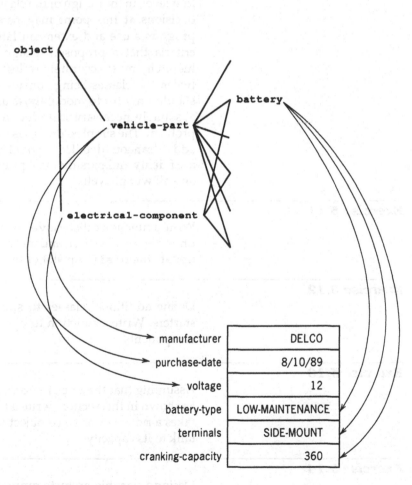

Figure 5-12 Inheriting Slots from a Mixin

Precedence Lists

The introduction of multiple inheritance raises an interesting question: When a class inherits a characteristic from more than one superclass, which superclass takes precedence? The principle is to always use the most specific method or default value available. When a CLOS class is defined, a precedence list of all superclasses is computed. When a precedence conflict arises, CLOS consults this list to determine which superclass is considered the most specific.

Design Criteria

In a procedural style of programming, an implementer can impose a level of abstraction on a program by relegating chunks of code to subroutines. The abstraction in an object-based system occurs at the first level, in the design of the class hierarchy. Hastily-made design decisions at this point may have adverse implications for the program's use and extension later on. There are two important criteria that a proposed design should satisfy. First, the class hierarchy must accurately reflect the real-world relationships between the classes being considered. Second, the class hierarchy should only try to model those aspects of the real world that are absolutely necessary in order to satisfy the requirements of the problem. The simplest design is usually the best; the temptation to add extraneous detail to a model must be resisted. The joint criteria are fidelity and parsimony. Apply them faithfully to your designs, and all will go well.

Exercise 5.11

Write a function called `move-piece` that will take as arguments a `chess-piece` object and new rank and file values. It should update the `position` slot of the piece.

Exercise 5.12

Define additional classes to support batteries, carburetors, and starters. Write a function to create an `auto` object with all of its components.

Exercise 5.13

Assuming that the `motor-vehicle` class has been implemented as shown in this section, write a function called `fill-er-up` that takes a `motor-vehicle` object as an argument and fills the fuel tank to its capacity.

Exercise 5.14

Design a class hierarchy to represent references like those found in the References section. Represent the authors and publishers as objects in their own right. You should be able to represent book and article citations.

Exercise 5.15

Write a function called set-up-pieces that will return a list of the 16 chess-piece objects comprising one side of a chess game (8 pawns, 2 rooks, 2 bishops, etc.). Set the contents of the position slot for each chess-piece to its appropriate position at the beginning of the game. The set-up-pieces function should take a single argument, specifying whether to set up the white side or the black side.

Exercise 5.16

You can summarize the status of a chess game given complete lists of the pieces (with their positions) for each side. Define a class to represent a chess game. Each chess-game object should have at least two slots to hold lists of white and black pieces. Viewed in this way, the chess-piece class has a part-of relationship to the chess-game class. Modify the definition of the chess-piece class, so that each piece will hold a pointer to its associated chess-game object. Chess-game objects should also have slots to hold a list of moves for each side. Chess moves can also be implemented as objects. A chess-move object should have two slots: a piece slot and a new-position slot. Moves resulting in the capture of a piece should be implemented as instances of a subclass of chess-move. They should have an additional slot to store the captured piece.

Exercise 5.17

As an alternative to representing the state of a chess board as two lists, as was done in the last exercise, a chess-game object could simply have a single slot containing an 8 x 8 array. The chess-piece objects could then be inserted in the appropriate cells of the array. The position of each object would be represented implicitly, and the position slot in chess-piece objects would become unnecessary. Which design do you prefer and why?

Exercise 5.18

Add a chess-board slot to the chess-game class and write a function called make-chess-game to construct instances of the class. You may use the set-up-pieces function from Exercise 5.15 to help set up the pieces in their positions at the beginning of the game.

Exercise 5.19 (*)

Define a class hierarchy with multiple inheritance. See if you can determine the rules by which CLOS computes the precedence list for each class.

SUMMARY

Common Lisp has a built-in facility for creating record-like data objects called *structures*. Common Lisp structures are defined using the defstruct macro. As a side effect of defining a structure with defstruct, a function for creating instances of the structure is automatically generated. Accessor functions for referencing the slots of the structure are generated at the same time. A structure can "inherit" slots from other structures using the :include keyword.

Objects are an alternative to using Common Lisp structures. Like structures, objects have predefined slots. Objects are organized into classes. Classes are defined using the defclass macro. Instances of a class are created using the make-instance function. The slot-value function is used to access the values stored in the slots of an object. There are two ways of initializing a slot of an object. One way is to provide an initialization form for the slot for the class at the time the class is defined. The second approach is to specify an initialization argument for the slot and then to provide an initialization value as an argument to make-instance.

Some care must be taken when designing the hierarchy of object classes to be used in an application. The designer must be clear on the relationship that exists between the classes of objects. Classes in Common Lisp can inherit slots from more than one superclass, a situation referred to as *multiple inheritance*.

NEW COMMON LISP DEFINED NAMES

```
defclass
defstruct
make-instance
*print-circle*
slot-value
```

FOR FURTHER READING

Common Lisp Structures are covered in Chapter 19 of *Common Lisp: The Language* (Steele, 1990). A more formal description of CLOS classes can be found in Chapter 2 of the Draft Standard (ANSI, 1990), in Chapter 28 of the Steele book, or in Chapter 1 of the CLOS Specification (Bobrow et al., 1988). See Chapter 6 in the Keene book (Keene, 1989) for a detailed discussion of inheritance in CLOS.

General background material on object-oriented programming in Lisp can be found in the Moon (Moon, 1986; Moon, 1988), and Stefik (Stefik et al., 1983; Stefik and Bobrow, 1986a) works. A more elaborate discussion of is-a relationships can be found in the Brachman article (Brachman, 1983). For an up-to-date view of what is being done in the area, see the proceedings of the Conference on Object-Oriented Programming Systems, Languages and Applications (OOPSLA). The OOPSLA Conference, sponsored by the ACM Special Interest Group on Programming Languages (SIGPLAN), has been held annually since 1986 and is the leading forum for the exchange of ideas about object-oriented programming.

Project 5.1

Write a function to solve the Knight's Tour problem. As shown in Figure 5-13, chess knights move in an *L*-shaped fashion. The

Figure 5-13 Possible Moves for a Chess Knight

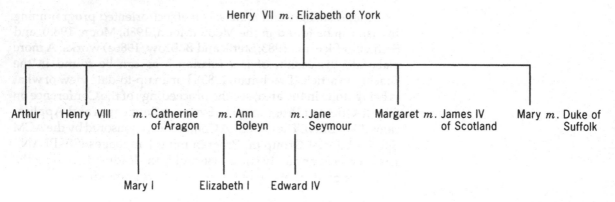

Figure 5-14 Genealogy of the Tudors

Knight's Tour problem is to move a knight to a given position in the fewest number of moves. Assume that your function will be passed a knight object and a destination position (implemented as a Common Lisp structure). It should return a list of the intermediate positions visited on the way to reaching the goal.

Project 5.2

Figure 5-14 shows the Tudor family tree. Define a class to represent a royal person. Create a data structure that will hold the information shown in the family tree. Write the following set of predicates:

a. married-p

b. daughter-of-p

c. mother-of-p

d. ancestor-of-p

Each predicate should accept a pair of royal-person objects and a family tree as arguments and should return the value t or nil.

Project 5.3

Design classes to represent airports and airline flights. A flight object should have slots for a carrier, departure and arrival times, an airport of origin, and a destination airport. Build a database of airline-flight objects and write a function to plan a trip given a point of origin and a destination.

6

Methods

Though this be madness,
yet there is method in't.
William Shakespeare, Hamlet

6.1 GENERIC FUNCTIONS

In Chapter 5, you were introduced to the idea of defining new data types using structures and objects. You learned how to define class hierarchies and how to create instances of classes. You learned that object-oriented programming involves organizing your programs around the objects the program is meant to model. So far, we have only discussed the structural aspects of object-oriented programming—how to define classes and create instances of them. In this chapter, you will learn about the functional side of object-oriented programming—that is, the use of methods and generic functions.

Methods

CLOS methods offer two important advantages over regular CL functions: Methods can be specialized to work with one or more specific classes, and methods can be inherited like slots. Each CLOS method represents a specialized way of performing a particular

173

procedure for a specific class of objects. A collection of methods with the same name is referred to as a *generic function* in ANSI Common Lisp. The terminology may be novel, but the idea is quite simple. In everyday language, we may use the same verb for a collection of related activities, but how the subject performs the activity may vary, depending on the object on which it is being performed. When you say that you are going to eat something, for example, it is understood that the actual method used will vary, depending on what you are eating—an ice cream cone, a cup of gazpacho, a plate of spaghetti, crow, your hat, and so on. In all cases, the meaning of *eat* is the same, but the observed behavior can be quite different. So it is with CLOS generic functions; you can define families of related methods that will permit special handling for specific objects or classes of objects.

defmethod Macro

We could have defined `drive-vehicle`, from Exercise 5.6, as a method instead of a function. Method definition is very similar to function definition in Common Lisp. There are two major syntactical differences. First, you must use the system-defined macro, `defmethod`, instead of `defun` when defining methods. Second, in a method, any parameter in the parameter list can be specialized. The form of a call to `defmethod` is

```
(defmethod  method-name
            method-qualifier
            parameter-list
            body)
```

The `method-qualifier` is optional (its use will be described in the next section). Parameters are specialized in `defmethod` by specifying the name of the class or object to which the method should be applied. Any parameter in the parameter list can be specialized by providing a list of the form

```
(parameter specifier)
```

instead of a parameter symbol. The `specifier` is usually a class name.[1] For example, `drive-vehicle` could be defined as follows:

---

[1]Specifiers of the form

```
(eql object)
```

can be used to define private methods. A method defined in this way would be used only by *object*.

```
(defmethod drive-vehicle
            ((vehicle motor-vehicle) miles-driven)
 (setf (slot-value vehicle 'odometer)
 (+ (slot-value vehicle 'odometer)
    miles-driven)))
```

Other than the changes to the parameter list, this method definition probably seems fairly similar to the drive-vehicle function that you wrote for Exercise 5.9. As a method, however, it will be used only when the object passed as the value of vehicle is an instance of the motor-vehicle class.

with-slots

When defining methods, there is a macro called with-slots that can help to clean up the appearance of the method. It is related to the let special form in that it creates a set of local variables. When you use with-slots, though, the local variables correspond to the slots in a specified object. This saves you the need to do an explicit call to slot-value every time you wish to access the contents of a slot. For example, drive-vehicle could be rewritten as follows:

```
(defmethod drive-vehicle ((vehicle motor-vehicle) miles-driven)
  (with-slots (odometer) vehicle
    (setf odometer (+ odometer miles-driven))))
```

The first argument to with-slots is a list of the slots that you wish to access; the second parameter is the object. The remaining arguments are forms that you would like to evaluate. By using with-slots, you can reference the contents of the odometer slot by simply using odometer as a variable name. This reduces the coding somewhat and makes the method easier to read.

Invoking Methods

Sending a message in Common Lisp is syntactically indistinguishable from calling a function. You could invoke the previous method by typing

```
(drive-vehicle old-faithful 100)
```

Since the method is specific for instances of the motor-vehicle class, and since old-faithful is an instance of that class (because auto is a subclass of motor-vehicle), the system will use the method definition.

Generic Functions

Methods allow us to define a family of routines that are selected at runtime based on the types of the arguments passed. The family of methods taken as a whole is referred to as a *generic function*. Generic functions in Common Lisp represent an idea in language design called *polymorphic procedures*. A polymorphic procedure is one that displays different characteristics in different contexts. The behavior evoked by calling a generic function will be determined by the nature of the arguments passed, just as the way you eat is determined by what you are eating.

Applicable Methods

If you invoke a generic function on a set of arguments, the interpreter must first determine which (if any) of the methods of the generic function is applicable. When `drive-vehicle` was called on the object `old-faithful`, the interpreter first looked to see if there was a private `drive-vehicle` method for `old-faithful`. Because none was defined, the interpreter looked to the `auto` class and then to the `motor-vehicle` superclass, seeking a `drive-vehicle` method. This process of walking up the class hierarchy looking for applicable methods is presented graphically in Figure 6-1. There was only one method to be found in this case: the `drive-vehicle` method specialized for the `motor-vehicle` class. Frequently, however, the interpreter may find two or more applicable methods. It must then determine which one is appropriate.

Determining the Effective Method

The proposed ANSI specification refers to the method that is finally selected and executed by the interpreter as the *effective* method. The most specific applicable method is selected to be the effective method. This is an intuitively reasonable approach, since in all cases the interpreter should use the most detailed and specialized method available.

In the simplest case, where each class has only one superclass, selecting the effective method is quite simple. When mixins are

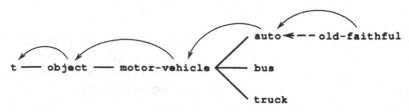

Figure 6-1   Walking Up the Class Hierarchy Seeking Applicable Methods

included and some of the classes have multiple superclasses, however, the selection can be more involved. If methods have been defined for two or more superclasses of a class, the interpreter will have to consult the precedence list for the class to determine which method to choose.

Multimethods

The situation can be further complicated if the methods of a generic function are specialized on two or more parameters. One of the powerful features of CLOS is that any or all of the parameters in the `lambda-list` can be specialized. Because of this capability, CLOS methods are sometimes referred to as *multimethods*. In this case, the determination of the most specific method becomes less intuitive.[2]

Method Inheritance

Because of the selection rules used by the interpreter, methods, like slots, are inherited by an object. If there is a method defined with a parameter that is specialized for a class, that method will be applied to all instances of that class and any class that is directly or indirectly a subclass of that class, provided that none of the subclasses supply their own method definitions. If there is a method that is specialized for a subclass of that class, then that method will take precedence over the method defined for the superclass. The method of the superclass is shadowed by the more specific method. For example, if there were a `drive-vehicle` method specialized for the class `auto`, it would shadow the method specialized for the class `motor-vehicle`.

Accessors Functions

As you recall from Chapter 5, when you create a structure using `defstruct`, slot accessor functions are created for each of its slots. These functions are then used to access the contents of the slots. The `defclass` macro does not automatically provide this service, though you can request it using the `:accessor` keyword. For example, you can redefine the `chess-piece` class as follows:

```
(defclass chess-piece ()
  ((color :initarg :color
          :accessor color)
   (position :initarg :position
             :initform (make-position)
```

---

[2]In situations in which different methods are specialized on different parameters of equal specificity, the interpreter uses the order of the parameters in the *lambda-list* to select the effective method. The leftmost parameter would have priority.

```
                                :accessor board-position)
                        (game :initarg :game)))
```

Adding the new keyword arguments results in the definition of two new accessor functions: `color` and `board-position`. These functions can be used in place of `slot-value` to retrieve the values stored in the slots. For example:[3]

```
CL> (defvar my-queen
            (make-instance 'queen :color 'black))
MY-QUEEN
CL> (color my-queen)
BLACK
```

Accessor functions created by `defclass` can be used to build *access-form*s for `setf` and can therefore also be used to write values into object slots. For example:

```
CL> (setf (board-position my-queen)
            (make-position :rank 3
                           :file 7))
#S(POSITION RANK 3 FILE 7)
```

Accessor functions created by `defclass` are implemented as generic functions. Knowing now how to define methods, you could define them by hand, if you wished, by creating an appropriately named method specialized for the class. The `board-position` accessor could be defined as follows:[4]

```
(defmethod board-position ((piece chess-piece))
    (slot-value piece 'position))
```

But why bother with accessor functions at all? Why not just use the `slot-value` function and avoid the overhead of another method call?

Private and Public Views of an Object

Many programmers like to maintain two views of an object—a

---

[3]The accessor functions are available to instances of the `queen` class because it is a subclass of `chess-piece`.

[4]This method of implementing an accessor method will work for reading a slot but will not allow you to write to a slot as a generic variable. To use the accessor function with `setf`, you would also have to define a `setf` form. See the Keene book (Keene, 1989) for details.

private view and a public view. There may be aspects of an object that the user need not be aware of. The programmer who defines a class and its associated methods is privy to all of its secrets, but it may not be necessary or desirable to burden the user with all the details of an implementation. For this reason, many programmers like to define an external view of an object that describes which parts of the object are visible to the public. Other parts may be concealed from public view. Using accessor functions helps to maintain the separation between the public and private parts of an object. Only the slots with accessor functions should be accessed by the user, and only the implementor should access slots using `slot-value`.

Defining a Public View

Object-oriented programming simplifies the process of establishing and maintaining private and public views. The public view of an object would consist of a set of generic functions used for creating and manipulating the objects. For the chess game application, a minimal public interface might consist of accessors for the `black-pieces` and `white-pieces` slots, a constructor function for building a game (like the one you defined in Exercise 5.18), and the generic function for moving `chess-piece` objects. Other slots, not meant to be used by anyone but the implementor, would not have accessors. Only the person designated to maintain the object should be writing procedures that use the low-level `slot-value` and `make-instance` functions.

Procedural Abstraction

As mentioned in the last chapter, the notion of obscuring parts of an application from a user's view is referred to as creating an *abstraction barrier*. The object itself is a kind of data abstraction. Its public view reveals a simple data structure with named slots. The user of the object (in this case, the programmer) does not need to see how the object is actually implemented as long as he or she is able to access the parts of the object when needed. Generic functions allow another kind of abstraction—procedural abstraction. They allow the system implementor to draw a screen around the details of the implementation of a procedure. Users of the procedure need only know the name of the generic function and the order of its arguments. The protocol for invoking the generic function constitutes a contract between the developer and the users of the function. Behind the abstraction barrier may be a complicated collection of specialized methods, but the view provided to the external world is a very simple one. This not only facilitates the sharing of software but also allows the implementor to modify the implementation without disrupting the performance of external routines that depend on the protocol. Procedural abstraction can be a powerful tool for constructing large, complex applications.

Exercise 6.1

Rewrite the `fill-er-up` function from Exercise 5.13 as a method specialized for `motor-vehicle` objects. Add a `fuel-type` parameter to the method. The value passed as `fuel-type` (e.g., regular or super-premium) should be stored in the fuel slot of the `motor-vehicle` object.

Exercise 6.2

Add a new method for motor vehicles called `prepare-for-sale`. The method will take a `motor-vehicle` object as an argument and, as a side effect, will reduce the value shown in the odometer slot by one-half. (Those of you who are not from Chicago may not be familiar with this procedure.)

Exercise 6.3

Write a `drive-vehicle` method for `auto` objects that updates not only the odometer, but the `fuel-volume` slot of the `fuel-tank` as well.

Exercise 6.4

One central theme of object-oriented programming is *data encapsulation*. This implies that each object is an entity unto itself and that only the object can change its internal state. To what degree does CLOS offer data encapsulation? What features of CLOS would help to enforce data encapsulation in an application?

Exercise 6.5

In Exercise 5.16 you were asked to define a set of classes to represent a chess game. These classes are summarized in Figure 6-2. Assume that a method for moving a `chess-piece` object has been defined as follows:

```
(defmethod move ((piece chess-piece) new-position)
  (with-slots (position) piece
    (when (legal-move-p piece new-position)
      (let* ((captured-piece (captured-piece-p piece new-position))
             (move (if captured-piece
                     (make-instance 'capture
                               :piece piece
                               :new-position new-position)))
                               :captured-piece captured-piece
                  (make-instance 'chess-move
                               :piece piece
                               :new-position new-position))))
```

```
(add-to-move-list move)
(if captured-piece (remove-captured-piece move))
  (change-piece-position move)))))
```

Write the method `change-piece-position` to record the move on the appropriate list of moves for the game.

Exercise 6.6

Write the `change-piece-position` method to update the game board and the `position` slot of the `piece` object.

Exercise 6.7

The `captured-piece-p` method checks to see if the destination square is occupied and if so, returns the occupying piece. The `remove-captured-piece` method simply removes the occupying piece from the appropriate list of pieces. Define these two methods.

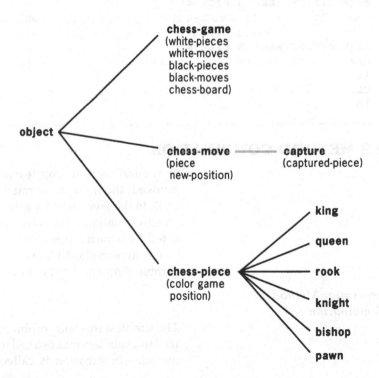

Figure 6-2 The Class Hierarchy (with Associated Slot Lists) for the Chess Example

Exercise 6.8

The `legal-move-p` generic function is a predicate that returns a non-`nil` value if, within the rules of chess, it is possible for a given piece to move to a specified position. A bishop, for example, can move to a new position diagonal to its original position, whereas a rook cannot. Implement the generic function `legal-move-p` for the six subclasses of the class `chess-piece`. Note that in so doing, you will have encoded many of the rules for playing chess. For example, the following are the opening moves of a chess game:

```
CL> (defvar my-chess-game (make-chess-game))
CL> (move (nth 11 (slot-value my-chess-game 'white-pieces))
          (make-position :rank 4 :file 3))
#S(POSITION RANK 4 FILE 3)
CL> (move (nth 11 (slot-value my-chess-game 'black-pieces))
          (make-position :rank 4 :file 4))
#S(POSITION RANK 3 FILE 3)
CL> (move (nth 12 (slot-value my-chess-game 'black-pieces))
          (make-position :rank 3 :file 4))
#S(POSITION RANK 3 FILE 4)
CL> (move (nth 11 (slot-value my-chess-game 'white-pieces))
          (make-position :rank 3 :file 4))
#S(POSITION RANK 3 FILE 4)
CL> (length (slot-value my-chess-game 'white-pieces))
16
CL> (length (slot-value my-chess-game 'black-pieces))
15
```

6.2 METHOD COMBINATION

In the last section, you learned that when a generic function is invoked, the interpreter must identify which methods are applicable to the given set of arguments and select one of them to be the effective method. The situation in CLOS is a little more complicated, because it is possible to combine several methods to produce an effective method. CLOS supports two different styles of method combination and has facilities for defining additional ones.

Imperative Method Combination

The simplest method combination occurs when a method specialized to a subclass makes a call to the next most general method. This method combination is called *imperative* because you explicitly invoke the more general method (Keene, 1989).[5] CLOS provides a built-in function called `call-next-method` for invoking the next most general method.

Suppose you wish to add the notion of gas consumption to the `drive-vehicle` method from Section 6.1. You could do this by writing a new method for the `auto` class that computes the amount of gas used when a vehicle is driven. The code would look something like this:

```
(defmethod drive-vehicle ((automobile auto) miles-driven)
   (with-slots (fuel-tank mileage-rating) automobile
      (let* ((fuel-volume (slot-value fuel-tank 'fuel-volume))
             (range (* fuel-volume mileage-rating)))
        ;;enough gas?
       (if (>= miles-driven range)
          ;;deplete tank
          (setf (slot-value fuel-tank 'fuel-volume) 0)
          ;;adjust gas level
          (setf (slot-value fuel-tank 'fuel-volume)
             (- fuel-volume
                (/ miles-driven
                   mileage-rating)))))))
```

If `drive-vehicle` is now invoked on an instance of the `auto` class, this code would be used in preference to the more generic version of `drive-vehicle` defined for the `motor-vehicle` class.

What would you do if you wanted the odometer to be updated for autos as well? One solution would be to add the code for resetting the odometer to our method for `auto` objects. If you later changed the definition of `drive-vehicle` for the `motor-vehicle` class but neglected to update the code for the `auto` class, however, you might introduce some unwanted differences between the behavior of `auto` objects and other motor vehicles. A better way would be to have all `motor-vehicle` objects share the same code for updating the odometer. The `call-next-method` function facilitates this code sharing. The `drive-vehicle` method could be rewritten as follows:

```
(defmethod drive-vehicle ((automobile auto) miles-driven)
   (with-slots (fuel-tank mileage-rating) automobile
      (let* ((fuel-volume (slot-value fuel-tank 'fuel-volume))
```

---

[5]This is similar to the method combination used in the object-oriented language LOOPS (Stefik et al., 1983).

```
            (range (* fuel-volume mileage-rating)))
     ;;enough gas?
     (cond ((>= miles-driven range)
            ;;deplete tank
            (setf (slot-value fuel-tank 'fuel-volume) 0)
            ;;update odometer
            (call-next-method automobile range))
           ;;adjust gas level
           (t (setf (slot-value fuel-tank 'fuel-volume)
                    (- fuel-volume
                       (/ miles-driven mileage-rating)))
              (call-next-method))))))
```

If `call-next-method` is invoked without any arguments (as it is here), the next most general method is passed the same arguments that were passed to the current method. The `call-next-method` function returns the value returned by the invoked method. Although it is not done here, this value could be used for further computation by the calling method. By the way, what will this version of `drive-vehicle` return?

Declarative Method Combination

The second type of method combination in CLOS uses the *method-qualifier* parameter of `defmethod` to define special-purpose methods known as `:before`, `:after`, and `:around`. This method combination is referred to as *declarative* because you declare through the *method-qualifier* parameter when the method is to be used (Keene, 1989).[6] Methods that have method qualifiers are referred to as *auxiliary methods*. The most specific method without method qualifiers for a particular set of arguments is termed the *primary method*. All applicable `:before` methods are executed before the primary method; all applicable `:after` methods are executed after the primary method; all applicable `:around` methods are invoked "around" the primary method. (In most cases, `:around` methods use `call-next-method` to invoke the primary method or the next most general `:around` method.)

As a simple example of the use of auxiliary methods, consider the oxygen sensor warning light feature of many new cars. When the car has been driven a specific number of miles (say, 50,000), the warning light is activated to warn the driver to replace the sensor. You could modify the `drive-vehicle` method to simulate this

---

[6]This is similar to the method combination used in the Flavors language (Moon, 1986).

behavior using an auxiliary method. After the more general method has been invoked and the odometer reading has been updated, an :after method could be invoked to test to see if the warning light should be lit.

```
(defmethod drive-vehicle :after ((automobile auto) miles-driven)
   (with-slots (odometer) automobile
      (if (>= odometer 50000)
          (print "Replace Oxygen Sensor!"))))
```

When drive-vehicle is called on an auto object, the applicable primary method will be invoked first, using call-next-method to invoke the more general method for updating odometers of motor vehicles. When control returns from the primary method, this auxiliary method will then be called. As you can see, the use of method combination can produce a fairly complicated pattern of behavior at execution time.

Modifying Accessor Functions

Accessor methods were presented in the last section as the preferred means for allowing users of an object to access slots. The easiest way of modifying an accessor function generated by defclass is to write an auxiliary method to augment its standard behavior. Using the :before and :after methods, you could add additional behavior to read and write accesses of a slot.[7] You could, in fact, write a :before method that would actually compute and store a new value in the slot every time someone accessed the slot!

The technique of computing a slot value every time it is needed begins to blur the distinction between slots and methods. In effect, the slot contents are replaced by a procedure that knows how to get the value when it is needed. For example, you could define the fuel-volume slot for the motor-vehicle class as follows:

```
(defclass motor-vehicle ()
    ((make      :initarg :make)
     (odometer :initform 0
               :type 'integer
               :initarg :odometer)
     (fuel      :initform 'gasoline
               :initarg :fuel)
     (fuel-tank :initarg :fuel-tank
                :initform (make-instance 'fuel-tank))
```

---

[7]You now have the tools to write auxiliary methods for read access. Doing the same for write accesses is a little more complicated. See the Keene book (Keene, 1989) for details.

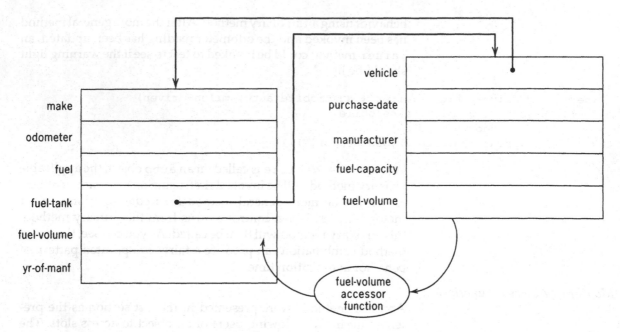

Figure 6-3 The `fuel-volume` Accessor Function Connects the Like-Named Slots in `motor-vehicle` and Its Associated `fuel-tank` Object

```
(fuel-volume :accessor fuel-volume)
(yr-of-manf  :initarg :yr)))
```

This slot would need to be kept consistent with the `fuel-volume` slot of the `fuel-tank` object associated with the motor vehicle. An easy way to do this would be to define a `:before` method that would get a new value from the `fuel-tank` object every time it was needed (Figure 6-3). This method could be defined as follows:

```
(defmethod fuel-volume :before ((vehicle motor-vehicle))
  (with-slots (fuel-tank fuel-volume) vehicle
    (setf fuel-volume (slot-value fuel-tank 'fuel-volume))))
```

Using this accessor method would greatly simplify getting the fuel volume for a vehicle. For example:

```
CL> (fuel-volume old-faithful)
0
```

Note that this technique requires that the `fuel-volume` slot *always* be accessed using the preceding accessor. If `slot-value` is used directly to fetch the contents, the value returned may be different from the one stored in the `fuel-tank` object.

Access-Oriented Programming

Computing slot values on demand is an example of a style of programming known as *access-oriented programming* (Skefik et al., 1986b). In this style of programming, storage locations may have attached procedures that are triggered by read and write accesses. The attached procedures can be easily implemented in CLOS, using method combination on accessor functions.

This technique is most useful when dependencies exist between the values stored in two or more slots. In the previous example, the contents of the `fuel-volume` slot in `motor-vehicle` objects depend on the current value of the `fuel-volume` slot in its associated `fuel-tank` object. Access-oriented programming allows the programmer to decide when to update the contents of the dependent slot. The dependent slot can be updated simultaneously, or the update can be deferred until someone tries to read the dependent slot. Your decision should be based on two factors: how frequently the dependent slot is read and how large a computation is involved to update the second slot. If the dependent slot is rarely read, it would be more efficient to compute the value only when it is needed. If the first value is updated frequently and the effort required to compute the dependent value is large, it may be wise to delay updating of the second slot. If, on the other hand, the dependent slot is read much more frequently than the other slot is updated, then it would probably be best to update them both at the same time.

Exercise 6.9

The `position` slot of a `chess-piece` could be computed when needed by consulting the `chess-board` slot of the `chess-game` object. Would this be a reasonable way to update this slot?

Exercise 6.10

Write an `accessor` method for the mileage-rating slot of `auto` objects called `get-mileage-rating`. Consider the value stored in the slot to be a manufacturer's suggested rating. If the value stored in the fuel slot is not the symbol `super-premium`, the accessor should return a mileage rating reduced by 10%.

Exercise 6.11

When testing the legality of chess moves, there are some general issues that apply to all types of chess pieces. For example, the new position must be on the board, and it must be different from the old position. Also, if the square associated with the new position is already occupied, it must be occupied by a piece of the opposite color. Write a `legal-move-p` method specialized for the `chess-`

piece class that will check to make sure that all of these requirements are satisfied. Use `call-next-method` in your `legal-`
`move-p` methods from Exercise 6.8 to invoke this more general
method.

6.3 CLOS PROGRAMMING PRACTICE

Although object-oriented programming techniques in Lisp have
been used for over a decade, the facilities for object-oriented programming in CLOS are so new that it is too early to try to formulate
clear guidelines for its use. This is because there is no wide body of
experience using CLOS and because CLOS is sufficiently different
from the other Lisp-based object-oriented languages to make it
difficult to generalize from their experience.[8] It is not too early,
however, for you, as programmers and system designers, to begin
to think about where you might use these facilities to support future
implementation efforts. There are several issues to consider: how to
choose whether to use structures or CLOS objects, when procedures should be implemented as generic functions, when it is
advisable to use multimethods, and how one should best use
method combination.

Structures versus Objects

Common Lisp structures have existed since the introduction of the
language. Experienced Common Lisp programmers are quite
comfortable using structures, and much existing code uses structures as well. There are also well-known techniques for their
efficient implementation. CLOS objects, on the other hand, are
relatively new. Although the defining objects using `defclass` are
reasonably straightforward, CLOS as a whole is considerably more
complicated than the built-in facilities for handling structures.
Common Lisp implementors are just beginning to develop efficient
implementations for CLOS. This means that, in the short run, there
are likely to be performance differences between systems using
CLOS and those using structures. For these reasons, it is unlikely
that CLOS objects will completely replace structures in the near
future.

---

[8]This is not to suggest that there has been no experience using CLOS.
Xerox PARC has been distributing a portable version of an object-
oriented language based on CLOS since early 1986. See the *Proceedings of
the First CLOS Users and Implementation Workshop* (PARC, 1988) for
examples of some of the work that has been done in CLOS.

CLOS and the Common Lisp Type Hierarchy

There is an interesting sort of reciprocity between the Common Lisp type hierarchy, which you studied in Chapter 4, and the CLOS object hierarchy. Classes can be used as though they were Common Lisp types. For example, you could type

```
CL> (typep old-faithful 'auto)
T
CL> (typep old-faithful 'motor-vehicle)
T
```

Coming from the other side, most Common Lisp required-types can be used in place of class names as specializers for method parameters. This means that generic functions can be defined to operate on most types of Common Lisp data objects. This close integration between CLOS and the Common Lisp language definition greatly expands the range of applications that can be addressed in an object-oriented fashion. It makes it possible, for instance, to do systems programming in an object-based style.

One of the elegant features of CLOS is that CLOS itself was defined using CLOS classes. Figure 6-4 shows part of the CLOS object hierarchy. CLOS classes, methods, generic functions, and slot descriptions are implemented as CLOS objects. When you create a method using `defmethod`, you are creating an instance of the class `standard-method` (and an instance of the class `generic-function`, if this is the first method defined with that specific name). When you define a class with `defclass`, an instance of the class `standard-class` is created. The class object has slots to store things like a list of superclasses for the class and a list of slot descriptions. Class objects can be both instances of and a subclass of other class objects. This is a confusing notion for many programmers learning to program in an object-oriented style. The class of which a class object is an instance is referred to as the *metaclass* for that class object.

In CLOS, every class object has at least one superclass and a metaclass. A metaclass is a class for which all of its instances are class objects. There is a keyword, `:metaclass`, for the `defclass` macro which allows the programmer to specify the metaclass for a class. The default metaclass is `standard-class` just as the default superclass is `object`. A class object inherits its own slots (e.g., a slot for its list of superclasses, a slot to store a list of slot descriptions for the class, etc.) and methods (e.g., methods for initializing instances of the class) from its metaclass. It inherits application-specific data from its superclass. Metaclasses, then, determine how an object-oriented system works. In CLOS it is possible to define your own metaclasses. This is useful when you wish to do something fancy, like emulate another object-oriented language. You could emulate Smalltalk in CLOS, for example, by creating your own standard metaclass and rewriting some of the methods. Programming with metaclasses is an advanced technique and will not be covered in this book.

Are you still confused about the distinction between superclasses and metaclasses? Let's go over it once more. As seen in Figure 6-4, the class object is a subclass of the class t. The class class is a subclass of object, and standard-class is obviously a subclass of class. If you think about it for a moment, that should make perfect sense. It gets a little more baffling, however, when we consider the metaclasses of the upper-level system classes. The class object is an instance of the class standard-class, class is an instance of the class standard-class, and standard-class is an instance of itself! Figure 6-5 portrays all of this graphically. (The dashed lines go from an instance to its class.) The rather incestuous relationships between the upper classes are sometimes referred to collectively as the "Eternal Golden Braid" (with apologies to Douglas Hofstadter). The "Braid" has always been the most confusing part of object-oriented programming. If you still find the distinction between superclasses and metaclasses confusing, let it go for a while and reread this section again later. You don't really have to understand the "Braid" completely in order to program in an object-oriented style, but it does help to give you an appreciation for the internal workings of CLOS.

As you are a newcomer to the scene, however, there are several reasons why you might wish to standardize on using CLOS objects. From a didactic standpoint, it is easier to become conversant with the use of one facility than to learn two. Since CLOS objects offer more capabilities than Common Lisp structures, they are the logical choice if you plan to learn only one. CLOS objects also allow you to capitalize on the advantages of programming in the object-oriented style. Finally, the argument in favor of structures as being more efficient is likely to diminish in time as developers begin to generate more optimized implementations of CLOS.

Using Generic Functions

The second issue concerning the use of CLOS is when to implement

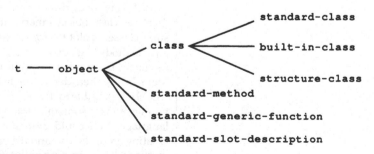

Figure 6-4   The Upper-Level CLOS Class Lattice

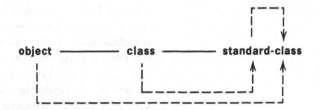

Figure 6-5 The Eternal Golden Braid

procedures using methods and generic functions. Generic functions and CLOS methods offer built-in type checking, are readily extensible, and offer convenient facilities for accessing the slots of CLOS objects. However, it is possible to have too much of a good thing. Just as there is a trade-off between the expressive simplicity of a recursive form and the computational efficiency of an iterative expression, there are costs associated with the use of generic functions. The need to compute and dispatch to an effective method places an extra burden on the system that is not present with standard functions. A simple guideline might be to always define procedures that operate on CLOS objects as generic functions. Even if the generic function will have only one method, it may be desirable to implement it as a generic function to ensure future extensibility.

Some programmers are beginning to use generic functions to define procedures that operate on standard Lisp objects. Because of the way that CLOS is integrated into the Common Lisp type hierarchy, it is possible to specialize parameters using Common Lisp types as specializers rather than CLOS classes. This means that complicated procedures that operate on Common Lisp built-in types like lists and numbers can be implemented in an object-oriented style. It is difficult to predict how large an impact the introduction of generic functions will have on Common Lisp programming practice as a whole, but its effect may become pervasive.

Multimethods

A third issue in CLOS programming practice concerns the use of multimethods. The notion of multimethods is novel to CLOS. Traditional object-oriented languages like Smalltalk only allow a method specialized to a single class (Goldberg and Robson, 1983). This was true of earlier Lisp-based, object-oriented languages as well (Stefik and Bobrow, 1986a). Permitting methods to specialize on multiple parameters generalizes the notion of object-oriented programming in a potentially very powerful way. Using multimethods, it is possible to create concise, well-structured generic functions (see Exercise 6.15 for an example). The use of multimethods, however, increases the complexity of a generic function for both the system and the programmer. For this reason, multimethods should not be used capriciously. Don't specialize parameters just because they can be specialized. On the other hand, if you find yourself resorting to type testing within your methods, you should probably be considering an implementation based on multimethods.

Method Combination

The fourth and final area of concern in CLOS programming involves the use of method combination. Method combination is one of the most complicated aspects of programming in CLOS. The method combination facilities in CLOS represent a union of ideas from several earlier languages (Stefik and Bobrow, 1986a). Method combination in CLOS is considerably more complicated than described in this chapter. It is also possible to define your own types of method combination and use them in conjunction with the built-in facilities. All of these facilities require the system designer, however, to act responsibly. It is very easy, using method combination, to produce large, ungainly, and baroque pieces of code that are difficult to read and impossible to maintain.

Programming in Style

The suggestions for programming in a good style, introduced in Chapter 3, are as valid for object-oriented programming as for procedure-based programming. The rule "Make every function you write easily comprehensible" could be applied to methods as well. The ways of achieving comprehensibility are generally the same: make your methods small, name them intelligently, provide sufficient documentation, and so forth.

Object-oriented programming offers important advantages for the implementation of large projects, particularly those that are implemented using a team of developers. It provides a means of sharing work between members of the team and supports the development of abstraction barriers between project subsystems. The real power of object-oriented programming becomes apparent, however, when you are required to extend an implemented system. Object-oriented systems can be extended through class specialization and method combination without requiring the programmer to change (and understand) existing code.

Exercise 6.12

What facilities in CLOS support the development of abstraction barriers between project subsystems?

Exercise 6.13

Define a class of objects to represent dates with slots for the day, the month, and the year. Define a generic function called date-arithmetic that will have the following behavior:

- When passed two date objects, it will return the number of intervening days (inclusive).
- When the first argument is a date object and the second argument is a positive integer *n*, it will return a new date object corresponding to the day *n* days after the specified date.
- When the first argument is a date object and the second argument is a negative integer *n*, it will return a new date object corresponding to the day *n* days before the specified date.

SUMMARY

In this chapter, the notion of programming with methods was introduced. CLOS methods offer two important advantages over standard CL functions: Methods can be specialized to work with one or more specific classes, and methods can be inherited like slots. Each CLOS method represents a specialized way of performing a particular procedure for a specific class of objects. A collection of methods with the same name is referred to as a *generic function* in CLOS.

Method inheritance makes object-oriented applications very simple to extend. Systems can be expanded to include new classes of objects by specializing existing classes. The new classes inherit slots and methods from the existing superclasses. In this way, new functionality can be added to a system without modifying any existing (and presumably working) code.

Methods are defined using the CLOS defmethod macro. Methods differ from functions in that elements of the parameter list for a method can be specialized to work only with objects of a specific class. If a method is defined with a parameter specialized for a given class, that method will be applied to all instances of that class and to any class that is directly or indirectly a subclass of that class. If there is a method that is specialized for a subclass, that method will take precedence over any method of the same name specialized for a superclass. Common Lisp types can be used in place of CLOS classes as parameter specializers for methods.

CLOS methods can be combined to produce an effective method. Methods defined without a *method-qualifier* are referred to as *primary* methods. Methods with qualifiers such as :before,

:after or :around are referred to as *auxiliary* methods. Generic functions are called just like standard Common Lisp functions. When a generic function is invoked, the system must determine which of the applicable methods to execute. The effective method is produced by performing the following steps:

1. Execute all applicable :around methods (most specific first).
2. Execute all applicable :before methods (most specific first).
3. Execute the most specific primary method (and possibly others if this method contains a call to call-next-method).
4. Execute all applicable :after methods (most specific last).

Access-oriented programming is easy to implement in CLOS. It involves attaching procedures to specified storage locations (i.e., slots of objects) that are executed whenever someone tries to access the specified location. A simple way to implement this is to define accessor functions for specified slots that have been augmented to perform the attached procedures.

NEW COMMON LISP DEFINED NAMES

```
call-next-method
defmethod
with-slots
```

FOR FURTHER READING

A detailed description of how effective methods are computed can be found in Chapter 2 of the Draft Standard (ANSI, 1990), in Section 28.1.7 of Steele's book (Steele, 1990) or in Chapter 1 of the CLOS Specification (Bobrow et al., 1988). See Chapter 5 of the Keene book (Keene, 1989) for a readable discussion of CLOS method combination. Access-oriented programming is described in an article by Stefik, Bobrow, and Kahn (Stefik et al., 1986b).

Project 6.1

Extend the move method for chess pieces to handle all legal moves, including pawn captures (including *en passant*), castling, pawn promotion, testing to make sure that the move does not place you in check, and so forth.

Project 6.2

Construct an object-oriented graphics system. Minimally, have classes to represent line objects, rectangular objects, and circular objects. Graphic objects should have slots to represent their location, color (or pattern), border width, and so on. Write methods to display, move, and erase the objects. If possible, do this as a team project. Devise a scheme for dividing the work evenly among team members. If you implement the system correctly, you should be able to add retroactively classes for new types of graphic objects (e.g., triangles, polygons, Bezier curves) without changing any of the existing code. (Note: In order to display the graphic objects, you will have to use implementation-dependent graphic routines. Consult the programmer's reference manual for your implementation.)

7

Gently Down the Stream

Row row row your boat
Gently down the stream,
Merrily merrily merrily merrily
Life is but a dream.
Traditional

7.1 LISP INPUT/OUTPUT (I/O)

There is another data type in Common Lisp that has not yet been discussed. It is called a stream. All I/O in Lisp is done by manipulating streams. Input streams provide sequences of characters for processing; output streams are repositories into which sequences of characters can be fed.

read-eval-print Loop

The read-eval-print loop was mentioned in Chapter 1. The normal behavior of the Lisp top level is to read an expression from the standard input stream, evaluate it, and print the result to the standard output stream, as shown in Figure 7-1. The default streams used for I/O are bound to the global variables *standard-input* and *standard-output*.[1]

---

[1]In most implementations, you may examine them using the inspect function.

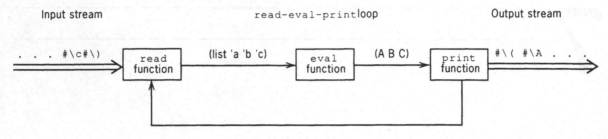

Figure 7-1   The `read-eval-print` loop (shown with an input and an output stream)

Because Lisp automatically does its own reading of expressions and printing of results, you have not had to concern yourself up to now with the details of Lisp I/O. This is another feature of Lisp that makes it attractive as a prototyping language: the task of handling simple I/O, such as typing of data elements and storage management, is delegated to the system. There are situations, however, where you may wish to exercise more control over how I/O is handled. Common examples include situations where you wish to read input from a file instead of from the terminal or where you would like to produce specially formatted output. This chapter will show how to manage tasks of this kind.

read Function

You have already used the `read` function in some of the exercises. The `read` function is often referred to simply as the *reader* in the same way that the `eval` function is known synonymously as the *interpreter*. It is the most commonly used function in Lisp for inputting data. The form of a call to `read` is

```
(read stream)
```

If no `stream` argument is given, it defaults to the current assignment of `*standard-input*`. In contrast to languages like Fortran that are record based, the Lisp `read` function always reads a full Lisp expression. If the expression extends over more than one line, the Lisp reader treats the intervening carriage return characters as spaces. For example:

```
CL> (defun read-test-1 ()
   (read))
READ-TEST-1
CL> (read-test-1)
((a b c)
```

```
          (d e f)
          (h i j))
    ((A B C) (D E F) (H I J))
```

However, read can also read multiple expressions from a single line. For example:

```
CL> (defun read-test-2 ()
      (list (read)(read)(read)))
READ-TEST-2
CL> (read-test-2)
a b c
 (A B C)
```

The job of the reader, then, is to recognize the type of expression appearing in the stream, capture the full sequence of characters in the expression, and return the expression. We call this *parsing* the expression.

read-char *and* **read-line**
Functions

If for some reason you wish to bypass the reader, there are lower-level input functions in Common Lisp that you can use. The read-char function can be called to read a single character from a stream. Doing input using read-char resembles doing input in assembly-level code. It does, however, give the programmer full control over how data are to be read. If you need to scan over a line of input you can write a function that will call read-char from inside a loop until it encounters a #\Newline character and then returns the accumulated string of characters. Since this is a fairly standard maneuver, Common Lisp provides a function that does just that, called read-line.

print *Function*

The Common Lisp read function is a stream *consumer*: it consumes the stream of characters typed in by the user. The Common Lisp print function is a stream *producer*: it produces the stream of characters that are displayed on the screen. At the Lisp top level, the print function takes the result returned by the interpreter and converts it into a stream of characters for display. The print function can be called directly with a call of the following form:

```
(print object stream)
```

where *object* can be any Lisp form. The stream argument is optional; if not specified, the output is directed to the current contents of *standard-output*. When invoked, the print function performs the following steps:

1. It evaluates *object*.

2. It converts the result into a sequence of characters.

3. It adds a #\Newline character to the beginning of the sequence and a #\Space character to the end.

4. It feeds the resulting sequence to the output stream.

5. It returns the value of *object*.

The write function works essentially the same way, except that it skips the third step. To supply a stream argument for write, you must use the :stream keyword.

Print Control Variables

The way that Lisp forms actually appear on the output stream is controlled by a number of global variables. For example:

```
CL> (defvar my-tree '(a(b(d)(e(f)(g)))(c)))
MY-TREE
CL> my-tree
(A (B (D)(E (F)(G)))(C))
CL> (setf *print-pretty* T)
T
CL> my-tree
(A (B (D)
      (E (F)
         (G)))
   (C))
CL> (setf *print-level* 2)
2
CL> my-tree
(A (B # #) (C))
CL> (setf *print-length* 2)
2
CL> my-tree
(A (B # ...) ...)
```

The *print-pretty* variable controls the printing of nested structures.[2] The *print-level* and *print-length* variables are useful when working with large and/or deeply nested

_____

[2]Pretty printing can also be achieved using the pprint function. Calling pprint will cause the value of its argument to be pretty printed but will have no effect on the global value of *print-pretty*.

lists. Often when debugging code, one is more interested in the structure of the output than in its actual contents. By setting these print control variables, you can suppress some of the detail and still see what you need to see. The effect of setting *print-level* to some value is that the more deeply nested sublists will be replaced by sharp-signs (#) in the printout. Setting the *print-length* variable to some numeric value will cause the tails of longer lists to be replaced with ellipsis points (...) when displayed. The *print-circle* variable controls the handling of self-referencing data structures.

Ensuring *read-ability*

There are situations where you would like to be able to read the sequence of characters that have been sent to an output stream and get a form identical to the one that was printed. For example, you might wish to write a Lisp expression into a file so that you can recreate it at some point in the future. Problems come up, however, when you have symbols with unusual names—names containing embedded blanks or lowercase characters. The default behavior of the system is to insert appropriate escape characters into the output so that the symbol will read in properly. If you are trying to generate a report, however, you may not want to see those escape characters. There is a printer control variable called *print-escape* that allows you to override the default behavior of the system.[3] For example:

```
CL> (write '|A weird symbol with embedded blanks|)
|A weird symbol with embedded blanks|
|A weird symbol with embedded blanks|
CL> (setf *print-escape* nil)
NIL
CL> (write '|A weird symbol with embedded blanks|)
A weird symbol with embedded blanks
A weird symbol with embedded blanks
```

The symbol name is printed twice because the write function returns the value of its argument, which then is printed once again as you complete the read-eval-print loop.

Un-*read*-able Data Objects

Some Common Lisp data types are printed in a way that precludes their being successfully read back in. Data types that fall into this

---

[3]In previous versions of Lisp, there was a function called princ for suppressing escape characters in output. For backward compatibility this function is also provided in Common Lisp.

category include hash tables, read tables, packages, and streams. Common Lisp implementations use the #<...> printed representation for printing objects of these types. For example:

```
CL>(print *package*)
#<PACKAGE "USER">
#<PACKAGE "USER">
CL> #<PACKAGE "USER">
Reader error: "#<" encountered.
```

The Common Lisp read function will signal an error whenever it encounters a #<...> expression.

Printing Numbers

The printing of numbers is also controlled by global variables in Common Lisp. The *print-base* variable determines the radix in which rational numbers will be displayed.[4] It can assume any value between 2 and 36 (inclusive). Whether or not the radix is displayed is controlled by the *print-radix* variable. For example:

```
CL> (setf hundred 100)
100
CL> (setf *print-radix* t)
T
CL> (setf *print-base* 8)
#o10
CL> hundred
#o144
CL> (setf *print-base* 2)
#b10
CL> hundred
#b1100100
```

Local Print Control

The write function accepts keywords other than :stream. The keywords :circle, :level, :length, :pretty, :escape, :base, and :radix correspond to the global print control variables described earlier. When the print control characteristics are set using the optional keywords to write, the setting applies only to the current write expression. Hence, it is often more convenient to use

---

[4]Floating-point numbers are always printed in base 10 in Common Lisp. An analogous variable called *read-base* controls the radix in which rationals are read in.

the write print control keywords rather than to do an assignment and a deassignment of one of the global variables.

write-char *Function*

For the programmer who wants to exert greater control over the handling of output, there is a Common Lisp printing function complementary to the read-char function. The write-char function accepts a single character as an argument and directs it to an output stream.

Exercise 7.1

Write your own version of read-line using read-char.

Exercise 7.2

Write a function using read-char that will read a sequence of characters representing a hexadecimal number and return the corresponding decimal value. For example:

```
CL > (read-hex)
face
64206
```

(Hint: The digital-char-p function takes an optional radix argument and will return the "weight" of the passed character in the specified radix.)

Exercise 7.3

Write a function called write-bases that displays its integer argument in binary, octal, decimal, and hexadecimal. For example:

```
CL> (write-bases 100)
2:1100100
8:144
10:100
16:64
NIL
```

Exercise 7.4

Write your own version of terpri.

Exercise 7.5 (*)

Write a fortran-to-lisp function that will read a Fortran assignment statement (using read-line) and translate it into a Lisp expression. You can assume that the Fortran statement will contain no parentheses. For example:

```
CL> (fortran-to-lisp)
x = B + C - D
(SETF X (+ B (- C D)))
```

7.2 FORMATTED OUTPUT

Common Lisp provides a function for doing fancy formatted output. Those who have programmed in Fortran will recognize a strong resemblance to the Fortran FORMAT facility. In fact, the Common Lisp function for doing formatted output is called format. Many consider the Common Lisp format facility to be a language unto itself. We will only touch on some of its basic features here. Look at the end of the chapter for additional sources if you are interested in writing code to do some particularly fancy output.

format *Function*

The general form of a call to format is as follows:

```
(format stream
  format-string
  output-arg(s))
```

If the *stream* argument is set to T, format will return NIL and cause a string of formatted output to be directed to the *standard-output* stream as a side effect. If the stream argument is NIL, format will return a formatted string as its result. Unlike the other I/O functions covered in the previous section, the *stream* argument is required for a call to format. It is a common mistake to forget the *stream* argument, and the effect can be unpredictable.

The *format-string* argument is just a normal Common Lisp string enclosed in double quotation marks. It may, however, include special format directives. The format directives are always preceded by a tilde character (~). Some of the more commonly used format directives are listed in Table 7-1.

Consumer Directives

There are a number of format directives that can be used to display data objects in certain formats. Among others, there is a ~d directive for displaying integers in decimal format, ~e and ~f directives for displaying floating-point numbers, and an omnibus ~a directive for displaying all types of Lisp data objects. Generally there is a one-to-one correspondence between consumer directives and *output-args*. For example:

```
CL> (format t "~d is an integer." 100)
100 is an integer.
NIL
```

TABLE 7-1 *Format Directives*

Consumer directives

~a	any Lisp object
~c	characters
~d	decimal integers
~e	floating-point numbers in exponential format
~f	floating-point numbers in fixed format
~s	any Lisp object (with escape characters)

Carriage control directives

~t	tab
~%	new line

Flow control directives

~{	start loop
~}	end loop
~^	exit loop

We say that the ~d directive "consumes" one argument because there must be one *output-arg* that evaluates to an integer for every occurrence of a ~d directive in the *format-string*.

The ~a directive displays the value of its corresponding *output-arg* as though the value of *print-escape* had been locally set to NIL. The ~s directive, on the other hand, displays its *output-arg* with escape characters. For example:

```
CL> (defvar foo '|schwalabar|)
foo
CL> (format t
        "~a is a ~a.~%~s is a ~s."
        foo
        (type-of foo)
        foo
        (type-of foo))
schwalabar is a SYMBOL.
|schwalabar| is a SYMBOL.
NIL
```

The ~f directive takes two optional arguments specifying the width of the field and the number of digits to appear after the decimal point, respectively. The number is displayed right justified within the field. For example:

```
CL> (format t "~10,4f" pi)
  3.1416
NIL
CL> (format t "~6,4f" pi)
3.1416
NIL
```

The list of all the consumer directives is too lengthy to report here. There are, for instance, directives for displaying integers in radices other than decimal.

Carriage Control Directives

The carriage control directives do not consume an *output-arg*; instead, they are used to insert carriage control characters. The ~t directive tabulates to a specified column. It takes a single numeric argument specifying the column. The ~% inserts a #\Newline character into the constructed string.

Flow Control Directives

As with a full-scale programming language, there are other format directives that allow the programmer to specify the order in which the elements of the *format-string* will be processed. This flow of control directives can get quite complicated, but the directives for iterating over lists are not very difficult to learn, and they can come in handy at times.

The ~{ and ~} directives allow the programmer to specify special formatting for each element of a list. The substring, consisting of these two directives and all that they enclose, will consume one list argument from the *output-args*. This is a very convenient way of looping over the elements of a list. In fact, using these directives is conceptually similar to making an implicit call to dolist, with the enclosed format substring representing the body of the loop. For example:

```
CL> (format t "~{<~a>~%~}" '(a b c))
<A>
<B>
<C>
NIL
```

The ~^ directive can be used to effect an early exit from the loop when the list has been exhausted. It is used primarily in situations where you wish to treat the last element of the list as some sort of exception.

Exercise 7.6

Is the format function called for result or for effect?

Exercise 7.7

What will the following `format` expressions return?

a. (format t "~5,3f~%~e" pi pi)

b. (format nil "~c~d~a~d" #\X 3 'j (1+ 12))

Exercise 7.8

Write a `format` expression to display a Lisp list as a Prolog list. Prolog lists are enclosed in square brackets, and the items are separated with commas. For example:

```
(A B C) => [A,B,C]
```

```
CL> (draw-board (make-array ' (8 8)
              :initial-contents
              '((nil nil nil nil nil QN nil nil)
                (nil nil nil nil nil nil nil QN)
                (nil QN nil nil nil nil nil nil)
                (nil nil nil QN nil nil nil nil)
                (QN nil nil nil nil nil nil nil)
                (nil nil nil nil nil nil QN nil)
                (nil nil nil nil QN nil nil nil)
                (nil nil QN nil nil nil nil nil)))))
```

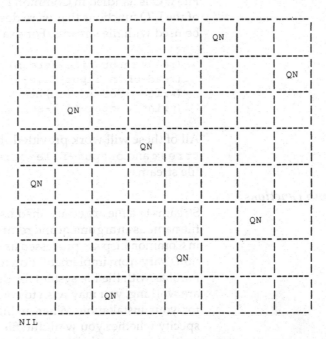

NIL

Figure 7-2 The output of the `draw-board` function

Exercise 7.9

Write a function `draw-board` to display the chessboard for the 8-Queens problem, as shown in Figure 7-2.

Exercise 7.10

Write a `display-moves` method to display all the moves for a `chess-game` object (as defined in the previous chapter). For example:

```
CL> (display-moves my-chess-game)
   White         Black
   1.P-e         P-e5
   2.P-d4        P-d5
   3.PxP         PxP
   4.Kn-f3       Kn-f6
NIL
```

Note that by convention, the chess board ranks are labeled with the letters "a" through "h."

7.3 FILE STREAMS

File I/O is handled in Common Lisp by the use of file streams. All of the I/O functions that were described earlier in the chapter can be used with file streams. For example:

```
(read input-file-stream)
(read-char input-file-stream)
(write :stream output-file-stream)
(print output-file-stream)
```

All of these will work provided that the variables `input-file-stream` and `output-file-stream` were properly initialized to file streams.

open and close Functions

Streams to a file are established using the `open` function. It takes a file name as an argument and returns a file stream object. File names in Common Lisp are processed as strings. The file naming conventions vary from implementation to implementation. If you are not familiar with the file system for the implementation in which you are working, you may wish to consult the programmer's manuals for your installation. When using the `open` function, you may specify whether you want the file to be opened for reading or for writing by using the optional `:direction` keyword. File streams are terminated using the close function. It takes a file stream as an argument. Usually when working with file streams, you will use a local variable to serve as a handle for accessing the stream object returned by the open function.

Suppose that you need to store the current binding of a variable out to a file so that you can restore that definition at some point in the future by reading the file. Of course, in order to restore the variable, you will need to write more than just its current binding; you will also need to write out to the file an appropriate expression that will cause the variable to be properly assigned when the file is read. To store the current value of foo out to the save-file.lisp file we could type

```
(let ((output-stream
        (open "save-file.lisp"
              :direction :output)
(format output-stream
        "(defvar ~s ~s)~%"
        'foo
        foo)
(close output-stream))  ;NOT RECOMMENDED!
```

Although this would work, it is not the way that most experienced Common Lisp programmers would do it.

with-open-file

Most Common Lisp programmers open and close files using a macro called with-open-file. The problem with the preceding form is that if an error occurs while executing the format expression, you would never get to the call to close and the file stream would remain open. The with-open-file macro guarantees that the stream will be closed when you exit the form, even if the exit is the result of an error. The general form of a call to with-open-file is

```
(with-open-file (stream-name
  file-name
  file-options)
  body)
```

Using with-open-file, the preceding form could be rewritten as follows:

```
(with-open-file (output-stream
                 "save-file.lisp"
                 :direction :output)
```

```
(format output-stream
          "(setf ~s ~s)~%" 'foo foo))
```

This will do just what you wanted. You could read the expressions back in again using the following form:

```
(with-open-file (input-stream
                    "save-file.lisp"
                    :direction :input)
   (eval (read input-stream))
```

Data-Driven Looping

What if there were more than one expression in the file being read? You would have to invoke read for every expression in the file. This would necessitate knowing in advance how many expressions to expect. It would be much more convenient if you could simply read expressions until there were no more and then stop. The read function has some optional arguments that make this possible. The more complete form of a call to read is

```
(read stream eof-error-p eof-value)
```

If the value NIL is passed as the *eof-error-p* argument, read will not signal an error when the end of file (eof) is reached. Instead, it will return one more value, the value passed as the *eof-value* argument. This enables the programmer to test the value returned by read to see if the end of the file has been reached. You could easily write a loop now that will be controlled by the number of expressions stored in the file. The form of this loop would be as follows:

```
(with-open-file (input-stream "save-file.lisp"
                                :direction :input)
   (do ((next-item (read input-stream
                        nil
                        input-stream)
                    (read input-stream
                        nil
                        input-stream))
       ((eq next-item input-stream)
    (eval next-item))
```

Notice that the *eof-value* used is the local binding for the input stream. It is very important that the value chosen for the *eof-value* not be an expression that could ever appear in the file that you are reading lest it cause you to stop reading the file prematurely. It is a standard programming trick (Brooks, 1984) to use the input stream object as the *eof-value*, since it will always be unique.

Exercise 7.11

Write a function called `save-vars` that will accept as arguments a list of variables and a file name. The function should write a `defvar` expression to the file for every variable on the list so that when the file is read, all of the variables will be defined and initialized to their original values.

Exercise 7.12

Write a function called `load-vars` that will read the files written by `save-vars`. It should accept a file name as an argument.

SUMMARY

All I/O in Common Lisp is done through streams. Input streams provide sequences of characters for processing; output streams are repositories into which sequences of characters can be fed.

The `read` function is the most frequently used form for input in Common Lisp. Each call to `read` will return one entire Lisp expression from the input stream.

The Common Lisp `print` function is a stream producer; it produces the stream of characters that are displayed on the screen. The way that Lisp forms appear on the output stream can be controlled by changing the assignments of the following global variables: `*print-circle*`, `*print-pretty*`, `*print-level*`, `*print-length*`, `*print-escape*`, `*print-base*`, and `*print-radix*`.

Fancy formatted output can be done in Common Lisp using the `format` function. This function allows the programmer to control the appearance of the output using format directives.

File I/O in Common Lisp is handled through the use of file streams. The standard practice is to use the `with-open-file` macro to open file streams, as this ensures that the stream will always be closed properly on exit.

NEW COMMON LISP DEFINED NAMES

```
close             *print-escape*     read-line
digital-char-p    *print-length*     *standard-input*
format            *print-level*      *standard-output*
```

```
open              *print-pretty*    terpri
print             *print-radix*     with-open-file
*print-base*      *read-base*       write
*print-circle*    read-char         write-char
```

FOR FURTHER READING

Steele (Steele, 1990) discusses streams in Chapter 21, I/O functions in Chapter 22 and File I/O in Chapter 23 (see specifically Section 23.2). Other format directives are described in Section 22.3.3.

Project 7.1

Write a program to solve the 8-Queens problem. Your program should search for all solutions. Use the draw-board function from Exercise 7.9 to display each solution as it is computed. After displaying a solution, prompt the user to see if he or she would like to see another solution before computing a new solution. Each solution displayed should be unique.

(Hint: You may find the safe-squares function from Exercise 4.23 useful for evaluating potential solutions.)

Project 7.2

Build an online bibliographic data base. Represent citations as objects (as in Exercise 5.14). Prompt the user for an author's name and then print out all citations by that author. Implement the procedure for printing citations as a generic function.

8

Functions Revisited

Multiplication is vexation,
Division is as bad.
The Rule of Three perplexes me,
And practice drives me mad.
Anonymous

8.1 ADVANCED FEATURES OF FUNCTIONS

Recall that, by the Second Rule of Evaluation, when the interpreter encounters a list, it treats it as a function call. The evaluation of a function call in Common Lisp has the following steps:

1. The interpreter fetches the functional definition associated with the first element of the list from its `symbol-function` cell.

2. It evaluates the arguments to the function in left-to-right order.

3. The returned values are bound to the elements of the parameter list. This is referred to as *spreading* the arguments (Teitelman, 1983).

4. The functional definition is executed with its parameters appropriately bound.

213

5. The value of the last expression in the function is returned as the result.

In this chapter, you will learn how to exercise greater control over this evaluation process. Specifically, you will learn how to control the evaluation and spreading of arguments and how to specify the number of values that will be returned by a function.

Up to this point, the number of arguments passed to a function had to correspond exactly to the number of parameters in the parameter list. If you defined a function with two parameters and later called that function with any number other than the two prescribed arguments, the interpreter would signal an error. There are situations, however, where it would be useful to be able to vary the number of arguments passed to a function, and Common Lisp provides this kind of flexibility. Common Lisp syntax allows the inclusion of so-called *lambda-list keywords* in the parameter list of a function definition. Lambda-list keywords modify the spreading of arguments to the parameters of a function.

Optional Parameters

The simplest case occurs when you wish to define a function with one or more optional parameters. If the function is called without the optional argument(s), no error is signaled. The values bound to the optional parameters can be specified by the programmer. Optional arguments are specified using the lambda-list keyword `&optional`. All lambda-list keywords have an ampersand (&) prefix instead of a colon.[1] All parameters appearing after the `&optional` keyword are considered to be optional parameters. For example:

```
CL> (setf x 1 y 2 z 3)
3
CL> (defun fun-with-optional-argument (arg1 &optional arg2)
      arg2)
FUN-WITH-OPTIONAL-ARGUMENT
CL> (fun-with-optional-argument x y)
2
CL> (fun-with-optional-argument x)
NIL
```

In the first call to `fun-with-optional-argument`, arg2 is

---

[1]Lambda-list keywords are not true keywords. They do not reside in the KEYWORD package.

bound to the current value of y. In the second call, the second argument is not provided. Unless specified otherwise, the default value for unsupplied parameters is nil.

You could rewrite the days-in-month function from Exercise 3.2 to have an optional parameter for passing the year. This would permit you to deal with leap years in the appropriate fashion. The way the arguments would be spread is displayed in an example in Figure 8-1. The revised version of days-in-month would look something like this:

```
(defun days-in-month (month &optional year)
  (case month
    (february (if (and year
                       (leap-year-p year) 29 28))
    ((april june september november) 30)
    (t 31)))
```

If the year argument is provided, you can test for leap years (using the leap-year-p function from Exercise 3.4). We are depending on the value of year to be nil when the second argument is not supplied. There are other situations where this would not work quite as dependably. In the preceding function, nil could not serve as an appropriate value for the year parameter, but in other situations you might have difficulty discriminating between a value of nil actually passed as an argument and a value of nil generated because an optional argument was not supplied. In situations of this sort, you can use a more elaborate form to specify the optional parameter and provide a default value for the parameter. The form is

```
(var initform supplied-p-var)
```

where *var* is the name of the parameter, *initform* is a Lisp

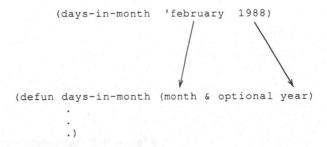

Figure 8-1 Spreading arguments in a function with an optional argument

expression, and *supplied-p-var* is a symbol. If no corresponding argument is supplied, the *initform* will be evaluated to provide a default value for the parameter. When the optional parameter has been supplied, the *supplied-p-var* local variable will be bound to the constant t. For example, the lambda list for days-in-month could be rewritten as follows:

```
(month &optional (year 1990 year-supplied-p))
```

Using this parameter list, if the second argument was not supplied, the year variable would be bound to the value 1990 instead of nil. You could test the binding of the year-supplied-p variable to see if the argument had actually been supplied or not.

Variable-Length Argument Lists

Some functions, such as the Common Lisp + function, can take a variable number of arguments. It would be clumsy to use &optional parameters to write a function like + because you would have to provide optional parameters to accommodate the longest possible argument list. Common Lisp provides another lambda-list keyword, &rest, for dealing with variable-length argument lists. When the interpreter encounters the &rest keyword in a parameter list, it gathers the remaining argument values and binds them to the local variable associated with the &rest keyword. For example:

```
CL> (defun fun-with-variable-arg-list
                        (&rest arg-list)
       arg-list)
FUN-WITH-VARIABLE-ARG-LIST
CL> (fun-with-variable-arg-list x y z)
(1 2 3)
```

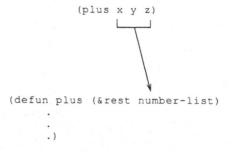

Figure 8-2   Spreading arguments in a function with a variable-length argument list

Note that the arguments are still evaluated before they are gathered in the list.

You could write your own version of the Common Lisp + function called `plus`, using the `&rest` keyword, as illustrated in Figure 8-2. The `plus` function could be implemented quite trivially, using the `sum-list` function (from Chapter 3) to sum the elements in the gathered list as follows:

```
CL> (defun plus (&rest number-list)
        (plus-list number-list))
PLUS
CL> (plus x y z)
6
```

The `&rest` keyword can be used with required parameters or optional parameters. The `&rest` keyword and its associated variable should follow all required and optional parameters.

Keyword Parameters

Many of the built-in Common Lisp forms, such as `write`, `open`, and `defclass`, use optional keyword parameters. You can set up your own parameters using the `&key` lambda-list keyword. For example:

```
CL> (defun fun-with-keyword (arg1 &key keyword-arg)
       keyword-arg)
FUN-WITH-KEYWORD
CL> (fun-with-keyword x :keyword-arg y)
2
```

The name of the parameter associated with the `&key` keyword is used both as the local variable name and as the keyword when calling the function.[2]

If you use `&key`, you can rewrite the `member-p` function from Exercise 3.8 so that the user of the function can specify the test used for comparing items in the passed list as follows:

```
CL>(defun member-p (item input-list &key (test #'eq))
  (if input-list
  (if (funcall test item (first input-list))
  item
```

[2]In Common Lisp, it is possible to have the keyword differ from the local variable name.

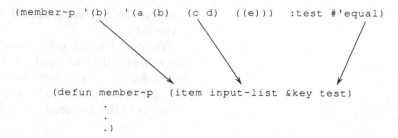

```
(member-p '(b)  '(a (b)  (c d)  ((e)))  :test #'equal)



          (defun member-p  (item input-list &key test)
                   .
                   .
                   .)
```

Figure 8-3 Spreading arguments in a function with a keyword parameter

```
(member-p item
(rest input-list)
:test test))))
MEMBER-P
CL> (member-p '(b)
'(a (b) (c d) ((e))))
NIL
CL> (member-p '(b)
'(a (b) (c d) ((e)))
:test #'equal)
(B)
```

You can provide an *initform* (and a *supplied-p-var*) for keyword parameters, just as you can for optional parameters. Figure 8-3 shows how the arguments to member-p would be spread. Note that the value of the optional parameter must be passed along in the recursive call to member-p.

Auxiliary Variables

There is a fourth lambda-list keyword called &aux for creating auxiliary variables. Auxiliary variables are simply local variables introduced within the lambda list instead of within an enclosed let form. For example, the following functional definition

```
(defun sum-list (number-list &aux (sum 0))
 (dolist (element number-list)
   (setf sum (+ sum
                     element)))
   sum)
```

would be equivalent to

```
(defun sum-list (number-list)
 (let ((sum 0))
```

```
(dolist (element number-list)
  (setf sum (+ sum
                element)))
sum))
```

Whether to use auxiliary variables or `let` expressions is a matter of personal preference, but many programmers consider the second form easier to read.

Multiple Values

You have now seen how the spreading of arguments can be controlled in Common Lisp; later in this chapter, you will discover that there are ways to control the evaluation as well. In Common Lisp you can also control the number of values returned by a function. Up to now, all of the functions you have encountered have returned exactly one value. It turns out that some of the Common Lisp built-in functions, like `get-decoded-time`, actually return more than one value. The `get-decoded-time` function returns nine values representing the current time and date.[3] For example:

```
CL> (get-decoded-time)
29
31
11
9
12
1988
4
NIL
5
```

Other Common Lisp functions that always return multiple values include the type-conversion functions `floor`, `ceiling`, `truncate`, `round` (and their floating-point equivalents: `ffloor`, `fceiling`, `ftruncate`, and `fround`), and `decode-float`.[4] In fact, most of the Common Lisp forms that you have studied will return multiple

---

[3]The values returned are, respectively, seconds, minutes, the hour, the day, the month, the year, the day of the week (0 = Monday, 1 = Tuesday, etc.), a Boolean constant specifying whether or not daylight savings time is in effect, and the time zone.

[4]The second value returned by `decode-float` is the exponent of its floating-point argument. For the other functions, the second value is the remainder when its first argument is divided by the second.

values if their last subform returns more than one value.[5] For example:

```
CL> (let ((x 10)
          (y 3))
      (floor x y))
3
1
```

Binding Multiple Values

There are several ways of capturing the extra values returned by some Common Lisp functions. There is a Common Lisp macro called multiple-value-bind that will create local variables corresponding to the returned values. The form of a call to multiple-value-bind is

```
(multiple-value-bind var-list
                      values-form
                      body)
```

where *var-list* is a list of symbols, *values-form* is a form that returns multiple values, and the *body* is one or more Common Lisp forms. For example:

```
CL> (multiple-value-bind (sec min hr day mon yr)
          (get-decoded-time)
        (print yr))
1988
1988
```

If, as in this case, the second argument returns more values than there are symbols in the *var-list*, the extra values are dropped. If the number of elements in the *var-list* exceeds the number of values returned by the second argument, the extra symbols are bound to nil.

There is another Common Lisp macro called multiple-value-list that can be used in place of multiple-value-bind. When called on a *values-form*, multiple-value-list will gather all returned values and return them as a list. For example:

```
CL> (multiple-value-list (get-decoded-time))
(39 7 12 9 12 1988 4 NIL 5)
```

---

[5]Exceptions to this rule include setq (and setf when assigning a value to a symbol), multiple-value-setq, prog1, and prog2.

This is particularly useful when you don't know how many values the *values-form* will return.

Now that you know how to capture more than one value, you may be interested in writing functions that return multiple values. This is quite easy to do in Common Lisp using the values function. This function evaluates all of its arguments and returns a value for each one. For example:

```
CL> (values 1 2 3)
1
2
3
```

If the call to values is the last expression evaluated within a function, then that function will return multiple values. For example, complex numbers are represented as a special data type in Common Lisp. You can create a complex number by typing sharp-sign-C followed by a list consisting of the real part and the imaginary part of the number. The Common Lisp functions realpart and imagpart can be used to recover the components of a complex number. For example:

```
CL> (realpart #c(5 1))
5
CL> (imagpart #c(5 1))
1
```

You could use these two functions in conjunction with values to write a function to decode a complex number as follows:

```
CL> (defun decode-complex-number (number)
       (values (realpart #c(5 1))
               (imagpart #c(5 1))))
DECODE-COMPLEX-NUMBER
CL> (decode-complex-number #c(5 1))
5
1
```

Of course, if you write functions that return multiple values, you will have to use one of the preceding multiple-value capturing forms when you call it, or the extra values will be lost. In general, when a call to a function that returns multiple values is used as an argument to another function, only the first value will be passed to the surrounding function as follows:

```
CL>(+ (decode-complex-number #c(5 1)) 3)
8
```

Exercise 8.1

Rewrite the `write-bases` function (Exercise 7.3) so that the radix can be provided as an optional argument. For example:

```
CL> (write-bases 100 'binary)
2: 1100100
NIL
CL> (write-bases 100)
2: 1100100
8: 144
10: 100
16: 64
NIL
```

Exercise 8.2

Write a function that takes a variable number of numeric arguments and computes their arithmetic mean. For example:

```
CL> (mean 11 13 15 13 11)
63/5
```

Exercise 8.3

Rewrite the `insert-sorted` function from Chapter 3, using an optional keyword for the test, so that it can be used with lists of characters and strings. For example:

```
CL> (insert-sorted #\d '(#\a #\b #\c #\e) :test #'char<=)
(#\a #\b #\c #\d #\e)
```

Exercise 8.4

Write a function called `get-date/time-string` that will return the current date and time in the following format:

```
CL> (get-date/time-string)
"Friday, December 9, 1988, 11:38:26-EST"
```

Exercise 8.5

Write a function called `get-decoded-date` that will return three values: the current month, day, and year.

```
CL> (get-decoded-date)
12
18
1988
```

Exercise 8.6

Rewrite the `days-in-month` function so that if the year is not supplied, it will default to the current year.

(Hint: Write a function called `get-decoded-current-year` to fetch the current year.)

Exercise 8.7 (*)

Rewrite the `combinations` function from Exercise 3.18 so that it will work with a variable number of input lists.

8.2 INTRODUCTORY MACROLOGY

After reading Chapter 2, you know that some built-in Common Lisp forms are implemented as functions while others have been implemented as macros or special forms. You may have noticed that some built-in macros and special forms seem to violate the Second Rule of Evaluation. Examples include the built-in forms `setf`, `if`, `let`, and `quote`. When the interpreter executes a function call, all of the arguments are evaluated first; but when a call to a macro or a special form is executed, some or all of the arguments may not be evaluated.

From time to time, you may encounter situations where it is desirable to write your own forms that do not evaluate all of their arguments. Although you are not permitted to define any new special forms in Common Lisp, you may define your own macros. In this section you will learn how macros really work and will see how they are defined.

Avoiding Argument Evaluation

Suppose that you must frequently set variables to `nil`. To save typing and to make your programs easier to read, you want to define a simple form `nil!` (read *nil-bang*) to perform this operation. Unfortunately, `nil!` cannot be defined as a function. If you defined `nil!` as follows:

```
(defun nil! (arg)
  (setf arg nil))
```

it would not work the way you wished. For one thing, if you called nil! on a variable that had no prior binding, you would get an *unbound variable* error message when the interpreter tried to evaluate the argument. Quoting the argument could solve that problem, but there is an even more fundamental flaw here. Because Lisp follows the convention of pass-by-value for symbols, an assignment to the parameter does not affect the binding of the variable outside of the function. For example:

```
CL> (defvar x 99)
X
CL> (nil! x)
NIL
CL> x
99
```

Defining Macros

To work properly, nil! needs to be implemented as a macro. The argument-passing convention used by Common Lisp macros is to pass the argument itself. Implementing nil! as a macro therefore allows you to access the argument before it is evaluated.

Macros are defined using the macro defmacro. The syntax for a call to defmacro is very similar to the syntax of a call to defun. The nil! macro can be defined as follows:

```
(defmacro nil! (var)
  (list 'setf var nil))
```

The behavior of macros is quite different from the behavior of functions, however. When a macro is called, it is evaluated to produce an expression, which, in turn, is executed. In this case, if the macro nil! is called as follows:

```
CL> (nil! x)
```

it will generate the expression

```
(setf x nil)
```

Figure 8-4   The steps in the evaluation of a macro call

which, when evaluated, will do exactly what you want. What makes the macro version work is that the `var` parameter is bound to the unevaluated argument. The steps in evaluating a macro call are summarized in Figure 8-4. Let us look at these steps in greater detail.

Evaluation of a Macro Call

Earlier in this chapter, the steps for evaluating a function call were presented. The steps for evaluating a macro call are as follows:

1. The macro expansion function associated with the macro name is fetched.

2. The arguments to the macro are spread (without evaluation) to the parameters in the macro's lambda list.

3. The expansion function is executed to produce an expression known as the *expansion of the macro*. This process is called *expanding the macro*.

4. The expression generated by the macro expansion function is then evaluated.

5. The value(s) of the last expression in the expansion of the macro is (are) returned as the result.

As you saw in the `nil!` example, there are two important differences between the evaluation of a macro call and a function call. First, whereas functions are simply executed, macros are expanded to produce a piece of code, which in turn is evaluated. The second major difference is that the arguments to the macro are not automatically evaluated before spreading.

Manipulating Lists with Macros

As an example of a slightly more complicated macro, try to write your own version of the `pop` macro for destructively removing the first element of a list. A functional version would look somewhat like this:

```
(defun my-pop (input-list)
  (let ((first-element (first input-list)))
    (setf input-list (rest input-list))
    first-element)) ;doesn't work!
```

This seems to do what you want:

```
CL> (defvar my-list '(a b c d))
MY-LIST
CL> (my-pop my-list)
A
```

until you check the value of my-list and discover the following:

```
CL> my-list
(A B C D)
```

Unfortunately, assigning the tail of the list to the input-list local variable does not have any effect on the my-list global variable. To make this macro work correctly, you must have access to the my-list variable itself, not to its value.

Writing Macros

Often a good first approximation for coding a macro can be achieved by hand-coding the desired macro expansion and then working backward to write the code that will generate the expansion. In the case of my-pop, you would like to generate some code that resembles the functional definition of my-pop given previously, except that references to the input-list local variable should point directly to the variable passed as an argument instead of to its value. The functional version of my-pop could be converted into a macro as follows:

```
(defmacro my-pop(input-list) ;works, but hard to read
  (list 'let
        (list (list 'first-element
                    (list 'first input-list)))
        (list 'setf
              input-list
              (list 'rest
                    input-list))
        'first-element))
```

When called, my-pop will now expand into an expression that will pop the first element off a passed list. You can check this using the macroexpand function. This function shows how a macro call will be expanded. For example:

```
CL> (macroexpand '(my-pop my-list))
(LET ((FIRST-ELEMENT (FIRST MY-LIST)))
(SETF MY-LIST (REST MY-LIST))
FIRST-ELEMENT)
T
```

The `macroexpand` function will recursively expand all macro calls inside your macro as well. In this case, there were no macros, but if you had used `do`, `dolist`, `return`, or any other form implemented as a macro in your implementation of Common Lisp, they would also be expanded. If you only want to see the top-level macro expanded, use `macroexpand-1` instead.

The Backquote Character

Although the preceding version of `my-pop` seems to be correct, all those nested calls to `list` make it difficult to read. Common Lisp provides an enhanced version of the `quote` special form that is very useful for writing macros. The backquote character (') permits you to easily construct the code to generate other code. Backquote by itself has the same behavior as the `quote` special form. For example:

```
CL> (defvar list-var '(une deux trois))
LIST-VAR
CL> list-var
(UN DEUX TROIS)
```

If you invoke backquote on a list like this:

```
CL> `(list-var list-var list-var)
(LIST-VAR LIST-VAR LIST-VAR)
```

its behavior will be the same as that of

```
(list 'list-var 'list-var 'list-var)
```

The difference between `quote` and `backquote`, however, is that backquote allows the programmer to disable quoting temporarily for specified elements of the backquoted expression. Elements of the backquoted expression are marked for evaluation using the comma (,) character. For example, if you typed

```
CL> `(list-var ,list-var list-var)
(LIST-VAR (UN DEUX TROIS) LIST-VAR)
```

the comma before the second element disables quoting and causes that item to be evaluated. It is treated as though you had typed

```
(list 'list-var list-var 'list-var)
```

If, instead of a comma, an element within the backquoted expression is preceded by a comma and an at-sign (@), that element is "spliced" into the list. For example:

```
CL> `(list-var ,list-var ,@list-var)
(LIST-VAR (UN DEUX TROIS) UN DEUX TROIS)
```

behaves as if you had typed

```
(append (list 'list-var list-var) list-var)
```

The my-pop macro could be rewritten, using backquote, as follows:

```
(defmacro my-pop (input-list) ;works most of the time
  `(let ((first-element (first ,input-list)))
     (setf ,input-list (rest ,input-list))
     first-element))
```

This version is much easier to read. (Satisfy yourself, using macroexpand, that both versions expand into the same expression.)

The Variable Capture Problem

There is an additional problem with our my-pop macro. It is an insidious problem because it will show up only under very special circumstances. Notice what happens if you call my-pop with a variable called first-element:

```
CL> (defvar first-element '(a b c d))
FIRST-ELEMENT
CL> (macroexpand '(my-pop first-element))
(LET ((FIRST-ELEMENT (FIRST FIRST-ELEMENT)))
(SETF FIRST-ELEMENT (REST FIRST-ELEMENT))
FIRST-ELEMENT)
T
```

In this example, first-element is rebound locally to the first element of the passed list. Since the original value of first-element is then lost, the call to setf cannot possibly work. This phenomenon is referred to as *variable capture within a macro*. It occurs when a local variable created in a macro expansion conflicts with a passed variable. The problem can be avoided by using a variable name that can never conflict with any other variable name. The gentemp function will generate a new variable name that is guaranteed to be unique. Using gentemp, the my-pop macro would look like this:

```
(defmacro my-pop (input-list)
  (let ((var (gentemp))) ;create a unique variable
```

```
`(let ((,var (first ,input-list)))
   (setf ,input-list (rest ,input-list))
   ,var)))
```

This version of `my-pop` neatly avoids the variable capture problem
found in the previous version, as you can see when the macro is
expanded:

```
CL> (macroexpand '(my-pop first-element))
(LET ((T3 (FIRST FIRST-ELEMENT)))
(SETF FIRST-ELEMENT (REST FIRST-ELEMENT))
T3)
T
```

*Macros and Lambda-List
Keywords*

The lambda-list keywords, discussed in the last section, work for
macros just as they do for functions, with the important exception
that the arguments are passed unevaluated. You can, for instance,
define macros using `&optional` and `&rest` that can handle a
variable number of arguments (see Exercise 8.8 for an example).
You frequently see the lambda-list keyword `&body` used in macro
definitions. It works exactly the same way as the `&rest` keyword,
with which you are already familiar.

Guidelines for Using Macros

Since macros give you a capability not offered by Lisp functions
(namely, the ability to access elements of the argument list directly),
they can be considered a more general way of defining forms. There
is also a performance advantage to using macros. The reason is that
when a macro call is compiled, it is replaced by its expansion.[6] The
expansion is executed immediately, without the overhead of a
function invocation. The question therefore arises, why not define
everything as a macro?

Generally, macros are always a little more complicated to write
and debug than functions because of the indirect way in which they
are defined. Also, there are some forms that must be implemented
as functions. Macros cannot be passed as functional arguments to
`apply`, `funcall`, or `map`, for example.

The following can be used as guidelines when deciding whether
or not to implement something as a macro:

- Use macros when you must access passed arguments directly.
  Macros are the only mechanism provided in Common Lisp for

---

[6]Compilation in Common Lisp will be discussed later in this chapter.

accessing arguments before they have been evaluated. The two examples given in this section, nil! and my-pop, can only be implemented as macros.

- Use macros to implement utilities that help to simplify coding. Many Lisp programmers have private libraries of little routines, often referred to as utilities, that simplify coding and help to reduce typing. The nil! macro is an example of a utility routine. Experienced programmers like to implement utilities as macros because they know that they can then use the utilities freely without incurring the cost of a function call. The macro facility in Common Lisp is one of the features that makes the language easily extensible. It makes it possible to customize the language for specific applications or to accommodate personal programming styles.

- Avoid using macros to implement large or important components of your programs. Macros can be difficult to debug, and they can produce obscure and unreadable code. Macros are handy and in some cases essential tools, but they should be used in moderation.

Exercise 8.8

Write a new version of if that uses the symbols then and else to separate its clauses (just like the IF statement in Pascal). For example:

```
CL> (pif t then "consequent-1" else "consequent-2")
"consequent-1"
```

Exercise 8.9

What do the following macros do?

a. (defmacro mystery-macro-1 (var)

```
`(setf ,var (1+ ,var)))
```

b. (defmacro mystery-macro-2 (var1 var2)

```
(let ((temp1 (gentemp))
      (temp2 (gentemp)))
  `(let ((,temp1 ,var1)
         (,temp2 ,var2))
     (setf ,var1 ,temp2)
     (setf ,var2 ,temp1)))))
```

Exercise 8.10

Write a `while` macro for conditional looping. Its form is:

```
(while conditional-clause
 exit-form
 body)
```

It should loop over the forms in the *body* while the value of the *conditional-clause* is non-nil. The *conditional-clause* should be tested prior to each pass through the loop. The *exit-form* should be evaluated once, when exiting the loop.

Exercise 8.11

Define a `macro-factorial` macro that will expand and compute the factorial of a number.

Exercise 8.12

Rewrite `my-pop` to work with sequences instead of lists.

Exercise 8.13

Try implementing `pull` (from Exercise 4.13) as a macro.

Exercise 8.14 (*)

Sometimes variable capture in a macro can be a good thing. For example, you could write yet another version of `if` that binds the value of the *conditional-clause* to the local symbol `it`. This symbol could then be referenced within the *then-clause* or the *else-clause*. This could be useful when the *conditional-clause* is either computationally expensive or has side effects. An example of this version of `if`, called `aif` (for *anaphoric if*), is

```
(aif (read some-stream nil nil)
  (process it))
```

Exercise 8.15 (*)

In the chess program (see Appendix D), the `legal-move-p` method tests to see if a piece can move to a specified destination. For certain classes of pieces (i.e., rooks, bishops, and queens) you must also check to make sure that the path from the current position to the new position is not obstructed. A `clear-path-p` method could be described as follows:

```
(defmethod clear-path-p ((piece chess-piece) new-position)
   ;;make sure the path between the piece and the new-position
   ;;is clear of obstructing pieces
```

```
(with-slots (position game) piece
  (let ((new-rank (position-rank New-position))
        (old-rank (position-rank position))
        (new-file (position-file new-position))
        old-file (position-file position))
        (board (slot-value game 'chess-board)))
    (let ((rank-init (cond ((= old-rank new-rank)
                             old-rank)
                           ((> old-rank new-rank)
                            (1- old-rank))
                           ((< old-rank new-rank)
                            (1+ old-rank))))
          (file-init (cond ((= old-file new-file)
                             old-file)
                           ((> old-file new-file)
                            (1- old-file))
                           ((< old-file new-file)
                            (1+ old-file))))
          (rank-step (cond ((= old-rank new-rank)
                             'rank)
                           ((> old-rank new-rank)
                            '(1- rank))
                           ((< old-rank new-rank)
                            '(1+ rank))))
          (file-step (cond ((= old-file new-file)
                             'file)
                           ((> old-file new-file)
                            '(1- file))
                           ((< old-file new-file)
                            '(1+ file)))))
      (construct-do rank-init rank-step file-init file-step
                    board new-position)))))
```

The construct-do macro takes the computed initialization and step forms and constructs a do expression between the current position and the new position for obstructing pieces. Write the construct-do macro and modify the legal-move-p generic function to use clear-path-p.

8.3 LEXICAL CLOSURES

In Chapter 3, a function called generate-number was defined to generate a new number every time it was called. It used a global variable to keep track of the last number generated between invocations of the function. It was suggested at the time that this was not the best way to write a generator function in Common Lisp. In this section, you will discover another mechanism for preserving the state of a function using a feature of Common Lisp called *lexical closures*.

Before explaining what the term *lexical closure* means, let's see how `generate-number` could be rewritten. First, you must define a new function called `make-generator` to define and return a new functional object. This is done as follows:

```
(defun make-generator ()
  (let ((last-value 0))
    #'(lambda ()
        (setf last-value (1+ last-value)))))
```

The code in the lambda expression is basically the same as the code in the old version of `generate-number`, except that it replaces all references to the `*last-value*` global symbol with references to the `last-value` local variable. The functional object (which is actually a lexical closure) returned by `make-generator` can be assigned to a symbol as follows:

```
CL> (defvar *my-generator* (make-generator))
*MY GENERATOR*
```

You can then write a new version of `generate-number` using the lexical closure as follows:

```
(defun generate-number2 ()
  (funcall *my-generator*))
```

This version of `generate-number` behaves exactly the same way as the old version, but it uses a lexical closure instead of a global variable to store the state of the function.

```
CL> (generate-number2)
1
CL> (generate-number2)
2
CL> (generate-number2)
3
```

Free Variables

The `last-value` variable is not local to the lambda form defined in `make-generator`. Nonlocally defined variables, that are referenced within the definition of a function are referred to as *free* variables. In this case, the `last-value` variable is defined in the surrounding function (its so-called lexical environment). When you create a new functional object, information is stored about the lexical environment in which the object was defined. In particular, if any free variables defined in the functional object have bindings within the surrounding definitional environment, those bindings are preserved for future use.

Dealing Cards

A more interesting example of a lexical closure uses sampling without replacement. In Exercise 5.7, you wrote a function to deal a hand of cards. Cards were represented as instances of the CLOS class defined as follows:

```
(defclass playing-card ()
  (suit :initarg :suit
   rank :initarg :rank))
```

Assume that cards in a deck are mapped to the set of integers between 0 and 51 as follows:

```
(defun compute-suit (number)
  (elt *card-suits* (floor number 13)))
(defun compute-rank (number)
  (elt *card-ranks* (mod number 13)))
```

where the following two vectors have been previously defined as global constants:

```
(defconstant *card-suits*
             '#(hearts clubs diamonds spades))
(defconstant *card-ranks*
             '#(ace 2 3 4 5 6 7 8 9 10 jack queen king))
```

You could then define a function to create a deck of cards implemented as a lexical closure as follows:

```
(defun make-deck (deck-size)
  (let (dealt-cards)
    #'(lambda ()
        (if (< (length dealt-cards) deck-size)
            (let ((card (pick-card dealt-cards
                                   deck-size)))
              (push card dealt-cards)
              (make-instance 'playing-card
                             :suit (compute-suit card)
                             :rank (compute-rank card)))))))
```

where `pick-card` is defined as

```
(defun pick-card (dealt-cards deck-size)
  (do ((s (random deck-size)(random deck-size)))
      ((not (member s dealt-cards)) s)))
```

The `pick-card` function randomly selects a number in the range and then tests to see if it was previously chosen.

A `deal` function could be defined to operate on the lexical closure objects generated by `make-deck`:

```
(defun deal (deck)
  (funcall deck))
```

Every time we call the `deal` function on a deck, it will return a new, randomly selected card. For example:

```
CL> (setf my-deck (make-deck 51))
#<A Lexical Closure>
CL> (let ((card (deal my-deck)))
      (values (slot-value card 'rank)
              (slot-value card 'suit)))
KING
HEARTS
```

Functional Composition

Lexical closures can be used to create new functions that combine the behavior of other, previously defined functions. This is referred to as *functional composition*. For example, the `cadr` function combines the behavior of the `car` and `cdr` functions (or the `first` and `rest` functions, using the more mnemonic function names). When the `cadr` function is invoked on a list, it returns the first element of the rest of the list as follows:

```
CL> (cadr '(a b c d))
B
```

You could define a function that would take two functions as arguments and return a lexical closure consisting of their composition. This function would look like this:

```
(defun compose (fun1 fun2)
  #'(lambda (arg)
      (funcall fun1 (funcall fun2 arg))))
```

You could then use this function to define your own version of cadr like this:

```
(defun my-cadr (arg)
   (funcall (compose #'first #'rest) arg))
```

This would have the same behavior as the system-defined version of cadr, that is:

```
CL> (my-cadr '(a b c d))
B
```

complement Function

The complement function defined in the ANSI standard is implemented using functional composition. It takes a functional object (usually a predicate) as an argument and returns a new functional object that is the logical complement of the passed predicate. For example, the count-if function takes a predicate and a sequence as arguments. It returns the number of sequence elements that satisfy the predicate:

```
CL> (defvar mixed-list '(x y z 100 3.12))
MIXED-LIST
CL> (count-if #'numberp mixed-list)
2
```

You could use the complement function to find out how many of the sequence elements fail to satisfy the predicate. For example:

```
CL> (count-if (complement #'numberp) mixed-list)
3
```

This is the same result that you would have obtained had you used the built-in count-if-not function.

Lexical Closures

Lexical closures offer another way of abstracting data. They are unusual in that they blur the traditional distinction that we maintain between data and code. A lexical closure is both a data object and an executable entity. Lexical closures are a rather exotic feature of the language. You will probably not use them every day. They are good to know about, though, as they occasionally come in very handy and provide some insight into how Common Lisp works. We will take up the topic of lexical closures in the next chapter when we discuss scope and extent.

Exercise 8.16

How do you explain the difference in behavior between `test-fun-1` and `test-fun-2`?

```
CL> (defun test-fun-1 ()
       (let ((my-generator (make-generator)))
         (values (funcall my-generator)
                 (funcall my-generator))))
TEST-FUN-1
CL> (test-fun-1)
1
2
CL> (defun test-fun-2 ()
       (values (funcall (make-generator))
               (funcall (make-generator))))
TEST-FUN-2
CL> (test-fun-2)
1
1
```

Exercise 8.17

Write a function called `create-new-account` that generates a lexical closure to represent a savings account. Write `account-withdrawal` and `account-deposit` functions that accept an account object and a dollar amount as arguments. For example:

```
CL> (setf my-account (create-new-account 1000.00))
#<A Lexical Closure>
CL> (account-withdrawal my-account 100.00)
900.0
CL> (account-deposit my-account 250.00)
1150.0
```

Exercise 8.18

Blackjack dealers in casinos deal from *shoes* that contain four or more decks shuffled together. Modify the card dealer example to deal from a shoe instead of from a single deck.

Exercise 8.19

Write your own version of the `complement` function called `my-complement`.

Exercise 8.20 (*)

Rewrite the `compose` function so that it works with a variable number of functional arguments. For example:

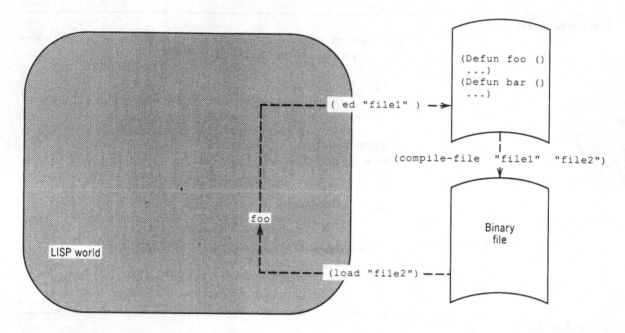

Figure 8-5 Compiling and loading Lisp source files

```
CL> (funcall (compose #'car #'cdr #'cdr) '(a b c d e))
C
```

8.4 THE COMPILER

Up to now, you have used the interpreter to execute everything you have written, but Common Lisp functions can also be compiled. Unlike languages such as Fortran, Common Lisp does not require you to compile your code to run it, but you can if you wish. Functions are compiled to make them run faster. The usual strategy is to run the function interpreted until it is debugged and then compile it. This process is known as *incremental compilation*. Incremental compilation is possible because Lisp allows you to have calls to both compiled and interpreted functions within a single application.

The `compile` *Function*

The Lisp compiler is implemented as a Lisp function. You compile a function in Common Lisp by calling the `compile` function on the specified function.[7] For example:

```
CL> (defun cube (n)
    (* n n n))
CUBE
CL> (compile 'cube)
CUBE
```

After a call to compile, the symbol-function slot of the file name is altered to point to the compiled rather than the interpreted definition. Subsequent calls to the cube function then execute the compiled version.

The `compile-file` Function

If you have stored one or more functions in a file, you can use the compile-file function to compile all the functions and create a binary file containing compiled definitions of the function(s). As shown in Figure 8-5, the contents of a binary file can be brought into the Lisp world using the load function. Using the compile-file function to create a binary file saves you the effort of recompiling functions every time you reload them.

Macros and the Compiler

Calls to a macro are treated differently from function calls by the compiler. When the compiler encounters a reference to a macro, it replaces the macro call with the expansion for the macro. This has two important implications for the programmer. First, if you are storing your code in a file, you must be certain that the compiler reads the macro definition before it encounters any calls to that macro. The compiler cannot discriminate syntactically between a function call and a macro call; if you haven't notified it in advance that a certain form is to be treated as a macro (by providing a macro definition),,calls to that form will not be compiled properly. Second, if you change a macro definition, you must make sure that all code that calls that macro is recompiled; otherwise, some of your compiled code will continue to contain an expansion of the obsolete macro definition.

Code Optimization

Functions run faster after compilation because the compiler translates the body of the function into the underlying machine language

---

[7]In some implementations of Common Lisp (such as Apple Common Lisp), functions are automatically compiled when they are defined.

for the machine on which you are working.[8] This means that the function can be executed directly without any further translation. Smart compilers, known as *optimizing compilers*, can sometimes improve performance even further by cleverly modifying the translated code in such a way that it runs faster but has the same behavior as the original Lisp function. For example, the overhead of performing a function call can sometimes be avoided by *open-coding* a function. This means that the compiler inserts the body of the function itself in place of the function call. A related technique is to convert recursive calls within a function into an iterative form, thereby avoiding multiple function calls. Common Lisp syntax allows the programmer to make certain declarations at the time that a function is defined, making it possible for the compiler to better optimize the compiled code.

Common Lisp Declarations

When defining a function, declarations follow the `lambda-list`. For example:

```
(defun cube (n)
  (declare (type integer n))
  (* n n n))
```

Declarations assume the form of a list. The first element of the list is the `declare` symbol; the remaining elements are *declaration-spec*s. A *declaration-spec* is itself a list whose first element is a declaration type. There are several types of declarations: those that specify data types for variables and forms used in the function, those that specify which functions can or cannot be open-coded, and declarations that determine how the function should be optimized.

type Declaration

The preceding declaration stipulates that only integer values will be passed for the n parameter. Knowing this, the compiler needn't generate any code to test for the type of the argument at runtime. This will make the function slightly smaller and faster. You can also specify that the function * will return an integer value by typing

```
(defun cube (n)
  (declare (function * (integer integer integer)
                      integer))
  (* n n n))
```

[8]If you're curious about what this code looks like for your machine, you can call the `disassemble` function on a compiled function to see the translated version.

inline Declaration

You can tell the compiler to open-code a function code using the `inline` declaration. For example, you can suggest that the call to `*` in cube be open-coded by typing

```
(defun cube (n)
  (declare (inline *))
  (* n n n))
```

If, on the other hand, you wish to guarantee that a function call will not be open-coded you can use the `notinline` declaration. Note that declaring a function to be `inline` does not necessarily mean that the compiler will open-code the function. It only relays the information that the programmer has no objection to the function's being open-coded.

optimize Declaration

Programmers have different notions about how they want their functions optimized by the compiler. For instance, the programmer may be more concerned about making the function as small as possible, even at the cost of making it slower. Or the programmer may want to ensure, at all costs, that the function returns a reliable result. The `optimize` declaration can be used to advise the compiler about the programmer's optimization priorities. Common Lisp recognizes three kinds of optimization: for execution speed, for the size of the function at runtime, and for runtime error checking. These three types of optimization are associated with the symbols `speed`, `safety`, and `size`. You may specify a numeric priority (0 to 3, inclusive) for each type of optimization. For example, to pull out all the stops and make your cube function really perform, you could type

```
(defun cube (n)
  (declare (optimize (speed 3) (safety 0) (size 0)))
  (* n n n))
```

Performance Tuning

The features described in this section make it possible to take a completed, logically correct program and make it run faster, which is a completely reasonable objective. Your strategy, however, should be to attain correctness first and address performance later. You may wonder why both issues cannot be dealt with concurrently. For small, simple applications this may be possible, but as the complexity of the application increases, the programmer's efforts should be concentrated on making the program work. Declarations are meant to provide clues to the compiler about how the programmer intends the code to be used, but declarations also impose constraints on how the code *can* be used. To some degree, then, the use of declarations is antithetical to the notion of Lisp as an exploratory programming language. As you will recall from Chapter 1, one of the features of Lisp is that it allows programmers to defer many design decisions up to the time of execution. This provides great flexibility in solving large, poorly-structured problems. The designers of Common Lisp hoped to create a language that could be used both for exploratory programming and to deliver a finished application. Because Common Lisp can be used in both ways, it is the programmer's responsibility to ensure that it is used properly.

Exercise 8.21

Write a recursive function to compute the factorial of a number. Declare that the value passed to the function will always be an integer and that the internal call to * can be open-coded. Compile and run your function.

Exercise 8.22

There is a macro called `time` in Common Lisp that can be used to compute the amount of elapsed time needed to evaluate a Common Lisp form. Evaluate the following call to the `tak` function (from Exercise 3.12) before and after compiling the `tak` function in your Common Lisp implementation:

```
(time (tak 18 12 6))
```

Timings for other implementations of Lisp can be found in Gabriel, 1985.

Exercise 8.23 (*)

One type of optimization used by Lisp compilers is called *tail recursion* optimization. It speeds up the execution of recursive code by translating it into an efficient iterative form. A function is considered tail recursive if the value returned by the function is the value of the recursive call within the function. Conduct a little experiment to see if your compiler uses tail recursion optimization. Write iterative and recursive versions of a tail recursive function. Compare their performance running both interpreted and compiled, using the `time` macro. Does your compiler perform this type of optimization?

8.5 VERIFYING CORRECTNESS

As you start writing larger and larger applications, you may discover that it becomes increasingly difficult to get your programs to work correctly. In this section, we will discuss what it means to produce a correct program and describe some strategies for achieving this goal with a minimum of effort. The term *program* is used here loosely to mean a piece of code developed to serve a specific purpose. A simple Lisp expression could meet this definition, but more commonly when we talk about a program, we are thinking of a larger body of code consisting of many functions (and possibly macros) designed to work together to solve a particular problem.

Correctness

When is a program correct? Minimally, a correct program should have the following properties:

1. It should load and/or compile without error.
2. Given an appropriate set of input, it should run to completion without breaking.
3. It should produce correct output.

Naturally, this definition raises additional questions, such as what constitutes *an appropriate set of input* and what *correct output* means? These terms are meaningful only in the context of the advertised features of the program. The external documentation should define the behavior of the program and specify the domain over which it operates. Assuming that such documentation exists, it may still be a non-trivial task to produce a program that has the preceding properties. However, there are certain general programming strategies that serve to simplify this process. Common Lisp provides some general-purpose debugging tools that can be used to implement these strategies.

Debug in Isolation

The first and possibly most important strategy for developing correct programs is to develop the program in pieces and to debug each piece as it is developed. It is much easier to debug a small function by itself than it is to debug a large program with hundreds of functions and thousands of lines of code. Just as a mason constructs a wall one brick at a time; so must you as a programmer construct your programs one form after another. Structured programming techniques endorse a *top-down* design strategy, but coding and debugging should be done from the *bottomup*.

step Macro

Because Lisp is an interpreted language, it lends itself easily to this sort of incremental debugging process. Individual forms can be evaluated in isolation in Lisp, allowing you verify the performance of a function expression by expression. Common Lisp has a macro called step to facilitate this kind of testing. It is called with an unquoted form as an argument and allows you to see each subexpression evaluated independently. The way this information is displayed and the options that are available at each step vary greatly from implementation to implementation. Experiment with the stepping facilities available on your system to see exactly how step works.

Divide and Conquer

A second strategy that can be employed in debugging is to try to localize faults by dividing the code into pieces. As an example, suppose that you have a program that fails and gives you an error message, but you don't have a clue as to where the problem is occurring. Rather than stepping through the code, which can be quite tedious with a large program, you can rerun the program with a breakpoint inserted. If the program reaches the breakpoint without issuing the error message, then the problem must reside further along in the code. If the error occurs prior to the breakpoint, then you need to move the breakpoint further ahead in the program.

break *Function*

Common Lisp provides a function called break that can be used to establish breakpoints in a program. The syntax of a call to break is

```
(break format-string arg-1 arg-2 . . . arg-n)
```

All of the arguments are optional. If provided, break behaves as though it were a call to format with the *format-stream* argument set to t (that is, it will evaluate *arg-1* through *arg-n*, display a string formatted according to the *format-string*, and return nil). This offers a convenient mechanism for printing the values of local variables.

In all cases, evaluation of a break form will cause the execution of the program to be interrupted. Most Common Lisp implementations allow several options from this interrupted state, such as reassigning variables, evaluating expressions, or continuing or aborting the execution. Once again, you will have to do some experimenting to see how the break facility works in your implementation. In some implementations, the break facility is quite elaborate and can be very powerful. Learning how to use it productively can simplify the debugging process.

Dispatching Macros

One trick that some programmers use is to flag their breakpoints with a read macro. For example, you could insert the following break into a form:

```
#+debug (break "foo is ~a" foo)
```

The dispatching #+debug macro controls the reading of the subsequent form. At read time, if the debug symbol was stored on the list associated with the *features* global variable, the break form would be read in; otherwise, it would be ignored. This allows you to switch debugging on and off globally by manipulating the value of the *features* list.

Data Probes

Another testing strategy is to install probes in your code that allow you to check variable bindings periodically as the program executes. This can be done in a number of ways. Some programmers simply insert format or print statements at strategic points in the code, which they then remove (or comment out) when debugging is finished. Using the break function with a *format-string* and a list of variables is a better approach because it enables you to take advantage all of the features of the break facility.

trace Function

The trace function, described in Chapter 3, can also be used to display intermediate results. The advantage of using trace to monitor the performance of the program is that it does not require any changes to the actual code. The trace function only displays values passed and returned by functions, however, so it is not useful for monitoring local variables; nor can it be used to debug macros.

inspect Function

Simply printing a data structure may not be very enlightening if the data structure is large and complicated. If you are working with arrays or large data tables, or with structures and CLOS objects containing components; the inspect function can be very useful. For example, if you were debugging a function that is supposed to return a three-dimensional array, you can wrap a call to inspect around the call to the function in order to view the generated data structure more easily. As with step and break, the behavior of the inspect function varies among implementations. Samples of how inspect displays an array and a structure in one Common Lisp implementation were shown in Chapters 4 and 5. Try a few test cases in your implementation to see how it works.

Access-Oriented Programming

When working with objects that use accessor functions (as discussed in Chapter 6), it is possible to install data probes by creating auxiliary methods for the accessor function. You could, for example, create a `:before` method that would notify you every time someone tried to read or to write into a specified slot. This is a very handy way to monitor the contents of an object's slots, because the probe can be established and removed without touching any of the code being tested. This technique assumes, of course, that all users will access the slot only through the accessor function. There is no way to monitor accesses if the slot is accessed directly using `slot-value`.

Developing Test Suites

Many experienced programmers like to develop sets of sample inputs, called *test suites*, when they code. This is a good thing to do, not only for the program as a whole, but also for individual functions within the program. There is an art to designing good test suites. In general, you want to make sure that all of the code is exercised and that the boundary cases are covered. Boundary cases are examples that occur at the limits of the domain over which your program operates. If you are writing a factorial function, which should work over the domain of natural numbers, you might want to have some test cases to make sure that it work for 0 and 1. A good set of test cases should not be discarded after the program appears to be debugged. An old test suite can often be very handy for future programmers. It can be reused, after the program has been modified, to see if it still works. Test suites for a program should be preserved with the source codes or in the documentation.

Program Verification

In this section, four strategies were discussed for establishing program correctness: debugging incrementally, partitioning code using breakpoints, using data probes and developing test suites.

TABLE 8-1   *Summary of Common Lisp Defining Forms*

	Arguments Evaluated	Arguments Not Evaluated
Fixed Number of Arguments	defun	defmacro
Variable Number of Arguments	defun with &rest	defmacro with &body

These strategies can only establish incorrectness, not correctness. This is because, regardless of how many test cases you run, you cannot prove that a program is correct, although you can prove incorrectness with a single test. However, after thorough testing, your confidence will grow that the program is *likely* to be correct, and in most cases that is sufficient. Formal techniques, based on induction, do exist for proving correctness (Manna, 1974), but these have not yet found their way into general practice.

SUMMARY

This chapter provided further detail about how functions are evaluated in Common Lisp. There are features in the language that enable the programmer to exert some control over how the arguments to a function are spread, whether or not the arguments will be evaluated, and the number of values that are returned by a function. A summary of the Common Lisp defining forms described in this chapter is found in Table 8-1.

The spreading of arguments can be controlled in Common Lisp using lambda-list keywords. The most important keywords are &optional, &rest, and &key. The &optional keyword permits the inclusion of optional arguments, &rest allows you to define functions with variable-length argument lists, and &key can be used to define functions that allow keyword arguments.

Some of the built-in functions in Common Lisp, such as get-decoded-time and round, return more than one value. Using the Common Lisp values function, you can write functions that return multiple values. The multiple-value-bind and multiple-value-list macros are used to capture multiple values.

The only way to define a form in Common Lisp that does not evaluate its arguments is to implement the form as a macro. Macros are defined using the defmacro macro. Macros are expanded before they are executed. When you write a macro, you write code that is evaluated to generate a new piece of code (i.e., the macro expansion), which is then evaluated. The backquote macro character can often simplify the process of writing code that generates code. Within a backquoted form, it is possible to force evaluation by preceding subforms with a comma.

Lexical closures consist of a functional object and a set of bindings for all free variables within the function. Because lexical closures can retain these bindings between calls to the function, they are often used to implement functions that work like generators. Generators need to store information about their state between invocations. Generators implemented as lexical closures need not resort to using global variables to store their state.

You can improve the performance of Common Lisp functions by compiling them. Individual functions can be compiled by calling the Lisp `compile` function. Incremental compilation is the strategy whereby each function is debugged in an interpreted form and then compiled. Lisp allows you to have calls to both interpreted and compiled functions within a common program. By inserting declarations in your functions, you can provide clues to the compiler about how the code can be optimized.

Four strategies were discussed for verifying the correctness of programs: coding and debugging incrementally, partitioning the body of code using breakpoints to isolate faults, using data probes to monitor data values during execution, and developing test suites. Common Lisp provides a number of helpful built-in forms like `break`, `trace`, `step`, and `inspect` to aid in debugging new code.

NEW COMMON LISP DEFINED NAMES

break	disassemble	multiple-value-bind
ceiling	fceiling	multiple-value-list
compile	*features*	realpart
compile-file	ffloor	round
complement	floor	step
count-if	fround	truncate
count-if-not	ftruncate	values
declare	imagpart	` (backquote character)
decode-float	macroexpand	
defmacro	macroexpand-1	

FOR FURTHER READING

Further information about the lambda-list keywords can be found in Section 5.2.2 of Steele's book (Steele, 1990). Multiple values are discussed in Section 7.10. Steele's book has a whole chapter (Chapter 8) devoted to macros. Additional information about writing macros can be found in the Graham article (Graham, 1988b). Lexical closures are discussed briefly in Steele in Section 7.1.1 and in Chapter 3. The Common Lisp compiler is described in Section 25.1; declarations are covered in Chapter 9; read dispatch macros in 22.1.4; and debugging facilities in Section 25.3. For background reading on compiler design and code optimization consult a compiler text (e.g., Aho et al., 1986 or Trembly & Sorenson, 1986). The Manna text (Manna, 1974) describes formal program verification.

Project 8.1

Write a program to simulate a blackjack game. The program should play as the dealer. It should deal cards to all players and to itself, and then play out the hand. The complete rules of the game can be found in Appendix E.

Project 8.2

Put together a suite of benchmark programs that exercise different aspects of a Lisp implementation (e.g., constructing lists, deep recursion, floating-point arithmetic, etc.). You may consult (Gabriel, 1985) for some ideas. Time your benchmark suite on a variety of Common Lisp implementations. If possible, try to compare a range of hardware architectures, such as Lisp machines, PCs, mainframes, and high-speed workstations.

9

Program Structure

Beauty from order springs.
William King, The Art of Cookery (1708)

9.1 STRUCTURING CODE

Earlier dialects of Lisp had a form known as `prog`, which Steele refers to as the *Program Feature* (Steele, 1990). Although Common Lisp supports `prog` as a macro, its use is not encouraged. Using `prog`, it was possible to write completely inscrutable code that was difficult to read and maintain. The designers of Common Lisp sought a way to offer programmers many of the capabilities of `prog`, but in a way that would foster a more structured style of programming.

The `prog` macro and its relative, `prog*`, do three things: they allow the ordered execution of a sequence of forms, they permit the embedding of labels within Lisp code for the purpose of branching, and they introduce local variables. There are individual language constructs in Common Lisp for accomplishing each of these goals independently without using `prog`.

251

Sequencing

For example, Common Lisp has a special form called `progn` that allows the sequential execution of a set of forms. The `progn` special form should not be confused with the more elaborate `prog` and `prog*` forms. It does not allow the incorporation of labels, nor does it introduce local variables. A call to `progn` has the following form:

```
(progn form-1 form-2 . . . form-n)
```

The forms in a call to `progn` are evaluated in left-to-right order. The value (or values) of the last form is (are) returned. As an example of the use of `progn`, consider the problem of the multi-consequent `if`. Suppose that you have more than one form that you would like to have evaluated when a condition is satisfied. Rather than testing the condition several times, you could wrap a call to `progn` around all of the consequents to produce a single form for use in the call to `if`:

```
(if (listp var)
  (progn
    (print (first var))
    (setf var (rest var))))
```

Implicit `progns`

Simple sequencing occurs frequently in Common Lisp code, even when you do not issue an explicit call to `progn`. You can have more than one form in the body of a call to `let`, for example. When the body is executed, the `let` form returns the value(s) of the last form in the body. This is an example of what is known as an *implicit* `progn`. Many Common Lisp forms were designed to behave as if they contained a nested call to `progn`.

`prog1` and `prog2`

Occasionally you may prefer to have a sequence of forms return the value of the first form rather than the last. For example, the `pull` macro from Exercise 7.12 could be written as follows:

```
(defmacro pull (input-list)
  (let ((var (gentemp)))
    `(let ((,var (first (last ,input-list))))
       (setf ,input-list (nbutlast ,input-list))
       ,var)))
```

The local variable statement generated in the macroexpansion is needed to capture the value of the last element of the list before the reassignment. There is a macro called `prog1` that returns the value of the first form in the sequence. Using `prog1`, the definition of `pull` could be simplified to[1]

```
(defmacro pull (input-list)
  `(prog1
     (first (last ,input-list))
     (setf ,input-list (nbutlast ,input-list))))
```

In the unusual situation where you want to return the value of the second rather than the first form, there is another macro called `prog2` that will serve your needs.

block Special Form

An alternative way of doing sequencing in Common Lisp is to use the `block` special form. The form of a call to `block` is as follows:

```
(block block-label form-1 form-2 . . . form-n)
```

where *block-label* is usually a symbol. As with `progn`, the forms in a call to `block` are evaluated from left to right and the value of the last form is returned. The big difference is that you can exit the body of a block form prematurely by evaluating a call to `return-from`. Exiting will be discussed in some detail later in this chapter.

tagbody Special Form

Another feature of the `prog` macro is that it allows you to insert tags into code that can be used as targets for branching. The `go` special form can be used within a `prog` to branch to the specified tag. The `prog` macro is implemented using the `tagbody` special form . This special form permits branching to tags within its body but does not support the other features of the `prog` macro (e.g., introducing variables). Within the body of a `tagbody`, lists are evaluated as always, but free-standing symbols or numbers (for you old Basic programmers) are treated as tags and are not evaluated. When the form

```
(go tag)
```

is evaluated, control branches to the next form within the `tagbody` following the specified *tag*. Only tags defined within the surrounding `tagbody` are accessible for branching.

---

[1]The macroexpansion for `pull` may look the same for both versions depending on how your implementation of Common Lisp expands the `prog1` macro.

As an example of how you could use `tagbody`, consider how you would write your own version of the Common Lisp `loop` macro. As you may recall from Chapter 3, the Common Lisp `loop` macro produces simple looping behavior. The following expression loops indefinitely:

```
(let ((counter 0))
  (loop
   (setf counter (1+ counter))
   (print counter)))
```

You could write your own version of `loop` as follows:

```
(defmacro my-loop (&body body)
;;;not quite correct
   `(tagbody top-of-loop
             ,@body
             (go top-of-loop)))
```

The macro wraps a call to `tagbody` around the body of the loop.[2] It also defines a tag before the body of the loop so that after the body has been processed, control can be directed to the top of the loop again. The expansion of this macro is

```
CL> (pprint (macroexpand '(my-loop
                           (setf counter
                                (1+ counter))
                           (print counter))))
(TAGBODY TOP-OF-LOOP
         (SETF COUNTER (1+ COUNTER))
         (PRINT COUNTER)
         (GO TOP-OF-LOOP))
```

This gives you the behavior you are seeking. There is a minor variable capture problem here, however, which could be corrected by redefining `my-loop` in this way:

```
(defmacro my-loop (&body body)
;;;the better way
   (let ((top-of-loop (gensym)))
     `(tagbody ,top-of-loop
               ,@body
               (go ,top-of-loop))))
```

---

[2]The `&body` keyword is frequently used in macro definitions. Basically, it does the same thing as the `&rest` keyword.

The macroexpansion now becomes

```
CL> (pprint (macroexpand '(my-loop
                            (setf counter
                                  (1+ counter))
                            (print counter))))
(TAGBODY #:G31
         (SETF COUNTER (1+ COUNTER))
         (PRINT COUNTER)
         (GO #:G31))
```

The Nefarious goto

The go special form is Common Lisp's version of the nefarious goto statement. The use of goto statements in other languages has been criticized as an unstructured way to program (Dahl, et al., 1972). The argument is that the undisciplined use of gotos make it difficult to discern the logic of a program. A program with a flow of control that resembles a plate of spaghetti is very hard to read. Advocates of *structured* programming prefer to use control constructs such as if-then-else rather than goto. Experienced Common Lisp programmers seldom use the special form go for many of the same reasons. Where possible, it is preferable to use the built-in control constructs such as case, if, cond, and when. In situations where a specialized type of control is needed, it is best to define a macro utility that conceals the actual call(s) to go and the surrounding tagbody.

Variable Introduction

The third service provided by the prog macro is variable introduction. The prog macro permits the programmer to create and optionally initialize local variables. In this book, you have been using the let special form for this same purpose. Like tagbody, let provides a subset of the capabilities of prog. It allows you to create local variables, but does support the use of return-from or go.

There is a special version of prog called prog* that binds its variables sequentially rather than in parallel, as is done in prog and let. This is similar to the difference between let and let*.

Using prog

The prog macro has the combined capabilities of the block (allows return-from), tagbody (allows go), and let (variable-introducing) special forms. In most cases, only one of these capabilities is needed. It is more efficient and is considered better style to use the simplest construct or set of constructs that serves your needs. For example, one shouldn't use block when progn would suffice, and one should avoid using prog when a simple call to block, let, or tagbody would serve as well.

Exercise 9.1

Can you rewrite the following function in order to make it easier to read?

```
(defun spaghetti-fun (some-list)
  (let ((to-do some-list))
    (tagbody
      top-of-loop
      (if (null to-do) (go out))
      (print (first to-do))
      (setf to-do (rest to-do))
      (go top-of-loop)
      out)))
```

Exercise 9.2

It is considered bad form to use a prog when it is not necessary. Rewrite the following without using prog:

```
(defun unnecessary-prog-fun (number-list)
  (prog ((result 0)
         (to-do number-list))
    top-of-loop
    (if (null to-do) (return result))
    (setf result (+ result (first to-do)))
    (setf to-do (rest to-do))
    (go top-of-loop)))
```

Exercise 9.3

Write an until macro for conditional looping. Its general form should be

```
(until conditional-clause
       exit-form
       body)
```

It differs from the while macro (in Exercise 8.10) in the two following ways: the conditional-clause is tested at the bottom of the loop, and it should continue to loop until the value of the conditional-clause is non-nil.

Exercise 9.4

The form of a call to prog is as follows:

```
(prog variable-list
      declarations
      body)
```

Assuming that there are no declarations, write a macro called my-prog that has the same behavior as prog.

Exercise 9.5

Repeat Exercise 9.4 for prog*.

9.2 LEXICAL VERSUS DYNAMIC SCOPING

Consider the following code:

```
CL> (defun mumble (foo)
        (fumble))
MUMBLE
CL> (defun fumble ()
        (grumble))
FUMBLE
CL> (defun grumble ()
        (print foo))
GRUMBLE
CL> (mumble 'Hi!)
```

The foo variable in grumble is referred to as a *free variable*. Free variables, as you may recall, are variables used in a function that are not locally bound. The foo variable is not free in mumble because it appears in the lambda list and is bound to an argument when mumble is called. Will the reference to foo in grumble use the binding from mumble? This is one of the fundamental differences between Common Lisp and some of the earlier Lisp dialects. In some versions of Lisp, that is indeed what would happen, but in Common Lisp an *unbound variable* error would be produced.

Scoping Rules

There are some simple rules that determine where a variable binding can be referenced in Common Lisp. The range of places where a variable binding is valid is referred to as the *scope* of the binding. Common Lisp uses what is known as *lexical scoping*. In a lexically scoped language, a binding can be used only inside its defining form. A defining form could be a defun, a defmethod, a let, a do, or any other variable-introducing form. Earlier versions of Lisp used dynamic scoping. Dynamic scoping allows a variable binding to be accessible, not only in its defining form, but also in any function called directly or indirectly within the defining form. Under dynamic scoping, when the interpreter encounters the free variable foo in grumble, it looks to see if foo has a binding in fumble; if not, it uses the binding in mumble. The binding of foo in mumble is accessible to the grumble function because grumble is called indirectly by `mumble`. Lexically scoped bindings can be resolved at the time that a form is defined or compiled; references to dynamic bindings, however, cannot be resolved until runtime, hence the name *dynamic*.

Special Variables

If necessary, you can make Common Lisp variable bindings operate under dynamic scoping rules. This is done by declaring a variable to be *special*. The bindings of special variables in Common Lisp subscribe to dynamic rather than lexical scoping rules. For example:

```
CL> (defun mumble (foo)
       (declare (special foo))
       (fumble))
MUMBLE
CL> (defun fumble ()
       (grumble))
FUMBLE
CL> (defun grumble ()
       (declare (special foo))
       (print foo))
GRUMBLE
CL> (mumble 'Hi!)
HI!
HI!
```

The special declarations in `grumble` and `mumble` force the interpreter to use a dynamic rather than a lexical scoping rule for references to the `foo` variable. This means that rather than issuing an error message when it encounters the reference to `foo`, the interpreter looks up the chain of functions that lead to the call to `grumble` in search of a binding.

Activation Frames

Every time a function is called, a data structure called an *activation frame* or a *stack frame* is generated. The local bindings for that function are stored in the activation frame. The interpreter keeps track of the activation frames on the *runtime stack.* The functions that appear above a given function on the runtime stack constitute the *activation environment* for that function. When a special variable is used *freely*, the interpreter seeks a binding at runtime in the activation environment. For example, look at the reference to `foo` in `grumble` in Figure 9-1. The rectangles represent activation frames on the runtime stack. The enclosing box represents bindings of global variables at the Lisp top level. Since `foo` has no binding in the stack frame for `grumble`, the interpreter would look up the stack for the first activation frame that contained a binding for `foo`.

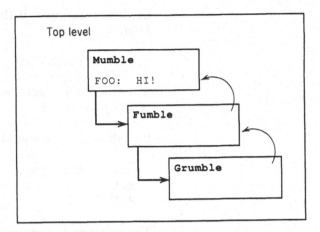

Figure 9-1   The activation environment for a dynamically scoped variable reference

Global Variables

Global variables also follow dynamic scoping rules. The original version of mumble/fumble/grumble could have been made to work by evaluating the form

```
(defvar foo 'Howdy!)
```

before the call to mumble.[3] The foo variable created by defvar will automatically be declared special.

Extent of a Binding

The period of time in which a binding is accessible is referred to as the *extent* of the binding. The extent of a binding differs from the *scope* of a binding. The scope determines *where* a binding can be referenced; the extent determines *when* it can be referenced. Bindings of global variables survive indefinitely. They have a different extent than bindings of local variables that have been declared special. These latter bindings remain in force only as long as the defining form resides on the runtime stack. The special binding of foo in mumble, for example, is undone once the call to mumble is completed.

Shadowing

If there is more than one special binding, the most recent one is

---

[3] It works because the free variable in grumble is assumed to be special.

used. For example, if the `fumble` function were redefined as follows:

```
(defun fumble ()
  (let ((foo 'Ho!))
    (declare (special foo))
    (grumble)))
```

the call to `mumble` would then return

```
CL> (mumble 'Hi!)
HO!
HO!
```

This situation is portrayed in Figure 9-2. The interpreter works its way back up the stack, looking for a special binding for `foo`. It now finds one in the `fumble` function, so the special binding in `grumble` and the global binding of `foo` are both ignored. We say that these bindings are *shadowed* by the binding in `fumble`.

Lexical Shadowing

Conflicting bindings can occur for lexically scoped variables as well. For instance, consider the following function definition:

```
(defun silly-but-fun (var)
  (let ((var (read)))
    (let ((var 'inner-binding))
      (print var))))
```

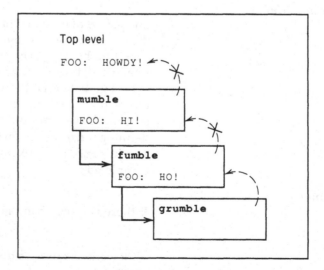

Figure 9-2 Shadowing of a dynamically scoped variable reference

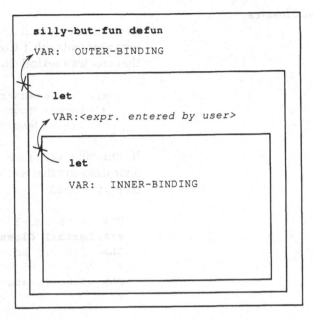

Figure 9-3   The definitional environment for a lexically scoped variable reference

In this contrived example, there are three bindings for var: the binding in the parameter list and the bindings in the two let forms. Which one takes precedence?

```
CL> (silly-but-fun 'outer-binding)
middle-binding
INNER-BINDING
INNER-BINDING
```

The accessible bindings for var are shown in Figure 9-3. This type of representation is sometimes referred to as a *contour plot* for the function. Each of the contours shows the lexical scope of a defining form. When a reference to a lexically scoped variable cannot be resolved within a defining form (such as a let or a do), the interpreter looks to the surrounding form for a binding. This process is repeated until a binding is found. If there is more than one binding (as in the case of silly-but-fun), the first binding encountered is used and the others are shadowed. The textual context of a defining form is known as its *lexical environment*. In resolving conflicts for a lexically scoped variable, the interpreter chooses the *contextually nearest* binding in the *lexical* environment; for a dynamically scoped variable, the most *recent* binding in the *activation* environment is used.

Lexical Closures

In the case of lexical closures, a function can carry its definitional environment with it. Consider, for example, the following function that creates a lexical closure:

```
(defun make-adder (addend)
  #'(lambda (num)
      (+ addend num)))
```

If you call `make-adder` with 3 as an argument, it will return a lexical closure that will have the following behavior when invoked using `funcall`:

```
CL> (setf add-3 (make-adder 3))
#<A Lexical Closure>
CL> (funcall add-3 4)
7
CL> (funcall add-3 6)
9
```

The `addend` variable is lexically scoped. It is bound in the definitional environment. A *lexical closure* consists of a functional definition and a set of bindings for the lexically scoped, free variables used in the function. Each time `make-adder` is called, it generates a new closure object that could conceivably have a different binding for `addend`. The bindings of the lexically scoped variables can be modified within the lexical closure object. Recall the `make-generator` function from Chapter 8:

```
(defun make-generator ()
  (let ((last-value 0))
    #'(lambda ()
        (setf last-value (1+ last-value)))))
```

The binding of the lexically scoped variable `last-value` is changed every time the lexical closure object is executed. The latest binding is retained within the closure object for later reference.

Lexical Function Definitions

So far, our discussion of lexical scoping has been confined to variable bindings, but there are circumstances where it would be useful for functional definitions to be lexically scoped as well. For example, suppose that you wish to write a function that takes a variable number of numeric arguments and returns their sum (which is exactly what the built-in + function already does). From the previous chapter, you know how to use the `&rest` lambda-list keyword to gather up the arguments in a list as follows:

```
(defun sum (&rest number-list)
  (sum-aux number-list))
```

The `sum-aux` helper function could then be used to CDR recursively down the list of numbers. It could be defined as

```
(defun sum-aux (numbers)
 (if numbers
    (+ (first numbers)
       (sum-aux (rest numbers)))
     0))
```

The problem with this approach is that since only `sum` ever calls `sum-aux`, there is no reason for the definition of `sum-aux` to be visible to the user.

`labels` Special Form

It would be nice to create local function definitions in the same way that you create local variables, and in fact, you already have the tools to do so. As you remember from Chapter 4, you can store a functional definition in the symbol-value cell of a symbol and invoke the function using `funcall` or `apply`. You could use `let` to create a local variable and initialize it to a functional definition. In practice, this is never done because it is clumsy (see Exercise 9.11) and because Common Lisp provides another special form for locally defining functions. The `labels` special form has the following syntax:

```
(labels ((name-1 arg-list-1 func-body-1)
         (name-2 arg-list-2 func-body-2)
           .
           .
           .
         (name-n arg-list-n func-body-n)
    lexical-body)
```

where *name-1* through *name-n* are locally defined symbols and *func-body-1* through *func-body-n* are their respective function bodies. The local functions so defined can be referenced only within the lexical scope of the `labels` form. For example, the preceding `sum` and `sum-aux` functions could be rewritten as

```
(defun sum-2 (&rest number-list)
  (labels ((sum-aux (numbers)
```

```
                            (if numbers
                              (+ (first numbers)
                                  (sum-aux (rest numbers)))
                              0)))
                         (sum-aux number-list)))
```

flet *and* macrolet

There are two other special forms that are closely related to the labels special form. The special form flet (pronounced *f-let*) is very similar to labels, except for the restriction that the local function names in a flet form can be referenced only in the *lexical-body*, not in the *func-bodies*. In a labels form, local function names can be used in the *func-bodies,* and the *func-bodies* can be recursive (as in the preceding sum-2 example). The flet form is most useful for locally redefining a global function name where you wish to reference the global definition when defining the local definition. The macrolet special form permits you to define macros locally.

Special versus Lexical Variables

In general, it is preferable to design your programs to use lexically scoped variables. One reason lexical scoping was chosen as the default in Common Lisp was that it is easier to read code when bindings are established within the lexical environment. This is in keeping with the principle of local transparency, discussed in Chapter 3, which holds that you should be able to understand the workings of a function without having to refer to external documentation or other pieces of code. Also, lexically scoped variables are protected from inadvertent modification, helping to make your programs more robust.

Dynamically scoped special variables, on the other hand, are subject to accidental modification. Variable name conflicts, for example, can lead to serious problems in large team programming projects. What is more, extensive use of special values is incompatible with the notion of local transparency. Does this mean that a good programmer should never use special variables? Not really. There are situations where global variables simplify the passing of information between functions and enhance the readability of code. With experience, you will develop some judgment concerning when their use is warranted and when it is not.

Exercise 9.6

Given the following function definitions:

```
(defun mumble (foo)
  (fumble))
```

```
(defun fumble ()
  (grumble))
(defun grumble ()
  (declare (special foo))
  (print foo))
```

would the following call work?

```
CL> (mumble 'Hi!)
```

Exercise 9.7

Consider the following definitions:

```
(defmacro mamba ()
  `(print foo))
(defun rumba (foo)
  (mamba))
```

As you can see in the following code, the free reference to `foo` in `mamba` works even though `foo` is not declared special:

```
CL> (rumba 'cha-cha)
CHA-CHA
CHA-CHA
```

Can you explain why?

Exercise 9.8

Write a function called `sum-of-squares` that takes a variable number of numeric arguments and returns the sum of their individual values. Implement `sum-of-squares` using the `labels` special form.

Exercise 9.9

Write another version of the the `sum` function that locally redefines the Common Lisp + function so that it treats missing values (i.e., `nil` values) as zeros. For example:

```
CL> (sum-3 12 nil 9 7)
28
```

Exercise 9.10

The `construct-do` macro written for Exercise 8.15 is only used by the `clear-path-p` method. Make `construct-do` be a locally defined macro within `clear-path-p`.

Exercise 9.11 (*)

Try rewriting `sum-2`, using `let` and `funcall` instead of `labels`. (Hint: The `let` special form allows declarations.)

9.3 EXIT STAGE LEFT

Earlier in the chapter, it was stated that the primary difference between using `block` and `progn` for simple sequencing was that you can exit from the body of a `block` form using the special form `return-from`. As you recall, `block` forms look like this:

```
(block block-label block-body)
```

The second argument in a `block` form is a symbol that is used as a label for the block. It is not evaluated. The forms within the *block-body* are evaluated sequentially unless a `return-from` is encountered.

return-from Special Form

The `return-from` special form may only be used within a *block-body*. When a `return-from` form is evaluated, an exit from the specified block occurs. Calls to `return-from` take the following form:

```
(return-from block-label result-form)
```

When a `return-from` expression is evaluated, the interpreter searches the surrounding lexical environment for a matching *block-label*. For this reason, exiting a block using `return-from` is referred to as a *lexical exit*.

In searching for a matching *block-label*, the interpreter selects the contextually nearest `block` form with a matching label. Intervening `block` forms with other labels are ignored. For example, consider the following code:

```
(block outer-block
  (block middle-block
    (block inner-block
      (return-from middle-block)
      (print 'inner-block))
    (print 'middle-block))
  (print 'outer-block))
```

What do you predict will be printed when this form is evaluated? When the interpreter encounters the `return-from` form, it exits not only from the block labeled `inner-block` but also from the surrounding block labeled `middle-block`. Consequently, only the `print` form in the outside block will ever be evaluated.

Value of a *block* Form

Ordinarily, a `block` form behaves like a `progn`. Each of the forms within the *block-body* is evaluated in sequence. The result of evaluating the last form in the *block-body* is returned as the value(s) of the call to `block`. When a `block` is exited via a `return-from` form, however, the value (or values) of the *result-form* for the `return-from` form is (are) returned as the value(s) of the `block`. If no *result-form* is supplied, the `block` simply returns `nil`.

Implicit *block* Forms

Implicit `block` forms are created every time you use one of the looping macros like `do`, `dolist`, `dotimes`, or `loop`.[4] The implicit `block` makes it possible to exit from the loops using the `return` macro. The `block` form that is created by the macros is labeled `nil`. The `return` macro effects a lexical exit from the first surrounding block with a `nil` label. The `return` macro behaves as though it were defined as follows:

```
(defmacro return (result-form)
  '(return-from nil result-form))
```

For example, you could write your own version of the `loop` macro as follows:

```
(defmacro my-loop (&body body)
  (let ((top-of-loop (gensym)))
    `(block nil
       (tagbody ,top-of-loop
         ,@body
         (go ,top-of-loop)))))
```

By wrapping the `block` form around the macroexpansion, you make it possible for future users of `my-loop` to exit using `return`. Understanding the internal workings of the Common Lisp looping macros is very helpful when you need to write your own looping macros with special behavior (see Exercise 9.3).

---

[4]An implicit block form is also created when the interpreter evaluates a call to `defun`. The *block-label* in this case is the same as the function name. This permits the programmer to use `return-from` within a function definition.

TABLE 9-1 *Lexical and Dynamic Exits*

	Lexical	Dynamic
Define Scope for Exit	`block`	`catch`
Effect Exit	`return-from, return`	`throw`

Dynamic Exits

Just as Common Lisp provides a way to circumvent the normal lexical scoping rules by using special variables, there is a way to exit a body of code in a nonlexical fashion. These are referred to as *dynamic, nonlocal* exits because the destination for the flow of control is determined at runtime. Dynamic exits are done using the Common Lisp `throw` special form. Instead of using a `block` form to establish a target for exiting, the `catch` special form is used for dynamic, nonlocal exits. The relationship between `catch` and `block`, `return-from`, and `throw` is shown in Table 9-1.

***catch* Special Form**

Syntactically, a `catch` special form resembles a `block` form. It looks like this:

```
(catch catcher-tag catch-body)
```

There are some important differences, however. A *block-label* is not evaluated, but a *catcher-tag* is evaluated within the lexical environment of the `catch` form. *Block-label*s are always symbols, but *catcher-tag*s can be any legal Lisp form.[5] The most important difference is that the `return-from` form for a `block` must appear within the text of the *block-body*, whereas the corresponding `throw` form for a `catch` can appear in any function called (either directly or indirectly) within the *catch-body*.

***throw* Special Form**

The syntax of a call to `throw` is also similar to the syntax of a call to `return-from`. The form of a call to `throw` is

```
(throw catcher-tag result-form)
```

---

[5] Even though you can use any legal Lisp form as a `catcher-tag`, in most cases it is still desirable to use symbols because *catcher-tag*s are compared using `eq`.

But there are important differences here as well. The *block-label* in a return-from form is never evaluated, but the *catcher-tag* in a call to throw is evaluated in the lexical environment of the throw.

Catchers

Calling catch results in the creation of a *catcher*. A catcher can be viewed as a type of tagged activation frame that is placed on the runtime stack. When a throw is evaluated, the interpreter searches up the runtime stack, looking for the most recent catcher with a matching *catcher-tag*. Catchers with tags that do not match the *catcher-tag* for the throw are ignored. If no catcher with an appropriate tag is found, an error is generated. Otherwise, the associated catch form is terminated and the value of the *result-form* from the throw is returned. For example, consider the following function definitions:

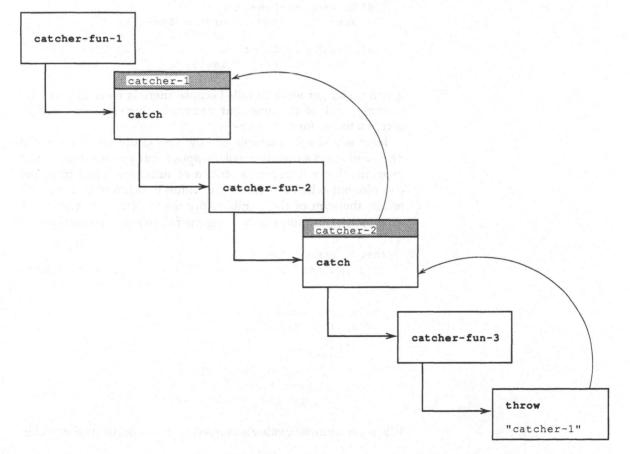

Figure 9-4 Seeking a catcher-tag in the activation environment

```
(defun catcher-fun-1 ()
  (catch 'catcher-1 (catcher-fun-2)))

(defun catcher-fun-2 ()
  (catch 'catcher-2 (catcher-fun-3)))

(defun catcher-fun-3 ()
  (throw 'catcher-1 'Ciao!))
```

When the throw in catcher-fun-3 is evaluated, the interpreter
moves up the runtime stack looking for a matching *catcher-tag*.
This can be viewed schematically in Figure 9-4. If you change the
definitions of catcher-fun-1 and catcher-fun-3 as follows:

```
(defun catcher-fun-1 ()
  (catch 'catcher-1 (catcher-fun-2))
  (catch 'catcher-4 (some-other-fun)))

(defun catcher-fun-2 ()
  (catch 'catcher-2 (catcher-fun-3)))

(defun catcher-fun-3 ()
  (throw 'catcher-4 'Ciao!))
```

it will no longer work. It fails because there is no catcher on the
runtime stack at the time that catcher-fun-3 is executed to
accept a throw for catcher-4.

Here is a simple example of how you could use catch and
throw to effect a dynamic exit. Suppose that you want to write a
program that will accept a stream of numbers typed in at the
console, but when a nonnumeric value is entered, you wish to
return the sum of the numbers previously entered. You could
accomplish this quite easily using the following two functions:

```
(defun summer-fun ()
  (format t "The sum is ~a" (catch 'as-catch-can
                                   (sum-numbers))))

(defun sum-numbers ()
  (let (num (sum 0))
    (loop
      (setf num (read))
      (if (not (numberp num))
        (throw 'as-catch-can sum)
        (setf sum (+ sum num))))))
```

When a nonnumeric value is entered, a throw occurs to the catcher tagged as-catch-can. The catch expression will return the sum of all numbers previously entered.

Value of a *catch* Form

If no throw expressions are directed to a particular catcher during the period that it resides on the runtime stack, the associated catch expression behaves like an implicit progn (that is to say, it returns the value of the last form in the *catch-body*). If, on the other hand, a throw does occur, the catch returns the value of the *result-form* of the throw. Catches and throws therefore perform two services: they can be used to divert the flow of control dynamically, and they provide an alternative channel for passing values back up the stack. They are probably most frequently used for handling error conditions, but they can be applied in other ways.

unwind-protect

Situations sometimes arise in coding in which you must ensure that certain processing steps are run to completion before you quit. A typical example occurs when you are doing file I/O and want to make sure that the file is closed properly when you exit. There is a special form in Common Lisp, known as unwind-protect, that guarantees that one or more clean-up forms will be evaluated after a specified form, whether or not that form runs to its normal completion. The form of a call to unwind-protect is as follows:

```
(unwind-protect protected-form clean-up-forms)
```

If the *protected-form* concludes normally, unwind-protect behaves like a prog1; all subforms are evaluated sequentially, and the value of the first subform (i.e., the *protected-form*) is returned. However, if, in the process of evaluating the *protected-form*, a throw is encountered to a catcher farther up the stack, unwind-protect causes the clean-up forms to be evaluated for effect before control is transferred to the catcher. If we revised the previous catch/throw example as follows:

```
(defun catcher-fun-1 ()
  (catch 'catcher-1 (catcher-fun-2)))

(defun catcher-fun-2 ()
  (unwind-protect (catch 'catcher-2 (catcher-fun-3))
    (print 'clean-up-form)))

(defun catcher-fun-3 ()
  (throw 'catcher-1 'Ciao!))
```

it would then behave as follows:

```
CL> (catcher-fun-1)
CLEAN-UP-FORM
CIAO!
```

The unwind-protect form intercepts the throw to catcher-1 and causes the clean-up form to be evaluated before control is relinquished to the catcher.

The unwind-protect form intercepts lexical exits as well. If the preceding nested-block example is rewritten as follows:

```
(block outer-block
  (block middle-block
    (unwind-protect
     (block inner-block
       (return-from middle-block)
       (print 'inner-block))
     (print 'clean-up-form))
    (print 'middle-block))
  (print 'outer-block))
```

the clean-up form will be executed before exiting from the middle-block.

The unwind-protect special form is used to implement the with-open-file macro described in Chapter 6. As you may recall, with-open-file is the recommended way of opening files in Common Lisp. You could now write your own version of with-open-file as follows:[6]

```
(defmacro my-with-open-file ((stream-name
                              filename
                              &rest options)
                             &body body)
 `(unwind-protect
    (let ((,stream-name (open ,filename
                              ,@options)))
      ,@body)
    (if ,stream-name (close ,stream-name))))
```

which would behave as follows:

---

[6]The way the lambda list for this macro is structured may look a little strange. It uses a feature of Common Lisp macros called *destructuring* that is not covered in this book.

```
CL> (pprint (macroexpand
       '(my-with-open-file (my-stream
                             "myfile.dat"
                             :direction :input)
           (read my-stream))))
(UNWIND-PROTECT
  (LET ((MY-STREAM (OPEN "myfile.dat"
                         :DIRECTION
                         :INPUT)))
    (READ MY-STREAM))
  (IF MY-STREAM (CLOSE MY-STREAM)))
```

The *protected-form* in this case is the let, which binds a file stream to my-stream and then reads from that stream. The clean-up form ensures that the file stream will be closed after the read.

Local Transparency

The concerns about violation of the principle of local transparency, which were discussed in the section on special variables, apply with equal relevance to dynamic exits. Undisciplined use of catches and throws can produce unreadable code. A reasonable policy for structured programming is to use dynamic exits only as a technique of last resort. In situations where dynamic exits are required, be sure to provide appropriate in-line documentation for both the catch and the throw.

Exercise 9.12

What will the following form return?

```
(block outer-block
  (block middle-block
    (block inner-block
      (return-from inner-block)
      (print 'inner-block))
    (print 'middle-block))
  (print 'outer-block))
```

Exercise 9.13

Rewrite the while macro from Exercise 8.10 without using loop.

Exercise 9.14

Assuming that catcher-fun-1, catcher-fun-2, and catcher-fun-3 are defined as follows:

```
(defun catcher-fun-1 ()
  (catch 'catcher-1 (catcher-fun-2)))
(defun catcher-fun-2 ()
```

```
          (catch 'catcher-2 (catcher-fun-3))
          (catch 'catcher-4 (catcher-fun-3)))
  (defun catcher-fun-3 ()
    (throw 'catcher-4 'Ciao!))
```

will the following call work?

```
  (catcher-fun-1)
```

Exercise 9.15

What does the following function do? Rewrite the function without using catch and throw.

```
(defun mystery-fun-99 (target tags)
  (if tags
    (1+ (catch (first tags)
          (mystery-fun-99 target (rest tags))))
    (throw target 0)))
```

9.4 HANDLERS AND RESTARTS

When writing robust code, it is often a good idea to write your functions in such a way that they can recognize and handle bad input data. For example, there is a problem with the following simple definition of the factorial function:

```
(defun factorial-1 (n)
  (if (zerop n)
    1
    (* n (factorial-1 (1- n)))))
```

The problem arises when you are passed a negative value. If the preceding function were passed the value -1, it would recurse indefinitely until a stack overflow occurred. Redefining the function to test for negative numbers only creates new problems, however. For example:

```
(defun risky-factorial (n)
  (cond ((zerop n) 1)
        ((and (integerp n)
              (plusp n))
         (* n (risky-factorial (1- n))))))
```

Now, if passed the value -1, the function would return the value

NIL. In effect, `risky-factorial` redefines the meaning of factorial as follows:

$$factorial(x) = \begin{cases} 1 & \text{when } x = 0 \\ x\big(factorial(x-1)\big) & \text{when } x > 0 \\ nil & \text{otherwise} \end{cases}$$

this is not consistent with its normal mathematical meaning. The factorial function should be defined only for the natural numbers, but `risky-factorial` will always return some value. What is more, this definition could be dangerously misleading, since it blithely rolls ahead even though it has been passed bad data. In a way, the first definition of `factorial` is better because, although it may break, one can at least be confident that it will not return an invalid result.

error *Function*

It is possible to test for bad data without returning a misleading result. You can cause an error condition to be signaled in Common Lisp by calling the `error` function. The `error` function, like the `break` function (described in Chapter 8), can accept an optional *format-string* with arguments. Unlike the `break` function, however, `error` always terminates the computation. It is used in situations where the program recognizes that it is on the road to perdition and can find no reasonable way to correct itself. For example, you could rewrite `risky-factorial` using `error` as follows:

```
(defun careful-factorial (n)
  (cond ((zerop n) 1)
        ((and (integerp n)
              (plusp n))
         (* n (careful-factorial (1- n))))
        (t (error "Factorial is undefined for ~a" n))))
```

This revised version will produce the same results as `factorial`, but it has two important advantages: it signals an error immediately when passed bad data (without having to overflow the stack), and it provides a more meaningful error message.

cerror *Function*

Sometimes you may wish to offer the user of the program the option of continuing the execution after an error has been signaled. Common Lisp has another version of `error`, called `cerror` (for continuable error), which can be used in this situation.[7] The `cerror` function has the syntax

```
(cerror continue-string
        format-string arg-1 . . . arg-n)
```

The *format-string* and arguments are used to generate an error message, just as in a call to `error`. The *continue-string* is used by the interactive debugger as a continuation option. For example, suppose that instead of just signaling an error when passed a negative value, you would like your factorial function to offer the option of computing the factorial of the absolute value (and then negate the result). This could be implemented using `cerror` as follows:

```
(defun tolerant-factorial (n)
  (cond ((zerop n) 1)
        ((and (integerp n)
              (plusp n))
         (* n (tolerant-factorial (1- n))))
        ((minusp n)
         (cerror "Compute -(|~D|)! instead."
                 "Factorial of ~D is not defined." n)
         (- (tolerant-factorial (abs n))))
        (t (error "Factorial of ~a is not defined." n)))))
```

Now if passed a negative value, the function will still break but it will give the user one way of recovering the computation. For example, an interaction with the function may now look like this (allowing for variations between implementations):

```
CL> (tolerant-factorial -5)
Error: Factorial of -5 is not defined.
While executing: TOLERANT-FACTORIAL
Options:
  1: Compute -(|-5|)! instead.
  2: Return to Lisp Toplevel.
Enter option... 1
Continuing...
-120
```

[7]The `cerror` function may seem to offer the same capabilities as the `break` function, but they are used in different ways. The `cerror` function is usually used in conjunction with specialized error-handling code; whereas `break` is used to enter the debugger unconditionally.

If the user opts to continue, `cerror` returns `nil` and control is passed to the next form in the function. In this case, if the user had selected the other option, the computation would simply be aborted.

Exhaustive Case Analysis

There is a fairly common scenario that arises when writing code. Suppose that you are writing an expression using the `case` macro. You would like to enumerate all of the valid cases and have an error signaled otherwise. This is called an *exhaustive* test because you have defined an action for all possible conditions. You could easily write the code to signal the error using `error` or `cerror`. For example:

```
(case reindeer
  ((dasher dancer prancer vixen)
   (format t "~%Now ~A!~%" reindeer))
  ((comet cupid donder blixen)
   (format t "~%On ~A!~%" reindeer))
  (rudolph (format t "~%Shine on, ~A!~%" reindeer))
  (otherwise (error "Unknown reindeer ~A." reindeer)))
```

This type of testing occurs so frequently, however, that Common Lisp has a built-in macro called `ecase` (for _e_xhaustive case) that allows you to achieve the same goal a little more succinctly. The preceding example could be rewritten, using `ecase`, as follows:

```
(ecase reindeer
  ((dasher dancer prancer vixen)
   (format t "~%Now ~A!~%" reindeer))
  ((comet cupid donder blixen)
   (format t "~%On ~A!~%" reindeer))
  (rudolph (format t "~%Shine on, ~A!~%" reindeer)))
```

Using `ecase`, the *otherwise-clause* is implicit. In fact, you are not allowed to have an *otherwise-clause* in a call to `ecase`.

ccase Macro

Common Lisp also has a `ccase` macro (for _c_ontinuable case). The `ccase` macro works as though it contained an implicit *otherwise-clause* that called `cerror`. For example:

```
CL> (defvar reindeer 'fred)
REINDEER
CL> (ccase reindeer
      ((dasher dancer prancer vixen)
       (format t "~%Now ~A!~%" reindeer))
```

```
    ((comet cupid donder blixen)
     (format t "~%On ~A!~%" reindeer))
    (rudolph (format t "~%Shine on, ~A!~%" reindeer)))
```
Error: CCASE key FRED is not any of the following:
  (RUDOLPH COMET CUPID DONDER BLIXEN DASHER DANCER PRANCER VIXEN)
While executing: CCASE
Options:
  1: Specify new key value.
  2: Return to Lisp Toplevel.
Enter option... 1
Enter expression for new key value... `cupid
Continuing...
On CUPID!
NIL

Exhaustive Type Testing

In the same vein, Common Lisp also has two special versions of the typecase macro, etypecase and ctypecase, for exhaustive type testing. Like ecase and ccase, they behave as though they contain an implicit *otherwise-clause* that signals an error. The factorial function could be rewritten using ctypecase as follows:

```
(defun accommodating-factorial (n)
  (ctypecase n
    (integer (cond ((zerop n) 1)
                   ((plusp n)
                    (* n (accommodating-factorial (1- n))))
                   ((minusp n)
                    (cerror "Compute -(|~D|)! instead."
                            "Factorial of ~D is undefined."
                            n)
                    (- (accommodating-factorial (abs n))))))
    (float (cerror "Truncate and compute."
                   "Factorial of ~d is undefined."
                   n)
           (accommodating-factorial (truncate n)))))
```

This version has different recovery strategies for different types of invalid input. For example:

CL> (accommodating-factorial pi)
Error: Factorial of 3.141592653589 is undefined.
While executing: ACCOMMODATING-FACTORIAL
Options:

```
 1: Truncate and compute.
 2: Return to Lisp Toplevel.
Option: 1
Continuing...
6
CL> (accommodating-factorial t)
Error: CTYPECASE key T is not of any of the following types:
 (FLOAT INTEGER).
While executing: ACCOMMODATING-FACTORIAL
Options:
 1: Specify new key value.
 2: Return to Lisp Toplevel.
Enter option... 1
Enter expression for new key value... nil
Continuing...
Error: CTYPECASE key NIL is not of any of the following types:
 (FLOAT INTEGER).
While executing: ACCOMMODATING-FACTORIAL
Options:
 1: Specify new key value.
 2: Return to Lisp Toplevel.
Enter option... 1
Enter expression for new key value... 10
Continuing...
3628800
```

Note that, in the latter example, the macro ctypecase applies the type test to the newly entered key value and returns control only if that value is valid. It is defined as a loop that will continue to signal errors until it receives a valid key value.

Object-Oriented Type Testing

There is a special technique for doing exhaustive case analysis in object-oriented applications. As discussed in Chapter 6, the most specific method for a set of input arguments is chosen to be the primary method. The most general possible method is one that has no specialized parameters. We term this the *default* method. Parameters without a specializer are specialized to type t, which is the supertype of all types and classes. Consequently, a default method, with all of its parameters specialized to the type t, is analogous to an *otherwise-clause* in a typecase form. It is the method of last recourse, used when no other more specific method is available. You may sometimes wish to use the default method for error signaling. It will be invoked only when the generic function has been passed one or more inappropriate arguments. (See Exercise 9.19 for an example.)

Other Continuable Errors

Common Lisp has other forms that will signal continuable errors. The check-type macro can be used to ensure the type of a generic variable. It takes an access form and a Common Lisp type specifier as arguments. Like ctypecase, check-type will continue to signal errors until it has a value of the appropriate type. For example, the factorial function could be rewritten using check-type as follows:

```
(defun concise-factorial (n)
   (check-type n integer)
   (if (zerop n) 1
       (* n (concise-factorial (1- n)))))
```

Unfortunately, concise-factorial no longer tests to see if the passed value is negative, leaving this version vulnerable to the stack overflow problem.[8]

assert Macro

There is another Common Lisp macro, called assert, that will test the value of any predicate and will signal errors until the predicate is satisfied. It takes a predicate and a list of generic variables as arguments. The assert macro optionally accepts an *error-string*, which will be used when prompting the user. Using the assert macro, concise-factorial could be rewritten as

```
(defun more-concise-factorial (n)
   (assert (and (integerp n)
                (or (zerop n)
                    (plusp n)))
           (n))
   (if (zerop n)
       1
       (* n (more-concise-factorial (1- n)))))
```

The assert macro is particularly useful in situations where you must test the relationship between two or more objects. For instance:

---

[8]Although it is not covered in this book, Common Lisp allows a way to construct type specifiers from predicates. For example, one could rewrite the check-type form to test for natural numbers by using

```
(check-type n (integer 0)
```
or
```
(check-type n (or (satisfies plusp)
                  (satisfies zerop)))
```

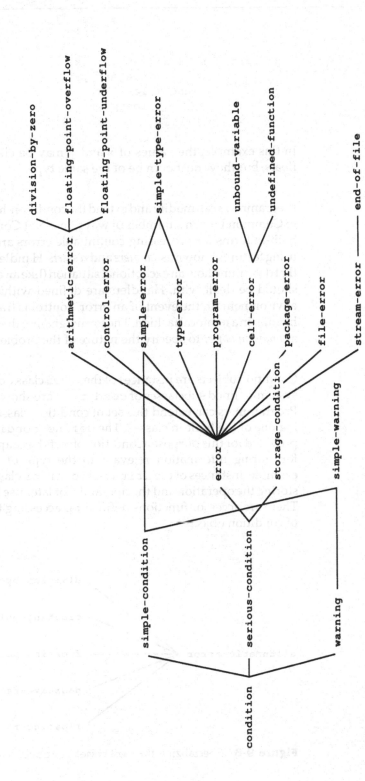

Figure 9-5 Class inheritance lattice for the condition system

```
(assert (or (and (integerp x)
                 (integerp y))
            (and (floatp x)
                 (floatp y)))
        (x y))
```

In this example, the values of x and y may be either integers or floats, but they must both be of the same type.

Condition System

Programmers can modify and extend the condition-handling system in Common Lisp in a number of ways. In ANSI Common Lisp, the built-in forms for processing continuable errors are implemented using features known as *handlers* and *restarts*. Handlers are functions that determine how an exceptional situation (like an error condition) should be dealt with. Handlers are defined within the dynamic environment. In the event of an error, control is transferred to the handler in a nonlocal fashion. The form signaling the error generates a *condition object* to specify the nature of the problem.

Conditions

Condition objects are instances of the CLOS class `condition`. The system-defined subclasses of `condition` are shown in Figure 9-5. Programmers can extend this set of condition classes by specializing one of the built-in classes. The `define-condition` macro is provided for this purpose. Condition objects have appropriate slots for storing information relevant to the type of condition. For example, instances of the `arithmetic-error` class have slots for storing the operation and the operands for later use by the handler. There are accessor functions defined for accessing the useful slots of condition objects.

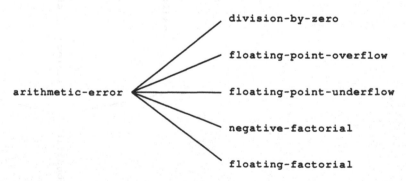

Figure 9-6 Specializing the `arithmetic-error` class.

Handlers

Handlers are selected on the basis of the class of the condition that has been generated. A handler can do only one of two things; it can handle the situation by explicitly transferring control or it can decline, in which case the system must seek another handler. The handler can inspect the slots of the condition object to determine which course of action to choose. For example, if you wish to have the program handle bad data problems without consulting the user, you will first have to create some new condition classes, as follows:

```
(define-condition negative-factorial (arithmetic-error))
(define-condition floating-factorial (arithmetic-error))
```

As shown in Figure 9-6, `negative-factorial` and `floating-factorial` are now subclasses of `arithmetic-error`. You could then redefine `accommodating-factorial` so that it would generate conditions of the appropriate class as follows:

```
(defun trusting-factorial (n)
  (ctypecase n
    (integer (cond ((zerop n) 1)
           ((plusp n)
                (* n (trusting-factorial (1- n)))))
           ((minusp n)
                (error (make-condition 'negative-factorial))
              (- (trusting-factorial (abs n))))))
    (float (error (make-condition 'floating-factorial))
         (trusting-factorial (truncate n)))))
```

Note that `error` and `cerror` will accept condition objects in place of a *format-string*. When this function is executed in a dynamic environment in which handlers for these conditions are active, control will be transferred directly to the handler, bypassing the debugging facilities. To establish special handlers for the newly defined conditions, you would use the `handler-case` macro. For example:

```
CL> (handler-case (trusting-factorial -5)
       (negative-factorial () (continue))
       (floating-factorial () (continue)))
-120
```

The `handler-case` macro takes as arguments an expression to evaluate and then one or more *type-clauses*. A *type-clause* has the form

```
(condition-type arglist body)
```

where the *arglist* can contain a single variable that will be bound
to the passed condition.

Restarts

The handler function must invoke a restart to resume execution of
a program. Restarts, like handlers, are entities defined in the
dynamic environment. Restarts may have a name or they may be
anonymous. Generally, anonymous restarts are used as continuation options in the debugger facility. The handler may query the
system to see which restarts are available, using the `compute-`
`restarts` function. A restart is invoked using the `invoke-restart`
function. The Common Lisp functions `abort`, `continue`, `store-`
`value`, and `use-value` work by calling `invoke-restart` to
invoke the appropriate named restart.

As an example, suppose that you want to allow the user of
`accommodating-factorial` to choose how a floating-point value
will be converted to an integer (i.e., by rounding or by truncation).
Unfortunately, the `cerror` function only allows one continuation
option. To provide more options, you could use the `restart-`
`case` macro to establish additional anonymous restarts. You could
rewrite the function in this way:

```
(defun forgiving-factorial (n)
  (etypecase n
    (integer (cond ((zerop n) 1)
            ((plusp n)
              (* n (forgiving-factorial (1- n))))
            ((minusp n)
             (cerror "Compute -(|~D|)! instead."
                 "Factorial of ~D is undefined." n)
              (- (forgiving-factorial (abs n))))))
    (float (restart-case (error "Factorial of ~D is undefined." n)
            (nil () :report "Truncate and compute factorial."
                (forgiving-factorial (truncate n)))
            (nil () :report "Round and compute factorial."
                (forgiving-factorial (round n)))))))
```

A call to `restart-case` has the following syntax:

```
(restart-case expression
        clause-list)
```

where the *clause-list* is made up of clauses of the following
form:

```
(restart-name arglist :report report-string
              body)
```

The restarts defined earlier are anonymous, so their *restart-name* is set to nil.

As planned, the forgiving-factorial function offers the user two ways of converting a floating-point value to an integer. For example:

```
CL> (forgiving-factorial 5.6)
Error: Factorial of 5.6 is undefined.
While executing: FORGIVING-FACTORIAL
Options:
  1: Truncate and compute factorial.
  2: Round and compute factorial.
  3: Return to Lisp Toplevel.
Option: 1
Continuing...
120
CL> (forgiving-factorial 5.6)
Error: Factorial of 5.6 is undefined.
While executing: FORGIVING-FACTORIAL
Options:
  1: Truncate and compute factorial.
  2: Round and compute factorial.
  3: Return to Lisp Toplevel.
Option: 2
Continuing...
720
```

Error Checking Trade-offs

You probably wouldn't want to use any of the factorial functions defined in this section. They were used to demonstrate the built-in error-handling facilities, but as written, they are grossly inefficient. Once you have done the type check, there is nothing to gain by retesting the input data in every recursive call. A more efficient approach might be to apply the test once and then use a helper function to compute the factorial recursively (see Exercise 9.18).

In many cases, it may not be necessary to do testing at all. If your function will be used by only a fixed number of callers, and if the callers can guarantee that the value passed will always be a natural number, then there is no real reason for further testing. Error-handling techniques can help to make your programs more robust, but like everything else, they should be used in moderation. There is always a trade-off between safety and efficiency. As a program designer, you will have to weigh the benefits of careful error checking against the associated costs.

Exercise 9.16

Add error checking to the days-in-month function (from Exercise 3.2) to handle input that is not a symbol corresponding to a month.

Exercise 9.17

Redo the calculator function from Exercise 3.25 so that it will reprompt the user when given bad data.

Exercise 9.18

Write another version of the factorial function called fast-factorial. This one should do the type testing on entry to the function and then should use a helper function to compute the factorial.

Exercise 9.19

Develop an error-handling method (or methods) for the date-arithmetic generic function from Exercise 6.15. If the first argument is not a date object, the method should allow the user to enter one. If the second argument is neither a date nor a number, the user should be asked to provide one.

Exercise 9.20

There are other ways of converting a floating-point number into an integer. Common Lisp has built-in functions for computing the floor and the ceiling of a number as well. Modify your version of fast-factorial (from Exercise 9.18) so that if passed a floating-point number, it will offer the user the option of using any of the four techniques (i.e., rounding, truncating, taking the floor, or taking the ceiling).

9.5 STRUCTURING THE SYMBOL TABLE

Packages

Packages were mentioned in Chapter 4 in describing the cells of a symbol. In Common Lisp the set of symbol names is partitioned into a collection of subsets known as *packages*. Within a package, a name specifies a single unique symbol, although other symbols with the same name may reside in other packages. Technically, a package defines a mapping between a list of print names and a collection of symbols. Think of a package as a defstruct structure with slots for things like the package name, a list of aliases by which the package is known, an object list, and perhaps some others. The object list could be implemented as an a-list that associates a symbol name with a data object. This is not necessarily the way packages were actually implemented in your system, but it gives you an idea of what a package is and how it works. When a symbol is added to the object list for a particular package, we say that the symbol is *interned* in that package. Symbols that are not interned in any package (such as those created by `gensym`) are called *uninterned* symbols.

Built-In Common Lisp
Packages

Common Lisp has several built-in packages. You can see the packages in your system using the `list-all-packages` function as follows:

```
CL> (list-all-packages)
(#<PACKAGE "CL-USER"> #<PACKAGE "SYSTEM">
#<PACKAGE "COMMON-LISP"> #<PACKAGE "KEYWORD">)
```

All Common Lisp implementations are required to have at least the four packages named "COMMON-LISP", "CL-USER", "SYSTEM", and "KEYWORD". Reserved symbols that are used internally by the implementation are stored in the package named "SYSTEM". As an application programmer, you needn't be concerned with symbols in this package. The symbols for the forms and global variables that reside in the package "COMMON-LISP" provide an interface to the system itself. Symbols like `defun`, `let`, and `do` are owned by this package. Keywords, both built in and user defined, are all interned in the package named "KEYWORD". The symbols that you define while you are working in Lisp are usually interned in the package named "CL-USER".

package

At any given time, there is a distinguished package in which any new symbols that are created will be interned by default. This package is assigned to the `*package*` global variable. You can check its value by simply evaluating the symbol:

```
CL> *package*
#<PACKAGE "CL-USER">
```

You can change the distinguished package (as you did in Exercise 2.17) by reassigning this variable.

Package Names

Every Common Lisp package has a name, which is represented by a unique string of characters. You can use the Common Lisp `find-package` function to retrieve a package object, given its name. For example:

```
CL> (find-package "COMMON-LISP")
#<PACKAGE "COMMON-LISP">
```

The `package-name` function allows you to move in the opposite direction; that is, given a package object, it determines the package name. For instance:

```
CL> (package-name *package*)
"CL-USER"
```

You will find these functions to be very useful when you begin to work with packages.

Making Your Own Packages

You can expand on the set of built-in Common Lisp packages using the `defpackage` macro.[9] It returns a new package object and, as a side effect, defines the package to the system. For example, suppose you have a number of functions and macros that you like to have accessible while coding. Some useful utilities include the looping macros `while` and `until` that you wrote earlier in the chapter. It would be convenient to store these utilities in their own package. You can create a package to hold these commonly used constructs as follows:

```
CL> (setq *package* (defpackage "UTILITY-CLOSET"))
#<PACKAGE "UTILITY-CLOSET">
```

This creates a new package with the name "UTILITY-CLOSET" and makes it the current default. Until *package* is redefined, every new symbol created will be interned in this package.

Internal and External Symbols

Ordinarily, when a new symbol is created, it is accessible only in the package in which it was originally defined, its so-called *home package*. Symbols that are meant to be used only within a given package are referred to as *internal* symbols. This wouldn't work for symbols like `while` and `until` that need to be accessible to programs written in other packages. Symbols that can be easily referenced from other packages are known as *external* symbols. You specify that a symbol is to be treated as an external symbol by using

---

[9]The `defpackage` macro was introduced in the draft ANSI standard (ANSI, 1990). If you are working in an implementation that does not yet conform to this standard, this macro may not be available. All Common Lisp implementations support the lower-level `make-package` function, however.

the function `export`. For example, the macros `while` and `until` could be made accessible in other packages by typing

```
(export '(while until))
```

Qualified Symbol Names

To access one of these user-defined looping utilities from another package, you must prefix its name with its package name. For example, the full name for the `while` macro is `utility-closet:while`. The package name prefix is referred to as a *package qualifier*, and a symbol name complete with a package qualifier is called a *qualified name*.

Symbol Inheritance

If you always had to type the package qualifier every time you wished to use a symbol from another package, you would have to do a lot of extra typing. Fortunately, there is an easier method. If the current assignment to `*package*` was the package named "CL-USER", but you wished to use some of your utilities defined in the "UTILITY-CLOSET" package, you could issue the following call:

```
(use-package (find-package "UTILITY-CLOSET"))
```

This would cause the "CL-USER" package to inherit the external symbols of the package "UTILITY-CLOSET". Thereafter, when a reference was made to a symbol, the interpreter would look first in the current default package (i.e., the package named "CL-USER"), and if it was not found there, it would use the definition in the package named "UTILITY-CLOSET". This would allow you to use your utilities without having to refer to them by their full qualified names.

Handling Name Conflicts

Occasionally naming conflicts can arise when symbols are given different definitions in different packages. In these situations, the normal rules for symbol inheritance may not always give you what you want. Of course, you can make explicit which definition you want to use by typing the full qualified name. Common Lisp also provides some functions for controlling the inheritance of symbols. Rather than inheriting all of the external symbols of another package, you may want to specify which symbols you wish to inherit. This is done with the `import` function. Instead of calling `use-package`, as earlier, you could type

```
(import '(utility-closet:while
  utility-closet:until))
```

TABLE 9-2 *Common Lisp Functions for Sharing Symbols between Packages*

Function Name	Purpose
use-package	Inherit all symbols
import	Inherit specified symbols
shadowing-import	Shadow specified internal symbol
shadow	Shadow specified inherited symbol

This is a little more verbose, but it gives you full control over which symbols will be inherited.

Shadowing Symbols

What happens if the while symbol already had a definition in "CL-USER" before you imported the symbol from "UTILITY-CLOSET"? The prior definition would take precedence and would prevent you from having access to the definition in the external package. We say that the definition of while in "UTILITY-CLOSET" is *shadowed* by the definition in "USER".[10] You can exert some control over which definition is shadowed by using the two functions shadowing-import and shadow. The shadowing-import function will import a symbol from an external package and cause it to shadow the *internal* definition. The function shadow will cause an internal symbol (creating one if necessary) to shadow an *inherited* symbol. Table 9-2 provides a summary of the four Common Lisp functions used for sharing symbols between packages.

Using Packages

The primary motive for using packages is to avoid symbol naming conflicts. There is a constant danger in Lisp of redefining important forms or global variables, particularly when several programmers are working on a common project. The use of packages can help to alleviate the problem, because you can, to some degree, protect symbol definitions within a package by making them internal. For this reason, many experienced programmers prefer to keep their applications in private packages and use the external symbols as an interface to the outside world. The general strategy, then, is to build packages that import the symbols needed from "COMMON-LISP"

---

[10]This is, of course, different from the shadowing of variable bindings discussed in the section on lexical and dynamic scoping.

and elsewhere and to export the external symbols to "CL-USER".[11] Common Lisp has some tools to help set things up properly at load time. For example, Figure 9-7 shows the contents of a file that could be used to define a package called "UTILITY-CLOSET". This file, as constructed, defines the macros pull, until, and while in the appropriate package. The order of the calls to the various package manipulation functions is very important. If you use this file as a template, however, you shouldn't have any problems.

Initialization Files

To provide easy access to the external symbols in "UTILITY-CLOSET" from "CL-USER", you can use the use-package function. This is done in the initialization file shown in Figure 9-8. In many implementations, the file "INIT.LISP" is loaded automatically when the Lisp system is started. This is not part of the Common Lisp standard, though, so in some implementations you may have to load the initialization file yourself when you start up Lisp.

Package Pitfalls

Despite their intended benefits, many programmers find packages to be more of a nuisance than a help. Unless you know what you are doing, working with packages can sometimes begin to feel like the old shell game, where you find yourself constantly guessing where your symbols might be hiding.

Two problems are frequently encountered with packages. The order in which operations are done is very important. If you try to reference a symbol that is not defined in your current default package, you will get an error message, but the interpreter, in the process of looking for the symbol, will intern a new unbound symbol in the current package. If you intended that symbol to be inherited from another package, this will not occur because the internal symbol will shadow the inherited one. In the end, you can recover by calling shadowing-import, but the situation can be very confusing for the uninitiated.

A more obscure problem arises when you have an internal symbol defined as a function and an inherited symbol of the same name defined as a variable (or vice versa). As you will recall from

---

[11]Note that when a symbol is inherited within a package, it is treated an an *internal* symbol. This means that inheritance of symbols between packages is not a transitive operation. If package A uses the external symbols of package B and package B uses the external symbols of package C, this does not imply that you can access the external symbols of C within package A.

Chapter 4, a Common Lisp symbol can name a function and a variable at the same time. Shadowing can cause problems here, though, and conceal either the value or the functional definition of

```
;;;;A Few Cherished Utilities

;;;;Timothy Koschmann
;;;;SIU School of Medicine
;;;;3/5/89

(in-package "Utility closet")

;;;;<<insert shadow/shadowing-import forms here>>

;;;;define public interface for "UTILITY CLOSET"
(export '(pull until while))

;;;;<<insert use-package forms here>>

;;;;<<insert import forms here>>

;;;;Define actual utilities

;;;conditional looping constructs
(defmacro while (condition exit-form &body body)
  (let ((top-of-loop (gensym)))
    `(block nil
       (tagbody
         ,top-of-loop
               (if (not ,condition)
                     (return ,exit-form)
         ,@body
         go, top-of-loop))))))

(defmacro until (condition exit-form &body body)
   (let ((top-of-loop (gensym)))
            `(block nil
                 (tagbody
                       ,top-of-loop
                       ,@body
                       (if ,condition
                             (return ,exit-form)
                             (go ,top-of-loop))))))
;;;queue manipulation macros
(defmacro pull (input-list)
  (let ((var (gentemp)))
    `(let ((,var (first (last ,input-list))))
       (setf ,input-list (nbutlast ,input-list))
       ,var)))
```

Figure 9-7 A properly constructed file for establishing the utility-closet package.

```
;;;;initialization file

;;;;Timothy Koschmann
;;;;SIU School of Medicine
;;;;5 March, 1989

;;;;initialize important global variables
(setq *print-base* 10)
(setq *print-pretty* T)
(setq *print-case* :upcase)
(setq *read-default-float-format* double-float)

;;;load up my favorite utilities
(load "UTILITIES.LISP")
(use-package (find-package "UTILITY CLOSET"))
```

Figure 9-8 An example of an initialization file.

the inherited symbol. These are relatively minor problems, however, and they should not prevent you from taking advantage of the Common Lisp package facilities.

SUMMARY

Common Lisp has facilities for structuring code. The prog macro provides three services: it allows the sequential execution of a block of forms with an optional exit, it is a variable introducing form, and it permits branching to specified tags within the body of the prog form. Unless you need all three of these services, it is stylistically preferable to use one of the block, tagbody, or let special forms, which each provide one of these services.

The bindings of local variables follow a lexical scoping rule in Common Lisp. Assignments made at the top level and variables declared special abide by a dynamic scoping rule. In seeking a binding for a lexically scoped variable, the interpreter chooses the contextually nearest binding in the lexical (i.e., definitional) environment; for a dynamically scoped variable, the most recent binding in the activation environment is used. Lexically scoped function and macro definitions can be created using the labels and macrolet special forms.

Lexical exits from blocks of code are done using the return-from special form in Common Lisp. Dynamic, nonlocal exits are performed using the catch and throw special forms. The unwind-protect special form will intercept both dynamic and lexical exits in order to ensure that certain clean-up forms will be executed.

Common Lisp has some built-in facilities for signaling and error handling. The error function can be used to signal an error situation. If the program designer wishes to allow continuation after the error, cerror may be used instead. There are special Common Lisp forms for signaling an error when doing exhaustive case or type processing. The condition system in ANSI Common Lisp is implemented in an object-oriented style. It is designed to allow the programmer great flexibility when writing portable code for handling errors and resuming execution.

The space of symbol names is partitioned into packages in Common Lisp. The full qualified name of a symbol can include the package name as a prefix. New symbols are interned in the package designated by the *package* global variable. Minimally, every conforming Common Lisp implementation must have four built-in packages named "SYSTEM", "COMMON-LISP", "KEYWORD", and "CL-USER". Other packages can be defined using the make-package function.

NEW COMMON LISP DEFINED NAMES

abort	error	prog1
assert	etypecase	prog2
block	flet	prog*
catch	floor	progn
ccase	go	restart-case
ceiling	handler-case	return
cerror	import	return-from
check-type	invoke-restart	round
compute-restarts	labels	store-value
continue	list-all-packages	tagbody
ctypecase	macrolet	throw
define-condition	make-condition	truncate
defpackage	package-name	unwind-protect
ecase	prog	use-value

FOR FURTHER READING

The code structuring forms are presented in Chapter 7 of the Steele book (Steele, 1990). The simple sequencing forms progn, prog1 and prog2 are discussed in Section 7.4, block in Section 7.7, tagbody and prog in Section 7.8.5, and let in in Section 7.5. Chapter 3 of Steele's book is devoted to lexical and dynamic scope.

Lexically scoped function and macro definitions are treated in Section 7.5. Lexical exits are discussed in Section 7.7 and dynamic, non-local exits in Section 7.11. The condition system is covered in Chapter 29. Packages are handled in Chapter 11. For background about the philosophy behind the condition system, see Pitman's working paper (Pitman, 1985).

For historical information about computer chess (for Project 9.2) see the books by Welsh (Welsh, 1984; Welsh, 1985) and Levy (Levy, 1982). These works also provide good background on position evaluation strategies. Searching algorithms for computer chess are covered in the Welsh (1985) book and in the book by Newborn (Newborn, 1975). The standard search algorithm for two-person games is called the *alpha-beta procedure*. See the Nilsson text (Nilsson, 1971) for a description.

Project 9.1

Create your own library of useful utilities. Define your utilities within your own package. Create an initialization file so that your utilities are loaded every time you run Lisp.

Project 9.2

Using the code from Appendix D as a starting point, design and implement a computer chess game. You will need to add the following components:

- A database of opening moves. (Consult one of the many books on chess openings for listings of the standard "book" openings.)
- A position evaluation facility for selecting new moves.
- An efficient search strategy.
- A gracious human interface for accepting moves from the user and for displaying the status of the game.

Have the symbols used by your program reside in one or more packages of your own definition.

10

Programmation et Logique

Die Welt is alles, was der Fall ist.[*]
Ludwig Wittgenstein, Tractus Logico
Philosophicus

"Contrariwise," continued Tweedledee,
"if it was so, it might be, and if it were so, it
would be;
but if it isn't, it ain't. That's logic."
Lewis Carroll, Through a Looking Glass

10.1 LOGIC PROGRAMMING

This chapter has three goals: to introduce a new style of programming called *logic programming*, to demonstrate how easily another language can be implemented on top of Lisp, and to provide an extended example of Lisp coding. Logic programming is quite different from the functional/object-oriented style of programming that has been promoted in this book. In a conventional programming language, a program consists of a list of steps that describe how a computation should proceed. In a logic programming language, the programmer makes assertions about what will be true when the computation is complete. The details concerning how the computation will actually be performed are left to the

[*]"The world is everything that is the case."

interpreter. Prolog is the most widely used example of a logic programming language.

Prolog Databases

Prolog resembles, in some ways, a database query language. It permits you to create a database of assertions and then allows you to make queries against the database. For example, if you were writing a program to be used in a medical setting, you might wish to create a database of assertions concerning the patients' temperatures. This information could be represented in Prolog in the following way:

```
temp(paul,102).
temp(joan,98.6).
temp(jane,98.6).
temp(kathy,98.6).
```

These are referred to as *facts* in Prolog. The first of the preceding facts could be interpreted to mean "the patient Paul has a temperature of 102 degrees."

Prolog Queries

Once you have created a database of facts in Prolog, you can make queries against it. For example, you could ask whether Paul has a temperature of 105 degrees by typing

```
?- temp(paul,105).
no
```

A more interesting query might be, "What is Paul's temperature?" This could be done by typing

```
?- temp(paul,?temperature).
?temperature = 102
```

The symbol ?temperature is termed a *logical variable*. A convention will be followed in this chapter of treating all symbols that begin with a question mark as logical variables. All items in an argument list that are not logical variables are referred to as *literals*.
  A more complicated query might be

```
?- temp(?pat,?temp),gt(?temp,100).
?pat = paul
?temp = 102
```

This query asks, "Is there a patient for whom we have recorded a temperature *and* for whom his or her temperature is greater than 100 degrees?"

Prolog Rules

So far, Prolog may seem no different from a relational database language, but there is another aspect to the language that has yet to be introduced. In addition to facts, you can put rules in your Prolog database. An example of a rule is

```
fever(?patient)  :-
    temp(?patient,?temperature),
    gt(?temperature,100).
```

This rule states, "If a patient has a recorded temperature and that temperature is in excess of 100 degrees, then that patient has a fever." Prolog rules are if-then statements in which the conclusion is stated before the conditions. In the terminology of logic programming, the rule conclusion is referred to as the *head* of the rule and the list of conditions is termed the *body* of the rule. There is a requirement that the head of a rule must be a single term. In a sense, all Prolog assertions are rules, since Prolog facts may be considered rules without a body (i.e., they are unconditionally true).

Deductive Retrieval

If you made the query

```
fever(?patient).
```

after adding the preceding rule to the database, the Prolog interpreter would provide the appropriate answer. Although there are no facts in the database pertaining to which patients are running a fever, the interpreter is able to deduce that Paul has a fever by applying the fever rule. Recovering answers from a database using one or more rules is referred to as *deductive retrieval*.

Backward Chaining

Prolog follows a strategy of working backward from a goal when trying to find an answer. This process is called *backward chaining*. In order to satisfy the fever rule, the interpreter must find a binding for the variables ?patient and ?temperature that will satisfy both of the conditions in the body of the fever rule. Each of these conditions constitutes a subgoal that must be achieved prior to the actual goal. In a more complicated example, the subgoals may in fact have subgoals of their own.

```
parent_of (henry_VII,arthur).
parent_of (henry_VII,henry_VIII).
parent_of (henry_VII,margaret).
parent_of (henry_VII,mary).
parent_of (elizabeth_of_york,arthur).
parent_of (elizabeth_of_york,henry_VIII).
parent_of (elizabeth_of_york,margaret).
parent_of (elizabeth_of_york,mary).
parent_of (henry_VIII,mary_I).
parent_of (henry_VIII,elizabeth_I).
parent_of (henry_VIII,edward_IV).
parent_of (jane_seymour,edward_IV).
parent_of (ann_boleyn,elizabeth_I).
parent_of (catherine_of_aragon,mary_I).

married (henry_VII,elizabeth_of_york).
married (henry_VIII,catherine_of_aragon).
married (henry_VIII,ann_boleyn).
married (henry_VIII,jane_seymour).
married (james_IV,margaret).
married (duke_of_suffolk,mary).

male (henry_VII).
male (henry_VIII).
male (arthur).
male (edward_IV).
male (duke_of_suffolk).

female(elizabeth_of_york).
female (catherine_of_aragon).
female (ann_boleyn).
female (jane_seymour).
female (margaret).
female (mary).
```

Figure 10-1 Slolog Facts Representing the Tudor Family Tree.

Slolog

In this chapter, you will see how to implement a Prolog-like language that we will call Slolog.[1] Slolog has a syntax and semantics that resemble those of Prolog, but it lacks some of the features and

---

[1]This name was borrowed from "Lonesome Bob" Cheslow, formerly of Xerox AI Systems.

the performance attributes of a commercial Prolog. This extended coding example should serve to highlight some of the important issues involved in designing interpreters and compilers. The value of the design used here, however, should be considered to be instructional rather than practical. The Slolog interpreter was written to demonstrate some of the interesting capabilities of Common Lisp, not to develop a tool for doing large-scale logic programming.

The remainder of this chapter describes the implementation of the interpreter. It begins by discussing the data structures used to represent facts and rules. It then explains how queries are matched with stored facts and rules using a process called *unification*. The remaining machinery for effecting a search of the database is then described. The final section describes the design of a parser for Slolog queries.

Exercise 10.1

A set of Prolog facts representing the Tudor family tree (from Figure 5-14) can be found in Figure 10-1. Write a Prolog rule that whereas will define the relationship `mother_of`.

Exercise 10.2

Write a Prolog rule that will define the relationship `grandparent_of`.

Exercise 10.3

Write a Prolog rule that will define the relationship `sister_of` to be used in conjunction with the Tudor family tree.

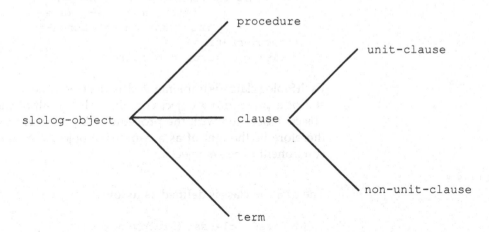

Figure 10-2 Class Hierarchy for the Slolog Database.

Write a Prolog rule (or rules) that will define the relationship `ancestor_of`.

10.2 REPRESENTING FACTS AND RULES

Facts and rules in the Slolog database will be implemented as CLOS objects. The class hierarchy of objects stored in the database are shown in Figure 10–2.

Slolog Procedures

Assertions in a Prolog database (i.e., facts and rules) are known as *clauses*. The name associated with a clause is called its *functor name*. The number of arguments to the head of a clause is called its *arity*. A collection of clauses that have the same functor name and arity is known as a *procedure*. The set of temperature facts in the previous section constitutes a procedure. Slolog procedures are implemented as instances of the `procedure` class. This class is defined as follows:

```
(defclass procedure (slolog-object)
  ((functor-name :initarg :functor-name
          :accessor get-functor-name)
   (arity :initform 0
          :initarg :arity
          :accessor get-arity)
   (clause-list :initform ()
              :initarg :clause-list
              :accessor get-clause-list)
  (attached-fn :initarg :attached-fn
             :initform #'try-clause
            :accessor get-attached-fn))
  (:documentation
  "Class of Slolog procedures"))
```

Each Slolog clause is implemented as an object. The `clause-list` slot of a `procedure` object contains a list of all of the `clause` objects associated with the procedure. A `procedure` object can therefore be thought of as a composite object with one or more component `clause` objects.

Slolog Clauses

The `clause` class is defined as follows:

```
(defclass clause (slolog-object)
  ((head :initarg :head
```

```
                          :accessor get-head)
              procedure
                (variable-list :initarg :variable-list
                               :initform nil
                               :accessor get-variable-list))
              (:documentation
               "Class of Slolog clauses"))
```

Assertions stored in the database are actually implemented as instances of one of the subclasses of the clause class. Slolog facts are stored as instances of the unit-clause class and rules as instances of the non-unit-clause class. They are defined as follows:

```
(defclass unit-clause (clause)
  ()
  (:documentation
    "Class of Slolog unit-clauses (i.e., facts)"))
(defclass non-unit-clause (clause)
  ((body :initarg :body
         :accessor get-body))
  (:documentation
    "Class of Slolog non-unit-clauses (i.e., rules)"))
```

Both subclasses inherit the head, procedure, and variable-list slots from the clause superclass. Instances of the non-unit-clause class have one additional slot: body. The procedure slot contains a pointer back to the procedure object with which the clause object is associated.

Slolog Terms

Clauses themselves are composite objects with pointers to one or more component term objects. The head of a clause is a term object, and the body of a non-unit-clause is implemented as a list of term objects. The rule

```
fever(?patient) :-
    temp(?patient,?temperature),
    gt(?temperature,100).
```

contains three terms. In the Slolog database, each term would be implemented as an instance of the term class. It is defined as follows:

```
(defclass term (slolog-object)
  ((arg-list :accessor get-arg-list
             :initarg :arg-list)
```

```
              (clause :accessor get-clause)
              (functor-name :accessor get-functor-name
                            :initarg :functor-name))
     (:documentation
      "Class of Slolog terms"))
```

Notice that the `term` class requires a slot to store the functor name, whereas the `clause` class does not. A clause always has the same functor name as its associated procedure, but a term (if it appears in the body of a non-unit clause) does not necessarily share the name of its associated clause. (Exercise 10.5 involves writing an accessor method for getting the functor name of a `clause` object.)

Slolog Database

The `procedure` objects in the Slolog database are stored in a hash table. The hash table is created when the program is loaded and it is associated with the `*slolog-database*` global variable as follows:

```
(defvar *slolog-database* (make-hash-table :size 1000
                                           :test #'eq))
```

The key for the hash table is a symbol constructed by concatenating the functor name with the arity for the procedure. For example, the key for the temperature procedure would be `temp/2`. You could install the temperature facts from the last section by first creating a `procedure` object as follows:

```
(defvar temp-procedure
        (make-instance 'procedure
                       :functor-name 'temp
                       :arity 2))
```

You would then create the `clause` objects and store them in the `clause-list` slot of the `procedure` object as follows:

```
(setf (slot-value temp-procedure 'clause-list)
      (list (make-instance 'unit-clause
                 :procedure temp-procedure
                 :head (make-instance 'term
                           :functor-name 'temp
                           :arg-list '(paul 101)))
            (make-instance 'unit-clause
                 :procedure temp-procedure
                 :head (make-instance 'term
                           :functor-name 'temp
                           :arg-list '(joan 98.6)))
```

```
(make-instance 'unit-clause
    :procedure temp-procedure
    :head (make-instance 'term
            :functor-name 'temp
            :arg-list '(jane 98.6))))
(make-instance 'unit-clause
    :procedure temp-procedure
    :head (make-instance 'term
            :functor-name 'temp
            :arg-list '(kathy 98.6))))
```

And finally, you could then insert the procedure object into the hash table as follows:

```
(setf (gethash 'temp-procedure *slolog-database*) temp-procedure)
```

Exercise 10.5

Write the get-functor-name accessor for a clause object. Note that the class definition for clause does not include a functor-name slot; the functor name is stored in the procedure object with which the clause is associated.

Exercise 10.6

Store the rule

```
fever(?patient) :-
    temp(?patient,?temp),
    gt(?temp,100).
```

in the *slolog-database* hash table.

10.3 UNIFICATION

When resolving queries, the interpreter must identify which facts and rules to use. A clause can be used only if its head matches the current goal. The process of matching goals and clauses is referred to as *unification*. A clause is selected if its head *unifies* with the goal.

Unifying Literals

The simplest kind of unification occurs when the two structures being compared have no logical variables. For example, if the goal is represented as the list

```
((temp paul 102))
```

it should (and does) unify with a clause head represented as

```
((temp paul 102))
```

Unifying two structures without variables can be accomplished by simply calling `equal` on the goal and the clause head.

Unifying Variables

The situation becomes a little more complicated when the goal contains logical variables. To unify a goal with logical variables, you must maintain a record of the variable bindings to make sure that the equivalency relationships are being maintained. For example, the goal represented as

```
((temp ?pat 98.6))
```

will unify with the clause head

```
((temp kathy 98.6))
```

if the logical variable `?pat` has no current binding (or if it happens to be bound to the `kathy` literal). However, if `?pat` has a previous binding in effect, then the goal will not unify with the clause head.

Dereferencing Variables

Unification is more complicated, however, because the clause heads may contain variables of their own. A variable may be bound to another variable, which in turn may be bound to a literal. In order to make sure that equivalency relationships are satisfied, the interpreter must determine to what a variable is actually bound, a process known as *dereferencing* the variable. For example, after the goal represented as the list

```
((fever ?person))
```

is unified with the clause head

```
((fever |?var23|))
```

the `?person` variable would be bound to the `?var23` variable. This binding would remain in effect while the subgoals in the body of the `fever/1` rule were being resolved. Consequently, when the `?var23` variable becomes bound to the `paul` literal, the `?person` variable is indirectly bound as well.

unify Function

A function for performing unification could be written as follows:

```
(defun unify (x y environment)
  ;;if x unifies with y, unify returns a
  ;;new environment, nil otherwise
  (let ((x (value-of x environment))
        (y (value-of y environment)))
   (cond ((equal x y) environment)
         ((logical-variable-p x)(bind-variable x y environment))
         ((logical-variable-p y)(bind-variable y x environment))
         ;;if both are lists, descend recursively
         ((and (listp x)(listp y))
         (let ((new-environment (unify (first x)(first y) environment)))
           (and new-environment
                (unify (rest x)(rest y) new-environment)))))))
```

The x and y parameters are the patterns to be matched. The environment parameter is a table of current variable bindings. It is implemented as an a-list. The function returns a new table of bindings, if unification of the patterns was possible, and nil otherwise. By convention, the empty environment (i.e., a table in which there are no current bindings) will be represented as the list

(nil).[2]

value-of *Function*

The value-of function is used to dereference the variables in the two patterns passed to unify. It could be defined as follows:

```
(defun value-of (x environment)
  (if (logical-variable-p x)
     (let ((binding (assoc x environment)))
       (if binding
          ;;recursively dereference all variables
          (value-of (rest binding) environment)
         x))
    ;;non-variables self-evaluate
    x))
```

The function first tests to see if the passed argument is a logical variable (the logical-variable-p function is left as an exercise for the reader). If it is a variable and has no binding in the current

---

[2]This is used so that a program calling unify will be able to discriminate between the situations of two patterns that do not unify and the situation in which the patterns unify but there are no variable bindings.

environment, it is simply returned. If it is bound to another variable, it returns the value of that variable. For example:

```
CL> (value-of '?x '((?y . fro)
                     (?z . baz)
                     (?x . ?y)
                       nil))
FRO
```

Unifying Patterns

The unify function tests to see if the values of the two patterns are equivalent. If so, it simply returns the old environment. For example:

```
CL> (unify '?x 'fro '((?y . fro)
                      (?z . baz)
                      (?x . ?y)
                        nil))
((?Y . FRO) (?Z . BAZ) (?X . ?Y) NIL)
```

If the value of the first pattern is a logical variable, it binds the variable and returns the new environment. (The bind-variable function is also left as an exercise.) For example:

```
CL> (unify '?x '?y '((?y . fro)
                     (?z . baz)
                       nil))
((?X . FRO) (?Y . FRO) (?Z . BAZ) NIL)
```

If neither pattern evaluates to logical variables, unify checks to see if both patterns are lists. If so, it recursively CDRs down the lists to see if the elements of the list unify. For example:

```
CL> (unify '(?x ?y) '(a b) '(nil))
((?Y . B) (?X . A) NIL)
```

Exercise 10.7

Write the logical-variable-p function used in both the value-of and unify functions. Symbols are considered Slolog logical variables if they begin with a question mark.

Exercise 10.8

Write the bind-variable function used in unify. Since unify is the only function that will ever use bind-value, you may want to implement it as a local function.

Exercise 10.9

What do you predict the following calls to `unify` would return?

a. `(unify '?x 'a '((?x . 99) nil))`
b. `(unify '((temp ?pat ?temp))`
        `'((temp bill 98.6))`
        `'(nil))`
c. `(unify '((foo ?x ?x))`
        `'((foo ?pat 101))`
        `'(nil))`
d. `(unify '((fever ?patient))`
        `'((?functor ?arg))`
        `'(nil))`
e. `(unify '((fever ?p)`
        `((temp ?p ?t) (gt ?t 100)))`
        `'((fever |?var23|)`
        `((temp |?var23| |?var24|) (gt |?var24| 100)))`
        `'(nil))`

10.4 BACKTRACKING SEARCH

Consider the following assertions:

```
temp(paul,101).
temp(joan,98.6).
temp(jane,98.6).
temp(kathy,98.6).

fever(?p) :-
    temp(?p,?t),
    gt(?t,100).
```

and this query

```
fever(?person).
```

The search tree for this query is shown in Figure 10-3. To resolve the query, the interpreter must decide which `temp/2` clause to try first. In theory, the choice is made in a nondeterminate fashion; in practice, the interpreter tries the clauses in the order in which they appear in the database. After reporting the first answer to the user, the interpreter queries the user to determine whether or not to continue the search for other solutions. If the user opts to go on, it is preferable to have the interpreter take up the search at the point where it left off rather than start from the beginning. The process of restarting the search from the point where it had been interrupted

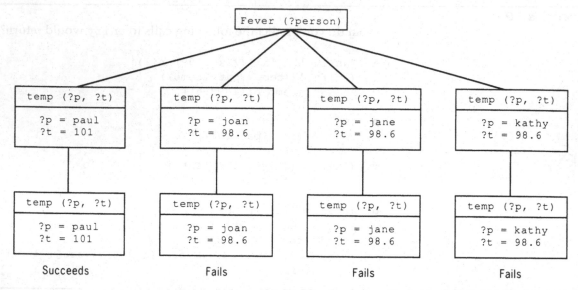

Figure 10-3   Slolog Search Tree.

is called *backtracking*. For this to work properly, the Slolog interpreter must have some means of retaining information about the state of the search.

Top-Level Loop

You could implement the top-level loop of the Slolog interpreter as follows:

```
(defun slolog ()
  (catch 'end-session
    (loop (format t "~%?- ")
          (catch 'end-query
            (satisfy (read)
                     '(nil)
                     #'display-results)
            (format t "~%no~%")))))
```

This function is analogous to the `read-eval-print` loop in Lisp. The reading of a user's query is actually done using the Lisp reader. The `satisfy` function accepts the query returned by `read`, resolves it, and displays an answer if an answer was found. If `satisfy` returns normally, then no solution was found and the answer "no" is reported to the user.

The Theorem Prover

The satisfy function is Slolog's theorem prover. It is defined as follows:

```
(defun satisfy (goals environment continuation)
   (if goals
      (let* ((procedure (get-procedure (caar goals)))
             (clause-list (get-clause-list procedure))
             (attached-fn (get-attached-fn procedure)))
         (funcall attached-fn clause-list (first goals) environment
                  #'(lambda (env)
                       (satisfy (rest goals) env continuation)))))
   ;;success! All goals are satisfied.
   (funcall continuation environment)))
```

It accepts three arguments: the list of goals to be proved (satisfied), the current binding environment (which is initially empty), and a continuation.

Continuations

The argument passed as a continuation is a lexical closure that is to be funcalled in the event that the list of goals is satisfied. Continuations are the mechanism in Slolog that allows the interpreter to perform a backtracking search. The top-level continuation is the display-results function, defined as follows:

```
(defun display-results (env)
   ;;display the results of a query and check to see if the user
   ;;would like to continue the search
   (cond ((equal env '(nil))
          (format t "~%yes~%") (throw 'end-query nil))
         (t
          (print env) (if (not (yes-or-no-p "Continue search?"))
                          (throw 'end-query nil)))))
```

If there are no variable bindings, it simply reports "yes" and returns (via a throw). Otherwise, the binding environment is printed and the user is queried to determine whether the search should continue. If the display-results continuation returns normally, the calling program will restart the search at the point at which it was interrupted.

Matching Assertions

The satisfy function fetches the procedure associated with the first goal in the goal list (the get-procedure function is defined in Appendix F). It funcalls the function stored in the attached-fn slot of the procedure object. Normally, the attached function is the try-clause function. It tries to match clauses from the database with the passed goal. The try-clause function is defined as follows:

```
(defun try-clause (clause-list goal env continuation)
  (if clause-list
    (let* ((clause (first clause-list))
           (new-names (make-new-names clause))
           (new-environment (unify goal
                                   (get-clause-head clause new-names)
                                   env)))
      (if (not (and new-environment
                    (satisfy (get-clause-body clause new-names)
                             new-environment
                             continuation)))
        (try-clause (rest clause-list) goal env continuation)
        new-environment)))))
```

The try-clause function tests one clause object at a time. It recursively calls satisfy to establish the terms in the body of the clause. If the body of the clause cannot be proven, try-clause CDRs down the list of remaining clauses.

Renaming Variables

The make-new-names method (called in try-clause) returns a list of replacement names for every variable in the clause. Logical variables are lexically scoped in Slolog (as in Prolog). The binding of a logical variable should only be visible in the clause in which it occurs. By renaming the variables, you can avoid any possible variable naming conflicts with other procedures called within the clause. The make-new-names method is defined as follows:

```
(defmethod make-new-names ((clause clause))
  (with-slots (variable-list) clause
    (if variable-list
      (let (new-names)
        (dolist (name variable-list new-names)
          (setf new-names
                (acons name (make-new-name) new-names)))))))
```

It calls a function called make-new-name to construct the new variable name. The make-new-name function is defined as

```
(defun make-new-name ()
  (funcall *slolog-name-generator*))
```

The name `generator` in Slolog is defined (naturally) as a lexical closure. When the interpreter is loaded, the global symbol `*slolog-name-generator*` is initialized as follows:

```
(defvar *slolog-name-generator*
          (make-name-generator "?var"))
```

The `make-name-generator` function is defined as follows:

```
(defun make-name-generator (&optional (prefix "?"))
  (let ((last-value 0))
    #'(lambda ()
        (multiple-value-bind (new-name)
            (intern (format nil "~a~d"
                      prefix
                      (incf last-value)))
          new-name))))
```

The lexical closure object returned by `make-name-generator` constructs a name and returns a new symbol. It uses the Common Lisp `intern` function to construct the new symbol rather than `make-symbol`. The `make-symbol` function creates an uninterned symbol, whereas `intern` creates a symbol in the current package if the symbol isn't already there. Note that `intern` returns two values: the symbol and a Boolean value that reports whether the symbol was found or created.

Substituting Variable Names

The `make-new-names` method returns an a-list with a replacement name for every variable in the clause. This a-list is used to substitute the new names for the old when the parts of the clause are actually retrieved. (See the accessor methods `get-clause-head` and `get-clause-body` in Appendix F.) The substitution of variable names is done using the `rename-variables` function defined as follows:

```
(defun rename-variables (term new-names)
  (if term
    (let ((first-item (first term)))
      ;;descend both the head and the tail
      (cons (if (listp first-item)
                (rename-variables first-item new-names)
              (if (logical-variable-p first-item)
                (rest (assoc first-item new-names))
                first-item))
            (rename-variables (rest term) new-names)))))
```

This renaming of variables has no effect on the `clause` object or its substituent `term` objects.

Slolog Queries

Using `try-clause`, the Slolog interpreter can now handle queries represented as Lisp lists. Each query has the following form:

```
(clause-1 . . . clause-n)
```

Each query is a list of clauses representing a conjunction of top-level goals. A clause is represented as a list consisting of a term (representing the head) and a list of terms (representing the body for non-unit clauses). Each term is itself represented as a list containing the functor-name and its arguments. For example, the compound query to find all patients with elevated temperatures could be entered as follows:

```
(((temp ?pat ?temp))((gt ?temp 100)))
```

Implementing Built-In Procedures

There are some procedures that cannot be implemented in Slolog using the `try-clause` function. Typically, these are procedures that have side-effects. For example, how would you write a procedure to halt the execution of the interpreter? Built-in procedures like `halt/0` are implemented by defining special attached functions. The attached function for `halt/0` could be written as follows:

```
(defun halt (&rest arg-list)
  (declare (ignore arg-list))
  ;;used by the halt/0 procedure.
  (throw 'end-session 'Ciao!))
```

It could be installed in the database as follows

```
(setf (gethash 'halt/0 *slolog-database*)
      (make-instance 'procedure
                     :functor-name 'halt
                     :arity 0
                     :attached-fn #'halt))
```

gt/2 Procedure

The `gt/2` procedure has no side effects, but it would be tedious (and ultimately impractical) to assert all of the facts that you would want the Slolog database to hold as true. For example,

```
(((gt 100 99)))
(((gt 100 98)))
(((gt 100 99.5)))
```

A special attached function for gt/2 could be defined as follows:

```
(defun gt (clause-list goal env continuation)
  (let ((x (value-of (second goal) env))
        (y (value-of (third goal) env)))
    (if (and (numberp x)
             (numberp y)
             (> x y))
      ;;success! goal is satisfied
      (funcall continuation env))))
```

If the assertion is satisfied—that is, if the value of x is greater than the value of y—the function signals success by invoking the continuation. The gt/2 procedure is installed in the database in the same manner as the built-in procedure for halt/0.

assert/1 Procedure

It would be very convenient if the user could assert new facts and rules without having to build the procedure objects by hand (as you did in Exercise 10.6). A function for asserting clauses could be defined as follows:

```
(defun asserta (clause-list goal env continuation)
  (declare (ignore clause-list))
  (let* ((head (caadr goal))
         (body (cadadr goal))
         (functor-name (first head))
         (arity (length (rest head)))
         (key (make-procedure-name functor-name
                                   arity))
         (procedure (or (gethash key *slolog-database*)
                        (make-instance 'procedure
                          :functor-name functor-name
                          :arity arity)))
         (clause-list (get-clause-list procedure))
         (clause (if body
                   (make-instance 'non-unit-clause
                     :procedure procedure)
                   (make-instance 'unit-clause
                     :procedure procedure)))
         (body-terms nil))
    ;;store the clause head in clause object
```

```
(setf (get-head clause)
      (make-instance 'term
          :clause clause
         :functor-name functor-name
         :arg-list (rest head)))
;;store the clause body in clause object
(when body
  (dolist (term body)
    (setf body-terms (cons (make-instance 'term
                                :clause clause
                                :functor-name (first term)
                                :arg-list (rest term))
                                body-terms)))
    (setf (get-body clause)
          (reverse body-terms)))
;;store the list of variables in the clause object
(setf (get-variable-list clause)
      (make-variable-list goal))
;;add clause to beginning of clause-list and install
;;clause-list in procedure
    (setf (get-clause-list procedure)
          (cons clause clause-list))
  ;;update the data base
  (setf (gethash key *slolog-database*)
          procedure))
 ;;;cause the goal to succeed
 (funcall continuation env))
```

Although it is long, there is nothing difficult about this function. The `make-variable-list` function is left as an exercise for the reader. The `asserta` function always adds the new clause at the beginning of the list of clauses. This same function can be used as the attached function for both the `asserta/1` procedure and the `assert/1` procedure (used when the user is indifferent about where the clause is added). The procedures are installed in the database in the usual way as follows:

```
(setf (gethash 'assert/1 *slolog-database*)
     (make-instance 'procedure
                    :functor-name 'assert
                    :arity 1
                    :attached-fn #'asserta))
(setf (gethash 'asserta/1 *slolog-database*)
     (make-instance 'procedure
                    :functor-name 'asserta
                    :arity 1
                    :attached-fn #'asserta))
```

```
CL> (slolog)
?- (((assert((temp paul 101)))))
yes
?- (((assert((temp jane 98.6)))))
yes
?- (((assert((temp kathy 98.6)))))
yes
?- (((assert((temp joan 98.6)))))
yes
?- (((assert ((fever ?person)
           ((temp ?person ?temp)
            (gt ?temp 100)))))))
yes
?- (((fever ?patient)))
((|?var4| . 101) (|?var3| . PAUL)
(?PATIENT . |?var3|) NIL)
Continue search? (yes or no)   yes
no
?- (((halt)))
CIAO!
```

Figure 10-4   A Sample Slolog Session.

A Sample Slolog Session

A sample session using the new built-in procedures can be found in Figure 10-4.

Exercise 10.10

Write the `make-procedure-name` macro used in the `get-procedure` function. It should accept a symbol representing the functor name and an integer representing the arity and return a symbol that can be used as a key for retrieving a procedure from the `*slolog-database*` hash table. For example:

```
CL> (make-procedure-name 'fever 1)
FEVER/1
```

Exercise 10.11

The `display-results` function simply prints the environment when there are bindings. This contains a lot of information that the user may not need to see. Modify `display-results` so that the output looks like this:

```
?- (((temp ?patient ?temperature)))
?PATIENT = JOAN
?TEMPERATURE = 98.6
Continue search? (yes or no)
```

Exercise 10.12

Write the `make-variable-list` function used by the `asserta` function.

Exercise 10.13

The `asserta/1` built-in procedure adds a new clause to the beginning of the clause list, where it will be the first to be encountered in a search. Implement a second procedure, `assertz/1`, that will place the new clause at the end of the clause list.

Exercise 10.14

Implement the built-in procedures `true/0` (it always succeeds) and `fail/0` (it always fails).

Exercise 10.15 (*)

For debugging purposes, it would be helpful to be able to trace the steps in a proof. Modify the interpreter so that a message is printed when a goal is called and again when it either succeeds or fails. Implement built-in procedures `trace/0` and `untrace/0` to turn the trace facility on and off. For example:

```
?- (((trace)))
  Succeed: (TRACE)
yes
?- (((fever ?p)))
  Call: (FEVER ?P)
  Call: (TEMP ?var5 ?var6)
  Succeed: (TEMP ?var5 ?var6)
  Call: (GT ?var6 100)
  Fail: (GT ?var6 100)
  Succeed: (TEMP ?var5 ?var6)
  Call: (GT ?var6 100)
  Fail: (GT ?var6 100)
  Succeed: (TEMP ?var5 ?var6)
  Call: (GT ?var6 100)
  Fail: (GT ?var6 100)
  Succeed: (TEMP ?var5 ?var6)
```

```
   Call: (GT ?var6 100)
   Succeed: (GT ?var6 100)
   Succeed: (FEVER ?P)
((|?var6| . 101) (|?var5| . PAUL) (?P . |?var5|) NIL)
Continue search? (yes or no) no
?- (((untrace)))
   Call: (UNTRACE)
yes
```

Exercise 10.16 (*)

Write a `retract/1` procedure that removes a clause or set of clauses from the database. It should remove all matching clauses, not just the first. As a goal, `retract/1` succeeds when it finds a matching goal and fails otherwise. For example:

```
?- (((retract((temp ?patient ?temp)))))
?PATIENT = JOAN
?TEMP = 98.6
Continue search? (yes or no) yes
?PATIENT = KATHY
?TEMP = 98.6
Continue search? (yes or no) yes
?PATIENT = JANE
?TEMP = 98.6
Continue search? (yes or no) yes
?PATIENT = PAUL
?TEMP = 101
Continue search? (yes or no) yes
no
```

10.5 PARSING A QUERY

Now that we have a working interpreter, it would be convenient if we could get it to accept input in a form that is a little more Prolog-like. This is achieved by writing a *parser*. The task of a parser is to take an expression such as

```
assert((fever (?p) :-
            temp(?p,?t),
            gt(?t,100))).
```

and transform it into

```
(((assert ((fever ?p)
           ((temp ?p ?t)
            (gt ?t 100))))))
```

On the surface, this appears similar to the task of converting Fortran assignment statements into Lisp `setf` expressions (as you did in an earlier exercise), and indeed, the tasks are conceptually very similar. However, the syntax of a Slolog query is substantially more involved than that of a Fortran assignment statement. Consequently, a more rigorous approach will be required to perform the current transformation.

read-query *Function*

The `read-query` function captures a query entered by a user and returns it in a form that can be processed by the `satisfy` function. The call to `read-query` can be substituted for the call to `read` in the top-level `slolog` function as follows:

```
(defun slolog ()
  (catch 'end-session
    (loop (format t "~%?- ")
          (catch 'end-query
            (satisfy (read-query)
                     '(nil)
                     #'display-results)
            (format t "~%no~%")))))
```

The `read-query` function itself is defined as follows:

```
(defun read-query ()
  (let ((input-string (get-input-string)))
    ;;set-up scanner for this input string
    (setf *slolog-scanner* (make-scanner input-string))
    ;;parse the input string
    (scan-token)
    (parse-query)))
```

Capturing the User's Input

A query typed by the user may continue over several lines. The Lisp reader will not parse a Slolog query properly, so we must use `read-line` instead of `read` to capture the user's input. The procedure is to read lines and concatenate them until a line is encountered that is terminated with a period. The `get-input-string` function performs this service. It returns a string containing the complete query. The definition of the `get-input-string` function is left as an exercise for the reader.

Scanner

The parser uses a scanner to break up the input string into pieces called *tokens*. The scanner function is implemented as a lexical closure object. A new scanner is created for each input string and bound to the `*slolog-scanner*` global variable. The `make-scanner` function is defined as follows:

```
(defun make-scanner (input-string)
  #'(lambda ()
      (if (not (equal input-string ""))
        (multiple-value-bind (token-text new-string)
            (scan-text input-string)
         ;;assign the next token to the global
         ;;variable *next-token*
         (if (member token-text
                '("," "." "(" ")" ":-")
                :test #'equal)
          (setf *next-token* (make-instance 'fiducial
                                             :value token-text))
          (let ((object (read-from-string token-text)))
            (typecase object
              (number (setf *next-token*
                            (make-instance 'numeric-constant
                                           :value object)))
              (symbol (setf *next-token*
                            (make-instance 'symbol-token
                                           :value object)))
              (t (cerror "Enter new query?"
                         "Unrecognized data object ~a" object)
                 (throw 'end-query nil)))))
         ;;advance pointer in the input string
         (setf input-string new-string))
        (error "Attempting to scan beyond end of input string")))))
```

The lexical closure created by `make-scanner` calls the `scan-text` function. This function reads down the string until it finds a break character. The break characters for Slolog are defined as follows:

```
(defconstant *slolog-breaks* '("(" ")" "," "." ":"))
```

The `#\Space`, `#\Newline` and `#\Tab` characters are ignored when scanning over an input string. The `scan-text` function returns two values: a string corresponding to the next token and the remainder of the input string with the token removed. (You will be implementing the `scan-text` function in Exercise 10.18.)

Parser Tokens

The lexical closure created by `make-scanner` creates an object to represent the token string returned by `scan-text`. Token objects are instances of one of the subclasses of the CLOS `terminal-token` class. The token classes are defined as follows:

```
(defclass terminal-token (slolog-object)
  ((value :initarg :value
          :accessor get-value))
  (:documentation
  "Class of terminal tokens for Slolog parser"))
(defclass fiducial (terminal-token)
  ()
  (:documentation
  "Class of fiduciary symbols for Slolog parser"))
(defclass symbol-token (terminal-token)
  ()
  (:documentation
  "Class of symbol tokens for Slolog parser"))
(defclass numeric-constant (terminal-token)
  ()
  (:documentation
  "Class of numeric-constant tokens for Slolog parser"))
```

Fiducial tokens correspond to the Slolog break strings (except for the break string ": , " which is really part of the token " : - "). Their value is always a string. Symbol tokens have Lisp symbols as values. Numeric constants have numeric values. The token object is stored in the `*next-token*` global variable.

The scanner is invoked in the program using the `scan-token` function. This function is defined quite simply as follows:

```
(defun scan-token ()
  (funcall *slolog-scanner*))
```

Parser Grammar

The work of actually transforming the input string into a Slolog goal list is performed by the parser. The parser is invoked by calling the `parse-query` function. The parser was designed to be used with a parser *grammar*, a table that describes how to parse a structure. It consists of a collection of *productions*, each of which defines a symbol in the grammar. For example, the production

```
QUERY -> CLAUSE QUERY-TAIL .
```

specifies that a `QUERY` consists of a `CLAUSE` and a `QUERY-TAIL` followed by a period. Additional productions would be required to define a `CLAUSE` and a `QUERY-TAIL`. Figure 10-5 shows a complete grammar for Slolog.[3] The epsilon symbol (ε) stands for the empty set. Study the grammar carefully and see if it corresponds to the way you would describe a Slolog query.

Implementing the Parser

The parser in Slolog is implemented by defining a function for each of the productions in the grammar. For example, the parse-query function corresponds to the first production in the grammar. It is defined as follows:

```
(defun parse-query ()
  ;;returns a list of clauses
  (cons
    (parse-clause)
    (parse-query-tail)))
```

Where there are two or more productions for one parser variable, the productions are combined in a single function. For example, the function for a QUERY-TAIL is defined as follows:

```
(defun parse-query-tail ()
  (when (equal (get-value *next-token*)
               ",")
    (scan-token)
    (cons (parse-clause)
          (parse-query-tail))))
```

Other parser functions are defined as follows:

```
(defun parse-clause ()
  ;;returns a term as a list
  (let ((term (parse-term)))
    (cond
    ;;non-unit clause?
    ((equal (get-value *next-token*)
            ":-")
    (scan-token)
    (let ((body-list (list (parse-term))))
      (list term
            (append body-list (parse-clause-tail)))))))
```

[3]This Slolog grammar is a little different from most Prolog grammars. The extra pair of parentheses around clauses used as arguments was added to allow assert/1 and retract/1 to work properly. Also, most Prologs define arguments recursively so that a term can be a argument.

```
QUERY -> CLAUSE QUERY-TAIL
QUERY-TAIL -> , CLAUSE QUERY-TAIL
QUERY-TAIL -> ε
CLAUSE -> TERM
CLAUSE -> TERM :- TERM CLAUSE-TAIL
CLAUSE-TAIL -> , TERM CLAUSE-TAIL
CLAUSE-TAIL -> ε
TERM -> symbol-token
ARG-LIST -> ( ARG ARG-LIST-TAIL )
ARG-LIST -> ε
ARG-LIST-TAIL -> , ARG ARG-LIST TAIL
ARG-LIST-TAIL -> ε
ARG -> ( CLAUSE )
ARG -> symbol-token
ARG -> numeric-constant
```

Figure 10-5 Grammar for the Slolog interpreter.

```
    ;;unit clause
    (t (list term)))))
(defun parse-term ()
  (cond
    ;;should be a functor name here
    ((eql (class-of *next-token*)
          (Find-class 'symbol-token))
     (let ((functor-name (get-value *next-token*)))
       (scan-token)
       (let ((arg-list (parse-arg-list)))
         (cons functor-name arg-list))))
    ;;if not, bail out
    (t (cerror "Enter new query?"
               "Illegal syntax at ~a"
               (get-value *next-token*))
       (throw 'end-query nil))))
(defun parse-arg-list ()
  (when
    ;;arg-list provided?
    (equal (get-value *next-token*)
           "(")
    (scan-token)
    (let ((first-arg (parse-arg)))
      (cons first-arg
            (parse-arg-list-tail)))))
(defun parse-arg-list-tail ()
  (let ((next-element (get-value *next-token*)))
```

```
(cond
 ;;more list elements?
 ((equal next-element ",")
  (scan-token)
  (cons (parse-arg)
        (parse-arg-list-tail)))
 ;;end of arg-list?
 ((equal next-element ")")
  (scan-token)
  nil)
 ;;otherwise, we're confused
 (t (cerror "Enter new query?"
            "Illegal syntax at ~a"
           (get-value *next-token*))
    (throw 'end-query nil)))))
```

The remaining two parser functions, `parse-clause` and `parse-arg`, are left as exercises for the student.

Recursive-Descent Parsers

Because the parser recursively descends into the structure being parsed, it is commonly referred to as a *recursive-descent parser*. The Slolog goal list structure is constructed when we unwind back up the stack. Informative error messages can be easily generated along the way if the parser is unable to parse part of the string.

A Sample Session

Figure 10-6 shows a sample session using the newly defined parser.

Exercise 10.17

The `get-input-string` function reads lines of text until it encounters a line terminated with a period; it then concatenates the entered lines into a single string and returns it. Implement the `get-input-string` function.

Exercise 10.18

Define the `scan-text` function used by the lexical closure stored in `*slolog-scanner*`. It should accept an input string as an argument and return two values: the next token in the string (returned as a string) and the input string with the token removed. Note that periods are break characters only when they occur at the end of a query.

Exercise 10.19

Write the `parse-clause-tail` parser function.

```
CL> (slolog)
?- assert((temp(paul,101))).
```
yes
```
?- assert((temp(jane,98.6))).
```
yes
```
?- assert((temp(kathy,98.6))).
```
yes
```
?- assert((temp(joan,98.6))).
```
yes
```
?- assert((fever(?p) :-
              temp(?p,?t),
              gt(?t,100))).
```
yes
```
?- fever(?patient).
```
?PATIENT = PAUL

Continue search? (yes or no)   yes

no
```
?- halt.
```
CIAO!

Figure 10-6   Sample Slolog Session (with Parser).

Exercise 10.20

Write the `parse-arg` parser function.
(Hint: The `class-of` function can be used to determine the class of an object.)

Exercise 10.21

Assert the facts from the Tudor family tree in Figure 10-1, and implement the procedures you designed for Exercises 10.1 through 10.4.

Exercise 10.22

In Prolog (and Slolog) it is an error for a functor name to be a logical variable. Add subclasses to `symbol-token` to represent logical variables and literals (i.e., symbols that are not logical variables). Modify the grammar to test for logical variables and literals. Make the necessary changes to the parser to handle these new types of tokens.

SUMMARY

This chapter introduced a new style of programming known as *logic programming*. In a logic programming language, the programmer builds a database of assertions about what is held to be true, and queries are made against the database. The interpreter for a logic programming language attempts to construct a proof in order to resolve a query.

The assertions in the database may be divided into two categories: those that are *facts* and those that are *rules*. Facts assert that some relationship is unconditionally true; rules assert that some relationship is true if certain qualifying conditions are met. In the terminology of logic programming, facts and rules are *clauses*. The name associated with a clause is called its *functor name*. The number of arguments that are required by a clause is referred to as the *arity* of the clause. A collection of clauses with the same name and arity are known as a *procedure*.

When resolving queries, the interpreter for a logic programming language must decide which facts and rules in the database to apply. The selection is done via a matching process known as *unification*. This is a form of pattern matching in which both patterns being tested can contain variables.

Typically, the result of a query is a stream of solutions. After reporting a solution, the user is asked whether or not to continue the search. In theory, you could compute all of the solutions at once and report only one at a time, but this would be very inefficient if the user is only interested in the first answer. Instead, most logic programming languages have the ability to *backtrack*, that is, to take up a search again at the point at which it was interrupted. One way of implementing backtracking is to use continuation arguments. Continuations can be implemented in Lisp as lexical closure objects.

The process of breaking down a textual object into its components is known as *parsing*. The set of rules that define the syntax of the object is called a *grammar*. A grammar consists of a collection of rules known as *production*, each of which defines a symbol in the grammar. A parser can be implemented by defining a function for each of the productions in the grammar. A parser implemented in this way is referred to as a *recursive-descent parser*.

NEW COMMON LISP DEFINED NAMES

```
class-of            string-trim-left
find-class          string-trim-right
intern              yes-or-no-p
string-trim
```

FOR FURTHER READING

The Slolog interpreter was based on the "downward success continuations" interpreter described in the article by Kahn and Carlsson (1984). The parser was inspired by the description of a recursive-descent parser in the Maier and Warren book (1988). Additional information about Prolog and logic programming can be found in the Malpas (1987) and the Sterling and Shapiro (1986) textbooks.

Project 10.1

The Slolog interpreter could be extended in a number of interesting ways. Try to add one or more of the following capabilities to the program:

a. Most Prolog implementations allow the programmer to store facts and rules in a disk file that can be read into the database using the `consult/1` procedure. The single argument to `consult` is a string specifying a file name. Define the `consult/1` procedure for the Slolog interpreter. It should succeed if the file is found and loads without error.

b. The `cut/0` built-in procedure (usually written as an exclamation point) is used to prune the search tree. It always succeeds when called but always fails on backtracking. It has the effect, therefore, of freezing the current bindings at the time the cut was encountered. See any current Prolog textbook (e.g., Malpas, 1987, or Sterling & Shapiro, 1986) for a more detailed description. Implement a cut facility in the Slolog interpreter.

c. Implement a procedure called `compile/1`. It should take a procedure name as an argument and should, as a side effect, Lisp compile the code that implements the procedure. It should succeed if the procedure was found and compiled without error.

11

Epilogue

*The policy of letting a hundred flowers
blossom and a hundred schools of thought contend
is designed to promote the flourishing of the arts
and the progress of science.*
Mao Tse-Tung

11.1 COMMON LISP: A REAPPRAISAL

It is interesting at this point to consider how Common Lisp has changed the way in which Lisp programmers program and what contributions it has made to the evolution of the language. At the same time, we need to consider some of the criticisms that have been raised with respect to the design of the language and attempt to anticipate how it might change in the future.

ANSI Common Lisp is the product of 30 years of language evolution. In its design, it builds on experiences gained with experimental Lisp dialects at MIT and elsewhere. Taken as a whole, Common Lisp is quite a different language from the earlier versions of Lisp used two decades ago. Some differences are cosmetic, such as the introduction of more mnemonic names (e.g., first, second, rest) for the functions that access the parts of a list, but other features have led to fundamental changes in programming practice.

Two features of Common Lisp that fall into this latter category are the choice of lexical scoping as the default scoping rule and a general trend toward greater abstraction. These features endorse and, to some degree, enforce a more structured style of programming.

Lexical Scoping

Older Lisp dialects utilized dynamic scoping rules. Although Common Lisp is not the first lexically scoped Lisp dialect, it is the first commercially important Lisp dialect designed to be lexically scoped.[1] Lexical scoping is important for two reasons: It permits the compiler to produce more efficient object code, and it improves the readability of programs. With dynamic scoping, one must often have knowledge of a function's callers in order to resolve variable references. Lexical scoping, in accordance with the principle of local transparency, ensures that all free variables are bound in their textual environment. Of course, there is nothing to prevent the programmer from declaring all variables special, if desired, and thereby defeat Common Lisp's default scoping rules. By making lexical scoping the default, however, the designers of Common Lisp are encouraging programmers to program in a more readable style.

Increasing Levels of Abstraction

Common Lisp, as a language, both reflects and supports abstraction. As an example, the generic variable facility in Common Lisp is a form of abstraction. Generic variables offer an abstracted means of updating elements of sequences, reassigning symbols, changing slot values in objects, and modifying other types of data objects. Rather than introducing different primitives for updating each type of data object, as was done in some earlier Lisp dialects, all of these data objects (or data locations) can be updated in Common Lisp using the `setf` macro. This helps to simplify coding and makes sources easier to read. The sequence data type is another form of abstraction introduced in Common Lisp. Sequences abstract the common features of vectors, lists, and strings and allow the programmer to write functions that will work with all three data types.

The proposed standard also permits programmers to create levels of abstraction within their own programs. Structures and CLOS objects provide built-in support for data abstraction. They

---

[1] The Scheme dialect and its relatives (T and NIL) are also lexically scoped, but they are primarily research and teaching languages and are not generally used to implement large commercial applications.

allow the programmer to define new data objects for specific applications. CLOS methods and generic functions also provide for a form of functional abstraction. Abstraction has long been a part of coding in Lisp, but the proposed ANSI standard for Common Lisp goes further than any other Lisp dialect in supporting this style of programming.

To Standardize or Not to Standardize

As suggested by its name, the primary rationale for creating Common Lisp in the first place was to provide a communal Lisp dialect, one that would allow applications developed in one hardware environment to migrate graciously to other environments. It has come a long way toward making it possible to write portable Lisp code. Despite its innovations and the fact that Common Lisp is the first truly portable Lisp dialect, it has had its detractors. Many have taken issue with particular design decisions that were made when Common Lisp was introduced (e.g., automatic conversion to uppercase, separate name spaces for variables and functions, the package system). A more fundamental criticism is that it was premature to try and standardize Lisp programming practice (Allen, 1987). There are really two arguments for this position. One argument holds that it is simply not possible to define a standard that will encompass current programming practice. The second states that, practical considerations aside, it is too early to even try to define such a standard. Let us look at these two issues in turn: whether we *can* define a workable standard and whether we *should* attempt to do so.

Difficulties in Standardizing Current Practice

Unfortunately, a number of things that programmers need are not covered by the proposed standard. For example, many programmers use windows and high-resolution graphics to develop sophisticated interfaces for their programs, but the Common Lisp standard is completely silent with respect to window handling and graphics. There are other important aspects of common programming practice that are also not standardized. Because of the wide variety of operating systems with which Common Lisp must operate, the proposed standard discusses only the simplest kinds of file management so that compatibility can be maintained with all possible operating environments.

Language Extensions

Functions and macros provided in an implementation that are not a part of the standard are called *language extensions*. Almost all

Common Lisp implementations provide some extensions. Built-in functions for creating windows, doing graphics, and manipulating file directories are all considered extensions. The problem with extensions is that they are not portable from one implementation to another.

Why not expand the standard to accommodate the features that are commonly handled as extensions? There are two reasons. Some things simply can't be standardized because we lack a consensus on the "right" way to do them. Window handling, graphics, and higher-level file management fall into this category. Other things can't be standardized in a language because, strictly speaking, they are not language issues. For example, it would be nice if the Common Lisp standard could be more specific about how characters are to be represented, but the representation scheme used in Common Lisp must be compatible with the scheme used by the operating system within which Common Lisp must work. Some operating systems use ASCII, some use EBCDIC, and some use 16-bit representations that support international character sets. Character representation conventions are also shared by languages. When you write a text file from a Lisp program, it is reasonable to expect to be able to read that same file using programs written in C or Pascal or Fortran. For these reasons, it would be inappropriate for the designers of Common Lisp to try to dictate their own standard for character representation. Such standards must be specified independently of any particular language definition.

Specification Inhibits Exploration

Even if we could specify everything we needed, some critics of Common Lisp would hold that it is wrong to try to develop a standard at this time. A language standard represents a contract between the designer of the language and the programmers who use it. The programmer assumes that upward compatibility will be maintained—that is, that code that conforms to the standard should continue to be compatible with all future revisions of the standard. Unfortunately, upward compatibility is maintained at a cost. It becomes very difficult to drop features from the language even if they are widely disliked. Ultimately, this may inhibit language designers from experimenting with new features. One of the things that programmers found attractive about Lisp in the past was its extensibility. It could be argued that the primary reason that Lisp has been able to survive and prosper is its ability to change with the times. The act of promulgating a standard has irrevocably changed the language, and this change has not been applauded by all members of the Lisp community.

Design by Committee

The standard is attacked from both sides; it is criticized both for not saying enough and for saying too much. Some developers would prefer to have the broadest possible standard to simplify porting of applications between hardware environments. Other programmers would probably prefer to have no standards at all. The proposed ANSI standard represents many compromises. It was designed by a committee representing implementors, users, and teachers of Common Lisp. The end result has been a fairly elaborate standard. Compared to the elegant simplicity of the earliest Lisp dialects, ANSI Common Lisp is a little daunting. The proposed standard is substantially larger than the version described in Steele (1984b). The sheer size of the standard is a problem for implementors, particularly those who would like to develop products for personal computers. It also increases the amount of material that new programmers are required to learn.

Utility of Common Lisp

Despite all its detractors, however, Common Lisp was necessary. Standardization was essential if Lisp was to develop a following outside of the research laboratories. The need for such a standard had grown more acute in recent years with the awakening of industrial interest in Lisp as a language for implementing AI applications.

Common Lisp is the "industrial-strength" Lisp. It derives its power from its size. Many of the new additions to the language in the ANSI standard add higher-level functionality. Examples include the loop system, the condition system, and CLOS. The more that is built into a language, the less that an implementor must write. Common Lisp will probably be used in a number of distinctly different ways, including the following:

- **Common Lisp as a prototyping language** As discussed in Chapter 1, Lisp is considered an excellent language for prototyping applications. Because of its power and portability, Common Lisp is a good candidate for a prototyping language.

- **Common Lisp as an implementation language** Except for AI applications, developers have shied away from using Lisp as an implementation language. Many programmers believe that one runs the risk of performance problems developing large applications in Lisp. Today, there is little basis in truth for this concern, but the misperception persists. As the notion of prototyping becomes accepted in industry, the use of Common Lisp as a general implementation language may increase.

- **Common Lisp as a teaching language**   Many computer science students are exposed to Common Lisp as part of the undergraduate curriculum. Although it is not a simple language to learn, once one acquires an understanding of its syntax, Common Lisp can be used to study a wide variety of topics in computer science. The fact that one can easily implement fairly complicated projects using built-in functionality makes Common Lisp useful for teaching a variety of topics such as AI, language design, algorithms, and data structures.

- **Common Lisp as a research language**   Lisp has always been, first and foremost, a language for use in research. Researchers who develop applications in Lisp such as expert systems are using the language to do research in other areas. Their needs have already been considered under "Common Lisp as a Prototyping Language" and "Common Lisp as an Implementation Language." Other researchers are interested in studying issues related to the design of computer languages themselves. Many researchers who fall into this category may also be attracted to Common Lisp. Their needs are not radically different from those of others doing exploratory programming in other areas. They need a high-level language with great expressive power. Portability is also important for this kind of research. What differentiates Common Lisp from other languages used in research is its widespread availability. This represents a big advantage over very specialized languages that are used at only one or two sites.

The Future

It is not clear what the future holds for Common Lisp and Lisp in general. Since the publication of the first edition of the Steele book (1984), Common Lisp has had an astounding growth in popularity. Whether its current popularity will be enhanced or weakened by the introduction of the ANSI standard remains to be seen. A second standards committee is currently developing a standard for Scheme (Rees & Clinger, 1986). Lisp is therefore in a period of transition from a single language with many semicompatible dialects to a family of related languages.[2] Whether Lisp will survive into the next century depends in part on whether it can succeed in branching out from the academic world to the commercial world. To do so, it will have to compete not only with well-entrenched languages like C and Ada but also with languages yet to emerge. Whatever the

---

[2]This is not unlike the situation with Pascal, which has branched out into a family of languages that includes Ada and Modula.

future holds, however, Common Lisp today represents the culmi-
nation of a long evolutionary history. It is an achievement worthy
of study in its own right.

FOR FURTHER READING

Background on the motivation for incorporating abstraction into
programs can be found in the Abelson and Sussman article (1988)
and in the textbook *Structure and Interpretation of Computer Programs*
(Abelson et al., 1985). See the Steele and Sussman (1979) technical
report for more information concerning the merits of lexical scoping. More about the debate concerning Common Lisp standardization can be found in Pitman (1988) and Allen (1987).

A

Common Lisp Vendors

VENDOR	HARDWARE
Apollo Computer, Inc. 330 Billerica Rd. Chelmsford, MA 01824 (617) 256-6600	Apollo Computers
Apple Computer, Inc. 20525 Mariani Ave. Cupertino, CA 95014 (800) 282-2732	Apple Macintosh
Artificial Intelligence Research & Systems, Ltd. 1914 N. 34th, #106 Seattle, WA 98103 (206) 547-9710	DEC Vax

Austin Code Works 11100 Leafwood Lane Austin, TX 78750 (512) 258-0785	DEC, Data General, Sun, IBM PC RT, 80386 PCs
Data General, Inc. 3400 Computer Drive Westboro, MA 01580 (800) 328-2436	Data General computers
Delphi S.P.A. Via della Vetraia, 11 I-55049 Viareggio, Italy (39) 584 395225	Suns, Apollo, NCube, Cray, and others
Digital Equipment Corp. 146 Main St. Maynard, MA 61754 (800) 344-4825	DEC Vax
Expertelligence 5638 Hollister Ave., Suite 302 Goleta, CA 93117 (800) 826-6144 (CA only) (800) 828-0113 (outside CA)	Apple Macintosh
Franz, Inc. 1995 University Avenue Berkeley, CA 94704 (415) 548-3600	Sun, DEC VAX, Apollo, 80386 PCs, Cray, and others
GigaMos Systems, Inc. 675 Massachusetts Ave. Cambridge, MA 02139 (617) 876-6819	LMI Lambda machines
Gold Hill Computers 163 Harvard St. Cambridge, MA 02139 (617) 492-2071	IBM-PC and Intel Hypercube
Harlequin, Ltd. Barrington Hall Barrington, Cambridge CB2 5RG U.K. 011 44 223 872522	Unix-based machines

Hewlett-Packard 19230 Prune Ridge Ave. Cupertino, CA 95014 (800) 752-0900	HP computers
IBM (Contact local sales rep.)	IBM MVS and IBM RT
Ibuki 1447 Stierlin Rd. Mt. View, CA 94043 (415) 961-4996	Sun, HP 9000/300, IBM RT, AT&T 3B2, MAD, Silicon Graphics, and others
NTT Intelligent Technology Comp., Ltd. 223-1 Yamashita-cho Naka-ku Yokoyama, Japan (45) 212-7447	ELIS Lisp machine
Prime Computer, Inc. Prime Park Natick, MA 61760 (617) 655-8000	Prime Computers (50 series)
Procyon Research, Ltd. Block B, Westbrook Centre Milton Rd. Cambridge CB4 14Q U.K. 011 44 223 65011	Apple Macintosh
Sun Microsystems, Inc. 2550 Garcia Avenue Mountain View, CA 94043 (415) 910-1300	Sun Workstations
Symbolics, Inc. Eleven Cambridge Center Cambridge, MA 02142 (800) 237-2401	Symbolics Lisp Machines, 80386 PCs, Mac II
Texas Instruments 13510 N. Central Expressway Dallas, TX 75266 (800) 527-3500	TI Explorer and Mac II

B

Common Lisp Defined Names

abort	restart, function
(abort)	
abs	function
(abs *number*)	
acons	function
(acons *key item a-list*)	
acos	function
(acos *number*)	
acosh	function
(acosh *number*)	
add-method	generic function
(add-method *generic-function method*)	
adjoin-item-list	function
(adjoin-item-list *item-list*)	
adjustable-array	type specifier
adjustable-array-p	function
(adjustable-array-p *object*)	

adjust-array	function
(adjust-array *array dims*)	
alpha-char-p	function
(alpha-char-p *char*)	
alphanumericp	function
(alphanumericp *char*)	
and	macro
(and *form-1 form-2* . . . *form-n*)	
append	function
(append *list-1 list-2* . . . *list-n*)	
apply	function
(apply *function arg-list*)	
apropos	function
(apropos *string-or-symbol*)	
apropos-list	function
(apropos-list *string-or-symbol*)	
aref	function
(aref *array subscripts*)	
array	type specifier
array-dimension	function
(array-dimension *array axis-number*)	
array-dimensions	function
(array-dimensions *array*)	
array-element-type	function
(array-element-type *array*)	
array-rank	function
(array-rank *array*)	
array-total-size	function
(array-total-size *array*)	
arrayp	function
(arrayp *object*)	
ash	function
(ash *integer count*)	
asin	function
(asin *number*)	
asinh	function
(asinh *number*)	
assert	macro
(assert *predicate*)	
assoc	function
(assoc *key a-list*)	
assoc-if	function
(assoc-if *predicate a-list*)	
assoc-if-not	function
(assoc-if-not *predicate a-list*)	
atan	function
(atan *number*)	
atanh	function
(atanh *number*)	

atom   function
   (atom *object*)
atom   type specifier
bit   function
   (bit *bit-array subscripts*)
block   special form
   (block *name body*)
boundp   function
   (boundp *symbol*)
break   function
   (break *format-string format-args*)
butlast   function
   (butlast *list*)
call-next-method   function
   (call-next-method)
car   function
   (car *list*)
case   macro
   (case *keyform*
       clause-list)
catch   special form
   (catch *tag body*)
ccase   macro
   (ccase *keyform*
       clause-list)
cdr   function
   (cdr *list*)
ceiling   function
   (ceiling *number*)
cerror   function
   (cerror *continuation-string*
       error-string args)
change-class   generic function
   (change-class *instance new-class*)
char   function
   (char *string index*)
character   type specifier
characterp   function
   (characterp *object*)
char-code   function
   (char-code *character*)
char-equal   function
   (char-equal *char-1 char-2*)
char-greaterp   function
   (char-greaterp *char-1 char-2*)
char-lessp   function
   (char-lessp *char-1 char-2*)
char-not-equal   function
   (char-not-equal *char-1 char-2*)

char-not-greaterp	function
(char-not-greaterp *char-1 char-2*)	
char-not-lessp	function
(char-not-lessp *char-1 char-2*)	
char/=	function
(char/= *char-1 char-2*)	
char<	function
(char< *char-1 char-2*)	
char<=	function
(char<= *char-1 char-2*)	
char=	function
(char= *char-1 char-2*)	
char>	function
(char> *char-1 char-2*)	
char>=	function
(char>= *char-1 char-2*)	
check-type	macro
(check-type *access-form type-spec*)	
class-name	generic function
(class-name *class*)	
class-of	function
(class-of *object*)	
close	function
(close *stream*)	
compile	function
(compile *name*)	
compile-file	function
(compile-file *file-spec*)	
compile-print	variable
compile-verbose	variable
complement	function
(complement *function*)	
complex	type specifier
complexp	function
(complexp *object*)	
compute-restarts	function
(compute-restarts)	
concatenate	function
(concatenate *seq-1 seq-2*)	
cond	macro
(cond *test-clauses*)	
conjugate	function
(conjugate *number*)	
cons	function
(cons *obj-1 obj-2*)	
cons	type specifier
consp	function
(consp *object*)	

constantly	function
(constantly *value*)	
constantp	function
(constantp *object*)	
continue	restart, function
(continue)	
copy-list	function
(copy-list *list*)	
cos	function
(cos *radians*)	
cosh	function
(cosh *number*)	
count	function
(count *item sequence*)	
count-if	function
(count-if *predicate sequence*)	
count-if-not	function
(count-if-not *predicate sequence*)	
ctypecase	macro
(ctypecase *keyform*	
type-clauses)	
decf	macro
(decf *access-form*)	
declare	special form
(declare *decl-spec*)	
decode-universal-time	function
(decode-universal-time)	
defclass	macro
(defclass *class-name*	
supers-list slot-spec-list)	
defconstant	macro
(defconstant *name initform*)	
defgeneric	macro
(defgeneric *function-name*	
lambda-list)	
define-condition	macro
(define-condition	
condition-name supers-list)	
defmacro	macro
(defmacro *lambda-list body*)	
defmethod	macro
(defmethod *lambda-list body*)	
defstruct	macro
(defstruct *structure-name*	
slot-description-list)	
defun	macro
(defun *lambda-list body*)	
defvar	macro
(defvar *name initform*)	

delete   function
   (delete *item sequence*)
delete-duplicates   function
   (delete-duplicates *sequence*)
delete-file   function
   (delete-file *file-spec*)
delete-package   function
   (delete-package *package*)
denominator   function
   (denominator *rational*)
describe   generic function
   (describe *object*)
disassemble   function
   (diassemble *function*)
do   macro
   (do *var-spec-list*
      (*end-test* (*result*))
      body)
do*   macro
   (do* *var-spec-list*
      (*end-test* (*result*))
      body)
documentation   function
   (documentation *symbol*)
dolist   macro
   (dolist (*var listform*)
        body)
dotimes   macro
   (dotimes (*var countform*)
         body)
ecase   macro
   (ecase *keyform*
      case-clauses)
ed   function
   (ed *file-spec*)
eighth   function
   (eighth *list*)
elt   function
   (elt *sequence index*)
encode-universal-time   function
   (encode-universal-time
        sec min hr date month yr)
endp   function
   (endp *list*)
eq   function
   (eq *obj-1 obj-2*)
eql   function
   (eql *obj-1 obj-2*)

equal	function
(equal *obj-1 obj-2*)	
equalp	function
(equalp *obj-1 obj-2*)	
error	function
(error *error-string arg-1 . . arg-n*)	
error-output	variable
etypecase	macro
(etypecase *keyform*	
type-clauses)	
eval	function
(eval *expression*)	
eval-when	special form
(eval-when *situations-list body*)	
evenp	function
(evenp *number*)	
every	function
(every *predicate sequence*)	
exp	function
(exp *number*)	
export	function
(export *symbols*)	
expt	function
(expt *base-number power-number*)	
fboundp	function
(fboundp *symbol*)	
fceiling	function
(fceiling *number*)	
features	variable
ffloor	function
(ffloor *number*)	
fifth	function
(fifth *list*)	
find	function
(find *item sequence*)	
find-class	function
(find-class *symbol*)	
find-if	function
(find-if *predicate sequence*)	
find-if-not	function
(find-if-not *predicate sequence*)	
find-package	function
(find-package *string*)	
first	function
(first *list*)	
flet	special form
(flet *function-def-list*	
body)	

float function
(float *number*)

float type specifier
floatp function
(floatp *object*)

floor function
(floor *number*)

fmakunbound function
(fmakunbound *symbol*)

format function
(format *destination*
format-string format-args)

fresh-line function
(fresh-line t)

fround function
(fround *number*)

ftruncate function
(ftruncate *number*)

funcall function
(funcall *function arg-1 . . arg-n*)

function special form
(function *function*)

function type specifier
functionp function
(functionp *object*)

gensym function
(gensym)

gentemp function
(gentemp)

get function
(get *symbol property*)

get-decoded-time function
(get-decoded-time)

getf function
(getf *access-form property*)

gethash function
(gethash *key hash-table*)

get-universal-time function
(get-universal-time)

go special form
(go *tag*)

handler-bind macro
(handler-bind *binding-list body*)

handler-case macro
(handler-case *expression type-clauses*)

hash-table type specifier
hash-table-p function
(hash-table-p *object*)

hash-table-size	function
(hash-table-size *hash-table*)	
hash-table-test	function
(hash-table-test *hash-table*)	
if	special form
(if *condition then-form else-form*)	
imagpart	function
(imagpart *complex-number*)	
import	function
(import *symbols*)	
in-package	function
(in-package *package-name*)	
incf	macro
(incf *access-form*)	
input-stream-p	function
(input-stream-p *stream*)	
inspect	function
(inspect *object*)	
int-char	function
(int-char *number*)	
integer	type specifier
integerp	function
(integerp *object*)	
intern	function
(intern *string*)	
intersection	function
(intersection *list-1 list-2*)	
invoke-restart	function
(invoke-restart *restart*)	
isqrt	function
(isqrt *integer*)	
keyword	type specifier
keywordp	function
(keywordp *object*)	
labels	special form
(labels *function-def-list* *body*)	
last	function
(last *list*)	
least-negative-double-float	constant
least-negative-long-float	constant
least-negative-short-float	constant
least-negative-single-float	constant
least-positive-double-float	constant
least-positive-long-float	constant
least-positive-short-float	constant
least-positive-single-float	constant

length	function
(length *sequence*)	
let	special form
(let *variable-binding-list body*)	
let*	special form
(let* *variable-binding-list body*)	
list	function
(list *item-1* . . . *item-n*)	
list	type specifier
list-all-packages	function
(list-all-packages)	
list-length	function
(list-length *list*)	
listp	function
(listp *object*)	
load	function
(load *filename*)	
load-print	variable
load-verbose	variable
log	function
(log *number*)	
long-float	type specifier
loop	macro
(loop *body*)	
lower-case-p	function
(lower-case-p *char*)	
macroexpand	function
(macroexpand *expression*)	
macroexpand-1	function
(macroexpand-1 *expression*)	
macrolet	special form
(macrolet *macro-definition-list body*)	
make-array	function
(make-array *dimension-list*)	
make-hash-table	function
(make-hash-table)	
make-instance	generic function
(make-instance *class*)	
make-list	function
(make-list *size*)	
make-package	function
(make-package *package-name*)	
make-sequence	function
(make-sequence *sequence-type size*)	
make-string	function
(make-string *size*)	

make-symbol   function
   (make-symbol *print-name*)
makunbound   function
   (makunbound *symbol*)
map   function
   (map *result-type function sequence*)
mapc   function
   (mapc *function list*)
mapcan   function
   (mapcan *function list*)
mapcar   function
   (mapcar *function list*)
mapcon   function
   (mapcon *function list*)
maphash   function
   (maphash *function hash-table*)
mapl   function
   (mapl *function list*)
maplist   function
   (maplist *function list*)
max   function
   (max *number-1 . . . number-n*)
member   function
   (member *item list*)
member-if   function
   (member *pred list*)
member-if-not   function
   (member *pred list*)
merge   function
   (merge *result-type*
       sequence-1 sequence-2)
min   function
   (min *number-1 . . . number-n*)
minusp   function
   (minusp *number*)
mismatch   function
   (mismatch *sequence-1 sequence-2*)
mod   function
   (mod *number divisor*)
most-negative-double-float   constant
most-negative-fixnum   constant
most-negative-long-float   constant
most-negative-short-float   constant
most-negative-single-float   constant
most-positive-double-float   constant
most-positive-fixnum   constant
most-positive-long-float   constant
most-positive-short-float   constant

`most-positive-single-float`	constant
`multiple-value-bind`	macro
(multiple-value-bind *var-list values-form*)	
`multiple-value-call`	special form
(multiple-value-call *function body*)	
`multiple-value-list`	macro
(multiple-value-list *values-form*)	
`multiple-value-prog1`	special form
(multiple-value-prog1 *body*)	
`multiple-value-setq`	macro
(multiple-value-setq *var-list expression*)	
`multiple-values-limit`	constant
`nbutlast`	function
(nbutlast *list position*)	
`nconc`	function
(nconc *list-1 list-2*)	
`next-method-p`	function
(next-method-p)	
`nil`	constant
`nil`	type specifier
`nintersection`	function
(nintersection *list-1 list-2*)	
`ninth`	function
(ninth *list*)	
`not`	function
(not *object*)	
`notany`	function
(notany *predicate sequence*)	
`notevery`	function
(notevery *predicate sequence*)	
`nreverse`	function
(nreverse *sequence*)	
`nset-difference`	function
(nset-difference *list-1 list-2*)	
`nset-exclusive-or`	function
(nset-exclusive-or *list-1 list-2*)	
`nsubst`	function
(nsubst *new-item old-item tree*)	
`nsubst-if`	function
(nsubst-if *new-item predicate tree*)	
`nsubst-if-not`	function
(nsubst-if-not *new-item predicate tree*)	
`nsubstitute`	function
(nsubstitute *new-item old-item sequence*)	
`nsubstitute-if`	function
(nsubstitute-if *new-item predicate sequence*)	

nsubstitute-if-not	function
(nsubstitute-if-not *new-item old-item sequence*)	
nth	function
(nth *index list*)	
nthcdr	function
(nthcdr *index list*)	
nth-value	macro
(nth-value *n form*)	
null	function
(null *object*)	
null	type specifier
number	type specifier
numberp	function
(numberp *object*)	
numerator	function
(numerator *rational*)	
nunion	function
(nunion *list-1 list-2*)	
oddp	function
(oddp *number*)	
open	function
(open *file-name*)	
or	macro
(or *form-1 form-2 . . . form-n*)	
output-stream-p	function
(output-stream-p *stream*)	
package	type specifier
package	variable
package-name	function
(package-name *package*)	
package-nicknames	function
(package-nicknames *package*)	
packagep	function
(packagep *object*)	
package-shadowing-symbols	function
(package-shadowing-symbols *package*)	
package-use-list	function
(package-use-list *package*)	
package-used-by-list	function
(package-used-by-list *object*)	
pairlis	function
(pairlis *key-list data-list*)	
pathname	function
(pathname *object*)	
pathname	type specifier
pathname-device	function
(pathname-device *pathname*)	
pathname-directory	function
(pathname-directory *pathname*)	

pathname-host	function
(pathname-host *pathname*)	
pathname-name	function
(pathname-name *pathname*)	
pathname-type	function
(pathname-type *pathname*)	
pathname-version	function
(pathname-version *pathname*)	
pathname-device	function
(pathname *pathname*)	
pathnamep	function
(pathnamep *object*)	
pi	constant
plusp	function
(plusp *number*)	
pop	macro
(pop *access-form*)	
position	function
(position *item sequence*)	
position-if	function
(position-if *predicate sequence*)	
position-if-not	function
(position-if-not *predicate sequence*)	
pprint	function
(pprint *object*)	
princ	function
(princ *object*)	
print	function
(print *object*)	
print-array	variable
print-base	variable
print-case	variable
print-circle	variable
print-escape	variable
print-gensym	variable
print-length	variable
print-level	variable
print-object	generic function
(print-object *object stream*)	
print-pretty	variable
print-radix	variable
prin1	function
(prin1 *object*)	
proclaim	function
(proclaim *decl-spec*)	
prog	macro
(prog *var-list body*)	
prog*	macro
(prog* *var-list body*)	

progn	special form
(progn *body*)	
prog1	macro
(prog1 *body*)	
prog2	macro
(prog2 *body*)	
push	macro
(push *item access-form*)	
pushnew	macro
(pushnew *item access-form*)	
quote	special form
(quote *object*)	
random	function
(random *number*)	
random-state	type specifier
random-state	variable
random-state-p	function
(random-state-p *object*)	
rassoc	function
(rassoc *item a-list*)	
rassoc-if	function
(rassoc-if *pred a-list*)	
rassoc-if-not	function
(rassoc-if-not *pred a-list*)	
ratio	type specifier
rational	function
(rational *number*)	
rational	type specifier
rationalize	function
(rationalize *number*)	
rationalp	function
(rationalp *object*)	
read	function
(read)	
read-base	variable
read-byte	function
(read-byte)	
read-char	function
(read-char)	
read-default-float-format	variable
read-from-string	function
(read-from-string *string*)	
read-line	function
(read-line)	
read-suppress	variable
readtable	type specifier
readtable	variable
readtablep	function
(readtablep *object*)	

realp	function
(realp *object*)	
realpart	function
(realpart *object*)	
reduce	function
(reduce *function sequence*)	
rem	function
(rem *number divisor*)	
remf	function
(remf *access-form indicator*)	
remhash	function
(remhash *key hash-table*)	
remove	function
(remove item sequence)	
remove-duplicates	function
(remove-duplicates *sequence*)	
remove-if	function
(remove *predicate sequence*)	
remove-if-not	function
(remove *predicate sequence*)	
remprop	function
(remprop *symbol property*)	
rename-file	function
(rename-file *old-name new-name*)	
rename-method	generic function
(rename-method *generic-function method*)	
rename-package	function
(rename-package *package new-name*)	
replace	function
(replace *sequence-1 sequence-2*)	
rest	function
(rest *list*)	
restart-bind	macro
(restart-bind *binding-list body*)	
restart-case	macro
(restart-case *expression restart-clauses*)	
return	macro
(return)	
return-from	special form
(return-from *block-name*)	
revappend	function
(revappend *list-1 list-2*)	
reverse	function
(reverse *sequence*)	
room	function
(room)	
rotatef	macro
(rotatef *access-form-1 . . . access-form-n*)	

round	function
(round *number*)	
rplaca	function
(rplaca *list item*)	
rplacd	function
(rplacd *list item*)	
scale-float	function
(scale-float *float power*)	
schar	function
(schar *string index*)	
search	function
(search *sequence-1 sequence-2*)	
second	function
(second *list*)	
sequence	type specifier
set	function
(set *symbol value*)	
set-difference	function
(set-difference *list-1 list-2*)	
setf	macro
(setf *access-form new-value*)	
setq	special form
(setq *var expression*)	
seventh	function
(seventh *list*)	
shadow	function
(shadow *symbols*)	
shadowing-import	function
(shadowing-import *object*)	
shiftf	macro
(shiftf *access-form-1 . . . access-form-2 value*)	
short-float	type specifier
signum	function
(signum *number*)	
simple-array	type specifier
simple-bit-vector	type specifier
simple-bit-vector-p	function
(simple-bit-vector-p *object*)	
simple-string	type specifier
simple-string-p	function
(simple-string-p *object*)	
simple-vector	type specifier
simple-vector-p	function
(simple-vector-p *object*)	
sin	function
(sin *radians*)	
single-float	type specifier
sinh	function
(sinh *number*)	

sixth	function
(sixth *list*)	
sleep	function
(sleep *seconds*)	
slot-boundp	function
(slot-boundp *instance slot-name*)	
slot-exists-p	function
(slot-exists-p *instance slot-name*)	
slot-makunbound	function
(slot-makunbound *instance slot-name*)	
slot-value	function
(slot-value *instance slot-name*)	
some	function
(some *predicate sequence*)	
sort	function
(sort *sequence predicate*)	
special-form-p	function
(special-form-p *object*)	
sqrt	function
(sqrt *number*)	
stable-sort	function
(stable-sort *sequence predicate*)	
standard-char	type specifier
standard-char-p	function
(standard-char-p *object*)	
standard-input	variable
standard-output	variable
step	function
(step *expression*)	
store-value	restart, function
(store-value *value*)	
stream	type specifier
stream-element-type	function
(stream-element-type *stream*)	
streamp	function
(streamp *object*)	
string	type specifier
string	function
(string *symbol*)	
string	type specifier
string-capitalize	function
(string-capitalize *string*)	
string-char	type specifier
string-char-p	function
(string-char-p *object*)	
string-downcase	function
(string-downcase *string*)	
string-equal	function
(string-equal *string-1 string-2*)	

string-greaterp	function
(string-greaterp *string-1 string-2*)	
string-left-trim	function
(string-left-trim *char-bag string*)	
string-lessp	function
(string-lessp *string-1 string-2*)	
string-not-equal	function
(string-not-equal *string-1 string-2*)	
string-not-greaterp	function
(string-not-greaterp *string-1 string-2*)	
string-not-lessp	function
(string-not-lessp *string-1 string-2*)	
string-right-trim	function
(string-right-trim *char-bag string*)	
string-trim	function
(string-trim *char-bag string*)	
string-upcase	function
(string-upcase *string*)	
stringp	function
(stringp *object*)	
string/=	function
(string/= *string-1 string-2*)	
string<	function
(string< *string-1 string-2*)	
string<=	function
(string<= *string-1 string-2*)	
string=	function
(string= *string-1 string-2*)	
string>	function
(string> *string-1 string-2*)	
string>=	function
(string>= *string-1 string-2*)	
sublis	function
(sublis *a-list tree*)	
subseq	function
(subseq *sequence start*)	
subsetp	function
(subsetp *list-1 list-2*)	
subst	function
(subst *new-item old-item tree*)	
subst-if	function
(subst-if *new-item predicate tree*)	
subst-if-not	function
(subst-if-not *new-item predicate tree*)	
substitute	function
(substitute *new-item old-item tree*)	
substitute-if	function
(substitute-if *new-item predicate tree*)	

substitute-if-not	function
(substitute-if-not *new-item predicate tree*)	
subtypep	function
(subtypep *type-1 type-2*)	
svref	function
(svref *simple-vector index*)	
sxhash	function
(sxhash *object*)	
symbol	type specifier
symbol-function	function
(symbol-function *symbol*)	
symbol-name	function
(symbol-name *symbol*)	
symbolp	function
(symbolp *object*)	
symbol-package	function
(symbol-package *symbol*)	
symbol-plist	function
(symbol-plist *symbol*)	
symbol-value	function
(symbol-value *symbol*)	
t	constant
t	type specifier
tagbody	special form
(tagbody *body*)	
tailp	function
(tailp *sublist list*)	
tan	function
(tan *radians*)	
tanh	function
(tanh *number*)	
tenth	function
(tenth *list*)	
terminal-io	variable
terpri	function
(terpri)	
throw	special form
(throw *tag result*)	
time	function
(time *expression*)	
trace	function
(trace *function-name*)	
trace-output	variable
tree-equal	function
(tree-equal *tree-1 tree-2*)	
truncate	function
(truncate *number*)	
type-of	function
(type-of *object*)	

typecase	macro
(typecase *keyform*	
type-clauses)	
typep	function
(typep *object type*)	
unexport	function
(unexport *symbols*)	
unintern	function
(unintern *symbol*)	
union	function
(union *list-1 list-2*)	
unless	macro
(unless *test body*)	
unread-char	function
(unread-char *char stream*)	
unsigned-byte	type specifier
untrace	function
(untrace *function-name*)	
unuse-package	function
(unuse-package *package*)	
unwind-protect	special form
(unwind-protect *form clean-up-forms*)	
upper-case-p	function
(upper-case-p *char*)	
use-package	function
(use-package *package*)	
use-value	restart, function
(use-value *value*)	
values	function
(values *val-1 . . .val-n*)	
values-list	function
(values-list *list*)	
vector	function
(vector *elem-1 . . . elem-n*)	
vector	type specifier
vector-pop	function
(vector-pop *vector*)	
vector-push	function
(vector-push item *vector*)	
vector-push-extend	function
(vector-push-extend item *vector*)	
vectorp	function
(vectorp *object*)	
warn	function
(warn *condition-or-string*)	
when	macro
(when *test body*)	

with-accessors	macro
(with-accessors *accessor-binding-list*	
instance-form	
body)	
with-input-from-string	macro
(with-input-from-string	
(*var string*)	
body)	
with-open-file	macro
(with-open-file	
(*var string*)	
body)	
with-open-stream	macro
(with-open-stream	
(*var string*)	
body)	
with-output-to-string	macro
(with-output-to-string	
(*var string*)	
body)	
with-slots	macro
(with-slots *slot-name-binding-list*	
instance-form	
body)	
write	function
(write *object*)	
write-byte	function
(write-byte *integer stream*)	
write-char	function
(write-char *char*)	
write-line	function
(write-line *string*)	
write-string	function
(write-string *string*)	
write-to-string	function
(write-to-string *object*)	
y-or-n-p	function
(y-or-n-p)	
yes-or-no-p	function
(yes-or-no-p)	
zerop	function
(zerop *number*)	
*	function
(* *number number*)	
+	function
(+ *number number*)	
-	function
(- *number number*)	

/   function
    (/ *number number*)

/=   function
    (/= *number number*)

1+   function
    (1+ *number*)

1-   function
    (1- *number*)

<   function
    (< *number number*)

<=   function
    (<= *number number*)

=   function
    (= *number number*)

>   function
    (> *number number*)

>=   function
    (>= *number number*)

Solutions for the Exercises

CHAPTER 1: INTRODUCTION

Exercise 1.1

Lisp symbols are like variables in other languages; they have names, and they can have associated values. A symbol evaluates to its current binding. Common Lisp strings are a type of constant. They cannot have an associated value. Strings, like all constants, evaluate to themselves.

Exercise 1.2

a. 5! = 120
b. 11/2 (Result is converted to a rational.)

Exercise 1.3

a. (/ 3 (* 2 3))
b. (* (/ 3 2) 3)
c. (/ (* .5 10) (+ 11 4))

Exercise 1.4

Remember that Lisp treats anything wrapped in parentheses as a list and that lists are evaluated as function calls. When you wrap the extra set of parentheses around a list, you create a new list with the former list as the first element. Lisp expects the first element of a list to be a function name, and it will object when it finds a list instead.

Exercise 1.5

All possible arithmetic combinations involving fixed-point (integer) operands will yield integer results except for division with two-integer operands, which may yield a ratio result. Whenever one or more floating-point operands are present, however, the result will always be of the floating-point type. This feature is sometimes referred to as floating-point contagion.

CHAPTER 2: THE RULE OF THREE

Exercise 2.1

a. No.

b. Yes.

c. No, but it could be made to work by typing

```
(+ (eval (defvar var5 4))
   (eval (defvar var6 3)))
```

d. Yes.

e. No, but once again, it is a problem of not evaluating far enough. It would work if changed to

```
(setf var8 'var9
      var9 3
      var10 (+ (eval var8)
               var9))
```

f. No, but this would work using the set function:

```
(set 'bad-guy 'bluto)
```

Exercise 2.2

When the Lisp interpreter encounters a function call, it first checks to see if a function by that name has already been defined. It then evaluates each argument sequentially from left to right and passes the values to the function. The function never sees the actual arguments that were passed, only the values they return after they are evaluated. The quote special form needs to return the original argument, not the value of the original argument, and therefore cannot be implemented as a function.

Exercise 2.3

a. Yes.

b. No.

c. No.

d. Yes.

Exercise 2.4

a. B

b. C

c. Z

d. COMMON-LISP

Exercise 2.5

a. `(second test-list)` or `(nth 1 test-list)`

b. `(rest test-list)`

   c. `(rest (rest test-list))` or `(nthcdr 1 test-list)`

   d. `(rest (rest (rest (rest test-list))))` or `(nthcdr 4 test-list)`

Exercise 2.6

Any list of the form `(( x ( y b)) z )` could be bound to `listx`, where *x*, *y*, and *z* could represent any Lisp expression.

Exercise 2.7

   a. `(symbolp x)`

   b. `(rationalp x)` and `(typep x '(or integer ratio))`

   c. `(typep x '(or character string))`

   d. `(atom x)`

   e. `(upper-case-p x)`

Exercise 2.8

   a. T

   b. T

   c. NIL

   d. T

   e. NIL

   f. NIL

   g. T

   h. T

   i. NIL

   j. T

Exercise 2.9 (a)

x	y	(and (not x) (not y))	(not (or x y))
t	t	nil	nil
nil	t	nil	nil
t	nil	nil	nil
nil	nil	t	t

Exercise 2.9 (b)

x	y	(not (or x y))	(or (not x)(not y))
t	t	nil	nil
nil	t	nil	t
t	nil	nil	t
nil	nil	t	t

Exercise 2.10

All of the arguments to a function are evaluated before the function is executed. The if special form evaluates its consequent (i.e., the second argument) only if the antecedent (i.e., the first argument) evaluates to a non-NIL value. Since this behavior would be impossible to produce in a function, it must be implemented as a macro or a special form.

Exercise 2.11

a. If the current binding of x is a list, return the tail of the list.

b. If the current binding of x is an integer, increment it and return the new binding.

c. Return ACE if rank is 1, JACK if rank is 11, QUEEN if rank is 12, and KING if rank is 13. Otherwise, return the current binding of rank.

d. If my-object is currently bound to a list, return the head of the list. Otherwise, construct a new list with the single element my-object. Note that the third clause is never used because the first two clauses are exhaustive.

Exercise 2.12

```
(defvar year 1980)
(if (= (mod year 400) 0)
 T
 (if (= (mod year 100) 0)
  NIL
   (if (= (mod year 4) 0)
    T
    NIL)))
```

Exercise 2.13

```
(defvar obj1 99)
(defvar obj2 100)
(typecase obj1
  (symbol (typecase obj2
            (symbol 'eq)
            (otherwise 'equalp)))
  (number (typecase obj2
            (number 'eql)
            (otherwise 'equalp)))
  (list (typecase obj2
          (list 'equal)
          (otherwise 'equalp)))
  (otherwise 'equalp))
```

Exercise 2.14

a. (cadr '(a b c))

    b.   `(cadddr '(a b c d e))`

    c.   `(cdddr '(a b c d e))`

    d.   `(cdadr '(a (b c d) e f g))`

Exercise 2.15

a. `(cond ((not (atom x)) (rest x)))` or, more succinctly,

    `(cond ((listp x) (rest x)))`

b. `(cond ((integerp x)`

         `(setf x (+ x 1))`

      `x))`

c. `(cond ((= rank 1) 'ace)`

        `((= rank 11) 'jack)`

        `((= rank 12) 'queen)`

        `((= rank 13) 'king)`

        `(t rank))`

e. `(cond ((typep my-object 'list)(first my-object))`

      `(t (list my-object)))`

Exercise 2.16

```
(cond ((string= (package-name *package*)
               "CL-USER")
       "Okay!")
      ((string= (package-name *package*)
               "SYSTEM")
       (setf *package*
             (find-package "CL-USER"))
       "Package changed to CL-USER")
      (t (package-name *package*)))
```

CHAPTER 3: FORMS AND FUNCTIONS

Exercise 3.1

```
(defun adiff (num1 num2)
  (abs (- num1 num2)))
```

Exercise 3.2

```
(defun days-in-month (month )
  (case month
    (february 28 )
    ((april june september november) 30)
    (t 31 )))
```

Exercise 3.3

a. Yes.
b. Yes.
c. No.
d. Yes.

Exercise 3.4

```
(defun leap-year-p (year)
  (cond ((= (mod year 400) 0) T)
        ((= (mod year 100) 0) NIL)
        ((= (mod year 4) 0) T)
        (T NIL)))
```

Exercise 3.5

You could easily write a sum-list that would work for lists of three elements as follows:

```
(defun sum-list (number-list)
  (+ (first number-list)
     (second number-list)
     (third number-list)))
```

A more general version, which would work for lists of any length, could be defined recursively as follows:

```
(defun sum-list (number-list)
  (if number-list (+ (first number-list)
                     (sum-list
                       (rest number-list)))
      0))
```

Exercise 3.6

	variables			returned value
	item	sorted-list	head	
[1]	12	(6 8 9 10 12 14)	6	(6 8 9 10 12 12 14)
[2]	12	(8 9 10 12 14)	8	(8 9 10 12 12 14)
[3]	12	(9 10 12 14)	9	(9 10 12 12 14)
[4]	12	(10 12 14)	10	(10 12 12 14)
[5]	12	(12 14)	12	(12 12 14)

Exercise 3.7

```
(defun my-length (input-list)
  (if input-list
    (1+ (my-length (rest input-list)))
    0))
```

Exercise 3.8

```
(defun member-p (item input-list)
  (if input-list
      (if (eq item
              (first input-list))
          item
          (member-p item (rest input-list)))))
```

Exercise 3.9

```
(defun insertion-sort (input-list)
  (if input-list
      (insert-sorted (first input-list)
      (insertion-sort (rest input-list)))))
```

Exercise 3.10

```
(defun squash-list (input-list)
  (if input-list
      (let ((item (first input-list)))
        (append (if (listp item)
                    (squash-list item)
                    (list item))
                (squash-list (rest input-list))))))
```

Exercise 3.11

```
(defun remove-redundancies (input-list)
  (let ((head (first input-list))
        (tail (rest input-list)))
    (if tail
        (if (member head tail)
            (remove-redundancies tail)
            (cons head
                  (remove-redundancies tail)))
        (list head))))
```

Exercise 3.12

a. This is a simple recursive countdown function. It prints the numbers as it counts down and returns the symbol LIFTOFF !

b. This function will reverse a list. Note that this is not necessarily the most efficient way to do a list reversal.

c. This function returns the nth element of the Fibonacci series. The Fibonacci series (named after an eleventh-century Italian mathematician) is defined recursively as follows:

$$fib(x) = \begin{cases} x \\ fib(x-1) + fib(x-2) \end{cases}$$

when x = 0, 1 or 2 for all other natural numbers

Exercise 3.13

The answer is 3.

Exercise 3.14

```
(defun build-infix-list (operator operand-list)
   (let (result-list)
      (dolist (operand operand-list result-list)
         (setf result-list
               (append result-list
                       (list operator operand)))))))
```

Exercise 3.15

```
(defun member-p (item input-list)
  (let (result)
     (dolist (element input-list result)
        (if (eq item element)
            (setf result item)))))
```

This works, but the following is more efficient. Do you see why?

```
(defun member-p (item input-list)
  (let (result)
     (do ((to-do input-list (rest to-do)))
         ((or result (null to-do)) result )
        (if (eq item (first to-do))
            (setf result item)))))
```

Exercise 3.16

a. This is an iterative version of the `factorial` function. You might be interested in doing some comparative timings on this function and on the recursive version in Exercise 3.9(a). Use a fairly large number as the argument and either time it by hand or use the Common Lisp `time` macro.

b. This function computes the length of a list.

c. This is an iterative list reversal function.

Exercise 3.17(a)

```
(let (element
      (to-do '(do re me fa sol la te do)))
  (loop
    (if (null to-do) (return 'Ciao!))
    (setf element (first to-do))
    (setf to-do (rest to-do))
    (print element)))
```

Exercise 3.17(b)

```
(let ((my-index -1))
  (loop
    (setf my-index (1+ my-index))
```

```
                              (if (> my-index 3) (return 'Ciao!))
                              (print my-index)))
```

Exercise 3.18

```
(defun combinations (list-1 list-2 list-3)
  (let (result-list)
    (dolist (element-1 list-1 result-list)
      (dolist (element-2 list-2 )
        (dolist (element-3 list-3)
          (setf result-list (cons (list element-1
                                         element-2
                                         element-3)
                                  result-list)))))))
```

Exercise 3.19

See the solution for Exercise 3.20.

Exercise 3.20

```
  (defun lisp-to-fortran-4 (expr)
;; this version extracts the rhs
  (let ((lhs (second expr))
        (rhs (third expr)))
    (write lhs)
    (write '=)
    (dolist (element (prefix-to-infix-4 rhs))
      (write element))
    (terpri)))
(defun prefix-to-infix-4 (expr)
;; handles unary operators
  (if (listp expr)
    (if (= (length expr) 2)
        (let ((operator (convert-operator (first expr)))
              (operand (second expr)))
          (list operator
         (prefix-to-infix-4 operand)))
        (let ((operator (convert-operator (first expr)))
              (new-expr (list (prefix-to-infix-4 (second expr)))))
          (dolist (element (nthcdr 2 expr) new-expr)
            (setq new-expr (append
                           new-expr
                           (list
                            operator
                            (prefix-to-infix-4 element)))))))
      expr))
(defun convert-operator (operator)
      (case operator
        (negate '-)
        (expt '** )
        (t operator)))
```

Exercise 3.21

This will not work for the same reason that

```
(scalar-arithmetic 5 '(5 10 15) '+)
```

will not work: The symbol + evaluates to its current binding, not to its functional definition.

Exercise 3.22

```
(mapc #'(lambda (x y)
           (print (list x y))
           (terpri))
      capitals
      states)
```

Exercise 3.23

a. This function will filter out all occurrences of the value passed in the parameter x from the list passed as y.

b. Trick question. This function is a no-op. Remember that mapc doesn't collect its results; it is only called for effect.

c. This function does a rotate left on the elements of the input list.

Exercise 3.24

```
(defun calculator ()
  (let ((result (read)))
    (do ((operator (read) (read)))
        ((eq operator '=) result)
      (setf result (funcall (symbol-function operator)
                            result
                            (read))))))
```

Exercise 3.25

```
(defun my-maplist (func input-list)
  (let (result-list)
    (do ((to-do input-list (rest to-do)))
        ((null to-do) result-list)
      (setf result-list
            (append result-list
                    (list (funcall func to-do)))))))
```

Exercise 3.26

This is a more readable version. What is more, it works!

```
(defun permute (var (if (> (length var) 1)
  (do ((n (length var) (1-n))
       (var2 var (rotate-list var2))
       (result ()))
      ((<= n 0) result)
```

```
    (setq result
        (append result
                (mapcar #' (lambda (x)
                             (append (list (first var2))
                                     x))
                    (permute (cdr var2))))))))
  (list var)))
(defun rotate-list (old-list)
  (append (rest old-list) (list (first old-list)))))
```

CHAPTER 4: INQUISITOR OF STRUCTURES

Exercise 4.1

A symbol is a complex data structure in Lisp; it can simultaneously hold a value and a functional definition. Strings are simply self-evaluating forms.

Exercise 4.2

```
CL> (setf (get 'foo 'time-of-creation) (get-universal-time))
2799344285
CL> (get 'foo 'time-of-creation)
2799344285
```

Exercise 4.3

```
(defun enumerate-list (input-list)
  (do ((to-do input-list (rest to-do))
       (counter 0 (1+ counter)))
      ((null to-do) (1- counter))
    (setf (get (first to-do) 'list-position)
          counter)))
```

Exercise 4.4

```
(defun my-set (symbol new-value)
  (if (boundp symbol)
      (setf (get symbol 'old-value)
            (symbol-value symbol)))
  (set symbol new-value))
```

Exercise 4.5

```
(defun generate-number ()
  (incf *last-number*))
```

Exercise 4.6(a)

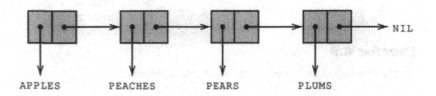

Exercise 4.6(b)

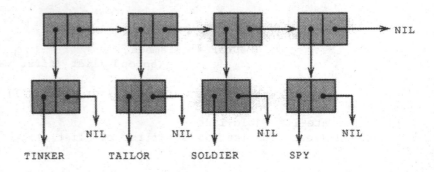

Exercise 4.6(c)

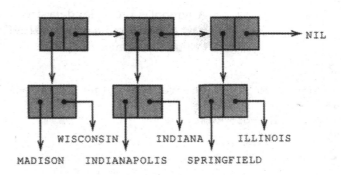

Exercise 4.7

The (nil nil nil) list is equivalent to

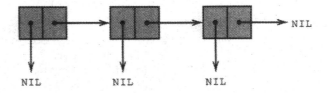

The empty list is simply represented as the nil constant.

Exercise 4.8

```
(defun swap-elements (n m input-list)
  (let ((nth-value (nth n input-list)))
    (setf (nth n input-list)(nth m input-list))
    (setf (nth m input-list) nth-value)
    input-list))
```

Exercise 4.9

```
(defun my-intersection (list-1 list-2)
  (let (intersection-list)
```

```
      (dolist (element list-1 intersection-list)
        (if (and (member-p element list-2)
                 (not (member-p element intersection-list)))
            (setf intersection-list
                  (nconc intersection-list (list element)))))))))
(defun my-union (list-1 list-2)
  (let ((union-list (append list-1 list-2)))
    (remove-redundancies union-list)))
```

Exercise 4.10

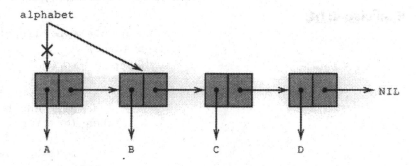

Exercise 4.11

```
(defun prefix-calculator ()
  (let ((stack (list (read)))
        result)
    (loop
      (if (null stack) (return result))
      (setf next (read))
      (if (numberp next)
          (if result
              (setf result (funcall (pop stack)
                                    result
                                    next))
            (setf result next))
        (push next stack)))))
```

Exercise 4.12

```
(defun squash-list (input-list)
  (let ((result-list))
    (do ((to-do (list input-list)))
        ((null to-do) result-list)
      (setf result-list
            (nconc result-list
                   (do ((item (pop to-do) (first item)))
                       ((atom item) (list item))
                     (if (rest item)
                         (push (rest item) to-do))))))))
```

Exercise 4.13

```
(defun pull (input-list)
  (let ((last-element (first (last input-list))))
    (nbutlast input-list)
    last-element))
```

This doesn't work, though. When the input list has fewer than two elements, the nbutlast function has no penultimate cons cell to modify. To get this to work, we need to implement pull as a macro. You will see how to do that in Chapter 7.

Exercise 4.14

```
(defun bubble-sort (input-list)
  (let (done)
    (loop
      (setf done t)
      (do ((to-do input-list (rest to-do)))
          ((equal(length to-do)1))
        (when (> (first to-do)
                 (second to-do))
          (swap-elements 0 1 to-do)
          (setf done nil)))
      (if done (return input-list)))))
(defun character-bubble-sort (input-list)
  (let (done)
    (loop
      (setf done t)
      (do ((to-do input-list (rest to-do)))
          ((equal(length to-do)1))
        (when (char> (first to-do)
                     (second to-do))
          (swap-elements 0 1 to-do)
          (setf done nil)))
      (if done (return input-list)))))
```

Exercise 4.15

```
(defun bft (tree)
  (do ((queue (list tree)))
      ((null queue))
    (let ((next (first (last queue))))
      (setf queue (butlast queue))
      (visit-node (first next))
      (dolist (subtree (rest next))
        (push subtree queue)))))
(defun visit-node (node)
  (print node))
```

Exercise 4.16

```
(defun inner-product (vector-1 vector-2)
  (reduce #'+
          (map 'vector
               #'*
               vector-1
               vector-2)))
```

Exercise 4.17

```
(defun sample (m n)
  (if (> m 0)
      (let ((selections (sample (1- m) (1- n)))
            (next (random n)))
        (if (member next selections)
            (cons n selections)
            (cons next selections)))))
(defun random-test (m n i)
  (let ((array (vector (1+ n)
                          :element-type 'integer
                          :initial-element 0)))
    (dotimes (count i array)
      (dolist (element (sample m n))
        (setf (aref array element)
              (1+ (aref array element)))))))
(inspect (random-test 5 10 10000))
```

Exercise 4.18

```
(defun palindrome-p (test-string)
  (equalp test-string
          (reverse test-string)))
```

Exercise 4.19

```
(defun translate-to-pig-latin (symbol)
  (let* ((new-string (symbol-name symbol))
         (end (length new-string)))
    (concatenate 'string
                 (do ((ptr 0 (1+ ptr)))
                     ((or (vowel-p (char new-string ptr))
                          (= ptr end)) (subseq new-string ptr))
                   (setf new-string
                         (concatenate 'string
                                      new-string
                                      (make-string 1
                                                   :initial-element
                                                   (char new-string ptr)))))
                 "AY" )))
(defun vowel-p (character)
  (find character '(#\A #\E #\I #\O #\U)))
```

Exercise 4.20

```lisp
(defun roman-numeral (n)
  (let ((number-table (make-array '(4 10)
                         :element-type 'string
                         :initial-contents
                         '(("" "I" "II" "III" "IV" "V" "VI" "VII" "VIII" "IX")
                           ("" "X" "XX" "XXX" "XL" "L" "LX" "LXX" "LXXX" "XC")
                           ("" "C" "CC" "CCC" "CD" "D" "DC" "DCC" "DCCC" "CM")
                           ("" "M" "MM" "MMM" "" "" "" "" "" "" ))))
        (result ""))
    (do ((left n (floor left 10))
         (row 0 (1+ row)))
        ((= left 0) result)
      (setf result
            (concatenate 'string
                         (aref number-table row (mod left 10))
                         result)))))
```

Exercise 4.21

```lisp
(defun outer-product (vector-1 vector-2)
  (let ((n (length vector-1))
        (m (length vector-2)))
    (if (= n m)
        (let ((matrix (make-array (list n n))))
          (dotimes (row n matrix)
            (dotimes (col n)
              (setf (aref matrix row col)
                    (* (elt vector-1 row)
                       (elt vector-2 col))))))
        "Vectors do not conform for multiplication")))
```

Exercise 4.22

```lisp
(defun matrix-multiply (array-1 array-2)
  (let ((i (array-dimension array-1 0))
        (j (array-dimension array-1 1))
        (n (array-dimension array-2 0))
        (m (array-dimension array-2 1)))
    (if (= j n)
        (let ((matrix (make-array (list i m))))
          (dotimes (row i matrix)
            (dotimes (col m)
              (setf (aref matrix row col)
                    (let ((sum 0))
                      (dotimes (ptr j sum)
                        (setf sum (+ (* (aref array-1 row ptr)
                                        (aref array-2 ptr col))
                                     sum))))))))
        "Matrices do not conform for multiplication")))
```

Exercise 4.23

```
(defun safe-squares (board)
  (let (safe-positions)
    (dotimes (rank 8 safe-positions)
      (dotimes (row 8)
        (if (and (rank-clear-p rank board)
                 (row-clear-p row board)
                 (diagonals-clear-p rank row board))
          (setf safe-positions (cons (cons rank row)
                                     safe-positions)))))))
(defun rank-clear-p (rank board)
  (let ((clear-flg t))
    (do ((row 0 (1+ row)))
        ((or (not clear-flg) (> row 7)) clear-flg)
      (if (aref board rank row)
        (setf clear-flg nil)))))
(defun row-clear-p (row board)
  (let ((clear-flg t))
    (do ((rank 0 (1+ rank)))
        ((or (not clear-flg) (> rank 7)) clear-flg)
      (if (aref board rank row)
        (setf clear-flg nil)))))
(defun diagonals-clear-p (rank row board)
  (and (upper-right-diagonal-clear-p rank row board)
       (upper-left-diagonal-clear-p rank row board)
       (lower-right-diagonal-clear-p rank row board)
       (lower-left-diagonal-clear-p rank row board)))
(defun upper-right-diagonal-clear-p (start-rank start-row board)
  (let ((clear-flg t))
    (do ((rank start-rank (1+ rank))
         (row start-row (1+ row)))
        ((or (not clear-flg)
             (> rank 7)
             (> row 7)))
      (if (aref board rank row)
        (setf clear-flg nil)))
    clear-flg))
(defun upper-left-diagonal-clear-p (start-rank start-row board)
  (let ((clear-flg t))
    (do ((rank start-rank (1- rank))
         (row start-row (1+ row)))
        ((or (not clear-flg)
             (< rank 0)
             (> row 7)))
      (if (aref board rank row)
        (setf clear-flg nil)))
    clear-flg))
(defun lower-right-diagonal-clear-p (start-rank start-row board)
```

```
     (let ((clear-flg t))
       (do ((rank start-rank (1+ rank))
            (row start-row (1- row)))
           ((or (not clear-flg)
                (> rank 7)
                (< row 0)))
         (if (aref board rank row)
             (setf clear-flg nil)))
       clear-flg))
   (defun lower-left-diagonal-clear-p (start-rank start-row board)
     (let ((clear-flg t))
       (do ((rank start-rank (1- rank))
            (row start-row (1- row)))
           ((or (not clear-flg)
                (< rank 0)
                (< row 0)))
         (if (aref board rank row)
             (setf clear-flg nil)))
       clear-flg))
```

Exercise 4.24

```
   (defun bubble-sort-2 (input-sequence)
     (let (done)
       (loop
         (setf done t)
         (dotimes (ptr (1- (length input-sequence)))
           (when (greater-p (elt input-sequence ptr)
                            (elt input-sequence (1+ ptr)))
                 (swap-elements-2 ptr (1+ ptr) input-sequence)
             (setf done nil)))
         (if done (return input-sequence)))))
   (defun swap-elements-2 (n m input-sequence)
     (let ((nth-value (elt input-sequence n)))
       (setf (elt input-sequence n)(elt input-sequence m))
       (setf (elt input-sequence m) nth-value)
       input-sequence))
   (defun greater-p (item-1 item-2)
     (typecase item-1
       (character (if (characterp item-2)
                      (char> item-1 item-2)))
       (number (if (numberp item-2)
                   (> item-1 item-2)))
       (string (if (stringp item-2)
                   (string> item-1 item-2)))
       (t (format t "Warning! Could not compare ~a to ~a ~%" item-1 item-2))))
```

Exercise 4.25

- Property lists are updated destructively; a-lists are not.
- Calling `getf` on a property list results in an item's being returned; calling `assoc` on an a-list causes a key-item pair to be returned.
- Association lists retain old key-item pairs; property lists do not.
- You can retrieve keys from an a-list using `rassoc`, given an item.
- The `assoc` function allows you to specify the equality test used, whereas `getf` always uses `eq`.

Exercise 4.26

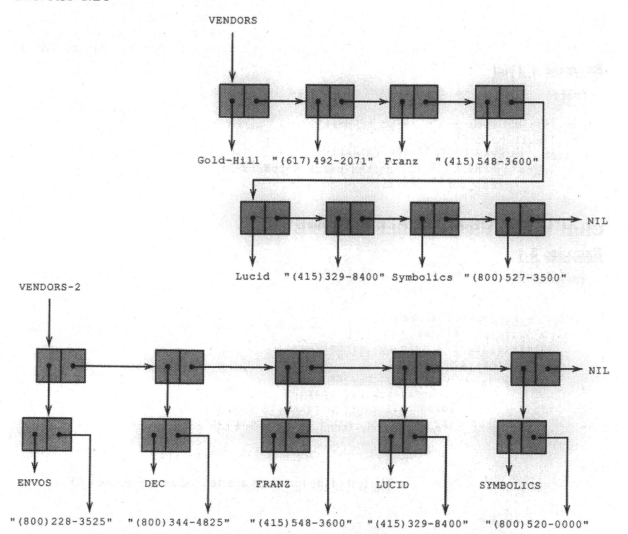

Exercise 4.27(a)

```
(defvar airports '(BOS "Boston,MA"
                   DCA "Washington, D.C."
                   JFK "New York, N.Y."
                   LAX "Los Angeles,CA"
                   ORD "Chicago,IL"
                   SEA "Seattle, WA"
                   SFO "San Francisco, CA"))
```

Exercise 4.27(b)

```
(defvar airports-2 '((BOS . "Boston,MA")
                     (DCA . "Washington, D.C.")
                     (JFK . "New York, N.Y.")
                     (LAX . "Los Angeles,CA")
                     (ORD . "Chicago,IL")
                     (SEA . "Seattle, WA")
                     (SFO . "San Francisco, CA")))
```

Exercise 4.27(c)

```
(defvar airports-3 (make-hash-table :size 100 :test #'eq))

(do ((to-do airports-2 (rest to-do)))
    ((null to-do))
  (let ((dotted-pair (first to-do)))
    (setf (gethash (first dotted-pair) airports-3)
          (rest dotted-pair))))
```

CHAPTER 5: OBJECTS ALL SUBLIME

Exercise 5.1

```
(defstruct position rank
                    file)

(defun safe-squares (board)
  (let (safe-positions)
    (dotimes (rank 8 safe-positions)
      (dotimes (row 8)
        (if (and (rank-clear-p rank board)
                 (row-clear-p row board)
                 (diagonals-clear-p rank row board))
            (setf safe-positions (cons (make-position :rank rank
                                                      :file row)
                               safe-positions)))))))
```

The rest of the functions are defined as in Exercise 4.23.

Exercise 5.2

```
CL> (setq *print-circle* t)
T
CL> (setf (dcons-predecessor second-element) first-element)
#1=#S(DCONS PREDECESSOR NIL CONTENTS JANUARY SUCCESSOR #S(DCONS PREDECESSOR
#1# CONTENTS FEBRUARY SUCCESSOR NIL))
CL> (setf (dcons-predecessor third-element) second-element)
#1=#S(DCONS PREDECESSOR #S(DCONS PREDECESSOR NIL CONTENTS JANUARY SUCCESSOR
#1#) CONTENTS FEBRUARY SUCCESSOR NIL)
CL> (setf (dcons-successor second-element) third-element)
#1=#S(DCONS PREDECESSOR #2=#S(DCONS PREDECESSOR #S(DCONS PREDECESSOR NIL
CONTENTS JANUARY SUCCESSOR #2#)
CONTENTS FEBRUARY SUCCESSOR #1#) CONTENTS MARCH SUCCESSOR NIL)
```

Exercise 5.3

```
(defstruct date day month year)
(make-date :day 27 :month 7 :year 89)
```

Exercise 5.4

```
(defstruct playing-card suit rank)

(defconstant card-suits '#(hearts clubs diamonds spades))
(defconstant card-ranks '#(ace 2 3 4 5 6 7 8 9 10 jack queen king))

(defun sample (m n)
  (let (selections )
    (do* ((j (- n m) (1+ j))
          (s (random j) (random j)))
         ((= j n) selections)
      (setf selections
            (cons (if (member s selections)
                      j
                      s)
                  selections)))))

(defun compute-suit (number)
  (elt card-suits (floor number 13)))

(defun compute-rank (number)
  (elt card-ranks (mod number 13)))

(defun deal-hand ()
  (let ((number-list (sample 5 51))
        hand)
    (dolist (number number-list)
      (setf hand
(cons (make-playing-card :suit (compute-suit number)
          :rank (compute-rank number))
                hand)))
    hand))
```

Exercise 5.5

```
(defun dft (tree)
  (when tree
    (visit-node (tree-node-contents tree))
    (dolist (subtree (tree-node-child-list tree))
            (dft subtree)))))

(defun visit-node (node)
  (print node))

(dft (make-tree-node
         :contents 'a
         :child-list (list (make-tree-node
                               :contents 'b
                               :child-list
                               (list (make-tree-node
                                       contents 'd
                                      child-list nil)
                                     (make-tree-node
                                       :contents 'e
                                      :child-list nil)))
                   (make-tree-node
                     :contents 'c
                    :child-list (list (make-tree-node
                                        :contents 'f
                                      : child-list nil)
                                   make-tree-node
                                         :contents 'g
                                  :child-list nil))))))))
```

Exercise 5.6

```
(defvar old-faithful (make-instance 'auto
                         :make 'Volkswagon
                         :model 'Bug
                         :year 1968
                         :fuel 'gas
                         :fuel-capacity 12
                         :odometer 100000
                         :mileage-rating 29))

(inspect old-faithful)
```

Note: Implementations that are not fully compatible with the ANSI standard may not support the inspection of CLOS objects.

Exercise 5.7

```
(defclass playing-card ()
  (suit :initarg :suit
   rank :initarg :rank))

(defun deal-hand ()
```

```
(let ((number-list (sample 5 51))
      hand)
  (dolist (number number-list)
    (setf hand
          (cons (make-instance 'playing-card
                   :suit (compute-suit number)
                   :rank (compute-rank number))
                hand)))
  hand))
```

The other function and constant definitions from Exercise 5.4 are unchanged.

Exercise 5.8

```
(defstruct location
  city
  state)

(defclass airport ()
  ((name :initarg :name)
   (location :initarg :location)))

(defvar airport-table (make-hash-table :size 100
                            :test #'eq))

(setf (gethash 'BOS airport-table)
      (make-instance 'airport
         :name "Logan"
         :location (make-location :city "Boston"
                       :state "Massachusetts")))
(setf (gethash 'DCA airport-table)
      (make-instance 'airport
         :name "Dulles"
    :location (make-location :city "Washington"
                 :state "District of Columbia")))
(setf (gethash 'JFK airport-table)
      (make-instance 'airport
         :name "Kennedy"
         :location (make-location :city "New York"
                                  :state "New York")))
(setf (gethash 'ORD airport-table)
      (make-instance 'airport
         :name "O'hare"
         :location (make-location :city "Chicago"
                       state "Illinois")))
(setf (gethash 'STL airport-table)
      (make-instance 'airport
         :name "Lambert"
  :location (make-location :city "St. Louis"
                 :state "Missouri")))
```

Exercise 5.9

```
(defun drive-vehicle (vehicle miles-driven)
  (setf (slot-value vehicle 'odometer)
        (+ (slot-value vehicle 'odometer)
           miles-driven)))
```

Exercise 5.10

```
(defclass chess-piece ()
  (color
   position))
(defclass king (chess-piece) ())
(defclass queen (chess-piece) ())
(defclass rook (chess-piece) ())
(defclass bishop (chess-piece) ())
(defclass knight (chess-piece) ())
(defclass pawn (chess-piece) ())
```

See Figure 5-9.

Exercise 5.11

```
(defun move (piece new-rank new-file)
  (setf (slot-value piece 'position)
    (make-position :rank new-rank :file new-file)))
```

Exercise 5.12

```
(defclass electrical-component ()
  ((voltage :initarg :voltage))
  (:documentation
   "Class of electrical components"))

(defclass battery (vehicle-part electrical-component)
  ((battery-type :initarg :type)
   (terminals :initarg terminals
              :initform 'side-mount)
   (cranking-capacity :initarg :capacity))
  (:documentation
   "Class of motor vehicle batteries"))

(defclass carburetor (vehicle-part)
  ((barrels :initarg :barrels
            :initform 2))
  (:documentation
   "Class of motor vehicle carburetors"))

(defclass starter (vehicle-part electrical-component)
  ((amperage :initarg :amperage))
  (:documentation
   "Class of motor vehicle starters"))

(defclass motor-vehicle ()
```

```
    ((make      :initarg :make)
     (odometer :initform 0
                :type 'integer
                :initarg :odometer)
     (fuel      :initform 'gasoline
                :initarg :fuel)
     (fuel-tank :initarg :fuel-tank
                :initform (make-instance 'fuel-tank))
     (battery :initarg :battery
                :initform (make-instance 'battery))
     (carburetor :initarg :carburetor
                :initform (make-instance 'carburetor))
     (starter :initarg :starter
                :initform (make-instance 'starter))
     (year :initarg :year))
    (:documentation
     "Class of motor vehicles"))

(defun make-auto ()
  (let ((auto (make-instance 'auto)))
    ;;fix the fuel tank to point to its auto object
    (setf (slot-value (slot-value auto 'fuel-tank) 'vehicle)
          auto)
    ;;fix the battery to point to its auto object
    (setf (slot-value (slot-value auto 'battery) 'vehicle)
          auto)
    ;;fix the carburetor to point to its auto object
    (setf (slot-value (slot-value auto 'carburetor) 'vehicle)
          auto)
    ;;fix the starter to point to its auto object
    (setf (slot-value (slot-value auto 'starter) 'vehicle)
          auto)
    auto))
```

Exercise 5.13

```
(defun fill-er-up (motor-vehicle)
  (let* ((fuel-tank (slot-value motor-vehicle 'fuel-tank))
         (fuel-capacity (slot-value fuel-tank 'fuel-capacity)))
    (setf (slot-value fuel-tank 'fuel-volume) fuel-capacity)))
```

Exercise 5.14

Exercise 5.15

See Appendix D.

Exercise 5.16

```
(defclass chess-game ()
  ((white-pieces :initarg :white-pieces
                     :initform (set-up-pieces 'white))
   (white-moves :initarg :white-moves
                   :initform nil)
   (black-pieces :initarg :black-pieces
                     :initform (set-up-pieces 'black))
   (black-moves :initarg :black-moves
                   :initform nil)))

(defclass chess-move ()
  ((piece :initarg :piece)
   (new-position :initarg :new-position)))

(defclass capture (chess-move)
  ((captured-piece :initarg :captured-piece)))
```

Exercise 5.17

The information content of both schemes is identical. The difference lies in how you access the information. To learn the position of a specified piece given the scheme used in Exercise 5.16, you need only access its position slot. Using the other scheme, you must search the array for the piece in order to find its indices. This would be quite inefficient. On the other hand, to check to see if a particular position is free would be a simple array reference in the latter scheme but could involve searching both lists of pieces in the former scheme. Your decision then should be based on which kind of access you need to do more frequently. If you need to perform both types of access fairly frequently (as you probably will), you might consider employing both storage schemes. This would solve your access problems, but it would introduce a new problem: how to ensure that both representations of the position remain consistent.

Exercise 5.18

See Appendix D.

Exercise 5.19

The class precedence rules are described formally in the CLOS Specification Document (Bobrow et al., 1988). To see how they work in a situation in which there is an inheritance conflict, try defining the following classes:

```
(defclass class-a ()
```

```
        ((slot-1 :initform 'foo)))
(defclass class-b ()
   ((slot-1 :initform 'bar)))
(defclass class-c (class-a)
   ())
(defclass class-d (class-c class-b )
   ())
```

If you were to create an instance of the class-d class, what would it hold in its slot-1 slot?

```
CL> (slot-value (make-instance 'class-d) 'slot-1)
FOO
```

However, if you had instead defined class-d like this:

```
(defclass class-d (class-b class-c )
   ())
```

its instances would be initialized with the other value:

```
CL> (slot-value (make-instance 'class-d) 'slot-1)
BAR
```

CHAPTER 6: METHODS

Exercise 6.1

```
(defmethod fill-er-up ((vehicle motor-vehicle) fuel-type)
   (with-slots (fuel-tank fuel) vehicle
      (let ((fuel-capacity (slot-value fuel-tank 'fuel-capacity)))
         (setf fuel fuel-type)
         (setf (slot-value fuel-tank 'fuel-volume) fuel-capacity))))
```

Exercise 6.2

```
(defmethod prepare-for-sale ((vehicle motor-vehicle))
   (with-slots (odometer) vehicle
      (setf odometer
            (/ odometer 2))))
```

Exercise 6.3

```
(defmethod drive-vehicle ((automobile auto) miles-driven)
   (with-slots (odometer fuel-tank mileage-rating) automobile
      (let* ((fuel-volume (slot-value fuel-tank 'fuel-volume))
             (range (* fuel-volume mileage-rating)))
         (cond
            ;;not enough gas!
```

```
   ((>= miles-driven range)
    (setf (slot-value fuel-tank 'fuel-volume) 0)
    (setf odometer (+ odometer range)))
  ;;otherwise, adjust odometer and fuel-volume
  (t
    (setf (slot-value fuel-tank 'fuel-volume)
          (- fuel-volume
             (/ miles-driven
                mileage-rating)))
    (setf odometer (+ odometer miles-driven)))))))))
```

Exercise 6.4

Some object-oriented languages do not permit an outside entity to change the internal state of an object. CLOS does not enforce this kind of data encapsulation. Any function can modify the state of a CLOS object using slot-value as an access-form for setf. Data encapsulation can be achieved in CLOS, however, if all programmers agree to access the slots of an object only through its advertised interface (i.e., through the use of its accessor methods). Data encapsulation is achieved as a convention in CLOS, therefore, rather than as an enforced requirement.

Exercise 6.5

```
(defmethod add-to-move-list ((move chess-move))
  (with-slots (piece new-position) move
    (let* ((color (slot-value piece 'color))
           (game (slot-value piece 'game))
           (moves-slot (if (eq color 'white)
                           'white-moves
                           'black-moves)))
      (setf (slot-value game moves-slot)
            (cons move (slot-value game moves-slot))))))
```

Exercise 6.6

```
(defmethod change-piece-position ((move chess-move))
  (with-slots (piece new-position) move
    (let ((old-position (slot-value piece 'position))
          (game (slot-value piece 'game)))
      (let ((old-rank (position-rank old-position))
            (new-rank (position-rank new-position))
            (old-file (position-file old-position))
            (new-file (position-file new-position))
            (board (slot-value game 'chess-board)))
        ;; vacate old position
        (setf (aref board old-rank old-file) nil)
        ;; install piece in new position
        (setf (aref board new-rank new-file) piece)
        ;; update position record in piece
        (setf (slot-value piece 'position) new-position)))))
```

Exercise 6.7

```
(defmethod captured-piece-p ((piece chess-piece) new-position)
  ;;this method will return the occupying piece object (if
  ;; any) from the new position
  (with-slots (game) piece
    (let* ((new-rank (position-rank new-position))
           (new-file (position-file new-position))
           (board (slot-value game 'chess-board))
           (captured-piece (aref board new-rank new-file)))
      captured-piece)))

(defmethod remove-captured-piece ((move chess-move))
  (with-slots (piece new-position captured-piece) move
    (let* ((game (slot-value piece 'game))
           (new-rank (position-rank new-position))
           (new-file (position-file new-position))
           (color (slot-value captured-piece 'color))
           (pieces-slot (if (eq color 'white)
                            'white-pieces
                            'black-pieces)))
      (setf (slot-value game pieces-slot)
            (remove captured-piece
                    (slot-value game pieces-slot))))
    captured-piece))
```

Exercise 6.8

See Appendix D.

Exercise 6.9

Computing a position from the 8 x 8 array stored in the chess-board slot of the chess-game object would be a fairly expensive undertaking. You would have to search through the array to try to find the piece. In the worst case, this could involve 64 array references. You would need to compute the position fairly frequently, so it would probably be better to store the value in the slot whenever you change it rather than when you need it.

Exercise 6.10

```
(defmethod get-mileage-rating ((auto auto))
  (with-slots (fuel mileage-rating) auto
    (if (not (eq fuel 'super-premium))
        (* .9 mileage-rating))))
```

Exercise 6.11

See Appendix D.

Exercise 6.12

Abstraction barriers represent a contract between a developer and a set of users. Each side is provided with a different view of a particular entity, be it a program, a data structure, or a procedure. The definition of a CLOS class can serve as an abstraction barrier if some slots are used only by the implementer and their presence is not advertised to the users. Generic functions serve as an abstraction barrier as well. Externally, they resemble a function and are invoked like a function. The implementer, however, is free to add and remove primary and auxiliary methods, provided that the generic function satisfies the terms of the agreement. Accessor methods are another interesting way to erect an abstraction barrier. The accessors are made public, but the implementer is free to decide how the slots will be defined. The slot may actually be in a different object (like the fuel-capacity slot in a motor-vehicle object), or there may be no slot at all.

Exercise 6.13

```
(defclass date ()
  ((day :initarg day
        :accessor get-day)
   (month :initarg month
          :accessor get-month)
   (year :initarg year
         :accessor get-year))
  (:documentation
   "Class to represent a date"))

(defmethod date-arithmetic ((date-1 date)(date-2 date))
  (let ((universal-time-1 (encode-universal-time 0
                                                 0
                                                 0
                                                 (get-day date-1)
                                                 (get-month date-1)
                                                 (get-year date-1)))
        (universal-time-2 (encode-universal-time 0
                                                 0
                                                 0
                                                 (get-day date-2)
                                                 (get-month date-2)
                                                 (get-year date-2))))
    ;;divide the difference between the two universal times
    ;;by the number of seconds in a day
    (/ (abs (- universal-time-1
               universal-time-2))
       86400)))
(date-arithmetic (make-instance 'date :day 1 :month 8 :year 1989)
                 (make-instance 'date :day 1 :month 7 :year 1989))

(defmethod date-arithmetic ((date date)(diff integer))
  (let* ((universal-time-1 (encode-universal-time 0
                                                  0
                                                  0
```

```
                                    (get-day date)
                                    (get-month date)
                                       (get-year date)))
       ;; multiply the difference in days by the number of
       ;; seconds in a day to compute the universal time
       ;; of the second day
       (universal-time-2 (+ universal-time-1
                            (* diff 86400))))
  (multiple-value-bind (sec min hr day month year)
                       (decode-universal-time universal-time-2)
    (make-instance 'date
                   :day day
                   :month month
                   :year year)))))
```

CHAPTER 7: GENTLY DOWN THE STREAM

Exercise 7.1

```
(defun my-read-line ()
;;assumes that the input string is < 80 chars
  (let ((accum-string (make-string 80)))
    (do ((next-char (read-char)(read-char))
         (index 0 (1+ index)))
        ((or (char= next-char
             #\Newline)
             (= index 80))
         (subseq accum-string 0 index))
      (setf (char accum-string index) next-char))))
```

Exercise 7.2

```
(defun read-hex ()
  (let ((next-char (read-char))
        (result 0))
    (loop
      (if (eql next-char #\Newline)
          (return result))
      (setf result
            (+ (* result 16)
               (digit-char-p next-char 16)))
      (setf next-char (read-char)))))
```

Exercise 7.3

```
(defun write-bases (number)
  (dolist (base '(2 8 10 16))
    (write base)
    (write-char '#\:)
    (write number :base base)
    (terpri)))
```

Exercise 7.4

```
              (defun my-terpri ()
                (write-char #\Newline)
                nil)
```

Exercise 7.5

```
(defun fortran-to-lisp ()
  (let ((parse-tree (infix-to-prefix (read-line))))
    (rplaca parse-tree 'setf)))

(defun infix-to-prefix (input-string)
   (let* ((parse-list (scan-for-operator input-string))
          (operand-1 (first parse-list))
          (operator (second parse-list))
          (operand-2 (third parse-list)))
     (if (null operator)
       operand-1
       (list operator
             operand-1
             (infix-to-prefix operand-2)))))

(defun scan-for-operator (input-string)
  ;;returns a list consisting of the first operand (as a symbol),
  ;;the operator (as a symbol) and the second operand (as a string)
  (let ((eos (length input-string)))
    (do ((i 0 (1+ i)))
        ((= i eos)(list (convert-to-symbol input-string)))
      (let ((next-char (char input-string i)))
        (if (member next-char *fortran-operators*)
          (return (list (convert-to-symbol (subseq input-string 0 i))
                        (intern (subseq input-string i (1+ i)))
                        (subseq input-string (1+ i)))))))))

(defvar *fortran-operators* '(#\= #\+ #\- #\* #\/))

(defun convert-to-symbol (name-string)
  (intern (string-trim '(#\Space) name-string)))
```

Exercise 7.6

When its stream argument is non-NIL, format is called for its side effect of directing a formatted string to an output stream; otherwise, it is called for its result.

Exercise 7.7(a)

```
        NIL
```

Exercise 7.7(b)

```
        "X3J13"
```

Exercise 7.8

```
(format t "[~{~a~^,~}]" '(a b c))
```

Exercise 7.9

```
(defun draw-board (board)
  (format T " ―― ―― ―― ―― ―― ―― ―― ―― ~%")
  (dotimes (row 8 )
    (draw-row board row)))


(defun draw-row (board row)
  (format T "|        |       |        |        |        |        |        |        | ~%")
  (format T "|")                    ; print out the third line of a square
  (dotimes (col 8)
    (format T " ~a |" (if (aref board row col)
                          'QN
                          " ")))
  (format T "~%|        |        |        |        |        |        |        | ~%")
  (format T " ―― ―― ―― ―― ―― ―― ―― ―― ~%"))
```

Exercise 7.10

The code for display-moves can be found in Appendix D.

Exercise 7.11

```
(defun save-vars (var-list output-file)
  (with-open-file (output-stream output-file
                                 :direction :output)
    (dolist (var var-list)
      (format output-stream "(setf ~s (quote ~s))~%" var (eval var)))))
```

Exercise 7.12

```
(defun load-vars (input-file)
  (with-open-file (input-stream input-file
                                :direction :input)
    (do ((next-item (read input-stream
                          nil
                          input-stream)
                    (read input-stream
                          nil
                          input-stream)))
        ((eq next-item input-stream))
      (eval next-item))))
```

CHAPTER 8: FUNCTIONS REVISITED

Exercise 8.1

```
(defun write-bases (number &optional radix)
  (case radix
```

```
                                      (binary (format t "2: ~b" number))
                                      (octal (format t "8: ~o" number))
                                      (decimal (format t "10: ~d" number))
                                      (hexadecimal (format t "16: ~x" number))
                                      (otherwise (dolist (base '(2 8 10 16))
                                                   (write base)
                                                   (write-char '#\:)
                                                   (write number :base base)
                                                   (terpri)))))
```

Exercise 8.2

```
                              (defun mean (&rest number-list)
                                (let ((sum 0)
                                      (n 0))
                                  (dolist (number number-list)
                                    (setf sum (+ sum number))
                                    (setf n (1+ n)))
                                  (/ sum n)))
```

Exercise 8.3

```
  (defun insert-sorted (item sorted-list &key (test #'<=))
     (if sorted-list
          (let ((head (first sorted-list)))
             (if (funcall test item head)
                 (cons item sorted-list)
                 (cons head (insert-sorted
                                item
                                (rest sorted-list)
                                :test test))))
          (list item)))
```

Exercise 8.4

```
  (defconstant days-in-week
    (vector "Monday" "Tuesday" "Wednesday" "Thursday" "Friday"
            "Saturday" "Sunday"))

  (defconstant months-in-year
    (vector nil "January" "February" "March" "April" "May" "June"
            "July" "August" "September" "October" "November" "December"))

  (defun construct-time-zone (time-zone-index daylight-savings-p)
    (let ((time-zone (case time-zone-index
                       (5 "EST")
                       (6 "CST")
                       (7 "MST")
                       (8 "PST")
                       (T "?ST"))))
       (if daylight-savings-p
         (setf (elt time-zone 1) #\D))
```

```
            time-zone))
  (construct-time-zone 6 NIL)

  (defun get-date/time-string ()
    (multiple-value-bind (sec min hour day month year day-in-week
                             daylight-savings-p time-zone)
                (get-decoded-time)
      (format nil "~a, ~a ~d, ~d, ~d:~d:~d-~a"
              (elt days-in-week day-in-week)
              (elt months-in-year (1- month))
          day
          year
          hour
          min
          sec
            (construct-time-zone time-zone daylight-savings-p)))))
```

Exercise 8.5

```
(defun get-decoded-date ()
  (multiple-value-bind (sec min hour day month year)
          (get-decoded-time)
    (values month day year)))
```

Exercise 8.6

```
(defun days-in-month (month &optional (year (get-decoded-year)))
  (case month
    (february (if (leap-year-p year) 29 28))
    ((april june september november) 30)
    (t 31)))

(defun get-decoded-year ()
  (multiple-value-bind (sec min hour day month year)
                (get-decoded-time)
    year))

(defun leap-year-p (year)
  (cond ((= (mod year 400) 0) T)
        ((= (mod year 100) 0) NIL)
        ((= (mod year 4) 0) T)
        (T NIL)))
```

Exercise 8.7

```
(defun combinations-2 (&rest input-lists)
  (let*
    ;;make a variable for each list
    ((var-list (mapcar #'(lambda (list)
                            (gentemp))
                        input-lists))
```

```
;;create an expression for the inner loop
(expr (list 'setf
            'result
             (list 'cons
                   (append '(list)
                            var-list)
                   'result)))))
;;build-up the nested loops
(do ((rest-lists input-lists (rest rest-lists))
     (rest-vars var-list (rest rest-vars)))
    ((null rest-lists) expr)
  (setf expr (list 'dolist
                   (list (first rest-vars)
                         (list 'quote
                               (first rest-lists)))
                   expr)))
;;wrap a let form around the expression and evaluate it
(eval (list 'let
            '(result)
            expr
            'result)))))
```

The readability of this function can be improved somewhat by using the backquote facility (described in the next section). For example:

```
(defun combinations-2 (&rest input-lists)
  (let*
    ;;make a variable for each list
    ((var-list (mapcar #'(lambda (list)
                           (gentemp))
                        input-lists))
     ;;create an expression for the inner loop
     (expr `(setf result
                  (cons (list ,@var-list) result))))
    ;;build-up the nested loops
    (do ((rest-lists input-lists (rest rest-lists))
         (rest-vars var-list (rest rest-vars)))
        ((null rest-lists) expr)
      (setf expr `(dolist (,(first rest-vars)
                           ',(first rest-lists))
                    ,expr)))
    ;;wrap a let form around the expression and evaluate it
    (eval `(let (result)
             ,expr
             result)))))
```

Code-generating forms of this kind, however, are more naturally written as macros. For example:

```
(defmacro combinations-3 (&rest input-lists)
  (let*
    ((result (gentemp))
    ;;make a variable for each list
      (var-list (mapcar #'(lambda (list)
                                   (gentemp))
                        input-lists))
    ;;create an expression for the inner loop
    (expr `(setf ,result
                 (cons (list ,@var-list) ,result))))
    ;;build-up the nested loops
    (do ((rest-lists input-lists (rest rest-lists))
         (rest-vars var-list (rest rest-vars)))
        ((null rest-lists) expr)
      (setf expr `(dolist (,(first rest-vars)
                           ,(first rest-lists))
                     ,expr)))
    ;;wrap a let form around the expression and evaluate it
    `(let (,result)
       ,expr
       ,result)))
```

Exercise 8.8

```
(defmacro pif (exp-1 then exp-2 &optional else exp-3)
  `(cond (,exp-1 ,exp-2)
         (t ,exp-3)))
```

Exercise 8.9(a)

This macro accepts a variable as an argument and increments it.

Exercise 8.9(b)

This macro accepts two variables as arguments and swaps their values.

Exercise 8.10

```
(defmacro while (condition exit-form &body body)
  `(loop
     (if ,condition
         (return ,exit-form))
     ,@body))
```

Exercise 8.11

```
(defmacro macro-factorial (num)
  (let ((n (eval num)))
    (if (zerop n)
        1
        `(* ,n
            (macro-factorial ,(1- n))))))
```

Exercise 8.12

```
(defmacro my-pop (input-seq)
  (let ((var (gentemp))) ;create a unique variable
    `(if (> (length ,input-seq) 0)
       (let ((,var (elt ,input-seq 0)))
         (setf ,input-seq (subseq ,input-seq 1))
         ,var)))))
```

Exercise 8.13

```
(defmacro pull (input-list)
  (let ((var (gentemp)))
    `(let ((,var (first (last ,input-list))))
       (setf ,input-list (nbutlast ,input-list))
       ,var)))
```

Exercise 8.14

The following definition comes from the Graham article (Graham, 1988a).

```
(defmacro aif (test-form &optional then-form else-form)))
  `(let ((it ,test-form))
     (if it ,then-form ,else-form)))
```

Exercise 8.15

```
(defmacro construct-do (w x y z bd new-pos)
  `(let ((init-1 ,w)
         (step-1 ,x)
         (init-2 ,y)
         (step-2 ,z)
         (board ,bd)
         (new-rank (position-rank ,new-pos))
         (new-file (position-file ,new-pos))
         (new-position ,new-pos))
     (eval `(do ((rank ,init-1 ,step-1)
                 (file ,init-2 ,step-2))
                ((and (= rank ,new-rank)
                      (= file ,new-file)) ',new-position)
                (if (aref ',board rank file)
                    (return nil)))))))
```

Modifications to the legal-move-p methods to call clear-path-p can be found in Appendix D.

Exercise 8.16

Every time make-generator is called, it creates a new lexical closure object with its own binding of the last-value variable. Therefore, test-fun-2 is calling two different, newly initialized closure objects.

Exercise 8.17

```
(defun create-new-account (current-balance)
  (function (lambda (x)
              (setf current-balance
                    (+ current-balance x)))))

(setf my-account (create-new-account 1000.00))

(defun account-withdrawal (account amount)
  (funcall account (* -1.0 amount)))

(defun account-deposit (account amount)
  (funcall account amount))
```

Exercise 8.18

```
(setf my-shoe (make-deck 208))
```

Exercise 8.19

```
(defun my-complement (fun)
  (compose #'not fun))
```

Exercise 8.20

```
(defmacro compose (&rest fun-list)
  `(function (lambda (arg)
               ,(build-comp-expr fun-list))))

(defun build-comp-expr (fun-list)
  (if fun-list
      `(funcall ,(first fun-list)
                ,(build-comp-expr (rest fun-list)))
      'arg))
```

Exercise 8.21

```
(defun factorial (n)
  (declare (type integer n)
           (inline *))
  (if (> n 1)
      (* n (factorial (1- n)))
      1))
```

Exercise 8.23

Ordinarily, the recursive version of your function will be less efficient than the iterative version due to the overhead of repeated function calling. However, if the compiler optimizes out recursive calls, the performance of the two functions when compiled should be about the same. As an example, take the div2 benchmark from the Gabriel book (Gabriel, 1985). The recursive version of the div2 function is

```
(defun recursive-div2 (l)
  (cond ((null l) ())
        (t cons (car l) (recursive-div2 (cddr l)))))
```

The iterative version is written as follows:

```
(defun iterative-div2 (l)
  (do ((l l (cddr l))
       (a nil (push (car l) a )))
      ((null l) a)))
```

You use the following definitions to actually run the benchmark:

```
(defun create-n (n)
  (do ((n n (1- n))
       (a () (push () a)))
      ((= n 0) a)))

(defvar ll (create-n 200.))

(defun test-1 (l)
  (do ((i 300. (1- i)))
      ((= i 0))
    (iterative-div2 l)
    (iterative-div2 l)
    (iterative-div2 l)
    (iterative-div2 l)))

(defun test-2 (l)
  (do ((i 300. (1- i)))
      ((= i 0))
    (recursive-div2 l)
    (recursive-div2 l)
    (recursive-div2 l)
    (recursive-div2 l)))
```

The test is run as follows:

```
(time (test-1 ll))
(time (test-2 ll))
```

CHAPTER 9: PROGRAM STRUCTURE

Exercise 9.1

```
(defun spaghetti-fun-2 (some-list)
  (dolist (element some-list)
    (print element)))
```

Exercise 9.2

```
(defun unnecessary-prog-fun-2 (number-list)
   (if number-list (+ (first number-list)
                      (unnecessary-prog-fun-2 (rest number-list)))
        0))
```

Exercise 9.3

```
(defmacro until (condition exit-form &body body)
   (let ((top-of-loop (gensym)))
     `(block nil
        (tagbody
           ,top-of-loop
           ,@body
           (if ,condition
              (return ,exit-form)
              (go ,top-of-loop)))))))
```

Exercise 9.4

```
(defmacro my-prog (var-list &body body)
  `(block nil
     (let ,var-list
        (tagbody
           ,@body))))
```

Exercise 9.5

```
(defmacro my-prog* (var-list &body body)
   `(block nil
      (let* ,var-list
         (tagbody
            ,@body))))
```

Exercise 9.6

No. In order for this example to work, foo must be declared special in mumble as well. Incidentally, if foo is declared special in mumble, but not in grumble, the example would still work. This is because free variables in Common Lisp are assumed to be special.

Exercise 9.7

The mamba macro is expanded and then executed in the lexical environment of the rumba function. Therefore, the reference to foo can be resolved.

Exercise 9.8

```
(defun sum-of-squares (&rest number-list)
   (labels ((ss-aux (numbers)
                (if numbers
                   (let ((num (first numbers)))
                     (+ (* num num)
                        (ss-aux (rest numbers))))
                   0)))
      (ss-aux number-list)))
```

Exercise 9.9

```
(defun sum-3 (&rest number-list)
  (flet ((+ (arg1 arg2)
           (let ((addend-1 (or arg1 0))
                 (addend-2 (or arg2 0)))
             (+ addend-1 addend-2))))
    (labels ((sum-aux (numbers)
               (if numbers
                   (+ (first numbers)
                      (sum-aux (rest numbers)))
                   0)))
      (sum-aux number-list))))
```

Exercise 9.10

See the definition of clear-path-p in Appendix D.

Exercise 9.11

MIDDLE-BLOCK
OUTER-BLOCK
OUTER-BLOCK

Exercise 9.12

```
(defmacro while (condition exit-form &body body)
  (let ((top-of-loop (gensym)))
    `(block nil
       (tagbody
          ,top-of-loop
          (if (not ,condition)
              (return ,exit-form))
          ,@body
          (go ,top-of-loop)))))
```

Exercise 9.13

No, because the catcher-4 catcher is not visible in the dynamic environment of catcher-fun-3.

Exercise 9.14

The mystery-fun-99 function performs a sort of membership test. It recursively creates a new catcher for each element in the list passed in tags. It is not a very good membership predicate, however, because it breaks whenever the target is not found.

Exercise 9.15

```
(defun days-in-month (month)
  (ccase month
    (february 28)
    ((april june september november) 30)
    ((january march may july august october december) 31)))
(days-in-month 'july)
```

Exercise 9.16

```
(defun calculator ()
  (flet ((read ()
            (let ((new-value (read)))
              (assert (or (numberp new-value)
                          (member new-value
                            '(+ - / * =)))
                      (new-value))
              new-value)))
    (let ((result (read)))
      (do ((operator (read) (read)))
          ((eq operator '=) result)
        (setf result (funcall (symbol-function operator)
                              result
                              (read)))))))
```

Exercise 9.17

```
(defun fast-factorial (n)
  (labels ((fact (n)
             (if (zerop n)
                 1
                 (* n (fact (1- n))))))
    (assert (and (integerp n)
                 (or (zerop n)
                     (plusp n)))
            (n))
    (fact n)))
```

Exercise 9.18

```
(defmethod date-arithmetic ((date date)(date-or-num t))
  (cerror "Enter a new value for the second operand."
          "Second operand must be a date or a number."
          date-or-num)
  (date-arithmetic date date-or-num))

(defmethod date-arithmetic ((date t)(date-or-num t))
  (cerror "Enter a date expression."
          "First operand must be a date object."
          date)
  (date-arithmetic date date-or-num))
```

Exercise 9.19

```
(defun fast-and-forgiving-factorial (n)
  (labels ((fact (n)
             (if (zerop n)
                 1
                 (* n (fact (1- n))))))
    (etypecase n
      (integer (cond ((zerop n) 1)
```

```
                            ((plusp n)
                             (* n (fact (1- n))))
                            ((minusp n)
                  (cerror "Compute -(|~D|)! instead."
               "Factorial of ~D is undefined." n)
                    (- (fact (abs n))))))
       (float (restart-case (error "Factorial of ~D is undefined." n)
   (nil () :report "Truncate and compute factorial."
              fact (truncate n)))
    (nil () :report "Round and compute factorial."
                   (fact (round n)))
  (nil () :report "Use ceiling to compute factorial."
     (fact (ceiling n)))
   (nil () :report "Use floor to compute factorial."
                  (fact (floor n)))))))))
```

CHAPTER 10: PROGRAMMATION ET LOGIQUE

Exercise 10.1

```
                        mother_of(?m,?x)  :-
                            parent_of(?m,?x),
                            female(?m).
```

Exercise 10.2

```
                        grandparent_of(?grandparent,?grandchild)  :-
                            parent_of(?grandparent,?parent),
                            parent_of(?parent,?grandchild).
```

Exercise 10.3

```
                        sister_of(?sister,?x)  :-
                            parent_of(?parent,?sister),
                            parent_of(?parent,?x),
                            female(?sister).
```

Exercise 10.4

```
                        ancestor_of(?ancestor,?x)  :-
                            parent_of(?ancestor,?x).

                        ancestor_of(?ancestor,?x)  :-
                            ancestor_of(?ancestor,?p),
                            parent_of(?p,?x).
```

Exercise 10.5

```
                        (defmethod get-functor-name ((clause clause))
                            (slot-value (slot-value clause 'procedure)
                                        'functor-name))
```

Exercise 10.6

```
  ;;Create a procedure object.
  (setf fever-procedure
```

```
        (make-instance 'procedure
          :functor-name 'fever
          :arity 1))
;;Create the necessary clause and term objects
(setf (slot-value fever-procedure 'clause-list)
      (list (make-instance 'non-unit-clause
               :procedure fever-procedure
               :variable-list '(?patient ?temperature)
               :head (make-instance 'term
                        :functor-name 'fever
                        :arg-list '(?patient))
               :body (list (make-instance 'term
                              :functor-name 'temp
           :arg-list '(?patient ?temperature))
                           (make-instance 'term
                              :functor-name 'gt
        :arg-list '(?temperature 100))))))
;;Install it in the data base
(setf (gethash 'fever/1 *slolog-database*) fever-procedure)
```

Exercise 10.7

```
(defun logical-variable-p (x)
  ;;symbols with names that begin with a question mark
  ;;are considered to be logical-variables
  (if (symbolp x)
    (let ((leading-char (char (symbol-name x) 0)))
      (if (char= leading-char #\?)
        x))))
```

Exercise 10.8

```
(defun unify (x y environment)
  (labels ((bind-variable (x y environment)
             (acons x y environment)))
    ;;if x unifies with y, unify returns a
    ;;new environment, nil otherwise
    (let ((x (value-of x environment))
          (y (value-of y environment)))
      (cond ((equal x y) environment)
            ((logical-variable-p x)(bind-variable x y environment))
            ((logical-variable-p y)(bind-variable y x environment))
            ;;if both are lists, descend recursively
            ((and (listp x)(listp y))
             (let ((new-environment (unify (first x)(first y) environment)))
               (and new-environment
    (unify (rest x)(rest y) new-environment)))))))))
```

Exercise 10.9

a. NIL

b. ((?TEMP . 98.6) (?PAT . BILL) NIL)

c. ((?PAT . 101) (?X . ?PAT) NIL)

d. ((?PATIENT . ?ARG) (?FUNCTOR . FEVER) NIL)

Note that unify will accept a variable as a functor name but Slolog will not.

e. ((?T . |?var24|) (?P . |?var23|) NIL)

Exercise 10.10

```
(defmacro make-procedure-name (functor-sym arity)
  `(multiple-value-bind (procedure-name)
(intern (format nil "~a/~d" ,functor-sym ,arity))
     procedure-name))
```

Exercise 10.11

```
(defun display-results (env)
  ;;display the results of a query and check to see if the user
  ;;would like to continue the search
  (cond ((equal env '(nil))(format t "~%yes~%")(throw 'end-query nil))
        (t (display-bindings env)(if (not (yes-or-no-p "Continue search?"))
             (throw 'end-query nil)))))

(defun display-bindings (env)
  (terpri)
  ;;present bindings in order of occurrence
  ;;(and drop the null environment from list)
  (let ((bindings (rest (reverse env))))
    (dolist (binding bindings)
      (let* ((variable (first binding))
             (var-name (symbol-name variable)))
        ;;also drop the system-defined variables
        (if (not (and (> (length var-name) 4)
                      (equal (subseq var-name 0 4)
                             "?var")))
          (format t "~a = ~a~%" variable (value-of variable env))))))
  (terpri))
```

Exercise 10.12

```
(defun make-variable-list (goal)
  ;;descends the structure of the goal and makes
  ;;a list of all logical variables, removing the
  ;;duplicates
  (labels ((list-vars (x)
             (if x
               (let ((item (first x)))
                 (if (listp item)
                   (append (list-vars item)
                           (list-vars (rest x)))
                   (if (logical-variable-p item)
```

```
                                       (cons item
                                         (list-vars (rest x)))
                                       (list-vars (rest x))))))))))
                        (delete-duplicates (list-vars goal))))
```

Exercise 10.13

See Appendix F.

Exercise 10.14

```
(defun slolog-true (clause-list goal env continuation)
   (declare (ignore clause-list goal))
   ;;this goal is always satisfied
   (funcall continuation env))

(defun slolog-fail (clause-list goal env continuation)
   (declare (ignore clause-list goal))
   ;;this goal is never satisfied
   nil)
```

Exercise 10.15

```
(defvar *slolog-trace-flg* nil)

(defun satisfy (goals environment continuation)
   (if goals
      (let* ((goal (first goals))
             (procedure (get-procedure goal))
             (clause-list (slot-value procedure 'clause-list))
             (attached-fn (slot-value procedure 'attached-fn)))
        (if *slolog-trace-flg*
          (format t " Call: ~a~%" goal))
        (funcall attached-fn clause-list goal environment
                 #'(lambda (env)
                     (if *slolog-trace-flg*
                       (format t " Succeed: ~a~%" goal))
                     (satisfy (rest goals) env continuation)))
      (if *slolog-trace-flg*
        (format t " Fail: ~a~%" goal)))
      ;;success! All goals are satisfied.
      (funcall continuation environment)))

(defun slolog-trace (clause-list goal env continuation)
   (declare (ignore clause-list goal))
   (setf *slolog-trace-flg* t)
   ;;this goal is always satisfied
   (funcall continuation env))

(defun slolog-untrace (clause-list goal env continuation)
   (declare (ignore clause-list goal))
   (setf *slolog-trace-flg* nil)
```

```
      ;;this goal is always satisfied
      (funcall continuation env))
```

Exercise 10.16

See Appendix F.

Exercise 10.17

```
(defun get-input-string ()
  (labels ((terminated-string-p (input-string)
             ;;check to see if terminated with a period
             (let ((last-char (1- (length input-string))))
               (equal (char input-string last-char)
                      #\.))))
    (let ((input-string (make-string 0)))
      (my-until (terminated-string-p input-string)
                input-string
                (setf input-string
                      (concatenate 'string
                                   input-string
                                   (read-line)))))))
```

Here my-until is defined as in Exercise 9.3.

Exercise 10.18

See Appendix F.

Exercise 10.19

```
(defun parse-clause-tail ()
  (when (equal (get-value *next-token*)
               ",")
    (scan-token)
    (let ((next-term (parse-term)))
      (cons next-term
            (parse-clause-tail)))))
```

Exercise 10.20

```
(defun parse-arg ()
  (let ((value (get-value *next-token*)))
    (cond
      ;;symbols or numeric constants are okay
      ((or (eql (class-of *next-token*)
                (symbol-class 'symbol-token))
           (eql (class-of *next-token*)
                (symbol-class 'numeric-constant)))
       (scan-token)
       value)
      ((equal (get-value *next-token*)
              "(")
       (scan-token)
       (parse-clause))
```

```
;;if not, bail out
(t (cerror "Enter new query?"
            "Illegal syntax at ~a"
            (get-value *next-token*))
    (throw 'end-query nil)))))
```

D

Sources for the Chess Application

```
;;;;Chess application
;;;;Timothy Koschmann
;;;;SIU, School of Medicine
;;;;8 August, 1989


;;;;;;;;;;;;;;;;;;;;;;;;;;;;;;;;;;;;;;;;;;;;;;;;;;;;;;;;;;;;;;;;;;;;;;;
;;;CL packages stuff
;;;;;;;;;;;;;;;;;;;;;;;;;;;;;;;;;;;;;;;;;;;;;;;;;;;;;;;;;;;;;;;;;;;;;;;
(in-package "CHESS")
(export '(make-chess-game move display-moves))


;;;;;;;;;;;;;;;;;;;;;;;;;;;;;;;;;;;;;;;;;;;;;;;;;;;;;;;;;;;;;;;;;;;;;;;
;;;define the structures
;;;;;;;;;;;;;;;;;;;;;;;;;;;;;;;;;;;;;;;;;;;;;;;;;;;;;;;;;;;;;;;;;;;;;;;
(defstruct position
   rank
   file)


;;;;;;;;;;;;;;;;;;;;;;;;;;;;;;;;;;;;;;;;;;;;;;;;;;;;;;;;;;;;;;;;;;;;;;;
;;;define the CLOS classes
;;;;;;;;;;;;;;;;;;;;;;;;;;;;;;;;;;;;;;;;;;;;;;;;;;;;;;;;;;;;;;;;;;;;;;;
(defclass chess-game ()
   ((white-pieces :initarg :white-pieces
                  :initform (set-up-pieces 'white))
    (white-moves :initarg :white-moves
                 :initform nil)
    (black-pieces :initarg :black-pieces
                  :initform (set-up-pieces 'black))
    (black-moves :initarg :black-moves
                 :initform nil)
```

```lisp
      (chess-board :initform (make-array '(8 8)
                                         :initial-element nil))))

(defclass chess-piece ()
  ((color :initarg :color
          :accessor color)
   (position :initarg :position
             :initform (make-position)
             :accessor board-position)
   (game :initarg :game)))

(defclass king (chess-piece)
  ((position :initform (make-position :rank 4))))

(defclass queen (chess-piece)
  ((position :initform (make-position :rank 3))))

(defclass rook (chess-piece)
  ((position :initform (make-position :rank 0))))

(defclass bishop (chess-piece)
  ((position :initform (make-position :rank 2))))

(defclass knight (chess-piece)
  ((position :initform (make-position :rank 1))))

(defclass pawn (chess-piece) ())

(defclass chess-move ()
  ((piece :initarg :piece)
   (new-position :initarg :new-position)))

(defclass capture (chess-move)
  ((captured-piece :initarg :captured-piece)))

(defclass castle (chess-move) ())

;;;;;;;;;;;;;;;;;;;;;;;;;;;;;;;;;;;;;;;;;;;;;;;;;;;;;;;;;;;;;;;;;;;;;
;;;define the macros
;;;;;;;;;;;;;;;;;;;;;;;;;;;;;;;;;;;;;;;;;;;;;;;;;;;;;;;;;;;;;;;;;;;;;
(defmacro neq (x y)
   `(let ((item-1 ,x)
          (item-2 ,y))
       (not (eq item-1 item-2))))
```

```lisp
;;;;;;;;;;;;;;;;;;;;;;;;;;;;;;;;;;;;;;;;;;;;;;;;;;;;;;;;;;;;;;;;;
;;;define the functions for setting up a game
;;;;;;;;;;;;;;;;;;;;;;;;;;;;;;;;;;;;;;;;;;;;;;;;;;;;;;;;;;;;;;;;;
(defun make-chess-game ()
  (let* ((game (make-instance 'chess-game))
         (pieces (append (slot-value game 'black-pieces)
                         (slot-value game 'white-pieces)))
         (board (slot-value game 'chess-board)))
    (dolist (piece pieces game)
      (let ((rank (position-rank (slot-value piece 'position)))
            (file (position-file (slot-value piece 'position))))
        (setf (aref board rank file) piece)
        (setf (slot-value piece 'game) game)))))

(defun set-up-pieces (side)
  (append (list (make-king side))
          (list (make-queen side))
          (make-rooks side)
          (make-bishops side)
          (make-knights side)
          (make-pawns side)))

(defun make-king (side)
  (let ((king (make-instance 'king :color side)))
    (setf (position-file (slot-value king 'position))
                        (if (eq side 'white)
                            0       ;white side
                            7))     ;black side
    king))

(defun make-queen (side)
  (let ((queen (make-instance 'queen :color side)))
    (setf (position-file (slot-value queen 'position))
                        (if (eq side 'white)
                            0       ;white side
                            7))     ;black side
    queen))

(defun make-rooks (side)
  (let ((rooks (list (make-instance 'rook :color side)
                     (make-instance 'rook :color side))))
    ;; fix position for queen-side rook
    (setf (position-file (slot-value (first rooks) 'position))
                        (if (eq side 'white)
```

```
                                  0          ;white side
                                  7))        ;black side
        ;; fix position for king-side rook
        (setf (position-rank (slot-value (second rooks) 'position)) 7)
        (setf (position-file (slot-value (second rooks) 'position))
                          (if (eq side 'white)
                              0          ;white side
                              7))        ;black side
      rooks))

(defun make-bishops (side)
    (let ((bishops (list (make-instance 'bishop :color side)
                          (make-instance 'bishop :color side))))
      ;; fix position for queen-side bishop
      (setf (position-file (slot-value (first bishops) 'position))
                          (if (eq side 'white)
                              0          ;white side
                              7))        ;black side
      ;; fix position for king-side bishop
      (setf (position-rank (slot-value (second bishops) 'position)) 5)
      (setf (position-file (slot-value (second bishops) 'position))
                          (if (eq side 'white)
                              0          ;white side
                              7))        ;black side
      bishops))

(defun make-knights (side)
    (let ((knights (list (make-instance 'knight :color side)
                          (make-instance 'knight :color side))))
      ;; fix position for queen-side knight
      (setf (position-file (slot-value (first knights) 'position))
                          (if (eq side 'white)
                              0          ;white side
                              7))        ;black side
      ;; fix position for king-side knight
      (setf (position-rank (slot-value (second knights) 'position)) 6)
      (setf (position-file (slot-value (second knights) 'position))
                          (if (eq side 'white)
                              0          ;white side
                              7))        ;black side
      knights))

(defun make-pawns (side)
    (let (pawns)
```

```
        (dotimes (rank 8)
          (let ((pawn (make-instance 'pawn :color side)))
            (setf (position-rank (slot-value pawn 'position))
                               rank)
            (setf (position-file (slot-value pawn 'position))
                  (if (eq side 'white)
                    1        ;white side
                    6))      ;black side
            (setf pawns (cons pawn pawns))))
        pawns))


;;;;;;;;;;;;;;;;;;;;;;;;;;;;;;;;;;;;;;;;;;;;;;;;;;;;;;;;;;;;;;;;;;;;
;;;define the methods for moving pieces
;;;;;;;;;;;;;;;;;;;;;;;;;;;;;;;;;;;;;;;;;;;;;;;;;;;;;;;;;;;;;;;;;;;;
(defmethod move ((piece chess-piece) new-position)
  (with-slots (position) piece
    (when (legal-move-p piece new-position)
      (let* ((captured-piece (captured-piece-p piece new-position))
             (move (if captured-piece
                     (make-instance 'capture
                                    :piece piece
                                    :new-position new-position
                                    :captured-piece captured-piece)
                     (make-instance 'chess-move
                                    :piece piece
                                    :new-position new-position))))
        (add-to-move-list move)
        (if captured-piece (remove-captured-piece move))
        (change-piece-position move)))))

(defmethod add-to-move-list ((move chess-move))
  (with-slots (piece new-position) move
    (let* ((color (slot-value piece 'color))
           (game (slot-value piece 'game))
           (moves-slot (if (eq color 'white)
                         'white-moves
                         'black-moves)))
      (setf (slot-value game moves-slot)
            (cons move (slot-value game moves-slot))))))

(defmethod change-piece-position ((move chess-move))
  (with-slots (piece new-position) move
    (let ((old-position (slot-value piece 'position))
          (game (slot-value piece 'game)))
```

```
        (let ((old-rank (position-rank old-position))
              (new-rank (position-rank new-position))
              (old-file (position-file old-position))
              (new-file (position-file new-position))
              (board (slot-value game 'chess-board)))
          ;; vacate old position
          (setf (aref board old-rank old-file) nil)
          ;; install piece in new position
          (setf (aref board new-rank new-file) piece)
          ;; update position record in piece
          (setf (slot-value piece 'position) new-position)))))

(defmethod captured-piece-p ((piece chess-piece) new-position)
  ;;this method will return the occupying piece object (if
  ;; any) from the new position
  (with-slots (game) piece
    (let* ((new-rank (position-rank new-position))
           (new-file (position-file new-position))
           (board (slot-value game 'chess-board))
           (captured-piece (aref board new-rank new-file)))
      captured-piece)))

(defmethod remove-captured-piece ((move chess-move))
  (with-slots (piece new-position captured-piece) move
    (let* ((game (slot-value piece 'game))
           (new-rank (position-rank new-position))
           (new-file (position-file new-position))
           (color (slot-value captured-piece 'color))
           (pieces-slot (if (eq color 'white)
                            'white-pieces
                            'black-pieces)))
      (setf (slot-value game pieces-slot)
            (remove captured-piece
                    (slot-value game pieces-slot))))
    captured-piece))


;;;;;;;;;;;;;;;;;;;;;;;;;;;;;;;;;;;;;;;;;;;;;;;;;;;;;;;;;;;;;;;;;;;;;;
;;;define the methods for testing the legality of a move
;;;;;;;;;;;;;;;;;;;;;;;;;;;;;;;;;;;;;;;;;;;;;;;;;;;;;;;;;;;;;;;;;;;;;;

(defmethod legal-move-p ((piece chess-piece) new-position)
  (with-slots (color position game) piece
    (let ((new-rank (position-rank new-position))
          (old-rank (position-rank position))
```

```
                  (new-file (position-file new-position))
                  (old-file (position-file position)))
         (if (and
                ;;new position is on the board
                (and (typep new-rank '(integer 0 7))
                     (typep new-file '(integer 0 7)))
                ;;new position is different from old
                (not (and (= new-rank old-rank)
                          (= new-file old-file)))
                ;;if new position is occupied, make sure
                ;;the occupant is of the opposite color
                (let ((occupant (aref (slot-value game 'chess-board)
                                      new-rank
                                      new-file)))
                  (or (null occupant)
                      (neq color (slot-value occupant 'color)))))
             new-position))))

(defmethod legal-move-p ((piece king) new-position)
  (and
    (call-next-method)
    (with-slots (position) piece
      (let ((delta-rank (adiff (position-rank new-position)
                               (position-rank position)))
            (delta-file (adiff (position-file new-position)
                               (position-file position))))
        (and (or (= delta-rank 1)
                 (= delta-rank 0))
             (or (= delta-file 1)
                 (= delta-file 0)))))))

(defmethod legal-move-p ((piece queen) new-position)
  (and
    (call-next-method)
    (with-slots (position) piece
      (let* ((new-rank (position-rank new-position))
             (old-rank (position-rank position))
             (new-file (position-file new-position))
             (old-file (position-file position))
             (delta-rank (adiff new-rank old-rank))
             (delta-file (adiff new-file old-file)))
        (or
          ;;move like a bishop
          (= delta-rank delta-file)
```

```lisp
        ;;move like a rook
        (or (= old-rank new-rank)
            (= old-file new-file)))))
    (clear-path-p piece new-position)))

(defmethod legal-move-p ((piece rook) new-position)
  (and
    (call-next-method)
    (with-slots (position) piece
      (let ((new-rank (position-rank new-position))
            (old-rank (position-rank position))
            (new-file (position-file new-position))
            (old-file (position-file position)))
        (or (= old-rank new-rank)
            (= old-file new-file))))
    (clear-path-p piece new-position)))

(defmethod legal-move-p ((piece bishop) new-position)
  (and
    (call-next-method)
    (with-slots (position) piece
      (let ((delta-rank (adiff (position-rank new-position)
                               (position-rank position)))
            (delta-file (adiff (position-file new-position)
                               (position-file position))))
        (= delta-rank delta-file)))
    (clear-path-p piece new-position)))

(defmethod legal-move-p ((piece knight) new-position)
  (and
    (call-next-method)
    (with-slots (position) piece
      (let ((new-rank (position-rank new-position))
            (old-rank (position-rank position))
            (new-file (position-file new-position))
            (old-file (position-file position)))
        (or (and (= (adiff old-rank new-rank) 1)
                 (= (adiff old-file new-file) 2))
            (and (= (adiff old-rank new-rank) 2)
                 (= (adiff old-file new-file) 1)))))))

(defmethod legal-move-p ((piece pawn) new-position)
  ;;does not handle capture en passant
  (and
```

```lisp
(call-next-method)
(with-slots (color position) piece
  (let ((new-rank (position-rank new-position))
        (old-rank (position-rank position))
        (new-file (position-file new-position))
        (old-file (position-file position)))
    (if (eq color 'white)
      (cond
        ;;standard pawn move (white)
        ((and (= old-rank new-rank)
              (= (- new-file old-file) 1)) t)
        ;;initial pawn move (white)
        ((and (= old-rank new-rank)
              (= old-file 1)
              (= (- new-file old-file) 2)) t)
        ;;pawn capture (white)
        ((and (= (adiff new-rank old-rank) 1)
              (= (- new-file old-file) 1)) t))
      (cond
        ;;standard pawn move (black)
        ((and (= old-rank new-rank)
              (= (- new-file old-file) -1)) t)
        ;;initial pawn move (black)
        ((and (= old-rank new-rank)
              (= old-file 6)
              (= (- new-file old-file) -2)) t)
        ;;pawn capture (black)
        ((and (= (adiff new-rank old-rank) 1)
              (= (- new-file old-file) -1)) t)))))))

(defmethod clear-path-p ((piece chess-piece) new-position)
  ;;make sure the path between the piece and the new-position
  ;;is clear of obstructing pieces
  (with-slots (position game) piece
    (let ((new-rank (position-rank new-position))
          (old-rank (position-rank position))
          (new-file (position-file new-position))
          (old-file (position-file position))
          (board (slot-value game 'chess-board)))
      (let ((rank-init (cond ((= old-rank new-rank)
                              old-rank)
                             ((> old-rank new-rank)
                              (1- old-rank))
                             ((< old-rank new-rank)
```

```
                                 (1+ old-rank))))
                   (file-init (cond ((= old-file new-file)
                                     old-file)
                                    ((> old-file new-file)
                                     (1- old-file))
                                    ((< old-file new-file)
                                     (1+ old-file))))
                   (rank-step (cond ((= old-rank new-rank)
                                     'rank)
                                    ((> old-rank new-rank)
                                     '(1- rank))
                                    ((< old-rank new-rank)
                                     '(1+ rank))))
                   (file-step (cond ((= old-file new-file)
                                     'file)
                                    ((> old-file new-file)
                                     '(1- file))
                                    ((< old-file new-file)
                                     '(1+ file)))))
              (macrolet ((construct-do (w x y z bd new-pos)
                           `(let ((init-1 ,w)
                                  (step-1 ,x)
                                  (init-2 ,y)
                                  (step-2 ,z)
                                  (board ,bd)
                                  (new-rank (position-rank ,new-pos))
                                  (new-file (position-file ,new-pos))
                                  (new-position ,new-pos))
                              (eval `(do ((rank ,init-1 ,step-1)
                                          (file ,init-2 ,step-2))
                                         ((and (= rank ,new-rank)
                                               (= file ,new-file)) ',new-position)
                                       (if (aref ',board rank file)
                                           (return nil)))))))
                (construct-do rank-init rank-step file-init file-step
                              board new-position)))))))


;;;;;;;;;;;;;;;;;;;;;;;;;;;;;;;;;;;;;;;;;;;;;;;;;;;;;;;;;;;;;;;;;;;;;;;
;;;define methods for displaying moves
;;;;;;;;;;;;;;;;;;;;;;;;;;;;;;;;;;;;;;;;;;;;;;;;;;;;;;;;;;;;;;;;;;;;;;;
(defmethod display-moves ((game chess-game))
  (with-slots (white-moves black-moves) game
    (format t "~%~6TWhite~16TBlack~%")
    (do ((to-do-white (reverse white-moves) (rest to-do-white))
```

```lisp
                (to-do-black (reverse black-moves) (rest to-do-black))
                (move-count 1 (1+ move-count)))
              ((null to-do-white))
            (let ((white-move (first to-do-white))
                  (black-move (first to-do-black)))
              (if black-move
                  (format t "~3D.~6T~A~16,8T~A~%" move-count
                                              (format-move white-move)
                                              (format-move black-move))
                  (format t "~3D.~6T~A~%" move-count
                                      (format-move white-move)))))))))

(defvar *chess-rank-names* '#(#\a #\b #\c #\d #\e #\f #\g #\h))

(defmethod format-move ((move chess-move))
  (with-slots (piece new-position) move
    (let ((rank (position-rank new-position))
          (file (position-file new-position)))
      (format nil "~a-~a~a" (piece-type piece)
                            (aref *chess-rank-names* rank)
                            (1+ file)))))

(defmethod format-move ((move capture))
  (with-slots (piece captured-piece) move
    (format nil "~ax~a" (piece-type piece)
                        (piece-type captured-piece))))


(defmethod piece-type ((piece chess-piece))
  (typecase piece
    (king "K")
    (queen "Q")
    (bishop "B")
    (knight "Kn")
    (rook "R")
    (pawn "P")))

;;;;;;;;;;;;;;;;;;;;;;;;;;;;;;;;;;;;;;;;;;;;;;;;;;;;;;;;;;;;;;;;;;;;;;
;;;define misc. functions
;;;;;;;;;;;;;;;;;;;;;;;;;;;;;;;;;;;;;;;;;;;;;;;;;;;;;;;;;;;;;;;;;;;;;;;
(defun adiff (num1 num2)
  (abs (- num1 num2)))
```

Official Rules of Black Jack

In this game, everyone plays against the dealer's "hand." The dealer starts the game by dealing each player two cards from the shoe, face up. The dealer's hand is dealt one card up and one card down. (The down card is called the *hole* card.) The dealer is not to look at the face of the hole card until all additional cards have been acted on.

The object is to draw cards that add up to 21 or as close to it as possible. You are responsible for computing the point count of your own hand. The Jack, Queen, and King count as 10. The Ace counts as 11 unless that would give you or the dealer a count in excess of 21, in which case the Ace counts as 1. All other cards are counted at their face value. Exceeding 21 is a *break*, and you automatically lose. Depending on the total of your original cards, you can *stand* (draw no more cards) or take a *hit* (draw one or more cards one at a time until you are satisfied with your count). If your total count is 21 or less and the point count of the dealer is in excess of 21, you win and the payout odds are 1 to 1. If your hand and the dealer's hand both total under 21 but your total count is higher, you win and the payout odds are 1 to 1. If you break (over 21) you lose, even if the dealer breaks. If your count is the same as the dealer's, it is a standoff. Should the dealer draw a 3 or more card 21, this does not beat your 2 cards 21 (Blackjack). If you have a 3 or more card 21 and the dealer has a 2 card 21 (Blackjack), you lose. If you achieve a score of 21 in two cards and the dealer achieves a score of 21 in more than two cards, you win. If the first two cards dealt to a player or dealer are any Ace and any 10, Jack, Queen, or King, the hand is considered a Blackjack.

Reprinted with permission of the Atlantic City Tropicana Hotel and Casino.

Blackjack

If the first face-up card dealt to the dealer is 2, 3, 4, 5, 6, 7, 8, or 9 and you have a Blackjack, the dealer shall announce and pay the Blackjack at odds of 3 to 2 and shall remove your cards before any player receives a third card.

If the first face-up card dealt to the dealer is an Ace, King, Queen, Jack, or Ten and you have Blackjack, the dealer shall announce the Blackjack but shall make no payment or remove any cards until all other cards are dealt to the players and the dealer receives his second card. If, in such circumstances, the dealer's second card does not give him Blackjack, your Blackjack shall be paid at odds of 3 to 2. If, however, the dealer's second card gives him Blackjack, the wager of the player having Blackjack shall be voided and constitute a standoff.

Insurance Wagers

Whenever the first card dealt to the dealer is an Ace, you have the right to make an *insurance wager* that wins if the dealer's second card is a King, Queen, Jack, or Ten and loses if the dealer's second card is an Ace, 2, 3, 4, 5, 6, 7, 8, or 9. Up to half of the initial wager may be bet as insurance after the second card is dealt and prior to any additional cards being dealt. Winning insurance wagers shall be paid at odds of 2 to 1.

Doubling Down

You may *double down* on any two cards of the first two of any split pair except for Blackjack or a count of 21 in two cards. You must make an additional wager not in excess of the amount of your original wager. Only one card is dealt to the hand. If the dealer obtains Blackjack after you double down, the dealer only collects the amount of the original wager and does not collect the additional amount wagered in doubling down.

Splitting Pairs

You may split two cards of identical value by making a wager on the second hand so formed in an amount equal to the original wager. You may not split again if the second card is identical in value to a card of the split pair. Only one card shall be dealt to each Ace of a split pair. If the dealer obtains Blackjack after you split pairs, the dealer shall only collect the amount of your original wager and shall not collect the additional amount wagered in splitting pairs. *Dealer must draw to 16 and stand on ALL 17's.*

F

Sources for the Slolog Interpreter

```
;;;;Slolog Interpreter

;;;;Timothy Koschmann
;;;;SIU School of Medicine
;;;;15 August, 1989


;;;;;;;;;;;;;;;;;;;;;;;;;;;;;;;;;;;;;;;;;;;;;;;;;;;;;;;;;;;;;;;;;;;;
;;;CL packages stuff
;;;;;;;;;;;;;;;;;;;;;;;;;;;;;;;;;;;;;;;;;;;;;;;;;;;;;;;;;;;;;;;;;;;;

(in-package "SLOLOG")
(export 'slolog)

;;;;;;;;;;;;;;;;;;;;;;;;;;;;;;;;;;;;;;;;;;;;;;;;;;;;;;;;;;;;;;;;;;;;
;;;define global constants and variables
;;;;;;;;;;;;;;;;;;;;;;;;;;;;;;;;;;;;;;;;;;;;;;;;;;;;;;;;;;;;;;;;;;;;

(defvar *next-token*)

(defconstant *slolog-breaks* '("(" ")" "," "." ":"))

(defvar *slolog-database* (make-hash-table :size 1000
                                           :test #'eq))

(defvar *slolog-scanner*)

(defvar *slolog-trace-flg* nil)

;;;;;;;;;;;;;;;;;;;;;;;;;;;;;;;;;;;;;;;;;;;;;;;;;;;;;;;;;;;;;;;;;;;;
;;;define the macros
;;;;;;;;;;;;;;;;;;;;;;;;;;;;;;;;;;;;;;;;;;;;;;;;;;;;;;;;;;;;;;;;;;;;
```

```lisp
(defmacro get-term (term)
  `(let ((term-obj ,term))
     `(,(get-functor-name term-obj)
        ,@(slot-value term-obj 'arg-list)))))

(defmacro make-procedure-name (functor-sym arity)
  `(multiple-value-bind (procedure-name)
        (intern (format nil "~a/~d" ,functor-sym ,arity)
                (find-package "SLOLOG"))
     procedure-name))

(defmacro my-until (condition exit-form &body body)
  (let ((top-of-loop (gensym)))
    `(block nil
       (tagbody
          ,top-of-loop
          ,@body
          (if ,condition
              (return ,exit-form)
              (go ,top-of-loop)))))))

;;;;;;;;;;;;;;;;;;;;;;;;;;;;;;;;;;;;;;;;;;;;;;;;;;;;;;;;;;;;;;;;;;;;;;;
;;;define the CLOS classes
;;;;;;;;;;;;;;;;;;;;;;;;;;;;;;;;;;;;;;;;;;;;;;;;;;;;;;;;;;;;;;;;;;;;;;;

(defclass slolog-object ()
  ()
  (:documentation
   "Class of objects that support the Slolog language"))

(defclass procedure (slolog-object)
  ((clause-list :initform ()
                :initarg :clause-list
                :accessor get-clause-list)
   (functor-name :initarg :functor-name
             :accessor get-functor-name)
   (arity :initform 0
          :initarg :arity
          :accessor get-arity)
   (attached-fn :initarg :attached-fn
                :initform #'try-clause
                :accessor get-attached-fn))
  (:documentation
   "Class of Slolog procedures"))

(defclass clause (slolog-object)
  ((head :initarg :head
         :accessor get-head)
```

```
      (procedure :initarg :procedure)
      (variable-list :initarg :variable-list
                    :initform nil
                    :accessor get-variable-list))
    (:documentation
     "Class of Slolog clauses"))

(defclass unit-clause (clause)
  ()
  (:documentation
   "Class of Slolog unit-clauses (i.e., facts)"))

(defclass non-unit-clause (clause)
  ((body :initarg :body
         :accessor get-body))
  (:documentation
   "Class of Slolog non-unit-clauses (i.e., rules)"))

(defclass term (slolog-object)
  ((arg-list :accessor get-arg-list
             :initarg :arg-list)
   (clause    :accessor get-clause
             :initarg :clause)
   (functor-name :accessor get-functor-name
                :initarg :functor-name))
  (:documentation
   "Class of Slolog terms"))

;;;classes used exclusively by the parser
(defclass terminal-token (slolog-object)
  ((value :initarg :value
          :accessor get-value))
  (:documentation
   "Class of terminal tokens for Slolog parser"))

(defclass fiducial (terminal-token)
  ()
  (:documentation
   "Class of fiduciary symbols for Slolog parser"))

(defclass symbol-token (terminal-token)
  ()
  (:documentation
   "Class of symbol tokens for Slolog parser"))

(defclass numeric-constant (terminal-token)
  ()
  (:documentation
```

```
        "Class of numeric-constant tokens for Slolog parser"))

;;;;;;;;;;;;;;;;;;;;;;;;;;;;;;;;;;;;;;;;;;;;;;;;;;;;;;;;;;;;;;;;;;;;
;;;top-level loop
;;;;;;;;;;;;;;;;;;;;;;;;;;;;;;;;;;;;;;;;;;;;;;;;;;;;;;;;;;;;;;;;;;;;

(defun slolog ()
  (catch 'end-session
    (loop (format t "~%?- ")
          (catch 'end-query
            (satisfy (read-query)
                     '(nil)
                     #'display-results)
            (format t "~%no~%")))))

(defun read-query ()
  (let ((input-string (get-input-string)))
    ;;set-up scanner for this input string
    (setf *slolog-scanner* (make-scanner input-string))
    ;;parse the input string
    (scan-token)
    (parse-query)))

(defun get-input-string ()
  (labels ((terminated-string-p (input-string)
             ;;check to see if terminated with a period
             (let ((last-char (1- (length input-string))))
               (equal (char input-string last-char)
                      #\.))))
    (let ((input-string (make-string 0)))
      (my-until (terminated-string-p input-string)
                input-string
                (setf input-string
                      (concatenate 'string
                                   input-string
                                   (read-line)))))))

(defun display-results (env)
  ;;display the results of a query and check to see if the user
  ;;would like to continue the search
  (cond ((equal env '(nil))(format t "~%yes~%")(throw 'end-query nil))
        (t (display-bindings env)(if (not (yes-or-no-p "Continue search?"))
                                     (throw 'end-query nil)))))

(defun display-bindings (env)
  (terpri)
  ;;present bindings in order of occurance
  ;;(and drop the null environment from list)
```

```
    (let ((bindings (rest (reverse env))))
      (dolist (binding bindings)
        (let* ((variable (first binding))
               (var-name (symbol-name variable)))
          ;;also drop the system-defined variables
          (if (not (and (> (length var-name) 4)
                        (equal (subseq var-name 0 4)
                               "?var")))
              (format t "~a = ~a~%" variable (value-of variable env)))))))
    (terpri))


;;;;;;;;;;;;;;;;;;;;;;;;;;;;;;;;;;;;;;;;;;;;;;;;;;;;;;;;;;;;;;;;;;;;;;;;;;
;;;define the theorem prover
;;;;;;;;;;;;;;;;;;;;;;;;;;;;;;;;;;;;;;;;;;;;;;;;;;;;;;;;;;;;;;;;;;;;;;;;;;

(defun satisfy (goals environment continuation)
  (if goals
      (let* ((goal (caar goals))
             (procedure (get-procedure goal))
             (clause-list (get-clause-list procedure))
             (attached-fn (get-attached-fn procedure)))
        (if *slolog-trace-flg*
          (format t "  Call: ~a~%" goal))
        (funcall attached-fn clause-list goal environment
                #'(lambda (env)
                      (if *slolog-trace-flg*
                        (format t "  Succeed: ~a~%" goal))
                      (satisfy (rest goals) env continuation)))
        (if *slolog-trace-flg*
          (format t "  Fail: ~a~%" goal)))
      ;;success! All goals are satisfied.
      (funcall continuation environment)))

(defun try-clause (clause-list goal env continuation)
  (if clause-list
      (let* ((clause (first clause-list))
             (new-names (make-new-names clause))
             (new-environment (unify goal
                                     (first (get-clause-head clause new-names))
                                     env)))
        (if (not (and new-environment
                      (satisfy (get-clause-body clause new-names)
                               new-environment
                               continuation)))
          (try-clause (rest clause-list) goal env continuation)
          new-environment))))

(defun unify (x y environment)
```

```
    (labels ((bind-variable (x y environment)
                (acons x y environment)))
      ;;if x unifies with y, unify returns a
      ;;new environment, nil otherwise
      (let ((x (value-of x environment))
            (y (value-of y environment)))
        (cond ((equal x y) environment)
              ((logical-variable-p x)(bind-variable x y environment))
              ((logical-variable-p y)(bind-variable y x environment))
              ;;if both are lists, descend recursively
              ((and (listp x)(listp y))
               (let ((new-environment (unify (first x)(first y) environment)))
                 (and new-environment
                      (unify (rest x)(rest y) new-environment)))))))))


(defun value-of (x environment)
  (if (logical-variable-p x)
    (let ((binding (assoc x environment)))
      (if binding
        ;;recursively de-reference all variables
        (value-of (rest binding) environment)
        x))
    ;;non-variables self-evaluate
    x))

(defun logical-variable-p (x)
  ;;symbols with names that begin with a question mark
  ;;are considered to be logical-variables
  (if (symbolp x)
    (let ((leading-char (char (symbol-name x) 0)))
      (if (char= leading-char #\?)
        x))))

(defun rename-variables (term new-names)
   (if term
     (let ((first-item (first term)))
       ;;descend both the head and the tail
       (cons (if (listp first-item)
               (rename-variables first-item new-names)
               (if (logical-variable-p first-item)
                 (rest (assoc first-item new-names))
                 first-item))
             (rename-variables (rest term) new-names)))))

(defmethod make-new-names ((clause clause))
  (with-slots (variable-list) clause
    (if variable-list
```

```lisp
      (let (new-names)
        (dolist (name variable-list new-names)
          (setf new-names
                (acons name (make-new-name) new-names)))))))

(defun make-name-generator (&optional (prefix "?"))
  (let ((last-value 0))
    #'(lambda ()
        (multiple-value-bind (new-name)
              (intern (format nil "~a~d" prefix (incf last-value))
                      (find-package "SLOLOG"))
          new-name))))

(defun make-variable-list (goal)
  ;;descends the structure of the goal and makes
  ;;a list of all logical variables, removing the
  ;;duplicates
  (labels ((list-vars (x)
             (if x
                 (let ((item (first x)))
                   (if (listp item)
                       (append (list-vars item)
                               (list-vars (rest x)))
                       (if (logical-variable-p item)
                         (cons item
                               (list-vars (rest x)))
                         (list-vars (rest x)))))))))
    (delete-duplicates (list-vars goal))))

(defvar *slolog-name-generator* (make-name-generator "?var"))

(defun make-new-name ()
  (funcall *slolog-name-generator*))

;;;;;;;;;;;;;;;;;;;;;;;;;;;;;;;;;;;;;;;;;;;;;;;;;;;;;;;;;;;;;;;;;;;;;;
;;;define accessors
;;;;;;;;;;;;;;;;;;;;;;;;;;;;;;;;;;;;;;;;;;;;;;;;;;;;;;;;;;;;;;;;;;;;;;

(defun get-procedure (goal)
  (let* ((functor-name (first goal))
         (arity (length (rest goal)))
         (key (make-procedure-name functor-name arity))
         (procedure (gethash  key *slolog-database*)))
    (cond ((null procedure)
           (cerror "Enter new query?"
                   "Unrecognized procedure: ~a" key)
           (throw 'end-query nil))
          (t procedure))))
```

```lisp
(defmethod get-clause-head ((clause clause) new-names)
  (with-slots (head) clause
    (list (rename-variables (get-term head) new-names)))))

(defmethod get-clause-body ((clause unit-clause) new-names)
  nil)

(defmethod get-clause-body ((clause non-unit-clause) new-names)
  ;;returns a list of terms representing the body of a clause
  (let ((term-list '()))
    (with-slots (body) clause
      (dolist (term body term-list)
        ;;be careful to preserve the order of the terms
        (setf term-list (cons (list (rename-variables (get-term term)
                                                       new-names))
                              term-list))))
    (reverse term-list)))

(defmethod get-functor-name ((clause clause))
  (slot-value (slot-value clause 'procedure)
              'functor-name))

(defmethod get-arity ((clause clause))
  (slot-value (slot-value clause 'procedure) 'arity))

(defmethod construct-clause-body ((clause unit-clause) new-names)
  nil)

(defmethod construct-clause-body ((clause non-unit-clause) new-names)
  ;;returns a list of terms representing the body of a clause
  (let ((term-list '()))
    (with-slots (body) clause
      (dolist (term body term-list)
        ;;be careful to preserve the order of the terms
        (setf term-list
              (cons (rename-variables (get-term term)
                                      new-names)
                    term-list))))
    (list (reverse term-list))))

;;;;;;;;;;;;;;;;;;;;;;;;;;;;;;;;;;;;;;;;;;;;;;;;;;;;;;;;;;;;;;;;;;;;;;
;;;define the parser
;;;;;;;;;;;;;;;;;;;;;;;;;;;;;;;;;;;;;;;;;;;;;;;;;;;;;;;;;;;;;;;;;;;;;;

(defun parse-query ()
  ;;returns a list of clauses
  (cons
```

```lisp
      (parse-clause)
      (parse-query-tail)))

(defun parse-query-tail ()
   (when (equal (get-value *next-token*)
                 ",")
      (scan-token)
      (cons (parse-clause)
            (parse-query-tail))))

(defun parse-clause ()
   ;;returns a term as a list
   (let ((term (parse-term)))
      (cond
         ;;non-unit clause?
         ((equal (get-value *next-token*)
                  ":-")
          (scan-token)
          (let ((body-list (list (parse-term))))
             (list term
                   (append body-list (parse-clause-tail)))))
         ;;unit clause
         (t (list term)))))

(defun parse-clause-tail ()
   (when (equal (get-value *next-token*)
                 ",")
      (scan-token)
      (let ((next-term (parse-term)))
         (cons next-term
               (parse-clause-tail)))))

(defun parse-term ()
   (cond
      ;;should be a functor name here
      ((eql (class-of *next-token*)
            (Find-class 'symbol-token))
       (let ((functor-name (get-value *next-token*)))
          (scan-token)
          (let ((arg-list (parse-arg-list)))
             (cons functor-name arg-list))))
      ;;if not, bail out
      (t (cerror "Enter new query?"
                 "Illegal syntax at ~a"
                 (get-value *next-token*))
         (throw 'end-query nil))))

(defun parse-arg-list ()
```

```
  (when
  _ ;;arg-list provided?
    (equal (get-value *next-token*)
           "(")
    (scan-token)
    (let ((first-arg (parse-arg)))
      (cons first-arg
            (parse-arg-list-tail)))))

(defun parse-arg-list-tail ()
  (let ((next-element (get-value *next-token*)))
    (cond
     ;;more list elements?
     ((equal next-element ",")
      (scan-token)
      (cons (parse-arg)
            (parse-arg-list-tail)))
     ;;end of arg-list?
     ((equal next-element ")")
      (scan-token)
      nil)
     ;;otherwise, we're confused
     (t (cerror "Enter new query?"
                "Illegal syntax at ~a"
                (get-value *next-token*))
        (throw 'end-query nil)))))

(defun parse-arg ()
  (let ((value (get-value *next-token*)))
    (cond
     ;;symbols or numeric constants are okay
     ((or (eql (class-of *next-token*)
               (Find-class 'symbol-token))
          (eql (class-of *next-token*)
               (Find-class 'numeric-constant)))
      (scan-token)
      value)
     ((equal (get-value *next-token*)
             "(")
      (scan-token)
      (parse-clause))
     ;;if not, bail out
     (t (cerror "Enter new query?"
                "Illegal syntax at ~a"
                (get-value *next-token*))
        (throw 'end-query nil)))))
```

```lisp
;;;;;;;;;;;;;;;;;;;;;;;;;;;;;;;;;;;;;;;;;;;;;;;;;;;;;;;;;;;;;;;;
;;;make a look-ahead scanner
;;;;;;;;;;;;;;;;;;;;;;;;;;;;;;;;;;;;;;;;;;;;;;;;;;;;;;;;;;;;;;;;

(defun make-scanner (input-string)
  #'(lambda ()
      (if (not (equal input-string ""))
          (multiple-value-bind (token-text new-string)
              (scan-text input-string)
            ;;assign the next token to the global
            ;;variable *next-token*
            (if (member token-text
                        '("," "." "(" ")" ":-")
                        :test #'equal)
                (setf *next-token* (make-instance 'fiducial
                                                  :value token-text))
                (let ((object (read-from-string token-text)))
                  (typecase object
                    (number (setf *next-token*
                                  (make-instance 'numeric-constant
                                                 :value object)))
                    (symbol (setf *next-token*
                                  (make-instance 'symbol-token
                                                 :value object)))
                    (t (cerror "Enter new query?"
                               "Unrecognized data object ~a" object)
                       (throw 'end-query nil)))))
            ;;advance pointer in the input string
            (setf input-string new-string))
          (error "Attempting to scan beyond end of input string"))))

(defun scan-text (input-string)
  ;;returns two values: the next token and the
  ;;input string with the token removed
  (let ((next-element (subseq input-string 0 1)))
    ;;if next element is a break character
    (if (member next-element *slolog-breaks*
                :test #'equal)
        (cond
          ;;handle ":-" case
          ((and (equal next-element ":")
                (equal (char input-string 1) #\-))
           (values
            (subseq input-string 0 2)
            (string-left-trim '(#\Space #\Tab #\Newline)
                              (subseq input-string 2))))
          ;;handle leading "."
          ((and (equal next-element ".")
```

```
                        (not (equal next-element input-string)))
             (multiple-value-bind (token new-string)
                 (scan-text-aux (subseq input-string 1))
               (values
                 (concatenate 'string next-element token)
                new-string)))
            ;;for all others, return the break string
            (t (values
                  next-element
                  (string-left-trim '(#\Space #\Tab #\Newline)
                                     (subseq input-string 1)))))
          ;;otherwise, read on
          (multiple-value-bind (token new-string)
              (scan-text-aux (subseq input-string 1))
            (values
              (concatenate 'string next-element token)
             new-string)))))

(defun scan-text-aux (input-string)
  ;;returns two values: the next token and the
  ;;input string with the token removed
  (let ((next-element (subseq input-string 0 1)))
    ;;if next element is a break character
    (if (member next-element *slolog-breaks*
                :test #'equal)
      (cond
        ;;handle embedded "."
        ((and (equal next-element ".")
              (not (equal next-element input-string)))
         (multiple-value-bind (token new-string)
             (scan-text-aux (subseq input-string 1))
           (values
             (concatenate 'string next-element token)
            new-string)))
        ;;for all others, return the break string
        (t (values
             (make-string 0)
             input-string)))
      ;;otherwise, read on
      (multiple-value-bind (token new-string)
          (scan-text-aux (subseq input-string 1))
        (values
          (concatenate 'string next-element token)
         new-string)))))


(defun scan-token ()
  (funcall *slolog-scanner*))
```

```
;;;;;;;;;;;;;;;;;;;;;;;;;;;;;;;;;;;;;;;;;;;;;;;;;;;;;;;;;;;;;;;;;
;;;specially-defined attached functions
;;;;;;;;;;;;;;;;;;;;;;;;;;;;;;;;;;;;;;;;;;;;;;;;;;;;;;;;;;;;;;;;;

(defun asserta (clause-list goal env continuation)
  (declare (ignore clause-list))
  (let* ((head (caadr goal))
         (body (cadadr goal))
         (functor-name (first head))
         (arity (length (rest head)))
         (key (make-procedure-name functor-name
                                   arity))
         (procedure (or (gethash key *slolog-database*)
                        (make-instance 'procedure
                             :functor-name functor-name
                             :arity arity)))
         (clause-list (get-clause-list procedure))
         (clause (if body
                    (make-instance 'non-unit-clause
                       :procedure procedure)
                    (make-instance 'unit-clause
                       :procedure procedure)))
         (body-terms nil))
    ;;store the clause head in clause object
    (setf (get-head clause)
          (make-instance 'term
            :clause clause
            :functor-name functor-name
            :arg-list (rest head)))
    ;;store the clause body in clause object
    (when body
      (dolist (term body)
        (setf body-terms (cons (make-instance 'term
                                 :clause clause
                                 :functor-name (first term)
                                 :arg-list (rest term))
                               body-terms)))
      (setf (get-body clause)
            (reverse body-terms)))
    ;;store the list of variables in the clause object
    (setf (get-variable-list clause)
          (make-variable-list goal))
    ;;add clause to beginning of clause-list and install
    ;;clause-list in procedure
    (setf (get-clause-list procedure)
          (cons clause clause-list))
    ;;update the data base
```

```lisp
        (setf (gethash key *slolog-database*)
              procedure))
  ;;;cause the goal to succeed
  (funcall continuation env))

(defun assertz (clause-list goal env continuation)
  (declare (ignore clause-list))
  (let* ((head (caadr goal))
         (body (cadadr goal))
         (functor-name (first head))
         (arity (length (rest head)))
         (key (make-procedure-name functor-name
                                   arity))
         (procedure (or (gethash key *slolog-database*)
                        (make-instance 'procedure
                           :functor-name functor-name
                           :arity arity)))
         (clause-list (get-clause-list procedure))
         (clause (if body
                     (make-instance 'non-unit-clause
                        :procedure procedure)
                     (make-instance 'unit-clause
                        :procedure procedure)))
         (body-terms nil))
    ;;store the clause head in clause object
    (setf (get-head clause)
          (make-instance 'term
             :clause clause
             :functor-name functor-name
             :arg-list (rest head)))
    ;;store the clause body in clause object
    (when body
      (dolist (term body)
        (setf body-terms (cons (make-instance 'term
                                  :clause clause
                                  :functor-name (first term)
                                  :arg-list (rest term))
                               body-terms)))
      (setf (get-body clause)
            (reverse body-terms)))
    ;;store the list of variables in the clause object
    (setf (get-variable-list clause)
          (make-variable-list goal))
    ;;add clause to end of clause-list and install
    ;;clause-list in procedure
    (setf (get-clause-list procedure)
          (append clause-list (list clause)))
    ;;update the data base
```

```lisp
        (setf (gethash key *slolog-database*)
              procedure))
  ;;;cause the goal to succeed
  (funcall continuation env))

(defun gt (clause-list goal env continuation)
  (let ((x (value-of (second goal) env))
        (y (value-of (third goal) env)))
    (if (and (numberp x)
             (numberp y)
             (> x y))
      ;;success! goal is satisfied
      (funcall continuation env))))

(defun halt (&rest arg-list)
  (declare (ignore arg-list))
  ;;used by the halt/0 procedure.
  (throw 'end-session 'Ciao!))

(defun retract (clause-list query env continuation)
  (declare (ignore clause-list))
  (labels ((retract-aux (clause-obj goal env continuation)
              (let* ((new-names (make-new-names clause-obj))
                     (clause (append (get-clause-head clause-obj
                                                         new-names)
                                     (construct-clause-body clause-obj
                                                         new-names)))
                     (new-env (unify goal clause env)))
                (when new-env
                  (retract-clause clause-obj)
                  ;;signal success
                  (funcall continuation new-env))))
           (retract-clause (clause)
              (let* ((procedure (slot-value clause 'procedure))
                     (clause-list (get-clause-list procedure))
                     (functor-name (get-functor-name procedure))
                     (arity (get-arity procedure))
                     (key (make-procedure-name functor-name arity)))
                ;;remove clause from clause list
                (setf (get-clause-list procedure)
                      (remove clause clause-list))
                ;;if this this procedure has other clauses, reassert
                ;;the procedure, otherwise remove it from the data base
                (if (get-clause-list procedure)
                    (setf (gethash key *slolog-database*)
                          procedure)
                    (remhash key *slolog-database*)))))
    (let* ((goal (cadr query))
```

```
              (head (first goal))
              (functor-name (first head))
              (arity (length (rest head)))
              (key (make-procedure-name functor-name
                                        arity))
              (procedure (gethash key *slolog-database*)))
         (if procedure
           (let ((clause-list (get-clause-list procedure)))
             (dolist (clause clause-list)
               (retract-aux clause goal env continuation)))))))))

(defun slolog-fail (clause-list goal env continuation)
  (declare (ignore clause-list goal))
  ;;this goal is never satisfied
  nil)

(defun slolog-trace (clause-list goal env continuation)
  (declare (ignore clause-list goal))
  (setf *slolog-trace-flg* t)
  ;;this goal is always satisfied
  (funcall continuation env))

(defun slolog-true (clause-list goal env continuation)
  (declare (ignore clause-list goal))
  ;;this goal is always satisfied
  (funcall continuation env))

(defun slolog-untrace (clause-list goal env continuation)
  (declare (ignore clause-list goal))
  (setf *slolog-trace-flg* nil)
  ;;this goal is always satisfied
  (funcall continuation env))

;;;;;;;;;;;;;;;;;;;;;;;;;;;;;;;;;;;;;;;;;;;;;;;;;;;;;;;;;;;;;;;;;;;;;;
;;;initialize the data base
;;;;;;;;;;;;;;;;;;;;;;;;;;;;;;;;;;;;;;;;;;;;;;;;;;;;;;;;;;;;;;;;;;;;;;

(setf (gethash 'assert/1 *slolog-database*)
      (make-instance 'procedure
                     :functor-name 'assert
                     :arity 1
                     :attached-fn #'asserta))

(setf (gethash 'asserta/1 *slolog-database*)
      (make-instance 'procedure
                     :functor-name 'asserta
                     :arity 1
                     :attached-fn #'asserta))
```

```lisp
(setf (gethash 'assertz/1 *slolog-database*)
      (make-instance 'procedure
                      :functor-name 'assertz
                      :arity 1
                      :attached-fn #'assertz))

(setf (gethash 'fail/0 *slolog-database*)
      (make-instance 'procedure
                      :functor-name 'fail
                      :arity 0
                      :attached-fn #'slolog-fail))

(setf (gethash 'gt/2 *slolog-database*)
      (make-instance 'procedure
                      :functor-name 'gt
                      :arity 2
                      :attached-fn #'gt))

(setf (gethash 'halt/0 *slolog-database*)
      (make-instance 'procedure
                      :functor-name 'halt
                      :arity 0
                      :attached-fn #'halt))

(setf (gethash 'retract/1 *slolog-database*)
      (make-instance 'procedure
                      :functor-name 'retract
                      :arity 1
                      :attached-fn #'retract))

(setf (gethash 'trace/0 *slolog-database*)
      (make-instance 'procedure
                      :functor-name 'trace
                      :arity 0
                      :attached-fn #'slolog-trace))

(setf (gethash 'untrace/0 *slolog-database*)
      (make-instance 'procedure
                      :functor-name 'untrace
                      :arity 0
                      :attached-fn #'slolog-untrace))

(setf (gethash 'true/0 *slolog-database*)
      (make-instance 'procedure
                      :functor-name 'true
                      :arity 0
                      :attached-fn #'slolog-true))
```

References

ABELSON, H., SUSSMAN, G. J., AND SUSSMAN, J. *Structure and Interpretation of Computer Programs*, MIT Press, Cambridge, MA, 1985.

ABELSON, H., AND SUSSMAN, G. J. Lisp: A Language for Stratified Design, *Byte*, **13**(2), 1988, 207 - 218.

AHO, A., SETHI, R., AND ULLMAN, J. *Compilers: Principles, Techniques and Tools*, Addison-Wesley, Reading, MA, 1986.

ALLEN, J. R. *Anatomy of Lisp*, McGraw-Hill, New York, 1978.

ALLEN, J. R. Speaking Lisp. *Computer Language*, **2**(7), 1985, 27 - 33.

ALLEN, J. R. The Death of Creativity: Is Common Lisp a Lisp-like Language? *AI Expert*, **2**(2), 1987, 48 - 61.

ANSI. *Working Draft American National Standard for Information Systems — Programming Language Common Lisp*, ANSI Document (in preparation).

BENTLEY, J. Programming Pearls: A Sample of Brilliance, *Communications of the ACM*, **30**(9), 1987, 754 - 757.

BERKELEY, E. L., AND BOBROW, D. (Eds.). *The Programming Language LISP: Its Operation and Applications*, Information International, Cambridge, MA, 1964.

BOBROW, D., DE MICHIEL, L., GABRIEL, R., KEENE, S., KICZALES, G., AND MOON, D. Common Lisp Object System Specification (ANSI X3J13 Doc. 88 - 002R), *ACM SIGPLAN Notices*, **23**, September 1988.

BRACHMAN, R. J. What IS-A Is and Isn't: An Analysis of Taxonomic Links in Semantic Networks, *IEEE Computer*, **16**, 1983, 30 - 36.

447

BROOKS, R. *Programming in Common Lisp*, Wiley, New York, 1985.

CHARNIAK, E., RIESBECK, C., McDERMOTT, D.V, AND MEEHAN, J. *Artificial Intelligence Programming*, Lawrence Erlbaum, Hillsdale, N.J., 1987.

CHURCH, A. *The Calculi of Lambda-Conversion*, Princeton University Press, Princeton, NJ, 1941.

DAHL, O., DIJKSTRA, E., AND HOARE, C. *Structured Programming*, Academic Press, London, 1972.

DUSSUD, P. H. Lisp Hardware Architecture: The Explorer II and Beyond. In C. Queinnec and J. Chailloux (Eds.), *Lisp Evaluation and Standardization: Proceedings of the First International Workshop*, ISO, Springfield, VA, 1988.

FRANZ, INC., *Common Lisp: The Reference*, Addison-Wesley, Reading, MA, 1988.

GABRIEL, R. P. *Performance and Evaluation of Lisp Systems*, MIT Press, Cambridge, MA, 1985.

GABRIEL, R. P., BELZ, F., DEWAR, R., FISHER, D., GUTTAG, J., HUDAK, P., AND WAND, M. Draft Report of Requirements for a Common Prototyping System, *SIGPLAN Notices*, **24**(3), 1989, 93 - 115.

GOLDBERG, A., AND ROBSON, D. *Smalltalk-80: The Language and Its Implementation*, Addison-Wesley, Reading, MA, 1983.

GRAHAM, P. Anatomy of a Lisp Machine, *AI Expert*, **3**(12), 1988a, 26 - 32.

GRAHAM, P. Common Lisp Macros, *AI Expert*, **3**(3), 1988b, 42 - 53.

HENNESSEY, W. *Common Lisp*, McGraw-Hill, New York, 1989.

HEWITT, C. Viewing Control Structures as Patterns of Passing Messages, *Journal of Artificial Intelligence*, **8**, 1977, 323 - 363.

HOFSTADTER, D. R. *Godel, Escher, Bach: An Eternal Golden Braid*, Basic Books, New York, 1979.

HOROWITZ, E., AND SAHNI, S. *Fundamentals of Data Structures*, Computer Science Press, Rockville, MD, 1976.

KAHN, K., AND CARLSSON, M. How to Implement Prolog on a Lisp Machine. In J.A. Campbell (Ed.), *Implementations of Prolog*. Halstead Press, New York, 1984.

KEENE, S. *Object-Oriented Programming in Common Lisp*, Addison-Wesley, Reading, MA, 1989.

KNUTH, D. E. *The Art of Computer Programming, Volume III, Sorting and Searching*, Addison-Wesley, Reading, MA, 1973.

LEVY, D. *All About Chess and Computers*, Computer Science Press, Rockville, MD, 1982.

MAIER, D., AND WARREN, D. S. *Computing with Logic: Logic Programming with Prolog*, Benjamin/Cummings, Menlo Park, CA, 1988.

MALPAS, J. *Prolog: A Relational Language and Its Applications*, Prentice-Hall, Englewood Cliffs, NJ, 1987.

MANNA, Z. *Mathematical Theory of Computation*, McGraw-Hill, New York, 1989.

MARTI, J. B., HEARN, A. C., GRISS, M. L.,, AND GRISS, C. Standard Lisp Report, *SIGPLAN Notices*, **14**(10), 1979, 48 - 68.

MATHIS, R. F. Organizational Progress Toward Lisp Standardization. In C. Queinnec, and J. Chailloux (Eds.), *Lisp Evaluation and Standardization: Proceedings of the First International Workshop*, ISO, Springfield, VA, 1988.

McCARTHY, J. Recursive Functions of Symbolic Expressions and Their Computation by Machine, *Communications of the ACM*, **3**(4), 1960, 184 - 195.

McCARTHY, J. History of Lisp, *ACM SIGPLAN Notices*, **13**, (8), 1978, 217 - 222.

McCARTHY, J., ABRAHAMS, P., EDWARDS, D., HART, T.P., AND LEVIN, M. *Lisp 1.5 Programmer's Manual*, MIT Press, Cambridge, MA, 1962.

MOON, D. Object-Oriented Programming with Flavors, *Proceedings of OOPSLA '86*, ACM Press, New York, 1986, 214 - 223.

MOON, D. The Common Lisp Object-Oriented Programming Language Standard. In W. Kim, and F. Lochovsky (Eds.), *Object-Oriented Concepts, Applications and Databases*, Addison-Wesley, Reading, MA, 1988.

NEWBORN, M. *Computer Chess*, Academic Press, New York, 1975.

NILSSON, N. J. *Problem-Solving Methods in Artificial Intelligence*, McGraw-Hill, New York, 1971.

PIER, K. A Retrospective on the Dorado, a High-Performance Personal Computer, Xerox PARC Technical Report, ISL-83 - 1, 1983.

PITMAN, K. M. Exceptional Situations in Lisp. MIT A.I. Laboratory working Paper 268, February 1985.

PITMAN, K. M. Interactions in Lisp. In C. Queinnec, and J. Chailloux (Eds.), *Lisp Evaluation and Standardization: Proceedings of the First International Workshop*, ISO, Springfield, VA, 1988.

Proceedings of the First CLOS Users and Implementation Workshop, Xerox Palo Alto Research Center, Palo Alto, CA, October 1988.

REES, J. AND CLINGER, W. (EDS.) Revised Report on the Algorithmic Scheme, *SIGPLAN Notices*, **21**(12), 1986, 37 - 75.

RETIG, M. Lisps with Class: Three Object-Oriented Lisps. *AI Expert*, **2**(4), 1987, 15 - 23.

SCHWARTZ, R. L., AND MELLIAR-SMITH, P. M. On the Suitability of Ada for Artificial Intelligence Applications, NTIS Report AD-A090 790, 1980.

SEARLE, S. *Matrix Algebra Useful for Statistics*, Wiley, New York, 1982.

SHEIL, B. Power Tools for Programmers, *Datamation*, **29**(2), 1983, 131 - 144.

STEFIK, M. AND BOBROW, D. Object-Oriented Programming: Themes and Variations, *AI Magazine*, **6**(4), 1986a, 40 - 62.

STEFIK, M., BOBROW, D. AND KAHN, K. Integrating Access-Oriented Programming into a Multiparadigm Environment, *IEEE Software*, **3**(1), 1986b, 10 - 18.

STEFIK, M., BOBROW, D., MITTAL, S., AND CONWAY, L. Knowledge Programming in LOOPS: Reprint on an Experimental Course, *AI Magazine*, **4**, 1983, 3 - 13.

STEELE, G. L. An Overview of Common Lisp, *Conference Record of the 1984 ACM Symposium on Lisp and Functional Programming*, 1984a, 98 - 107.

STEELE, G. L. *Common Lisp: The Language*, Digital Press, Bedford, MA, 1984b.

STEELE, G. L. *Common Lisp: The Language* (2nd Ed.), Digital Press, Bedford, MA, 1990.

STEELE, G. L., AND SUSSMAN, G. J. The Art of the Interpreter or, The Modularity Complex (Parts Zero, One, and Two), MIT AI Memo No. 453, May 1978.

STEELE, G. L., AND SUSSMAN, G. J. Design of LISP-Based Processors or, SCHEME: A Dielectric LISP or, Finite Memories Considered Harmful or, LAMBDA: The Ultimate Opcode, MIT AI Memo No. 514, March 1979.

STERLING, L., AND SHAPIRO, E. *The Art of Prolog: Advanced Programming Techniques*, MIT Press, Cambridge, MA, 1986.

STOYAN, H. Early Lisp History (1956 - 1959), *Conference Record of the 1984 ACM Symposium on Lisp and Functional Programming*, 1984, 299 - 310.

TEITELMAN, W. *Interlisp Reference Manual*, Xerox Corporation, Stamford, CT, 1983.

TOURETZKY, D. *Lisp — A Gentle Introduction*, Wiley, New York, 1984.

TOURETZKY, D. How Lisp Has Changed, *Byte*, **14**(2), 1988, 229 - 234.

TREMBLY, J., AND SORENSON, P. *The Theory and Practice of Compiler Writing*, McGraw-Hill, New York, 1985.

WELSH, D. *Computer Chess*, W.C. Brown, Dubuque, IA, 1984.

WELSH, D. *Computer Chess II*, W.C. Brown, Dubuque, IA, 1985.

YOSHINO, Y. *The Japanese Abacus Explained*, Dover Publications, New York, 1963.

Index